Northwestern University Studies in History

NUMBER III

A Whig in Power

THE POLITICAL CAREER OF HENRY PELHAM

John W. Wilkes

Northwestern University Press

1964

The publication of this book has been aided by contributions from friends of James Alton James and by the Warshauer Trust Fund.

TO MY FATHER

Acknowledgments

℣ IT IS IMPOSSIBLE to acknowledge all the many people who have aided by encouragement and information the preparation of this book. Their kindly words and thoughtful comments have been most valuable and greatly appreciated.

Special gratitude must be expressed to Leland H. Carlson, who suffered with great patience long hours of direction in the initial stages of the work. His endless help and encouragement made "straight the way" for a newcomer to the profession. In addition I most gladly recognize my debt to Gray C. Boyce, gentleman and scholar, whose constant kindness can never be put in words. I am only one of many who have found him an inspiration to achievement. Of the many individuals who provided intellectual and practical assistance to one more American who ventured to London for the first time, I can do little but say thank you. It is proper, however, to remember especially the generous efforts of Robert W. Greaves.

In a less personal way I am grateful to the many libraries and their staffs that have made pleasant the work of research. To the British Museum and the Public Record Office, where most of the research materials are deposited, I can only acknowledge my debt. The Bodleian Library of Oxford University granted permission to use portions of the North Papers. And the Henry E. Huntington Library in San Marino, California, provided many pleasant days as I culled its manuscripts.

To Earl Fitzwilliam and the trustees of the Wentworth-Woodhouse Settled Estates I extend thanks for permission to use manuscripts now deposited in the Sheffield City Library. A like indebtedness must be expressed to the Marquis of Cholmondeley for the use of the Cholmondeley-Houghton Manuscripts deposited in the Cambridge University Library. And again to the Duke of Newcastle I express gratitude for permission to see his manuscripts, deposited in the Nottingham University Library. To the librarians of all these institutions I am also deeply in debt.

It would be improper to close this lengthy list without expressing unending thanks to the History Department of Northwestern University, the Graduate School of Arts of the same university, and the Northwestern University Press for making the publication of the book possible. I have dedicated the volume to the one who made easy the years of study that also made the book possible.

J. W. W.

New York City
1963

Contents

Introduction

℣ THE SECOND QUARTER of the eighteenth century is a period of great importance to the political development of England. Its importance has been slighted by many historians because they have failed to grasp the fact that during these years the political parties of the Restoration era were destroyed. Most historians write of the growth of the power of the cabinet in the eighteenth century, but ignore the fact that the establishment of the great political parties of the nineteenth century, which began during the reign of George III, could never have occurred if the problems and prejudices of the Stuart government had dominated the eighteenth century. By 1725 these questions were things of the past and had been largely settled. The groups that had formed themselves into parties before and during the Revolution Settlement of 1689 had served their purposes and now had little to offer. The great problem of the period was, therefore, how to conduct a workable government without the old parties.

The Tory Party of Queen Anne's reign was discredited by charges of Jacobitism, which by 1725 were mostly untrue and unimportant. Even the opposing politicians used these accusations as an emotional issue to win elections, and the willingness to make deals for parliamentary seats was sufficient proof that most so-called Tories were recognized as being of the Hanoverian variety. The rebellion of 1745 was the final nail in the coffin of the legend of Jacobite strength. It was, as far as England was concerned, a complete fiasco, and, as will be discussed later, the invasion of the Stuart prince in itself was not regarded as dangerous by the government at Westminster. There was, therefore, little chance that the group opposed to the Glorious Revolution could provide a government. Its members were split, its leaders were in ill repute or actual exile, and it developed no program except opposition to the existing government.

The case of the Whigs of Queen Anne's time was much more complex. They won the political fight in 1714 and set to work to entrench themselves in power. There was a conscious leadership (though soon split into two factions). They had a program, at least the negative program of maintaining the Hanoverian dynasty, the Protestant religion, and their own position. There was a feeling of unity. The truth of these statements is best brought out by the defense of the Sunderland-Stanhope faction, after the collapse of the South Sea Bubble, by the Townshend-Walpole faction. After this event, however, the Whigs lost their superior position. Certainly by 1725, when Sir Robert Walpole forced William Pulteney from office, the disintegration of the Whigs, which Walpole not only used but also constantly developed, was well on its way. There is no question that the *raison d'être* of the earlier Whigs was gone, that any party in power had a hard time maintaining its position, and that the gradual decline of the Whigs would have begun during the period. The process of dissolution was definitely, and to a great extent, accelerated by Robert Walpole's ambition, which led him to attempt to assume all power to himself by excluding all possible rivals from the government. Thus from 1725 to 1741 the Whig Party was rent into many factions and groups whose only common end was to keep Tories out of power.

This policy of Walpole's, to gather all power into his own hands, had another result in addition to the fact that it rapidly speeded up the destruction of the Whig Party. It provided a solution to the problem of how to conduct a ministry and the general processes of government amid the difficulty caused by the absence of any party that could govern. Moreover, one-man control was quite in line with the tradition that had grown up with Marlborough, Godolphin, Oxford, Bolingbroke, and Stanhope, and therefore it was acceptable. However, it had a very serious flaw: It could be successful only as long as the Tory opposition was weak and, more important, as long as the great number of Whig opponents could not decide on a common policy and leader. By 1742, when these two conditions no longer prevailed, Walpole fell.

Another method of governing was tried during the following years when there were no real political parties. This was the method of Henry Pelham, who firmly believed that a careful balance of as many groups as possible, regardless of name, was the best method of maintaining a government and his own personal position. It was the only time in the eighteenth century when this method was employed, and under Pelham's leadership it was remarkably successful. The following pages will try to show just how the system worked under his guidance.

A third method (or rather, lack of method) of governing was rule by one of the small groups into which the big parties had split. This was essentially the manner of conducting the government from the death of Pelham until the time of the younger Pitt. It was one major cause for the political chaos that existed during these years, and proved to be successful only during a war period.

With this general political background in mind, we need to turn back in time and follow the early career of Henry Pelham in order to discover the way in which he arrived at a position of political power. Who was Henry Pelham, and from what sources did he derive his position? Few men who have held the office of Prime Minister of Great Britain are as little known as Pelham. Lord Liverpool is perhaps the nearest in comparison, for even the failures of history find poor fame in their failure. The clearest explanation seems to be that the shadows of Robert Walpole and William Pitt the elder blot out or obscure everything that occurred between their administrations. This is patently unfair to the other politicians of the time. Walpole's domestic policy may have been excellent, but his foreign policy was inept, to say the least. Pitt's brilliance as a foreign secretary and manager of the war are accepted, but he paid almost no attention to domestic affairs. These facts must always be borne in mind when the inevitable comparisons occur. Men who were not brilliant in any one sphere often conducted a much more balanced and successful ministry than those who were. Henry Pelham was one of the unspectacular men who managed to direct the government under great difficulties for more than ten years. How successful he was in this administration remains to be examined.

BOOK ONE

The Period of Training

CHAPTER I

Pelham's Apprenticeship under Walpole, 1717–1737

HENRY PELHAM was born in 1696, the second son of Thomas Baron Pelham and Lady Grace Holles. Baron Pelham was an important landholder in Sussex, and Lady Grace was the sister of John Holles, Duke of Newcastle, a wealthy and important member of the Whig aristocracy. The family connections of the boy were to play an important part in his future life, for through them he was to find easy access to the world of politics. Even more important to the young Henry was his older brother Thomas, who inherited the vast estates and titles of their father and uncle and used them to advance himself and his brother in the political sphere.[1] Between the two brothers there remained throughout their lives real friendship and love, which ultimately overcame any temporary quarrels. The power of the Pelhams rested, therefore, in typical eighteenth-century fashion, upon family, wealth, and landed interests that controlled the Houses of Parliament.

When the father of Thomas and Henry died in 1712, the younger son inherited £5,000 and various small annuities for life, while the bulk of the estate was left to the elder Thomas, who was created Earl of Clare in 1714 and Duke of Newcastle in 1715.[2] Henry Pelham thus was left with little but his wits to advance his career. He was forced to live largely on the bounty of his brother. This situation provoked several plans to increase the younger man's financial independence. As early as 1723 the solution was decided upon: Henry Pelham was to marry someone who would bring him a dowry of £30,000 in cash, which he could exchange for the family estates in Lincolnshire.[3] Such a marriage was arranged in 1726 with the Duke of Rutland, who gave the desired sum with his daughter, Lady Katherine Manners. The Lincolnshire estates, thus obtained, were the main financial resources of Henry Pelham and his family for the rest of his life, though the Duke of Newcastle often supplemented the income of his brother.[4] It is interesting to observe that the marriage, contracted in this calculating manner, proved to be a supremely happy one. Pelham was always deeply in love with his wife and children, and the least illness, to say nothing of death, threw him into sorrow and worry.[5]

3

He was, as a father, gay and cheerful, and it seemed that some of his happiest hours were spent in this role.[6]

The relationship between the brothers was further cemented by Henry's financial sense. Newcastle, who had an uncanny ability to get value returned for public money at election time, was prodigal of his own fortune. Henry Pelham was frequently called upon to unravel the duke's personal expenditures, even at the early age of twenty-three.[7]

Though these family relationships merely serve to establish a background for the political character of Pelham, they must never be forgotten, for they help to explain his future actions. Pelham's relative poverty, his happy home life, his family connections, and above all his love for Newcastle and the interdependence of the brothers in most affairs must always be kept in view. But life, and especially political life, in the eighteenth century was never that simple. One must turn to the expansion of these obvious facts to discern the origin and growth of Henry Pelham's political career.

On November 13, 1717, Pelham, a youth of twenty-one, returned to England from a trip of several months on the continent. He went immediately to London and quickly received attention from the Court.[8] The government responded rapidly because of the influence of Newcastle, who earlier in the year had been appointed Lord Chamberlain and was held in high esteem by the Earl of Sunderland, First Lord of the Treasury, and Earl Stanhope, Secretary of State. Newcastle made a move for the advancement of his brother in 1719, when a special election was held at Seaford in Sussex. This borough was safely in the hands of the Pelham family, and Newcastle produced the required votes to elect his brother to the House of Commons.[9] Pelham entered parliament, therefore, as a candidate of the Sunderland Whigs, and he supported that group until it was overcome by the Townshend-Walpole faction.[10] At the same time he formed a friendship with Sir Robert Walpole that was to last until the death of the great politician in 1745.[11] In 1720, through the influence of Townshend, Pelham was appointed Treasurer of the Chamber for the Prince of Wales and thus began a career in public office that continued until his death in 1754.[12] The real importance of this appointment was that a young man of twenty-four, without a title, had gained entrance to the political hierarchy.

The government crisis produced when the South Sea Bubble burst in 1721 gave the Townshend-Walpole faction of Whigs an opportunity to seize office. Newcastle and Pelham, who had family connections and friendships in both Whig groups, were continued in the government.[13] Newcastle received no advancement in office, but Pelham gained his first important position when he was appointed a member of the Treasury Board.[14] In this position Pelham became a financial understudy to Walpole, and the lessons he learned were to be of great advantage in later years when he became First Lord of the Treasury.[15] At the same time he showed his ability. Of the members of the Board—Richard Edgecomb, George Baily, Sir Charles Turner, and Pelham—he alone gained further advancement from Walpole in the realm of political office.[16] Certainly this office was of importance to him because it gave him the necessary training and contacts without which he could not have hoped for promotion to important office.

The South Sea Bubble scandal was critical for the entire group of men who were in office or striving to be in office. Almost all the politicians were involved to some degree in the financial corruption, and Pelham was no exception. When the crash came, he and Newcastle lost about £2,000.[17] Pelham, however, escaped any great public criticism, and when the new ministry was formed he took part in the parliamentary defense of Sunderland. Walpole, with the aid of Pelham and others, worked long and hard to defend Sunderland against prolonged attacks of illegal or unethical behavior. They were successful in procuring a majority of sixty-one in favor of Sunderland.[18] Walpole had been forced to this position of defense because his new ministry needed the prestige of Sunderland's wealth, family, and title to support the government. At no time during the remainder of Walpole's long term of office was the Whig Party so united. The very fact of his uninterrupted power was ultimately to be one of the chief causes of the party's collapse, but in 1722 the Whig Party was solidly behind the Norfolk squire. Pelham's contribution in the debates was important in consolidating his position with Walpole and therefore with the party.

In spite of the agreement within the ministry, there was much undercover discontent and struggle. The death of Sunderland in April 1722 brought matters to a critical state. Newcastle had remained closely connected with the Sunderland group, but he had carefully avoided any break with Townshend and Walpole.[19] The death of Sunderland, however, made Townshend and Walpole the obviously dominant ministers, and Newcastle shifted to their side in the ministerial quarrels. He was readily accepted for the same reason that Sunderland had been tolerated: his wealth and position increased the power of the group, especially with the king.[20] Pelham faced no such adjustment, since he had always agreed more fully with Walpole than with any other man, and Newcastle's change of position brought the brothers more closely together than ever before.[21] This worked to their mutual advantage, since it gave Pelham a greater assurance of maintaining office and afforded Newcastle an ally close to Walpole. The political advantage to Pelham was clear in the election of 1722, when Newcastle named him to represent the county of Sussex and secured his election.[22]

By 1723 the balance of political power within the cabinet had been established in favor of Townshend and Walpole, though remnants of the Sunderland group remained in the persons of the Duke of Roxburghe, the Earls of Cadogan and Berkeley, and Lords Carteret and Parker. The

Townshend-Walpole group was in control of most of the important offices and had gained a firm hold on the king's regard because of Walpole's financial ability. Newcastle was increasing his importance within that group, and with the advance of his position came a gradual promotion for Pelham. When George I went to Hanover in 1723 both Townshend and Carteret attended him. Newcastle was made a member of the Lords Justices to carry on the government.[23] Moreover, Townshend considered Newcastle to be the only member of the government worthy of the confidence of Walpole and himself. That this was the case is clear from the many letters Townshend wrote to Walpole, among which the following are examples:

> You see the niceness of this point, and the many hazards of having our secret apprehensions get abroad; and therefore I need not employ many words in desiring you to keep the secret entirely to yourself, and to make your dispositions for doing what shall be found necessary in the most private manner that may be. You know any hint of secrecy does not extend to his grace the duke of Newcastle.[24]

A few days later Townshend wrote:

> You will easily judge of what importance it is, that our apprehensions, and the provision of money necessary to be made in consequence of them . . . should remain an entire secret to every body, except the duke of Newcastle, to whom I desire you would communicate my letters.[25]

This great confidence in Newcastle was of importance to Pelham because through his brother he learned some of the most secret plans of the leaders of the government.[26] Later in the same year Walpole demonstrated his faith in Newcastle when he went to Norfolk and left the duke in London to direct the whole ministry.[27] This was not an isolated happening; it occurred several times.[28] Again, this was a definite advantage to Pelham, for he gained access to the inner working of the government.

The first indication of the eventual change that Walpole and Townshend were to make is seen in the following letter:

> I received an account last night, that Jack Smith [Teller of the Exchequer] was certainly dead, which tho' 'tis not yet known in town, is certainly true. This may give an opportunity of disposing of Treby [Secretary at War], and putting in Mr. Pelham. . . . I beg you will gett immediately a promise from the king not to dispose of it, nor to be ingaged to any body else; for I think by the things that are now vacant, we may settle our affairs in parliament to our content.[29]

It was clear that the loyal support of Pelham in the preceding two years had been appreciated, and he was to be rewarded as soon as the opportunity arose. The opportunity was deliberately provoked in the next year.[30]

The crisis of 1724 was caused by Townshend and Walpole in order to get rid of Carteret and the others of the Sunderland faction. Townshend had long complained of the actions of his fellow Secretary of State, who was favored by George I, and he was determined to get rid of his troublesome colleague. The brothers-in-law, Townshend and Walpole, taking advantage of an insignificant quarrel over French policy, threatened to resign. Since George I could not afford to lose the support of their parliamentary majority, he accepted Lord Carteret's resignation. As a result of the reshuffling of the cabinet two important offices were given to the Pelhams. Newcastle received the post of Secretary of State for the Southern Department, which Carteret had vacated, and became the third most important man in the ministry.[31] This position gave him and, through him, his friends a great influence in the making of policy. More important to Pelham was his own appointment to the office of Secretary at War.[32] Thus Pelham became at the same time a member of the ministry and, through the influence of his brother, one of the more powerful men in England.[33]

The next years were spent by the brothers in the consolidation of their positions. In order to prevent Carteret from joining the opposition, Walpole and Townshend decided to appoint him to the Viceroyalty of Ireland, which was held by the Duke of Grafton. Since Grafton did not wish to resign, Townshend and Newcastle wrote tactless letters which demanded his retirement. There was nothing for Grafton to do but resign and accept the office of Lord Chamberlain, which Newcastle had just given up. In this way the cabinet adjusted its organization and gave power completely to the Townshend-Walpole faction, but still satisfied the older group.[34] The French ambassador clearly recognized the new political alignment, for he wrote to Louis XV that the Duchess of Kendall "is closely united with the three ministers who now govern; and these three ministers are in strict union together." [35] Later he wrote, "The more I consider state affairs, the more I am convinced that the government is entirely in the hands of Mr. Walpole, lord Townshend, and the duke of Newcastle." [36] The ministry was firmly established by this move. Newcastle was recognized as one of the leading members, and Pelham held an important position.

Pelham held his place as Secretary at War for the next six years and therefore was forced to spend much time on the minutiae of that office. Many of the problems had to do with legal aspects of the army, and Pelham had to clear these through the appropriate legal officials. Such problems were quite varied, having to do with enlistments, courts-martial, mutiny, desertion, jurisdiction between army and civil magistrates, and the king's commutation powers.[37] In all, he gained a wide knowledge of the working of the army, which was to be very useful at a later date. It also gave him experience in the actual administration of an important department of the government.

The only man who had done much to help Townshend and Walpole

and had received no reward was William Pulteney. By 1725 his accumulated grievances burst forth in a quarrel over the issue of payment of the
excess Civil List debts. Pulteney launched an attack in Commons against
any proposal for payment until the books had been audited.[38] He was
answered by Sir William Yonge, Henry Pelham, and Sir Robert Walpole.
The motion to pay the debts was carried by 120 votes, and the ministry
successfully defeated the first major attack against it.[39] Pelham was an
important participant in these parliamentary maneuvers, and his share
was important training for the more critical debates to follow in the latter part of Walpole's administration and in his own administration. The
result of the attack by Pulteney was that he was dropped from his official
position of Cofferer at the end of the session. In his place the Earl of
Lincoln, brother-in-law of the Pelhams, was appointed.[40] Lincoln was an
unimportant man, but the significance of the event was that the Pelhams
gained another agent in the ministry.

Another phase of political life that Pelham had to learn was the technique of electioneering. This lesson was begun in 1719 when Pelham
worked to get Philip Yorke (later Lord Hardwicke) elected at Lewes,
where the Pelhams' interest was primary.[41] Moreover, Pelham helped Newcastle organize his entire Sussex election machine and soothed the quarrels within the Pelham family's many branches and their political
connections.[42] This chore of general election manager for Newcastle in
Sussex was taken over by James Pelham, a cousin, in 1721; so Henry Pelham's next major electioneering was in 1724, when he stood for reelection
after his appointment as Secretary at War.[43] In July 1725 he was hard at
work in the ministerial interest at Scrofton. During the campaign he had
to withstand popular feeling, which was strongly against the ministry. On
one occasion he had to be protected from the rage of the mob by the Tory
leader, Lord Gower.[44] This episode and others, less violent, were repeated
many times during the next thirty years, and in learning how to deal
with them Pelham gained experience important for any politician.

The first real test of Pelham as a minister did not come until 1729. On
January 27 of that year the Treaty of Seville (between England and
Spain) was debated in the Commons.[45] Pelham moved the next day that
an army of 17,000 land troops be maintained, and on February 3 he led
the debate to continue 12,000 Hessian troops in British pay for a year
longer.[46] These proposals were violently attacked by Shippen, the Jacobite
leader, who carried the attack further to a general denunciation of the
military policies of the ministry and especially of Henry Pelham.[47] Pelham
met these charges and defended himself with great ability and success.
Another lesson in the conduct of office was learned, and Pelham's edu-
cation was advanced.

Although the change of monarchs in 1727 had little effect on the control the ministry exerted, it did have an important effect within the cabinet. Walpole gained a greater amount of prestige because George II

recognized him as the one absolutely necessary man. From that time on the equality of power between Walpole and Townshend was gone. Walpole increased his power steadily until he was intervening regularly in Townshend's special domain of foreign affairs. Walpole had a strong ally in this move, for Newcastle had increased his dislike for Townshend because of the latter's continual efforts to direct both the Northern and the Southern Departments.[48] In 1730 Townshend gave up and retired. William Stanhope, newly created Baron Harrington, was picked by Newcastle as his new colleague.[49]

The retirement of Townshend was an obvious gain to Walpole and Newcastle, but it was also a clear sign of Pelham's advance. In the general change of offices that occurred at the time, Pelham resigned the office of Secretary at War and was appointed instead to the very lucrative employment of Paymaster-General of the Forces.[50] This position was one of the most desirable of all government posts, for it involved the possession of the army funds, from which vast personal profits could be obtained by investment.[51] Since this was the case, it was held only by the persons most favored by the ministry. The appointment of Pelham, therefore, showed his particularly close relationship with Walpole.[52] Whatever the cause, he had advanced considerably in the government, while Walpole had removed all men who might oppose his own leadership within the ministry.

During the remaining years of Walpole's administration, 1730–42, the strength of the parliamentary opposition steadily increased. Gradually the groups of people who resented one policy or another of the ministry joined together, forming a bloc within parliament that constantly voted against government measures. This situation was particularly distressing in the House of Lords.[53] There such people as Lords Carteret and Cobham, the Earls of Stair, Marchmont, and Chesterfield, and the Dukes of Bolton, Argyle, and Montrose represented important interests, and in the end all these men opposed Walpole. In the House of Commons the opposition was less well organized, but men like Pulteney and Samuel Sandys led groups that consistently opposed the ministry.[54] The actions taken by the ministry to meet this opposition were typical of the eighteenth century. New men—Philip Yorke, created Baron Hardwicke; Charles Talbot, made Lord Chancellor; and Lord John Hervey, created Baron Hervey—were promoted to the House of Lords, where their aid was a great help in debates. All pressure possible was exerted to prevent further defection from the administration ranks in the Commons, as the case of Lord Scarborough showed.[55] In these moves Pelham played an important part and took the lead with Walpole and Newcastle. Pelham's later actions showed that he learned to avoid any such critical situation when he became head of the ministry.

The question of revenue was the main source of difficulties for the cabinet during these years.[56] The Pelhams and Horatio Walpole were the main proponents of a scheme to reduce the interest on the national debt from 4 per cent to 3 per cent and thereby save current expenditure.[57] Robert Walpole was strongly against such a move, probably because of the pressure of the South Sea annuitants, though all fund holders, large and small, joined in the protests.[58] Pelham showed his first real independence of Walpole on a matter of principle on this issue, for both he and Horatio Walpole voted with the minority and against the Prime Minister. This is the only time on record that Pelham took such a stand while Walpole remained in office, but it presaged his later financial reorganization when he had the ultimate word in such matters. Walpole's plan was to increase the revenue by means of an excise tax, especially one on salt. A bill to this effect was submitted to Commons, where it met violent opposition, especially from Pulteney. The defense of the government's policy was entrusted to Pelham. In the debates he was so strong in his statements against Pulteney that the House publicly admonished him.[59] Thus, in spite of the fact that Pelham disagreed on the plan of financial reform, he completely supported Walpole's unpopular policy, even to the point of receiving a public rebuke. Finally, in 1733, Walpole proposed his plan for reduction of the land tax by means of the sinking fund. Again Pulteney led the attack on the policy.[60]

The intensity of the opposition was reported by Pelham in a letter to the Earl of Essex, wherein he apologised for being a poor correspondent.[61] Later he reported to the same man that he was sure the uproar over the excise would be overcome and that all other measures were assured of a large majority. "This has been worked up by a few people very skillfully," was his final remark.[62] The popular appeal against the measure that had been stirred up, as Pelham said, was the greatest worry of the government, for an election campaign was then in progress. Two letters from Pelham indicate his estimate of the situation:

> Story came from thence [Rye] yesterday and says they are all zealous for us, but I find we must not name excise or Sr Robert. I am sorry to find our friend is so unpopular; I wish we don't find it so in other countrys also.[63]

And a few days earlier:

> tho' I must own to you, I had a great deal more trouble about the excise there [Robertsbridge], than in any place where I have been. . . . Jemmy [James Pelham] has done most incomparably, and so have all his Agents.[64]

These indicate that the strength of the opposition lay in the country rather than in parliament, so that the various measures were carried, even though with greatly decreased majorities. Walpole was so unpopular with the mob that Pelham and Hervey had to carry word of the successful vote to the king, so that Walpole could remain off the streets and away from the people.[65] In April 1733 Walpole went to Norfolk and left Pelham in charge of the House of Commons. In Walpole's absence the younger man continued the parliamentary battle over the "excise scheme." [66] The great popular outcry, however, caused the ministers to drop the entire financial plan late in April. The opposition thought that this move would cause the fall of the ministry, but Walpole, Pelham, Yorke, and Onslow made a brilliant defense, and the administration was preserved. [67] The entire experience was a lesson that was not lost on Pelham or any other minister. Pelham's friendship for Walpole was consolidated during these trying times, and his visits to Houghton, Walpole's home, were much more frequent from 1733 to 1735 than at any other time. [68]

As the above remarks on the excise indicate, the real worry of the government was the election that took place in 1734. Of all the county elections of Pelham's career, this one is the most fully documented. With all his activities in Westminster, Pelham spent much time in Sussex in his own and his family's interest. In September 1733 he spent at least two weeks testing the political sentiment, which he found favorable to his own reelection as well as to his allies. There also appeared the close cooperation of Lord Wilmington, Lord President of the Council, with the Pelhams. Moreover, the lesser members of the Pelham family were very active in the campaign. James Pelham, Sir John and Lady Mary Shelley (sister of Newcastle and Pelham), and Lord Ashburnham contributed their share. The greatest political ally of the Pelhams, the Duke of Richmond, also gave his required support. In April, at least, Pelham was back in Sussex again for the actual elections. [69] The result of the usual fights, job distributions, house seizures for voting rights, juggling of the Poor Books, and free food and drink was that Pelham and his colleague, James Butler, were reelected. Pelham was happy with the result, for he wrote:

> I should not have been so lazy a correspondent, had I had any leisure, but elections have taken up my whole time of late; in which, altho' we have had a great deal of trouble, and much more expence than I thought I should ever have been put to, yet we have this satisfaction that the enemy was beat handsomely, not only in Sussex, but in every burrough where my Brother or any of his family have the least concern. [70]

At no time in the future was Pelham put to such a hard time to get elected. He became something of an institution to the Sussex voters and worried little about the possibility of defeat as he moved to the top of the political ladder.

The various problems of the government—administrative, electioneering, political, financial, and parliamentary—had all been experienced by Pelham before 1737 under the capable guidance of Walpole. The young man of twenty had grown into the mature adult of forty. Pelham had gained a more extensive training in government than any other political figure of the eighteenth century. The question that the next few years held for him was what use would he make of his training. [71]

CHAPTER II

The Disintegration of Walpole's Ministry, 1737–1742

℥ THE SUDDEN DEATH of Lord Chancellor Talbot on February 14, 1737, produced the conditions necessary to cause an eventual break in the solid front of the Walpole ministry. Newcastle had been increasing his power and position ever since the dismissal of Townshend. He had disagreed with Walpole's attitude of isolation with regard to the War of the Polish Succession and had resented Walpole's interference in the office of the Secretary of State. He knew that his local political strength was superior to Walpole's, for he had spent hours of time and great amounts of money and paper on organizing his political alliances. He therefore was ready to contest direction of the government with Walpole when he could get assurance of help from his friends. This personal support appeared in 1737 when Baron Hardwicke was promoted to the chancellorship. Hardwicke and Newcastle were the greatest of friends, and the former gave Newcastle the feeling of strength and ability he needed. Moreover, the promotion left Newcastle and Hardwicke dominant in the House of Lords; in fact, Walpole had to depend on them to get his measures through the upper house.[1]

Since these two men and Henry Pelham made up the core of the Pelham faction within the cabinet, it was easy to guess at the potential strength of the group if it ever wished to act. Walpole had placed himself in a weak position, having alienated most alternative ministers from himself. Still, early in 1737 it was clear that these men were on good terms, for on the problem of the Prince of Wales they were agreed:

> The next day the Dukes of Grafton, Devonshire, & Newcastle, & Mr. Pelham dined at New Park with Sir Robert Walpole, who told them that I had made him a long Visit the Day before, and had talked to him like an Angel for an Hour together on the Subject of the Prince, but he thought all my Arguments [for reconciliation of the prince and his family] made for *his Conclusion* rather than *mine*. . . . On Monday the 5th of September I was desired to meet Sir Robert Walpole at Hampton Court, with only the Duke of Newcastle & Mr Pelham.[2]

Hardwicke, Newcastle, and Pelham were for moderate treatment of the Prince of Wales, and Walpole gave in to their view. The whole cabinet

12

was to approve the position later. But from this time on, the attitudes of the men changed. The rest of 1737 was dominated by rapidly growing enmity between Walpole and Newcastle.

> At this time Lord Ilay and Lord Hervey on the one hand were always telling Sir Robert Walpole that the Lord Chancellor and the Duke of Newcastle were laying schemes to govern independently of him, and that they were certainly in good intelligence with Sherlock and Carteret.[3]

Walpole's answer to these accusations was, "They don't govern me, nor they shan't govern me; but you [Hervey] hate the Duke of Newcastle, and therefore never will imagine he can do anything right." [4]

There was much truth to Hervey's statement, for during the summer Newcastle suggested to Walpole that Carteret be brought into the ministry. Walpole's response was that Newcastle must make a choice between Carteret and himself, for he would have nothing to do with Carteret.[5] The quarrel was heightened by opposed views on a bill for the government of Scotland, in which Newcastle's position was defeated.[6] The culminating event was the death of Queen Caroline. At the time of the queen's sickness Walpole and Pelham were at Houghton in Norfolk, and Newcastle was in charge of affairs in London. He kept the two informed of the state of the queen's health, and in his excitable fashion sent frantic reports at first and then reported all was well.[7] At any rate Walpole and Pelham returned to London, but it was too late, for Caroline died shortly thereafter. This death deprived Walpole of his greatest influence over George II and weakened him in the struggle with Newcastle. All members of the opposition prepared to take advantage of Walpole's weakness.[8] From this point onward all men waited for the inevitable break between Walpole and Newcastle.

At the beginning of 1738 Pelham was seen as a definite ally of his brother by one of the opposition leaders:

> I love the chancellor much, and I should therefore be very sorry to see him become the crutch of a battered minister. If he has engaged to a certain degree with the Pelhams, and if the Duke of Newcastle's breach with Walpole is irreconcilable, why should not these circumstances be improved.[9]

There is also some evidence that the brothers were attempting to gain the Duke of Devonshire to their side, but it is not definite proof.[10] The hopes of the opposition were not to be attained at this time, for they had not taken the temperament of the cabinet members into account. Walpole knew that Newcastle was scheming against him; but he refused to take any active steps against the duke, for there was nothing to be gained thereby.[11] The power of Newcastle in the House of Commons was almost essential to Walpole's control of that body, and this effectively prevented any break.[12] The final and most important reason that no rupture occurred was that Pelham actually opposed it. He spent much time during 1738 calming his more emotional brother and patching the relations between Walpole and Newcastle.[13]

By September 1738 intracabinet relations were apparently good again.[14] In November Pelham accompanied Walpole to Houghton for several days, and his correspondence with Newcastle indicated that he was admitted into the secrets of Walpole's ideas on policy. These Pelham reported to Newcastle, and then he advised the Secretary of State how to conduct his foreign negotiations so that they would win Walpole's approval.[15] One possible explanation for the improved relations may be found in the state of Walpole's health. In September the Prime Minister was seriously ill for several days, and Pelham wrote his brother that he would keep a close watch and send regular reports. It was probable that the Pelhams thought Walpole might die, and they were carefully making peace so that they might profit politically from such an event.[16] At any rate, the reconciliation had been achieved by the efforts of Pelham, Hardwicke, and Horatio Walpole, who recognized the seriousness of a split at that time.

In 1739 the quarrel between Newcastle and Walpole broke out again because Walpole wished to give Lord Hervey the office of Lord Privy Seal. Newcastle was violently opposed to this step, and for the first time in his career threatened to resign. He disliked Hervey and felt the appointment would be a direct insult, and he refused to agree:

> I shall add one more Consideration upon this Head, which is in Common to us all, and that is, that Those who think, their Age, Health, or other Circumstances, may not permitt them to continue long in the Administration, will take effectual care by this Measure to make the Succeeding one as disagreeable to us four, as is possible. . . . my own Party, I think is taken, I have thoroughly weigh'd, and consider'd it, I shall not alone, abruptly, at the beginning of the Session, give up, because my Ld. H[ervey] is made Privy Seal, but I shall from that moment determine, to have nothing more to do, with Sr. R. W. and to take my opportunity of withdrawing from the administration.[17]

This serious quarrel had begun when Lord Godolphin gave his resignation of the Privy Seal for personal reasons. Godolphin refused to change his plan unless Walpole requested it,[18] and Walpole wanted the change. The crisis was again passed by the successful negotiations of Hardwicke, Pelham, and Horatio Walpole. It was only through the efforts of these men that the cabinet was preserved.[19] The immediate solution was that Godolphin should remain in office for another session of parliament in order to give the mediators time to find a final decision.[20] In April 1740 the solution was made final when Hervey received the Privy Seal with the approval of Newcastle. Pelham had been very much upset by this quarrel, and he expressed his utmost relief when it was resolved. He wrote to Hardwicke:

I can't sufficiently express the sense I have of your great goodness to my Brother his friends and family, you have given ease to my mind, and by your successfull negotiation, I hope procur'd what I almost despair'd of, a mutual inclination in both partys to live together in friendship and confidence for the future. I saw my Brother and Sr R[obert] together yesterday morning, and by their looks and behaviour, one would have thought, there had never been any coldness between them.[21]

The expectations of the opposition were again dashed, and its leaders were full of denunciations of the men who had solved the problems of the ministry and of those of their own fellows who had connived with the government.[22]

The preceding events make clear that Pelham was not prepared to break his long-standing relationship with Walpole. His great aim was to preserve the ministry as it existed. To achieve this end he joined with Horatio Walpole and Lord Hardwicke to bring the principal ministers to agreement. The three men did this not once but several times. Pelham's attitude may be explained partly by his great friendship and respect for Walpole and his love for, and dependence on, his brother. It may also be explained by Pelham's sincere belief that the existing government was the best possible one which could be arranged for England. The uneasy peace thus negotiated lasted throughout 1740 and was shaken only by differences over the direction of the war against Spain, though these were not serious enough to rouse Newcastle to the heat of temper.

The War of Jenkins' Ear had been building up for many years. The Asiento Treaty of 1713 had laid a basis of discord between Spain and England, and commercial problems had constantly occurred. Political incidents were the usual result, and they increased from 1713 through the Congresses of Cambrai and Soissons and the War of the Polish Succession until 1739, when war finally broke out. Each side felt that it was the aggrieved party and would make no concessions.[23] The English cabinet was split over the Spanish problem. Newcastle led the faction that demanded strong action against Spain and the fulfillment of popular demands. Walpole, as during earlier crises, worked for a peaceful settlement but was afraid that Newcastle would provoke a war. For this reason he interfered in the functions of Newcastle's department. As the first half of 1739 dragged on, it became apparent that France and Spain were tied closely together and the Family Compact which had functioned during the Polish War was to function again. The difference now was that its anti-English nature was seen by everyone. A war with Spain meant a war with France, and Newcastle felt justified in his long suspicion of Cardinal Fleury.[24] Once war was declared, Walpole gave in to the pressure of events and attached himself more closely to the policies of Newcastle.[25] In June, Walpole proposed a scheme for the augmentation of the British fleet at Cadiz, and he recognized that he or Newcastle was the only one who could press such a measure successfully.[26] In light of this it cannot be said, as Walpole later did, that the war was entirely Newcastle's doing and none of his own. The truth is that Walpole realized there was no other course available. The members of the cabinet were split into three groups over the war: first, Newcastle, Hardwicke, Pelham, and their followers; second, Wilmington, Dorset, and their friends; and third, Walpole, Devonshire, Grafton, and all Walpole's "posse." [27] It is interesting to observe that Pelham was listed, for the Paymaster-General was not a regular cabinet post.

Lord Egmont was probably correct in his inclusion of Pelham, since he had had some part in foreign affairs as early as the Polish war.[28] More especially, beginning in 1739, Pelham was almost always present at meetings held to discuss the war.[29] Admiral Norris revealed that in the private meetings he had with Walpole, Pelham was always present. Pelham must have been considered a person of major importance even though he held no major office. This assumption is borne out by lists of various meetings where Pelham was the only Commoner present besides Robert Walpole.[30] Another sign of his importance was the number of pleas for patronage or pensions that came to him from petitioners who sought his mediation because he had such great influence with Walpole.[31] All these support the belief that though Pelham supported Newcastle in cabinet quarrels, yet he always tried to solve them so that Walpole would not suffer. Having established this equivocal position for Pelham, until the end of 1740, one must determine the extent to which he altered his position and became part of the intrigue that brought about the fall of Sir Robert Walpole from power.

The ordinary processes of government had to continue in spite of the war, the conflicts within the ministry, the opposition attacks, and the ambitions of Newcastle. One of the major problems of 1740 was to provide a regency government during George II's trip to Hanover. Before the death of Queen Caroline, George had made her regent; but now some new form had to be invented, since neither ministers nor king desired, nor in fact would allow, the Prince of Wales to take her place. The final decision was to create a body, to be called the Lords Justices of Great Britain, to act as regent. It may readily be seen that the purpose of the ministers was to maintain power in their own hands, for every man named to the Lords Justices was a member of the cabinet.[32] This became the general rule for the rest of the reign.

The State Papers for the period of January through May 1740 reveal the great number of problems that came into the Secretary of State's office and consumed his time. There were innumerable petitions, pleas for mercy, messages from customs men, examinations into libels, inquiries from most officials of the government, and the respective answers to each.[33] These were typical of the entire period of the middle of the eighteenth century, and it is well to remember them when condemning the administrative slowness of the time. Another major interruption to the efficient

operation of the government was patronage. Almost every important official was beset by a stream of requests for help. Common requests were for
army positions, and Pelham found it a main duty of his job as Paymaster
to make decisions on these requests. Also most applications to Pelham, oɪ
to Newcastle for Pelham, show that Pelham's influence with Walpole was
an important reason for the number of requests he received.[34]

The most pressing problem in 1741 for the government was the elections. Newcastle and Pelham had begun to prepare for them the previous
July, when Pelham wrote:

> I am not at all surpris'd att Mr Campions being att this meeting [of Sussex
> opponents]; I rather think he will not be att the Races, for that he looks upon
> as disrespectfull to you, this he judges as only attending his party, which no one
> could ever think he would not. I can make no judgment at all from any of these
> letters who the candidates will be; Sr. Tho. Dyke told me last year it would not
> be Fuller; and I hope he is in the right, for tho' I believe he would Poll fewer
> than any other man in the County yet he would make some of our friends cool
> at least that would make you uneasy, and of consequence give us as much
> trouble as if it was never so dangerous. I cannot advise about any thing who
> should be wrote to, for I see you have wrote to almost all already. . . . don't
> think it signifies two pence who they set up, no[t] much what their meetings
> are, provided they have none of our friends among 'em. . . . The best place
> our friends can be in is Sussex, and if they don't do all they should, will do more
> good there than any where else.[35]

There are many letters which demonstrate the details of the management
of the Sussex elections, both county and borough.[36] Newcastle and Pelham
concentrated all their allies, and the result was a complete victory.[37] The
unfortunate death of James Butler, Pelham's colleague from Sussex
County, after the election, made a reelection for that seat necessary. Pelham and Newcastle went into immediate conferences with Lord Wilmington and the Duke of Dorset to select a person. The four decided on Lord
Middlesex, the son of Dorset, whose candidacy proved successful with
the aid of the Duke of Richmond, to the pleasure of all concerned.[38]

Besides the varieties of domestic concerns, there was the ever-present
question of the war. This presented two problems: first, the naval and
colonial war against Spain and, second, the continental war that broke
out in 1740 between Prussia and Austria. They must be dealt with separately in these early stages. With regard to the Spanish war, the English
efforts had been unsuccessful. Walpole never gave wholehearted support
to the conduct of the war, and the officers in the army and navy were
split by constant quarrels on the method of campaigning. In 1740 the
Lords Justices gave instructions to the admirals, as a general rule, for the
campaigns.[39] By 1741 the directions for the war were more likely to be
given by Newcastle after consultation with a few ministers, among whom
Pelham was usually numbered.[40] This did little to improve the rivalries

between the generals and admirals, but it does lay responsibility more directly on Newcastle. Pelham must also bear blame for the misfortunes, for he had a share in the directions.

The continental war was another matter. France entered this war as an auxiliary of Prussia, and England supported Austria in a like capacity. In this war George II took an active interest and knew more about the problems than most of his ministers. Once England entered the war, Walpole left the conduct almost entirely to Newcastle and Harrington. Although it was fought largely with subsidies for hiring armies to support Austria, the great fear of the cabinet was the French navy.[41] Until midsummer 1741, Pelham did not seem to be consulted on the conduct of the European fighting, and the ultimate responsibility rested on Newcastle, Hardwicke, Wilmington, Walpole, Harrington, and the king.[42] In fact, Pelham said that he only knew in a general way about the war.[43]

The summer of 1741, however, produced a change. The French threat to Hanover terrified George, and he sent urgent calls for help to England from the Electorate. The cabinet in England replied that they would send aid, but only what could be spared from England.[44] September was a bad month for Newcastle. He was left almost alone in London to run the government while the others retreated to the country.[45] George II and Harrington, in Hanover, negotiated the neutrality of that state with the French, leaving the English cabinet at a loss for the moment. It was at this point that Pelham began to figure prominently in the government's decisions. Newcastle was furious at the king's action, and Horatio Walpole and Pelham were seriously worried by the event that proved to be the occasion of the final quarrel between Newcastle and Walpole; for the Prime Minister undertook to defend the action of the king.[46] Nothing could have been worse for the cabinet at this critical point of the war. Newcastle was ready to resign and probably intended to carry out his threat.[47] Pelham argued the duke out of his temper and promised that the brothers would join and force a final decision with Walpole that would not give everything to the opposition.[48] At this time all members of the cabinet realized that they could not remain in office on the existing basis, especially since the parliamentary majorities were much too small for safety. It is necessary to turn back and gather together the stray items that led the Pelham faction to the decision to break with Walpole.

On May 13, 1740, the Earl of Egmont wrote that the king had rejected Walpole's desire that Horatio Walpole go to Hanover and had taken Harrington, "who is at no good understanding with Sir Robert, and that the Duke of Montagu had forced Walpole to give him the post of Master of Ordnance." [49] Walpole had thus angered two members of the cabinet. In June Horatio Walpole wrote to Hardwicke that unless Newcastle changed his attitude either Newcastle or Walpole would have to resign.[50] This did not help Newcastle's temper, though, as noted above, the immediate quarrel was patched up. In June 1741 Harrington was

Pelham persuaded him to remain in office so as not to make the settlement more confused.[69] Under pressure from the king, Newcastle and Walpole acted thereafter as if they had settled all arguments and were going to continue in office.[70] The result was that a united front was presented to the opposition during the negotiations on the composition of a new government.[71] When the negotiations slowed down, and it appeared there might be no change, Carteret launched a violent attack on Walpole's conduct of the war and presented a clear forecast of the steps he would take if he moved into office.[72] This speech sealed Walpole's fate as far as parliament was concerned, but he made one last move to save himself. He sent Bishop Secker to the Prince of Wales to offer a substantial bribe if the heir would support Walpole. Frederick was so opposed to Walpole that he rejected the offer and said he would have nothing to do with the ministry until Walpole was out of office.[73] In the prince lay Walpole's last possibility of reestablishing power, and this possibility was now lost. Walpole was forced to surrender to the opposition.

While these moves were taking place, there was much secret negotiation going on behind the scene. The government arranged a recess of parliament for the second week of January so that uninterrupted conferences could be held. When Commons reconvened, it took up the issue of a contested Scottish election. After the government failed to gain enough votes to prevent a defeat, it let the opposition have its way.[74] Walpole did not dare to chance a vote. On Thursday, January 22, Pulteney proposed a secret committee to examine anybody or anything the members should desire. The debate was long and intense, but the government managed to defeat the proposal by three votes.[75] These final votes made the negotiators work in seriousness to achieve a settlement.

Six men, with Walpole's approval, met at Pulteney's house to make the final settlement—Newcastle, Hardwicke, and Pelham for the government against Carteret, Pulteney, and Sandys from the opposition. The first issue was a date for adjournment, and they agreed upon Sunday, January 31. The most important issues were the distribution of offices and the fate of Walpole, which the Pelhams insisted was to "be attended with honour and security."[76] The Court party proposed, in the king's name, to make Carteret Secretary of State. He refused, saying that if he came into the administration he would be possessed of the *vis potentiae,* the management of the money, and therefore he insisted on being First Lord of the Treasury. They replied that the king intended that office for Pulteney, upon which, Carteret consented to become Secretary. Pulteney then upset matters by refusing to take any office. Carteret thereupon insisted that he have the Treasury post, with a commission of his own friends.[77] At this point the first conference ended. The government had gained one advantage by bringing Carteret and Pulteney to negotiate secretly, for this split the opposition. A second meeting was held shortly afterward, at which the government negotiators put forward Lord Wil-

mington as the king's nominee for the Treasury. Carteret again refused
that place to anyone but Pulteney, but the latter strongly supported
Wilmington, and Carteret finally accepted the compromise.[78] It is likely
that agreement was also reached at this meeting to make the Earl of
Winchelsea First Lord of the Admiralty. These matters were decided by
the six men, with reference to no one else on either side.

Wilmington and Dorset both objected to the admission of Carteret and
offered to resign. This the king, urged by the negotiators, refused to
allow, and the opposition within the old cabinet died.[79] The factions of
the opposition were not so easily satisfied. The confusion in their ranks
was great, and nothing was done to satisfy Argyle, Cobham, Chesterfield,
and others.[80] According to one contemporary:

> Chesterfield expected to have been Secretary of State, Pitt Secretary at War,
> and Bedford and Sandwich to have been in the Admiralty. When disappointed,
> they entered into the closest amity and intimacy with the leaders of the
> Jacobites. In writing, in conversation, and in their speeches, they expressed an
> insolent contempt and malevolence to the King and his Government, beyond
> what had appeared under the Walpole Administration.[81]

Richard Glover, a member of parliament, indicated that Bedford,
Carlisle, Chesterfield, Gower, Bathurst, and Argyle tried to negotiate
with Pulteney to keep him from making peace with the Pelhams. This
move failed, except that Argyle received back his old place in the
Ordnance.[82] Egmont expressed the general opinion of Carteret and
Pulteney when he said that the purpose of their opposition had always
been to gain high office for themselves and that, despite their contentions,
they had no respect for principles of honest government.[83] The Prince of
Wales was brought to accept the decision reached by the negotiations.
Though he accepted Newcastle and Pelham, he was angry with the dukes
of Richmond, Grafton, and Marlborough, whose support of the Pelhams
made the negotiations possible.[84]

The main changes in the cabinet as a result of the negotiations provided that:

Wilmington become First Lord of the Treasury,
Carteret become Secretary of State for the Northern Department,
Harrington become Lord President of the Council,
Sandys become Chancellor of the Exchequer,
Winchelsea become First Lord of the Admiralty,
Pulteney become Earl of Bath with a cabinet seat,
Walpole become Earl of Orford.

Thus only three main posts went to new members of the government;
the rest remained in the hands of the old Walpole cabinet members. In
addition, the Marquis of Tweeddale was made a Secretary of State for
Scotland, a re-creation of an old job that had been merged in the two
regular secretaryships.[85] The new Treasury Board (Wilmington, Sandys,

George Compton, Sir John Rushout, and Philip Gybbon) was appointed on February 18, 1742, and with this act Sir Robert Walpole was officially out of the government.[86] It had been arranged by the negotiators that the Chippenham election contest would be the decisive issue in parliament, and when Walpole lost that vote by one, he resigned and the changes discussed above were announced.

James Oswald, a Scottish member of parliament who was among the opposition, viewed the changes with a more balanced eye than more interested men. He reported that:

> As matters are settled, we are certainly not ill. Foreign affairs are certainly in the hands of an able man. The Treasury and Exchequer are, I think, in the hands of honest men. The Admiralty is no longer in the hands of those who have made us the jest of Europe; and the army is in the hands of one who, I hope, will make us all at least be respected in it.[87]

Another semi-outsider, the Duchess of Portland, gave a report of the changes that ended with a very important side remark, "All affairs are to be transacted by the advice of Pulteney and Pelham." [88]

Thus we are led back again to Henry Pelham. Throughout the negotiations his name appeared occasionally but never as prominently as those of Newcastle and Hardwicke. Nevertheless it is a safe assumption that he did much of the actual work, since Newcastle was too emotional to carry out the negotiations without the help of both Pelham and Hardwicke. Moreover, as noted above, Pelham was the one who pushed Newcastle into negotiation rather than resignation. And finally, there exists an important letter, written at the end of February, which indicates that Pelham did most of the organizing of the Walpolites and Pelhamites which made possible an effective negotiation of a new ministry:

> Upon what you said to me att parting last night and what I heard this morning from others. We call'd our few friends together, and after talking things over, it was determin'd to put off the meeting to morrow night. . . . I went to Mr. Pulteney to tell him of our resolution, and that what was done, was out of reguard to him. . . . this whole day I have been running about from place to place to satisfy our friends. . . . We have such difficultys and inconsistencys every day, that I own I am quite tir'd.[89]

He concluded by advising cooperation with Carteret for the session, as a trial. If things did not work out, then the Pelhams should leave office. Also it is important to note that Newcastle was in Sussex and that Pelham directed their joint interests in London. These indirect evidences all testify to the part Pelham played in the negotiation and reorganization. One definite and concrete evidence of Pelham's importance was the office he received in the new cabinet. He had been Paymaster for twelve years and he retained that post, but it was made of cabinet rank for him. Still more important was the fact that he became the leader of the House of Commons for the cabinet, even though Sandys, as Chancellor of the

Exchequer, sat in the lower house. There were no official acts recognizing this, since there was no such office, but all actions during the next two years reveal him as such. Therefore at least one of Walpole's main duties fell into his hands. It made him, whatever his official position, one of the most important members of the new cabinet. He alone, of all the members of the Walpole government, received a real promotion in power, though not in the usual manner.

There was one other problem involved in the alteration of the ministry —what was to be done about Sir Robert. The opposition factions were furious when they suspected that part of the compromise for the new cabinet was to be the promotion of Walpole to an earldom. They immediately proceeded to demand an investigation of the administration of Walpole, as had been originally demanded by Pulteney and Perceval. Pelham led the government in opposing any such demands in the strongest terms.[90] In this defense he was seconded by Henry Fox. In February the opposition groups that had been left out of the new ministry were so irate that they decided to impeach Walpole and to remove Newcastle and Pelham from office, since they claimed that the brothers were merely biding their time before returning Walpole to power. They had much proof of their contentions, for Pelham led the defense of the Walpolites in contested elections.[91] In March, Richard Glover introduced a motion condemning Walpole's neglect of merchants' safety. This Pelham also opposed, but Pulteney supported it, and it was carried. Yet Pulteney supported the measure with such moderation that his erstwhile friends began to realize that he had given up the investigation.[92] On March 9 the move to investigate the conduct of the last twenty years was defeated.[93] In this debate Pitt and Pelham were the active leaders for the two positions. By the middle of the month Egmont extended his suspicions from Pulteney to Carteret.[94] At the same time Hardwicke's son wrote to his brother that Pulteney would support an enquiry for appearances but that it would amount to nothing in the end.[95] The answer was clear to anyone who looked for it: the opposition had been outmaneuvered by the men who were interested in protecting Walpole.

When, on March 23, a motion was made to investigate the conduct of Robert, Earl of Orford, for the last ten years, it was passed by Commons. Walpole had collected his strength by appeals to his old allies, and Pelham was ready for the investigation.[96] Once the investigation was in process, the tactics of the defenders was clear: the committee was given no power to compel witnesses to testify or to protect those who did testify, and Henry Pelham was one of the most prominent members of the committee. Therefore little could be learned.[97] Some worry was expressed by various friends of Walpole during the course of the enquiry, but it gradually died a natural death. Interest died on the part of the public, and the committee was closed. By December, when Lyttelton tried to revive the enquiry, he was soundly defeated by a vote of 186 to 253.[98] The Walpole regime was then truly over, and Pelham had carefully guided the last phase of the investigation through Commons in a manner that satisfied a safe majority. He was at last ready to establish his own place in politics. At this time he had completed the most thorough preparation for office of any man of the eighteenth century.

CHAPTER III

The Period of Transition, 1742–1743

℣ THE DEFENSE OF WALPOLE through 1742, by Henry Pelham actively and by the rest of the ministry passively, improved relations between Pelham and Walpole beyond any earlier friendship. By this means Pelham paid the great political debt that he owed Walpole, and they could continue as friends and equals, not as leader and subordinate. In a way quite remarkable for the eighteenth century, Walpole resigned his office, once it became absolutely necessary and contented himself with an advisory role behind the scenes. He was, of course, fortunate in having a loyal friend to succeed him when age, health, and political enmity made it necessary for him to leave office. During the last three years of his life, therefore, Walpole kept in the background and gradually slipped into the shadows. He emerged from the darkness of Norfolk less and less often—and toward the end of his life only under pressure.

In the crisis of the reorganization of the ministry in February 1742, Henry Pelham had flatly refused to take either of the offices Walpole had held. There was some criticism of him for this refusal, but he justified himself by saying that he would not profit by Walpole's fall. In gratitude for this stand, Walpole promised that he would remain in London and assist the majority in the Lords.[1] The real reason Pelham wished to keep Walpole happy with the new political situation was that it would be almost impossible to direct any government without Walpole's advice. He alone knew many secrets of the last twenty years. Walpole supplied this information to Pelham, and it became one of Pelham's sources of strength.[2] Incidentally, it was significant that Pelham, not Newcastle, was the one who kept in contact with Walpole. By June 1743 Pelham was strongly enough entrenched in office to visit Walpole openly at Houghton, as he had been in the habit of doing during the 1730's.[3] During this visit Pelham returned to his habit of reading official dispatches with Walpole.[4] This was, naturally, a secret from all but Newcastle. It was important that Pelham have Walpole available for consultation, for many actions in Commons would have been most difficult without Walpole's knowledge of previous transactions.

26

Early in July 1743 the death of the Earl of Wilmington created a competition within the cabinet for his position as head of the Treasury Board. Horace Walpole, the son of Sir Robert, who disliked the Pelhams, voiced the opinion of his father when he said, "Lord Wilmington is dead, I believe the civil battle for his post will be tough. . . . You may imagine our Court wishes for Mr. Pelham." [5] For more than a month the position was vacant. Carteret, in Hanover with the king, was seeking to promote the Earl of Bath, and the Pelham faction was working to obtain the place for Pelham. In the end, George II was forced to place Pelham in the Treasury because the government absolutely had to keep the Pelhamites' parliamentary votes in order to continue in office.

On July 13 Walpole wrote to Pelham:

> In short, all this is saying nothing; but gain time, strengthen yourself; and enter into no hasty engagement.
>
> If you had taken the advice of a fool, and been made chancellor, under Wilmington, the whole had dropt into your mouth. Lost opportunities are not easily retrieved.[6]

In August, the day after the offer of the Treasury came from George II, Walpole wrote from Houghton to urge Pelham to take the position no matter what qualifications were attached to it.[7] These letters make it clear that Walpole constantly watched political events and supported Pelham against the other factions of the ministry. Late in August, Walpole wrote a letter of triumph to Pelham, declaring that regardless of obstacles that might arise, Pelham would win over anyone else. The letter ended with a long piece of advice on how to handle the king, Carteret, and the ministry in general.[8] Clearly Walpole had no hope or expectation of returning to power himself, and he was passing on the experience of a generation in politics to his chosen successor and friend.

The information and suggestions of Walpole would be of considerable use to anyone in Pelham's place, for quarrels immediately grew within the cabinet. Each of the two factions—that led by Carteret and that led by the Pelhams—continued to plan to rule without the other. Through the fall Pelham kept in close touch with Walpole on the specific problems of the time. The resignation of Lord Stair as commander of the army and the Treaty of Hanau were only two of the major questions. Walpole was informed of each of these, and Pelham asked him to estimate the prospect of the success of a negotiation with the Cobhamites, opposition Whigs, and even a few Tories.[9] Walpole responded with a forthright letter giving his way of dealing with the situation:

> To lay aside all preambles and unnecessary professions, I will only say, I doubt not in the least your making the old corps, and the Whig party, the foundation of your system. Upon that you must build, and make no use of other materials, farther than shall be necessary. . . .

It appears by your account, the Treasury board is awkward and cold, and as you say, lie by. That is lord Bath's plea with whom they are connected, and the declaration of *"keep your places and your temper, and all will go well; we have power, and when we come home we will shew it,"* can be the language of but one man, and from abroad. Is he then so strictly engaged with Bath? Can he satisfy him without undoing what cost him a month's labour in vain to prevent? Can he, in short, remove you, or put the other in your place? How, then, is this power to be shewn? Will he hope to keep you tied down to your present board? It cannot be. But, if they profess submission, it may probably be the first struggle. But then Carteret avowedly breaks with you.

The next great question is, if there be this secret conjunction, is the prince of Wales in it? And how is this to be reconciled? Cobham, with the Pitts, Lyttel-tons, etc., insists upon a total rout of Bath, etc. And the prince supports Bath. How far, then, will the Cobham squadron, who are to be gratified with a com-petency of Tories, extend? . . .

But there is one thing appears very strong. Carteret writes to none of you, and upon such an event as Lord Stair's quitting, says not a word. Lord Stair can have no imputation to lay upon any body, but the king, and, in form, upon Carteret; and upon such an event, no intimations are given to the king's ministers, to parry or soften the invidious insinuations that will be made. Can he be so drunk with wine and power . . . as to seek no resource upon such an event, and not to think of screening, or protecting the king? Hitherto, it is plain, he seeks no refuge with you. . . .

The secrecy of a correspondence with Houghton, will become every day more necessary: for your sake and for mine, it must not be known, that I enter at all into your affairs. Lord Bath, from the moment he was disappointed, turned his eye upon me. He thinks he shall be stronger upon stirring old questions, and reuniting numbers personally against me, than in any other light. He will try to fling my weight into your scale, in order to sink it. I write not out of any apprehensions; but my indiscretion will be thought very great, if it should be known that I begin to provoke valour; and I am too free with some persons, if I was not safe in your hands.[10]

The letter makes two main points: first, the inconsistencies of Carteret's position and, second, that Walpole's name must be kept out of the debate lest personal hatreds destroy an otherwise prosperous outlook. In other words, Pelham had nothing to fear from Carteret in the long run unless the personal dislike of Walpole was carried over and associated with Pelham by the politically articulate.

The question of political alliances available to the Pelhams was of major importance to them if they would be successful in ousting Carteret and his friends. The problem was often discussed, and Walpole was consulted. In September, Newcastle said that he did not see how the Cobhamite group could be gained to support the Pelhams unless a few Tories were also taken into the government—a step he personally dis-liked.[11] Walpole responded that Pelham should make the deal if possible with Cobham and some Tories while he had the prestige of his August victory, or else Carteret might do it and thereby control the ministry.[12]

This was sound advice, and Pelham took it to heart, though it was a year before he brought it to completion.

Another aspect of Walpole's relationship with Pelham was its effect on Newcastle. The duke had long considered himself the leader of the Pelhamite faction of the Whigs, and it was something of an insult to his jealous disposition to find that Walpole preferred his brother. By the end of 1743, Newcastle was expressing his resentment against Walpole. The duke especially resented Walpole's always putting Pelham first because he was in the House of Commons and got along well with George II. His anger was even greater because Walpole had persuaded the king of Pelham's superiority.[13] Newcastle did not carry his resentment further than complaints to Hardwicke, but his jealousy in this situation did not lessen during the lifetime of the brothers. It remained an undercurrent of the next eleven years. The same letter that shows Newcastle's anger indirectly indicates that the moral support Pelham needed to make him undertake the direction of the government had come from Walpole's faith and advice.

In 1744, Walpole's increasingly bad health made his availability to Pelham difficult. Occasional letters indicate that he was still consulted, though much less frequently. The great cabinet crisis of November made it clear that Walpole was still a force to be reckoned with and that he still strongly supported the Pelhams.[14] It was obvious that Walpole's death on March 18, 1745, was a loss to Henry Pelham more than to anyone else. The skillful old politician, besides freely giving Pelham his help and advice, had supported Pelham's position with the king, the ministers, and the public whenever he could do so with advantage. His actions had made it possible for the new ministry to take office easily, and he had made it easier for the Whigs who had been his friends to follow Pelham. Probably most important to Pelham was Walpole's constant belief and trust in the younger man's ability to direct a government. Pelham had always looked to Walpole as the leader, and the reversal of positions was only achieved because Walpole made Pelham feel that he could be successful. This was Pelham's last debt to Walpole, but in many ways it was his greatest. Never while he was in office did Walpole show himself a greater politician or diplomat than he did during the three years after his resignation. The death of Walpole made Pelham at last completely free to prove his own ability, but it also removed his best friend. This loss was never quite replaced.

The years 1742 and 1743, while Pelham was learning to get along without Walpole, also provide an interesting example of government by compromise. The cabinet was split from its inception, and Lord Carteret and the Duke of Newcastle had different notions about the policies to be pursued and the methods of achieving them. Each man had his own claim to leadership of the whole cabinet. Newcastle was the titular and in many ways the real leader of the greatest number of cabinet members, and he stood for the long Whig tradition of government. Carteret was the primary leader of the group that had destroyed Walpole's power and brought sufficient strength to form a new ministry. He had a definite policy for the prosecution of the war, which had dragged unsuccessfully along for three years. Behind these two stood, perhaps, three others: the Earl of Bath (William Pulteney), Henry Pelham, and Lord Hardwicke. Each had his own variations of the leaders' programs but took a secondary seat, at least in the public eye. Therefore it was clear that two or more solutions would be suggested for every problem. Before actually examining the relations among the various men, it is necessary to examine just how the cabinet functioned in the ordinary spheres of government.

In every administration of the eighteenth century the Privy Council was the widest administrative unit. It was an active organization through the first part of the century, though it lost its policy-making functions very early in the period. By its vote it very often decided many problems and was responsible throughout the middle of the century for approving colonial acts and decisions, Irish legislation, Channel Islands acts, and general decisions of the active cabinet.

The Privy Council acted in four general ways: it could meet as a full Council with the king or Lords Justices present; as the Privy Council without the king's presence; as a general committee of the Council, in which case anything could be discussed; or, finally, as a special committee of the Council to deal with a specific subject. The last of these functions was the most active, for there were regular Committees for Plantation Appeals, Plantation Affairs, Irish Bills, and Jersey and Guernsey Affairs. Membership on these special committees was not definite and changed constantly. It was, however, accepted practice that one of the legal members of the Privy Council (the Lord Chancellor or one of the Chief Justices) should be present, and very few meetings took place without one of them during the middle of the century.[15] The first and second forms of the Privy Council were different only in the degree of formality and prestige that the king's presence gave to its decisions. The functions in either case were to approve the cabinet's policies, and the meetings were attended faithfully by most members.[16] The third form of the Council was probably organized to get Privy Council approval for special orders of the cabinet that the ministers did not want to spread before the whole Council, where some members might be opposed to the ministers.[17] Attendance at these meetings was usually restricted to cabinet members and two or three special friends. The leaders of the government practically never attended the special committees, but they almost always attended the full Privy Council. It remains difficult to guess the importance of the general committee meetings, for the leaders of the cabinet attended about half the time. The subjects discussed lead one to believe that they were more important than any others. One other idea gained from examining the attendance at these meetings was the importance of the Lord President. He attended almost every meeting, no matter what type, of the Privy Council. Here, then, was the reason why all cabinets of the eighteenth century placed one of their strongest adherents in that position.

Henry Pelham attended the Privy Council and the general committee meetings with steadily increasing regularity after he became First Lord of the Treasury in August 1743. Obviously he was tightening his hold on all phases of the government after this promotion. Thus we know that the Privy Council had definite functions assigned to it as well as general power, inherited from the past, to issue orders to accomplish the king's business as suggested by the cabinet. The general business was what interested the cabinet leaders most, and they delegated other Council business to the Lord President to direct.

The next smaller unit of administration was the cabinet. Since it had become the center of any ministry, it was also the center of all quarrels within the government. It is sufficient at this point to indicate the relative position of the members of the Carteret-Newcastle ministry, for the disagreements will be discussed later. Newcastle retained his secretaryship of the Southern Department, and Carteret held the Northern Department. Because Carteret was interested mainly in foreign affairs, Newcastle directed most of the daily affairs in the domestic field. But Newcastle also refused to give Carteret any control over the Southern Department foreign affairs. This was the key to unhappy future events. Lord Harrington held the Presidency of the Council, which thus was directed by a Pelhamite. Lord Hardwicke, another Pelhamite, remained as Lord Chancellor and dominated the legal system. Samuel Sandys held the Exchequer post, but he had little real power. Lord Wilmington, a Walpolite and friend of the Pelhams, was the titular lead of the government and held office as First Lord of the Treasury. Last, Henry Pelham retained his position as Paymaster-General of the Forces. Because of the custom of the times, ministers seldom interfered in departments other than their own, especially when no one functioned as a Prime Minister. For this reason the departments operated quite separately during 1742–43.[18]

Pelham's main duties as Paymaster concerned the supplying of the army and its payment. While the Earl of Stair was commander of the army in Europe, Pelham had a friend with whom to work, and he was willing to follow Stair's lead in all matters except the actual cash transactions, as the following letter indicates:

> you will see the whole payment is refer'd to your Lordships further directions, and if there is anything that you would have alter'd or added, you may be assured I shall be pleas'd, all that I want is that the Troops may be paid honestly and punctualy. . . . I have directed Mr Hunter to keep an exact account of all for the benefit of the Publick.[19]

Pelham thus wanted to protect the public funds from waste and safeguard his own custodianship of the army money. This was consistent with his later ideas of keeping expenses as low as possible while keeping the departmental experts well supplied with the money necessary to do their jobs properly. He also had the reverse function to perform—to carry army financial and supply matters to the cabinet. Several incidents of this type occurred while Pelham held the Paymastership, but the outstanding one was Pelham's defense of the troops' plea to be paid in Dutch money and not in the currency of Flanders.[20] He won the approval of the government for his position.

More important than Pelham's position as Paymaster was his post as the First Lord of the Treasury, to which he was appointed in 1743. This had been held by Walpole, and during his long tenure it had been recognized as the chief cabinet post. The holder's prime duty was to preside over the Treasury Board, but in practice a strong individual like Walpole could alone direct the entire financial operation of the government. It was done by the simple expedient of appointing a subservient board, which did little but ratify the First Lord's decisions. This was not the case under Wilmington, when the board, as a whole, was active. The duties of the board were quite varied, for it had to investigate or pass on requests for such diverse things as rewards to Riding Officers for putting down smuggling, payments to the armed forces, payments for subsidies to foreign courts, payments for new roads or repair of existing ones, funds for secret service on the demand of the king, and the usual governmental expenses.[21] The First Lord also was responsible for producing the revenue necessary to run the government. In this task the Chancellor of the Exchequer had a large part, but Walpole held both jobs, and it was clear after August that Pelham intended to hold both. He arranged the necessary cabinet shifts to permit him to assume entire direction of the financial part of the government in December 1743. In this role of raising revenue Pelham took an active part and kept a close watch on the sources of money, especially of customs and the excise.[22] The routine business of the Treasury Office was only one of the duties. Just as important was the fact that the First Lord was either the principal cabinet official or one of the three or four principal ones. In either case the First Lord had to attend to many duties that, strictly speaking, were out of his province. These affairs were usually determined by discussion among several of the leading cabinet members.

One example of the nonfinancial duties of Wilmington and Pelham was the creation of the regency. In 1742, George II had wanted to go to Hanover but was prevented by the press of circumstances and the advice of all his ministers.[23] In the spring of 1743 the king had his way and left for the continent with Carteret. The government had reestablished the Lords Justices to act as a joint regency, and this consumed the time of all the members.[24] Since Carteret was gone with the king, the Regency Board was left under the orders of the Pelham faction, which helped counteract Carteret's influence with the king. In practice the departure of Carteret as minister in attendance on the king left all aspects of the government firmly in the hands of those who stayed at home, except the conduct of the war. This naturally increased the importance of Wilmington and then Pelham as well as Newcastle.

Other problems the cabinet faced were public attacks on the government, its policies, the war, the royal family, and especially accusations against Pelham.[25] There is no hint as to why Pelham was singled out for special attack. The only explanation, which seems reasonable, is that as leader of the Commons he was considered the spokesman of the cabinet most vulnerable to attack. When Pelham became First Lord of the Treasury he was subjected to constant accusations. In some manner the cabinet had to reply, and much effort was expended in these answers until 1744. The government also had the difficult task of raising the necessary manpower to fight the war. The "press gang" was used, but mutinies were not uncommon even after the men were in the army. One particularly ugly affair of this sort happened in May 1743.[26] It was settled shortly, but such occurrences made the easy direction of the government impossible. The question of personnel was an ever-present problem: death, quarrels, old age, and lack of ability always interfere with the process of government, but these were quite serious problems during the summer of 1743.[27] The death of Wilmington was only the last of several losses. All these things made administration very difficult, but that was not all. Parliament, patronage, and foreign affairs added to the difficulties of running a smooth and efficient ministry.

Any executive branch of a government has an important responsibility to see that the legislative branch functions to provide the laws considered necessary to efficient administration. Provision of the finances to run the king's government was, by the eighteenth century, an accepted function of the Commons. In the 1740's many excise duties were sold to private corporations in return for loans, or other financial considerations, to the government. Parliament was often called on to revise existing contracts or approve new ones. In Walpole's last years several moves were started to reduce the government's interest on such debts or to decrease the share of revenues that went to such corporations. In 1742 and 1743 these questions came up again.[28] No great success attended negotiations under either Wilmington or Pelham at this time, but they showed clearly the general interest of the government in its financial responsibilities. Two other recurring problems of parliament during the eighteenth century were the army and the care of the poor. The first of these involved manpower for the many wars and usually provoked strong opposition in parliament.[29] The opposition was usually opposed to whatever number of troops was to be supplied, and this was especially true in 1742 and 1743 when the ministry was divided as to the direction of the war. However, the cabinet generally got approval for its suggestions, despite the opposition. Care of the "Rogues, Vagabonds, and other idle and disorderly Persons" was constantly being changed, but no definite policy was adopted until the Speenhamland Act was passed in 1795.[30] As the 1742 parliamentary act showed, there were no real efforts to solve the social problems of the poor and unemployed. It merely attempted to tinker with, and give enforcement power to, the outdated Elizabethan Poor Laws. Neither Commons nor Lords was willing to attack the question with the necessary provisions. These three types of problems are fair examples of the kind of domestic legislation dealt with during the years of the mid-eighteenth century.

One peculiar problem of the English ministry was the preparation of the King's Speech at the opening of each session of parliament. In 1742 this duty was performed by the Pelhamite faction of the cabinet. Carteret made a tactical error by allowing his rivals to get the first voice in parliament. In October Hardwicke sent a rough draft of the speech to Newcastle and Pelham, so that they could study and revise it at leisure.[31] It was a month later that Pelham presided over a preview meeting of Whigs at which the speech was given out for approval of the party shortly before George II read it to parliament officially.[32] This speech required a great deal of attention, because even at that time it was regarded as the general outline of the policy to be pursued. It was particularly necessary that the speech be well done in 1742, in order not to cause quarrels within the cabinet or to provoke too much opposition. In 1743 Pelham took a more public part in directing the speech, for his position had been improved by his elevation to the Treasury.[33] Thus the authorship of the King's Speech was a difficult problem in the cabinet's relationship to parliament, but it also served in these two cases as an important part of the intracabinet struggle for power—one that the Pelhams won from Carteret almost by default.

One last problem that faced the cabinet at the beginning of each session of parliament was attendance. During the wars of the eighteenth century this was often a serious matter, for many army officers were also members of the House of Commons and could not be in Flanders and Westminster at the same time. Fortunately the ending of campaigns in the winter allowed these men to return to England for most of the parliamentary season. However, in 1742 the presence of the officers was considered essential to the safety margin of votes, and Henry Pelham sent what amounted to orders to the Earl of Stair to send the men to England.[34] He even listed them, and when six did not arrive he sent orders a second time.[35] This was really not a major problem, but it demonstrated the fact that Pelham was the accepted director of the Commons and especially indicated the careful and detailed work that was considered necessary to run the Commons in those years.

One of the most persistent and demanding issues before the government was patronage. Since so many aspects of government were based on personal relationships, questions of favors and friendly recommendations were extremely important. The usual requests might be divided into four main categories: army, church, government office, and pensions. Very often in the 1740's the ecclesiastical demands were the most numerous and difficult. Pelham, Newcastle, and Carteret had many such requests during their joint ministry, and Newcastle, who was considered the responsible official, never satisfied many of them.[36] The Treasury was constantly beset by requests for places in the Customs and similar agencies.[37] There were frequent appeals to the Secretaries of State for positions in their offices.[38] The Treasury received numerous demands for pensions, usually from important political allies, and these could not often be refused.[39] Often the leaders of the cabinet of the day were called upon to find military commissions for persons to whom they owed political debts.[40] Besides these ordinary types of petitions, there were many unusual requests—for houses, personal support for such men as Viscount Bolingbroke, and diplomatic places or shifts.[41] All these requests, petitions, and demands had to be answered in some tangible form, for they were the real sources of control of the House of Commons and often of the House of Lords. Patronage was one of the most time consuming of all duties of the cabinet leaders, and decisions almost always involved the possibility of disappointment for someone who could cause parliamentary trouble unless compensation was found. The government in 1742 and 1743 was not strongly enough entrenched in office to afford many defections, and therefore it was very careful when it made any decisions on patronage.

The most clear-cut problem of the cabinet in 1742 was the war. By this time the entire nature of the war had changed. The Spanish naval war was relegated to a secondary place, and the continental French war assumed the primary position. In part this was because Lord Carteret cared little about America but had a great interest in Europe. Moreover, France was a much larger threat to the position of England in the world. The naval war in the Caribbean Sea, therefore, bogged down for three main reasons: no central direction or control, slow and inefficient delivery of supplies, and disagreements among the local commanders. The first was plain from the almost complete lack of orders sent from the Secretaries in London to the area commanders. The second was a combination of distance and personality. The Duke of Montagu, Master-General of Ordnance, was a firm believer in the use of "proper channels" and refused to expedite any orders by cutting down delays. Moreover, he was frequently away from London, and without his direct order little could be done to send equipment.[42] The local naval and military commanders seldom decided on campaigns or expeditions, and some one of them invariably refused to cooperate with the decisions. Admirals Vernon and Ogle argued with General Wentworth, and all three argued with Governor Trelawny of Jamaica.[43] No success could be expected under such conditions. Finally London officials drew naval strength from the West Indies in order to be protected against a surprise attack by the French fleet in the Channel or in North America.[44] With all these defects, the naval war floundered along for several years, and the cabinet in London must jointly bear responsibility for the floundering.

The War of the Austrian Succession, in which England fought the first four years as an auxiliary of Austria, began without good relations between the members of the old Grand Alliance against Louis XIV. The Dutch were exhausted from the earlier struggle, and they refused to enter the new war actively lest their remaining commercial position be destroyed.[45] English ministers wanted the Dutch to fill their old place as a military and financial contributor. Carteret and Newcastle were so determined to gain the Dutch that the former made a special trip to the Hague to reinforce the seriousness of the situation.[46] Carteret conducted the negotiations alone but failed to gain more than the offer of troops partially subsidized by Britain.[47] The result of the 1742 negotiations was that in April 1743 England paid £40,000 to the Dutch to get their army into the field for the summer campaign.[48] These payments to the Dutch, and by both countries to others, continued to be a major cause of cabinet discussion, and the majority of the cabinet always held that the Dutch should contribute more money to the joint struggle.[49] The English believed throughout the war that the Dutch were not doing their full share. The longer the war dragged on, the more discontented the English government became, and this discontent was one of the main reasons for the final armistice.

The third major partner in the old Grand Alliance was Austria, and in the war of 1740–48 that country was the principal contender against Prussia. The English cabinet, as early as May 1742, was well aware of the poor resources available to the Hapsburgs. James Porter, official British minister to Vienna, in 1742 estimated that the Austrians could maintain themselves for only one campaign.[50] Carteret led the cabinet to support subsidies for the Austrians so that they could continue the war until victory.[51] The cabinet agreed, but the decision carried the seeds of future disagreements. Henry Pelham represented the feelings of these dubious cabinet members when he wrote:

no one can be more attach'd to the interests of the House of Austria, being fully persuaded they are inseparable from the true interest of this country. I might add that the great and amiable qualitys which have appeard in the Queen of Hungary, ever since Her accession, must raise in every generous heart, a warm concern for Her interest. What is to come of the confederate Army this winter, and what have been the political negotiations of this summer, we are as yet but imperfectly inform'd, but as His Majesty and Lord Carteret are soon expected here, we live in hopes of having every thing settled to the mutual satisfaction of the two Crowns.[52]

Because of the weakness of the Austrians, Carteret was active in trying to gain additional allies against France.[53] He did have a temporary success, however, in negotiating a peace between Austria and Prussia through Lord Hyndford, in order to concentrate forces against France.[54] Much time was also spent in negotiating with Sweden and Denmark to gain their support against France. He used subsidy treaties, marriage treaties, and dynastic problems to gain his ends.[55] None of the negotiations during 1742–44 was able to produce the strength necessary to meet France on equal terms as long as Prussia was allied to that country.

Carteret considered his negotiations of the spring of 1743, which led to the Convention of Worms, to be his master stroke. They brought the king of Sardinia into the war, but at the price of a large subsidy. This was a stumbling block and became one of the great points of contention between the cabinet factions. The treaty was signed by Carteret after approval by the king and the Lords Justices (Hardwicke, Harrington, Dorset, Grafton, Bolton, Montagu, Newcastle, Tweeddale, Winchelsea, Ilay, and Pelham) on September 2 and 13, 1743.[56] When the king and Carteret returned to England at the end of the summer campaign, the argument over the treaty broke out. Hardwicke kept a record of one cabinet meeting where Pelham led the group that opposed the treaty. His reason was that it could not possibly pass the Commons because of the subsidy commitments, and he was actively supported by Grafton, Richmond, Montagu, and Dorset. Carteret had the active support only of Winchelsea and Bolton.[57] Newcastle also preserved a record that he made of a cabinet meeting on the subject. He recorded that Hardwicke and Harrington had joined him in opposing ratification, and he added Tweeddale to Carteret's adherents.[58] The split indicated by the two records was representative of the voting strength of the two factions within the cabinet, and it left little doubt that the Pelhams could win on any cabinet vote they pressed, even in Carteret's special sphere of foreign affairs.[59] The Treaty of Worms was never ratified, and Carteret did not forgive the opposition of his colleagues for many years.

While Carteret was conducting his negotiations, the Battle of Dettingen was won by the allied armies, which gave a certain amount of prestige to England and Austria.[60] The battle, however, was the source of a series of events that had important political repercussions. The Earl of Stair, commander of the British forces, was overruled and practically ignored by George II and Carteret when they reached the army. Stair was furious and blamed Carteret for the failure to follow up the victory on the field.[61] This treatment led Stair to resign his command with bitterness and to return home a determined enemy of Carteret.[62] The entire affair was an example of Carteret's contempt for other officials and of the growing dissatisfaction among government leaders with the coalition of the Pelhams and Carteret. Foreign affairs and the war in particular were becoming more and more important as domestic political issues.

The most controversial question in the conduct of the war throughout 1742 and 1743 was the employment of Hanoverian troops by the British. Members of the opposition leaped upon the granting of money for this purpose and stirred up the most flagrant example of bitter antiforeign feeling of the eighteenth century. They played on this theme in their desperate attempt to overthrow those Whigs who were in office. A violent and often vulgar pamphlet campaign was set afoot by the opposition to undermine the administration, and the government responded in kind. The general theme of all the attacking pamphlets was that English ministers like Carteret had steadily sacrificed the interests of their own country to those of a "wretched little Electorate in Germany" in order to preserve their favor with the king.[63] These again indicated the close influence of foreign affairs on the domestic scene and the extent to which bitter political rivals would go in order to achieve their ambitions.

The utter folly of the entire attack was that England was engaged in an unsuccessful war and needed allies with manpower. Hanover had men available and was the most convenient source upon which to draw. The charges of favoritism, in spite of George II's yellow sash at Dettingen, were hardly true as far as any member of the cabinet was concerned. Carteret was usually singled out as the worst offender, but in 1742 Hardwicke, Harrington, Newcastle, Bolton, Tweeddale, Pembroke, Winchelsea, Ilay, Wilmington, Bath, Carteret, and Pelham had all agreed to the use of 16,000 Hanoverian and 6,000 Hessian troops.[64] Moreover, the warrant for the payment of these troops was passed in the usual fashion, as were estimates for 1743, which included further payments.[65] There can be no doubt that Carteret was primarily concerned in the decisions of foreign policy and to that extent was most responsible, but he was not alone in the final votes. In 1743 the same attacks were repeated with more success in parliament, for one bill to continue the employment of Hanoverian troops was defeated.[66] The Pelhams were quicker to read the temper of the country, and they began to amend their position on the subject. The troops were obtained for 1743, but Newcastle and Pelham began to make use of the Hanoverian charges against Carteret to their own advantage. This once again leads the investigation to the clash for domination of the cabinet that had been slowly growing since Walpole's fall, in spite of surface agreements on the day-by-day functions of the ministry.

CHAPTER IV

The Contest for the Treasury, 1742–1744

IT IS CLEAR from any examination of events during the coalition government from 1742 to 1744 that all was not well among the ministers. Almost every decision by the cabinet produced a quarrel of some sort. Plainly no single man or group directed the ministry, and there were several factions within the cabinet itself. It is safe to discount the importance of all the groups within the ministry except the one led by Lord Carteret and its great rival, led by the Pelham brothers. This competition for supreme position was typical of eighteenth-century politics, and it presented a fairly simple example of all the ingredients that went into political fights at that time.

The coalition had been in office about one month when the first rumors of trouble arose. This was a quarrel between William Pulteney and Henry Pelham over the distribution of minor offices of the government. Carteret and Pulteney threatened to quit if their list was not adopted and all Walpole's friends excluded from office.[1] Pelham held firm, and eventually the quarrel was compromised. No serious results came from the disagreement, and by May it seemed to be completely solved.[2] Both sides knew that they had to agree, or both would lose. Since neither wanted to leave the king's service and its rewards, both remained. The satisfactory relations thus settled lasted through the summer. Various lesser politicians like Lord Cobham, Earls Gower and Bathurst, and the Duke of Argyle were brought to support the cabinet by the usual method of bestowing jobs.[3] More important, Newcastle was pleased with Carteret's behavior. He indicated that at the time he felt Carteret, Pelham, and he were on the very best of terms and confidence.[4] The Duke of Bedford also indicated in a letter to Pulteney that the new members of the government were likewise satisfied with the prospects.[5] Clearly, after the initial troubles of setting up the cabinet, both factions were resolved to get along while feeling out the temper of parliament and the country.

By July small signs of quarrels showed here and there, though none was important in itself. Pelham absented himself from a vote in Commons on one of Pulteney's bills that he disliked.[6] Chesterfield was stirring up his old friend Lord Gower, the Lord Privy Seal, against Carteret, who had left Chesterfield out of the new ministry.[7] Hardwicke showed signs of wishing to be left solely to his legal office and removed from a policy-making position.[8] This particularly alarmed Newcastle, for he wrote that even with Pelham he would not be able to prevail in the cabinet without the Lord Chancellor's advice and support. The position of Gower seemed especially acute, for still existing are many comments on his discontent with Carteret.[9] Moreover, several letters indicate that Gower and Pelham formed a friendship and political alliance during this period.[10] This made Gower's discontent much more important than it otherwise would have been, for it joined him with the main rivals of Lord Carteret. One other small indication of these feelings was that Newcastle's jealousy was growing; he felt Carteret was persuading the king to ignore him.[11] In any cabinet of which Newcastle was a member, his personal tendency to be jealous of others can never be ignored, for it was an important part of his nature and caused great difficulties. At the very least, by the autumn of 1742, all was not well among the personnel of the cabinet, though no event had arisen to serve as a focal point for discontent.

The opening of parliament late in the year served to draw the cabinet members together for their mutual benefit. Thus internal quarrels remained suspended for a few months while both groups protected themselves as a whole from opposition attacks. Throughout the winter of 1742–43 Pelham's strength within the cabinet steadily increased. As Paymaster, he far exceeded the duties and importance of any previous or following Paymaster.[12] He was well aware of his position, for he wrote:

> Tho these affairs [promotions] are not properly in my department, yet as I have opportunitys of seeing His Majesty some-times, I shall take hold of every opportunity to facilitate your Lordships desires.[13]

Outsiders also knew that Pelham was more than an ordinary Paymaster. Horace Walpole the Younger wrote about the unsettled state of the ministry and concluded by saying that all expected Pelham to become head of the Treasury but that the Prince of Wales, Carteret, and Bath would not like it.[14] When unimportant politicians could speculate on the advance of Pelham to one of the main political positions six months before it became vacant, his importance to the government must have been extremely obvious to anyone who examined the political picture. The added comment that Carteret and Bath would not like the promotion makes it equally plain that the little disagreements of the previous year were still present and known in Westminster.

April 1743 brought another problem to the cabinet in creating the regency for the king's trip to Hanover. The Prince of Wales was again excluded, and his political allies were angry, especially when it was discovered that "the Earl of Bath and Mr. Pelham, neither of them in Regency-posts, are to be of the number."[15] It was a sign of the uneasy cabinet compromise that these two leaders were given positions as Lords Justices. At the same time, however, the list of regents included Lord

Gower. This caused a serious quarrel among Carteret's followers, who wanted Gower to be replaced by Lord Cholmondeley.[16] Cholmondeley blamed his rejection on the Pelhams, and the fight within the cabinet became public knowledge.[17]

The quarrel over the use of the Hanoverian troops caused further divisions among the ministers. The cabinet supported the continuation of the troops, but the Pelhams were willing to support the disbanding of them in the face of the strong opposition. In the several votes in the Lords on the issue, Newcastle and Hardwicke voted with Carteret, but Lord Gower voted with the opposition.[18] It is difficult to guess what the exact position of the Pelhams in relation to the issue could have been. The Duke of Newcastle voted for the troops, but the actions of the whole faction indicated rejection; and as soon as they were in a position to direct affairs, they disbanded the Hanoverian troops outwardly. The only logical explanation must be that they were playing for public support and alliances with the opposition against Carteret.

The first serious fight between Carteret and the Pelhams was provoked by the victory at Dettingen and Carteret's negotiations with Austria and Sardinia. Almost entirely on his own and the king's authority, he conducted the series of negotiations that led to the Convention of Worms. The cabinet in London recognized this as within his power but deeply resented the fact that he did not keep it informed of the developments and seek its advice and concurrence.[19] When Carteret sent the Convention for ratification, the cabinet delayed taking action. Moreover, Carteret demanded money for secret service uses in connection with the treaty in such terms that the cabinet resented the demand even though he was following previously agreed-upon terms.[20] The treatment of the Earl of Stair by Carteret and George II at Dettingen was a final cause of the quarrel. Stair kept stirring up the ministers in London throughout the entire summer by complaints and requests for support from his friends among them.[21] These two incidents were never really resolved and were in the background of all later developments.

In June the first open skirmishes appeared in the most serious contest between the Pelhams and Carteret. The Earl of Wilmington's health became so bad that it was obvious he could not long retain his office. The Duke of Richmond, who was with the king on the continent, wrote that Carteret was "double dealing" against Henry Pelham in his efforts to solve the problem to be caused by the removal of Wilmington from the Treasury.[22] Few steps were actually taken until Wilmington died early in July, but then both factions moved quickly to gain the position. Newcastle, as the ranking minister in London, wrote to inform the king and Carteret of the death. He concluded his letter to Carteret by saying:

I must refer you to Harry's [Henry Pelham's] Letter for Particulars. I understand you will have had earlier Notice of this Event from other Hands, and

That even, you have been prepared for it. You know my Thoughts already upon this Subject, as well as upon many others, and my Inclinations.[23]

Obviously Newcastle had made it clear to Carteret that he expected his brother to be promoted.

In spite of the knowledge that Pelham expected the position of First Lord of the Treasury, Carteret made no response to the letters sent him on the death of Wilmington. The Secretary of State was working on the king to promote his friend the Earl of Bath to the post. Richmond replied to Newcastle that Carteret and Bath were trying to persuade George of their superiority but that he hoped they would eventually give in to Pelham.[24] For the next few weeks things stood still. No decision was reached. Horace Walpole quipped, "Most people wish for Mr. Pelham; few for Lord Carteret; none for Lord Bath." [25] The Pelhams waited impatiently in London for some reply from Carteret. The longer they waited, the more their anger at Carteret grew.[26] It was fanned by the disagreement over the Treaty of Worms and the treatment of Stair. They felt they were in a strong position because of their strength in parliament, and they thought Carteret was not ready to create a split in the cabinet. On July 22 they still expected Carteret to write of Pelham's appointment without a fight.[27] Five days later their eyes were opened to the correct state of Carteret's plans, for then Richmond wrote that Carteret announced he had promised to support Bath for the position.[28] Richmond also noted that when he had objected to such a settlement, Carteret became enraged. By August, Carteret clearly had settled on a policy of delay to gain his ends. Richmond, who kept prodding the Secretary for a decision, wrote that he had had a stormy interview on the subject but had gained no answer to his questions.[29] Carteret wanted to delay settlement until he returned to England.

A few days later Newcastle wrote the following summary of the situation:

It is very true, that my Brother does say in His Letter to Lord Carteret, that He told Lord Bath, that Lord Carteret always declared, He must be for Him, if He desired it; and It is true in words that Lord Carteret did say so. But all our measures, all our Discourses, and Schemes, have gone, for some months past, upon a Supposition that My Brother was to be in the Treasury; and Lord Carteret even proposed to us the doing it before the King went. But what is said on this Side is quite forgot now; and I conclude, as Lord Carteret has no other View, but His own Absolute, Sole, Power, and as He thinks, by His Attendance abroad, and *Complaisance* there He has an Opportunity of getting His End; He is resolved to strike now; lest, when they come back, things may revert to their old Channel. Tho' it is easy to see, that all His Schemes are founded upon One Principle of *Power;* I own, We are much at a Loss here, how He intends finally to act in this great Point. By His Discourse to your Grace, He declares for Lord Bath: He has not yet sent back Rushout's Servant: and, by what we hear, He writes as little to them, as He does to Us. All His

Rants of P[ultene]y's personal Credit in the House of Commons; of My Brother's coming in, in Six Months, etc; are nonsense. Does He think, that We are now to acquiesce; and take their Leavings? I beg His Pardon; We are not yet drove so low; and, if We would, the Party would not let Us; For I do in my conscience believe, my Brother could not, if He would, support Lord Bath's Treasury, in this House of Commons.[30]

Newcastle thus indicated that he would resign if Carteret did not change his position. Pelham definitely agreed with this stand, for he wrote to Stair that he would not remain in office unless the matter of the Treasury was corrected.[31]

From Houghton, Walpole wrote to Newcastle that the brothers must not give up but continue the struggle. The old man urged that Pelham accept the offer of the Treasury if it came, no matter how conditioned it might be. He ended by saying that he knew there would be great difficulties but they could be overcome.[32] The lines were drawn between those who supported Pelham and those who preferred Bath or some other choice of Carteret.

While the lines hardened against him in England, Carteret delayed as long as possible. It is impossible to guess what he expected to gain from the fight. His position with the king was strong, but he had at most three or four friends in the cabinet and almost none in parliament. The scales were weighted against him, but he provoked a test of strength that he could not possibly win in the long run. George II saw the situation better than his favorite, and he agreed to choose Henry Pelham because only through him could the House of Commons be brought to support the war.[33] Carteret revealed his essential weakness, as he had in 1724 and would again in 1744 and 1746. He had no interest in the details of government, parliament, or a consistent policy. Carteret must stand as a brilliant dreamer and excellent diplomat who floated through more than forty years of British history without ever knowing what the results of his actions would be.[34]

Once the king's choice was made, Carteret put up a good face and told Richmond, who, he knew, would write to Newcastle.[35] The next day Carteret officially wrote to Newcastle to congratulate Pelham on his selection.[36] The letter was quite inept, for Carteret admitted he had wanted Bath and then reversed himself and declared he wanted a firm union with the Pelhams. However, the Duke of Newcastle was pleased with the letter, and all the Pelhamites were pleased that they had achieved their end.[37] Newcastle was right when he said, "It is plain we have got the better of him." Word of the victory was dispatched to various ministers and friends who were not in London, and the pleasure of the writers is clear in all of them.[38] Even the leaders of the opposition were puzzled by the delay and agreeable to the solution.[39] Walpole was happy at the success of Pelham and wrote him a long estimate of the political situation. The old master recommended that Pelham pamper the king for a while and,

You will treat the great man [Carteret] abroad, too, in his own way; give him
as good as he brings. . . . Your strength must be formed of your own friends,
the old corps, and recruits from the *Cobham* squadron, who should be persuaded, now Bath is beaten, it makes room for them. . . . Whig it with all
opponents that will parly; but 'wary Tory! I never mean to a person or so; but,
what they can bring with them will prove a broken reed.[40]

Walpole also commented on particular rising men as to their usefulness
to a cabinet. He assessed Henry Fox as necessary, Sir Thomas Winnington as essential, William Murray as safe and useful, Sir Dudley Ryder as
able and honest, and William Pitt as to be proved. These five men came
to be the core of Pelham's direction of the House of Commons in the
succeeding years. Plainly Walpole considered that Pelham had won the
essential fight with Carteret and could proceed to the post of Prime
Minister, which had been vacant since his own fall from office.

Carteret also recognized that he had lost a battle in the war to control
the cabinet. He wrote a summary of foreign affairs to Newcastle, which
put him more in agreement with the duke than ever before.[41] He tried to
reduce the criticism of himself, at least until he could recover some of
his lost prestige. Probably Carteret realized that his position as favorite
of George II was not quite so strong as he had believed, for the king
refused to give Bath the Garter, as Carteret had requested.[42] He also
realized that Pelham was in a position to demand some changes in the
ministry, and Carteret wished to keep his own position as firm as possible
by quickly making peace.[43] Both Pelham and Newcastle indicated that
they would go along with Carteret only as long as he was reasonable, and
he undoubtedly knew of their remarks.[44] Carteret never admitted that
he had lost to the Pelhams, only that he had suffered a setback.

The final step in the political fight was taken on September 2, when the
new Treasury Commission was officially opened and Pelham took his seat
as the head of that Board.[45] It was a satisfactory meeting, and all went
well between Pelham and the old members of the board who remained
from Wilmington's regime.[46] The split within the cabinet seemed to be
healed, but in reality it had deepened considerably. Each side was definitely committed to gaining power for itself. Carteret could not let the
victory of his rival remain uncontested long, nor could the Pelhams stop
at their halfway position. As soon as Henry Pelham was settled at the
Treasury, he, Newcastle, and Hardwicke began to try to solve the problem of their place in the cabinet in relation to Carteret.[47] The second
phase of the intracabinet fight began at this point.

CHAPTER V

The Crisis of 1744

℘ NEWCASTLE'S JEALOUS NATURE rose to bother the Pelham faction of the cabinet as soon as Henry was settled in his new employment. The duke expected to formulate the foreign policy of his friends without any question from them, but Pelham did not exactly agree with his brother's plans for the future.[1] He began to question seriously the conduct of foreign affairs. The two did not disagree on general policy but on the particular means to achieve that policy. During October the discussions among Newcastle, Pelham, and Hardwicke led to arguments, and finally the duke asked that he and his brother settle their disagreements by letter before the king returned.[2] The biggest problem to be settled was the use of Hanoverian troops for the next year. The opposition, within and outside parliament, was powerful, and Newcastle was prepared to abandon the troops in order to quiet criticism. Pelham was less inclined to refuse the hiring of the Electorate's troops, for Carteret was insistent on their use. Moreover, Pelham believed that if the troops were refused the reason should be the Dutch refusal to do their share in the war. Newcastle preferred to be more blunt with the king and tell him that it would be impossible to carry the measure through parliament.[3] He tried to get Hardwicke to side with him and exert pressure on Pelham to accept Newcastle's views. He felt Pelham wanted to assume the position of Walpole and be the "First Person upon all Occasions." [4] This jealousy was to recur many times during the next eleven years. It never provoked so serious a problem between Newcastle and Pelham as it did between Newcastle and others, but the possibility of a quarrel was always present. In this particular case the return of Carteret settled the disagreement, for the brothers could always submerge their personal differences in the face of a common enemy.

During September and October complaints steadily increased on the part of Newcastle and Hardwicke against Carteret. These cannot have been caused solely by the jealousy of Newcastle, for the Lord Chancellor was just as vehement as was the duke. Both men were particularly disturbed by the secret methods Carteret used in his conduct of diplomacy.[5] In November, after the king returned, Hardwicke was still firmly opposed to the Treaty of Worms and refused to put the Great Seal to it until alterations were made.[6] According to his son, the "Old Whigs," who voted to oppose the treaty as it stood, were Hardwicke, Harrington, Newcastle,

45

Dorset, Richmond, Montagu, Argyle, Grafton, and Pelham, and those who supported the treaty were Carteret, Winchelsea, Tweeddale, and Bolton.[7] This division represented the usual strength of the two factions, except that Argyle often switched sides. Pelham early in December committed himself to his brother's criticisms of Carteret and denounced their rival, though he still saw advantages in Carteret's ability.[8] The events of the previous summer still influenced the ministers, and Carteret was not forgiven for his attitude toward the vacant Treasury, Lord Stair, or consultation with the London cabinet. The quarrel was common knowledge by November, and the only possible surprise would be the time of the split between the factions.

Horace Walpole described the situation that autumn as follows:

> The Parliament meets the 22nd of November. All is distraction! no union in the Cabinet: no certainty about the House of Commons: Lord Carteret making no friends, the King making enemies: Mr. Pelham in vain courting Pitt etc. Pulteney unresolved. How will it end? No joy but in the Jacobites.[9]

"Pelham in vain courting Pitt etc." is the key line, for Horace Walpole was repeating knowledge that he must have gained from his father. The elder Walpole was urging Pelham and Newcastle to draw the Cobhamite group into the government, even with a few Tories. This, in Walpole's opinion, was the only way the Pelhams could retain their advantage over Carteret and Bath.[10] Hardwicke was included in the secret discussions, but he was more cautious than the others and warned them of Walpole's prejudices against Bath.[11] The Pelhams were, in a sense, divided, and they failed to gain the Cobhamites because they were not themselves sure what they wanted to do. At the same time that Newcastle and Pelham were attempting an agreement with Cobham, Pelham took a definite step toward the Chesterfield group of Whigs. He and Chesterfield had a secret meeting to reach an understanding.[12] The meeting failed to achieve an alliance because Pelham insisted that Tories could be admitted only as individuals, that only a few places would be available for Chesterfield's friends, and that if peace were unattainable, the Hanoverian troops must be kept.[13] Chesterfield rejected these conditions, but the two parted on good terms with an agreement to keep the meeting secret from all but Pitt, Murray, and Edmund Waller.

Since negotiations with various opposition groups failed to achieve the ends desired by the Pelhams, they sought to strengthen their own hands by promoting friends to vacant seats in the Commons and reinforcing alliances with officials throughout Great Britain.[14] When parliament opened, the opposition put on a bold front and threatened to cause serious trouble. In reality, the opposition was not strong enough to be much of a problem. It merely caused the ministers to smooth over their differences and function together.[15] The temporary peace between the Pelhams and Carteret lasted about two weeks. Pelham had to vacate his seat in Commons and stand for reelection because of his promotion to the Treasury.[16] This left the Commons without a recognized leader for almost three weeks and gave dissatisfied people a chance to work freely. William Pitt launched one of his sharp attacks on the government, but he concentrated on Carteret.[17] The attack served to strengthen the Pelhams. The autumn negotiations between Pelham and Cobham had achieved a working agreement, and Pitt's speeches were probably designed to facilitate the removal of Carteret.

In view of the parliamentary situation it becomes easier to explain why changes occurred in the ministry during the first two weeks of December. On the twelfth, Pelham was appointed Chancellor of the Exchequer, and his friend Henry Fox was made a member of the Treasury Board along with Lord Middlesex, a friend of the Prince of Wales.[18] Sandys was created a baron and made Cofferer of the Household, and Sir John Rushout was made Treasurer of the Navy. Both these promotions were designed to please Bath; they showed that the Pelhams were not worried about him and were working to weaken Carteret. The last change was that Sir Thomas Winnington took over Pelham's old position as Paymaster-General of the Forces, thus fulfilling one of Walpole's recommendations. One victory was won by Carteret when Lord Gower resigned the Privy Seal over the Hanoverian troops controversy. He had gradually swung to the Pelhams after he joined the ministry with Carteret, and his loss broke a connection between the brothers and some of the opposition. Carteret moved rapidly and persuaded George II to appoint the Earl of Cholmondeley to the vacancy.[19] Cholmondeley was a son-in-law of Robert Walpole, but he was disappointed with his treatment by the Pelhams and supported Carteret's policies. Carteret hoped that by this move he could regain his prestige and restore a better balance in the cabinet, and some of the Pelhamites feared that he had succeeded in his aims.

By the time parliament adjourned for the Christmas recess, it seemed as if a major crisis was at hand. The Duke of Richmond wrote of his fears:

> Linky [Earl of Lincoln] arrived here safe last night, & I am exceedingly concern'd to find by him that things go so ill. however I expected it, & if you dont or cant gett rid of your collegue [Carteret] they will & must go worse. this last stroke of his making Chomly Privy Seal, is in my opinion a strong one.[20]

The elder Horatio Walpole was also worried by the split among the cabinet members. He believed that the public service was suffering and the opposition would be the only possible gainer.[21]

The leaders of the opposition had been waiting for such an opportunity ever since Carteret and Bath had deserted their ranks. Various of them devised schemes and plots to bring down the coalition government, but all failed.[22] The bitterness of the attacks was considered by at least one foreign observer to be unheard of anywhere else.[23] Among even some of the

opposition the vehemence of Pitt against the government was thought to
be in very bad taste and based on the wrong facts.[24] In spite of all the planning and noise the ministry moved along in its own way. Benjamin Keene
(sometime ambassador to Spain) summed up the parliamentary scene
rather plainly:

> We have had a very easy sessions under the auspices of Mr. H. Pelham. Mr. Pitt
> is almost the only one in the opposition that is much attended to. Mr. Dodding-
> ton is very sleepy and very busy. And Mr. Waller collects matter and is called
> for that Reason the Commissary of Stores. These are the chiefs that enter the
> Lists against us. Terror therefore does not come from without, What I fear, is
> from within, From the difficulty of agreement of so many Persons as at present
> compose this administration whose Swords are pretty near of the same Length.[25]

The summer of 1743, therefore, became a critical time for the opposition.
They needed unity as much as did the cabinet, and they needed a common
policy even more.

At the death of Wilmington, Lord Bolingbroke advised the Earl of
Marchmont to observe carefully who replaced him.[26] Thus the elder states-
man of the opposition recommended no move at the critical time, but
careful waiting. Another problem was the victory at Dettingen, which had
increased the popularity of the government and helped undermine opposition to the war.[27] The answer of the opposition was to whip up
feeling against the Hanoverians and against the ministry for supporting
them. For the rest of the year the entire force of the opposition was concentrated on this one end, and especially on Carteret as the leader of the
policy.[28] This tactic won popular approval but did little to influence votes
in the House of Commons.

Moreover, hints appeared occasionally that the leaders of the opposition were not averse to a private deal with some part of the cabinet.
Dodington was accused of such subversion during 1743.[29] It has also been
seen that Chesterfield, with Waller's knowledge, negotiated with Henry
Pelham for entry into the cabinet of that faction.[30] Lord Bolingbroke
himself had much communication with Hardwicke and even offered to
send secret opposition plans to the Chancellor.[31] And finally Lord Gower
was in communication with the Duke of Bedford, planning to negotiate
an offer from some part of the cabinet, which he felt was sure to come.[32]
Thus the opposition was unstable, and many were willing to make a break
if invited to do so by one faction of the ministry. In fact, late in 1743 the
committee of leaders of the opposition took a definite step among themselves. They voted five to four to accept any offer made by the Pelhams.
Bedford, Chesterfield, Gower, Pitt, and Lyttelton voted to join the cabinet, and Cobham, Waller, Dodington, and Sir John Hynde Cotton voted
against it.[33] No one now can tell just exactly what was the reason for this
vote, but the fact that it was made is proof that the leaders were sure they
could not defeat the existing cabinet and could gain office only by com-

promise. Truly at the beginning of 1744 the opposition was much weaker than it appeared.

Though the opposition leaders realized their position, they found no convenient opportunity to make individual agreements with the cabinet members. Besides, the rank-and-file members of the opposition still believed the cabinet could be forced from office and that they could direct the entire government. These men saw only the quarrels between the factions of the cabinet and believed, therefore, that it was very weak. The leaders throughout the spring session of parliament continued to pursue the tactics they had followed in 1743: attack the ministry in general and Carteret in particular on the issue of the war and related topics. Thus the existing cabinet moved along its stormy path through the early part of 1744.

In January Sir John Shelley, brother-in-law of the Pelhams, told the Earl of Egmont that a break had definitely come between Carteret and the brothers.[34] Egmont further noted that the Pelhams intended to leave office, though he doubted that they would. Moreover, he reported that Carteret had personally insulted Henry Pelham by saying, "He [Pelham] was only a chief clerk to Sir Robert Walpole, and why he should expect to be more under me, I can't imagine: he did his drudgery and he shall do mine."[35] Whatever the provocation or intentions of the Pelhams, they remained in office, and Pelham directed the cabinet's policies through the House of Commons. In particular, Pelham defended the war and the army in Flanders and won a decisive vote in their favor.[36] A very interesting aspect of this debate was that Pitt and Lyttelton took no part for the opposition. The day after the debate Pitt rose in the Commons and made a speech against the entire idea of the war, but he carefully avoided any attack on Pelham and concentrated on Carteret.[37] Shortly afterward Sir George Lyttelton deserted the opposition and supported Pelham for the first time, a position he constantly maintained for several years.[38] Both the opposition and the Pelhams were slowly feeling their way toward possible future agreement, but they were not sufficiently pressed to hurry. Richard Glover preserved the attitude of the regular opposition when he accused Chesterfield, Gower, Marchmont, Pitt, and Lyttelton of keeping in touch with Pelham so that when a critical event took place they could take advantage of it and join hands.[39] It is clear that both sides were maneuvering to put themselves in an advantageous position for the crisis all expected.

At the end of January, Edmund Waller moved to examine all aspects of the Treaty of Worms. Again Pelham defended the policy of Carteret, though it had long been plain that he opposed the treaty in the cabinet.[40] This did not mean that the friction within the cabinet had been reduced, but merely that Pelham was still holding to his existing government rather than preparing for a change. Both Horatio Walpoles have left a steady record of discontent during the winter. Horace the Younger wrote:

> Don't fear from Lord Carteret's silence to you; he never writes: if that were a
> symptom of disgrace, the Duke of Newcastle would have been out long ere
> this: and when the Regency were not thought worthy of his notice, you could
> not expect it.[41]

His uncle, the elder Horatio, wrote:

> For you must know, that, notwithstanding the common danger, they are, if
> possible, greater enemies than ever; and that appears in all the deliberations in
> council, at this great and critical juncture.[42]

Trevor's answer to the above letter reflected the dissatisfaction of the under officials at the unsettled state of affairs. They could not be sure which
side of the quarreling cabinet should be obeyed, and the whole administration suffered as a result.[43] The elder Horatio Walpole also noted that
the divisions among the ministers and, partly, their want of capacity made
the administration "the weakest I ever knew." [44] The longer the quarrel
between the factions lasted, the more the king's service suffered. The
situation was becoming intolerable not only to the participants but also
to the whole English ruling class.

In March, Carteret was so irate at the rest of the ministers that he refused to attend formal dinners when the other men were present. Furthermore, Lord Bath split with Carteret and joined the Pelhams.[45] Carteret
pursued his course and began to insist on his views in all small matters of
governing. He even went so far as to provoke a new quarrel with Pelham
over three vacant army commissions.[46] This was the situation when word
arrived that the elder son of the Pretender had joined the French army
on the Channel. The English government was furious at this breach of
previous treaties and sent strong protests to the French. The reply of the
French government was to declare war on the English. The split within
the English ministry worked to the disadvantage of the whole allied force,
for the quarrel kept them from planning a campaign for the summer.[47]
The allied generals left England in disgust at the political feud that had
destroyed the chance of winning much military success during the summer, especially in view of the new threat.

While the foreign situation was deteriorating, Pelham rode out the
storm of opposition attacks on the conduct of the war.[48] He also took up
relations again with certain leaders of the opposition. This move led Lord
Marchmont to hope publicly that Pelham would gain the support of all
"honest" men without regard to party. In plain words he hoped that
Pelham would focus all men against Lord Carteret and lead a national
government.[49] By the end of April the bulk of the parliamentary work was
done for the session, and Pelham was commended for the way he had
handled the problems.[50] The opposition apparently gave up any attempt
to vote the cabinet out of office, after a decisive defeat on a war finance
issue that the government won by a majority of 114. The whole opposi-

tion then saw it had failed, and most of the leaders were ready to make a compromise. Carteret must have sensed his position to some degree, for he became more amenable to cooperation with his fellow ministers.[51] Moreover, Newcastle began to insist on a louder voice in foreign affairs, and Carteret gave in somewhat when Newcastle was backed by Pelham, Harrington, and Hardwicke.[52] At this very time another change occurred, for Henry Pelham began to suggest methods of foreign negotiation. Newcastle even attributed his success to Pelham's advice in convincing George II of the need for a new policy toward the Dutch.[53] Therefore at the end of the parliament a new situation had developed. The opposition was finally ready to compromise, Carteret was slightly on the defensive with regard to the Pelhams, and Newcastle, Pelham, Hardwicke, and Harrington were united and ready to move as a group to gain their ends. All that was needed for a final showdown was a particular crisis to start the three forces in motion.

Lord Carteret made the first move in the effort to bring some sort of a solution to the government impasse. He approached Newcastle, who reported their conversation to Hardwicke as follows:

> I had a very extraordinary Conversation with My Lord Carteret, going with him yesterday to Kensington; which, with the late Incidents that have pass'd between Us, produced a more extraordinary Declaration from Him, to My Brother, & me, last night. He said, that, if My Lord Harrington had not been gone, He intended to have spoke very fully to Us; That He would do it, when your Lordship, Lord Harrington, and We should be together. That Things could not remain, as they were; That They must be brought to some Precision; That He would not be brought down, to be overruled, and outvoted, upon every Point, by Four to One; That if We would take the Government upon us, We might; But if We could not, or would not, undertake it, There must be some Direction, and He would do it. Much was said upon what pass'd last year; upon the Probability of the King's Going abroad; etc. Every thing pass'd coolly, and civilly, but pretty resolutely, on both sides. At last, He seem'd to return to His usual Professions, and Submisssion. Upon this, My Brother, & I, thought it absolutely necessary, that We should immediately determine amongst Ourselves, what Party to take; and He has therefore desired Me to see Your Lordship, and talk it over with You, in the Course of this Day. We Both, look upon it, that either My Lord Carteret will go out, (which I hardly think, is His Scheme, or at least His Inclination) or that He will be uncontrollable Master. My Brother supposes, that, in that Case, He means, that We should go out. . . . Upon the whole, I think, The Event must be, that we must either take upon us the Government; or go out. I beg, Your Lordship would consider this Matter seriously, in the Course of the Day.[54]

The most important part of this passage is in the last four sentences, for in those Newcastle indicated that Pelham had the deciding voice in the policy the brothers were to pursue. This meant that Newcastle's jealousy was no longer to be the dominating force in the quarrels between the cabinet factions but that Pelham's more practical hand was to direct the inevitable crisis.

A few days later Newcastle was furious at the king because he felt that Carteret had completely captivated the monarch. He wrote to Pelham:

> My Intention therefore is, to remain, 'til the rest of My Friends shall think, they can go on no longer; and then, most heartily, willingly, & cheerfully, to go out with Them; and whilst I do remain, To confine Myself, singly, to the Business of the Southern Province which is singly now confined to the Court of Turin. . . . To go into the King's Closet, as seldom, as possible; and to avoid being there with Lord Carteret, whenever I can.[55]

One of the main reasons for this tirade was the king's desire, supported by Carteret, to go to Hanover. The Pelhams were strongly opposed to such a plan because of the experience of the previous summer. In the end the king gave in and decided to remain in England, but he did it angrily and told Hardwicke, "I know what this is, it is Contention for power, & from motives of that kind I am to be confined." [56] George was, of course, quite right in his suspicions, but the Pelhams stoutly denied any intention to "confine" him. In August the king was still angry over being prevented from going to Hanover and blamed the unsuccessful warfare on his own absence. Moreover, George blamed Newcastle and Pelham for keeping him in England by bad advice. Newcastle flared back that the king had three months before parliament opened to dismiss those of his ministers who had given dishonest advice.[57] George, for obvious reasons, made no reply.

While Newcastle was becoming more and more angry from personal slights and incidents, Pelham was working behind the scene to make a change of ministry possible. Through William Murray, the future Lord Mansfield, and the Earl of Stair he established communication with Lord Bolingbroke. Either directly or indirectly Pelham indicated to Bolingbroke and the Tories that he was ready to lead a "national government" if they would support him.[58] During the next four days Stair interviewed Lord Chesterfield upon the question of a new ministry led by Pelham. Chesterfield must have made objections to bringing his opposition Whig friends into such a government because of Pelham's attitude the year before during their negotiations. Stair, probably with the authority of Pelham, told Chesterfield that affairs were now changed and that the same conditions would not be insisted on.[59] While Pelham was working with Bolingbroke and Chesterfield separately, those two men met and agreed that union with the Pelhams was the only course open to them.[60] The Earl of Chesterfield was particularly worried about future jealousies of the Pelhams that might lead to difficulties. Bolingbroke convinced him that such fears were groundless in light of the present situation, and Chesterfield finally agreed.[61] The important aspect of these negotiations was that Pelham was accepted by the opposition as the leader of the government faction with whom they were willing to deal, and that he was accepted by them as the future leader of a coalition government.

At the time these secret political deals were being formed in England, foreign affairs took an unfortunate turn. Prussia declared war on Austria again, and the Austrian armies were withdrawn from Alsace to meet the new threat. Carteret and the king wanted to grant a subsidy to Saxony to gain help for the Austrians. This provided Pelham with the question of policy he wanted to provoke a ministerial crisis.

> My Brother had a longer Audience, and enter'd more fully into the matter [aid for Saxony] with the King; Shew'd a Disposition to do, what should be necessary for the support of the Common Cause: Insisted upon having the Concurrence of Holland, that It might appear to be a British Measure: Had several Flings at Lord Carteret's Conduct, & Manner, without Naming him: To which the King reply'd, that All that might be true, but did not relate to the present Question, which was the Necessity of the Thing. Upon the Whole My Brother told him, that We would seriously consider it amongst Ourselves: and that the King's Servants must tell him, What they would, & would not do.[62]

The two brothers, Hardwicke, and Harrington had a special emergency meeting to determine their final action with regard to Lord Carteret's new policy. The stand taken by the Pelhamites against Carteret made the king even more angry with them than he had been.[63] Pelham was as irritated with the king's behavior as was Newcastle, but insisted they must resign on a public issue and not on a private quarrel.[64] He urged that the subsidy to Saxony be made the issue, and desired a meeting of their faction at the Duke of Grafton's house to determine their policy before a cabinet meeting Carteret had called. It is clear that Hardwicke and Harrington sided with Pelham and wanted to have an issue of policy on which to provoke the crisis with Carteret.[65] By the first of September the Pelhamite faction had made its decision to cause a split with Carteret on a public issue and to do it before the opening of the next parliament.

The first active cooperation between the Pelhams and the opposition groups came at the election of Lord Stair as one of the sixteen Scottish peers. Carteret, in league with the Marquis of Tweeddale, was secretly working to elect Lord Aberdeen. Stair won the election when Pelham discovered Carteret's scheme and stirred his old and new friends to support their political ally.[66] The great coalition against Carteret was finally working.

Lord Bolingbroke suggested that the issue to force the removal of Carteret should be the Secretary's Convention of Worms. If the Pelhams used this issue, Bolingbroke promised them Tory support in parliament.[67] The leaders of the opposition were sure that they would not have to worry about Carteret because the rank and file of the government Whigs were so angry at him that Pelham could not save him under any circumstances. Furthermore, Lord Bath had completely deserted his erstwhile ally and joined the intrigue against him.[68] Carteret had no possible prospect of gaining strength from any source. It seemed only a matter of days until he would fall.

Pelham moved carefully, however, and refused to be hurried. Neither the opposition's eagerness nor the jealous urgings of Newcastle could make him speed his preparations to oust Carteret from the cabinet.[69] There can be no question that Pelham disliked, if not actually hated, Carteret, for this personal attitude was commented on at the time and later events supported the truth of the comments.[70] In spite of his personal feelings, Pelham had learned from Robert Walpole's experiences not to force quarrels to a breaking point until the opponent had been rendered politically harmless. Carteret was not to be ousted until Pelham was absolutely sure that the Secretary would be unable to become a parliamentary force in opposition to the government.

Pelham's slowness to force a showdown with Carteret led many of the opposition to doubt his sincerity. Even the Duke of Dorset, Lord Steward, was sometimes afraid that the Pelhams were not absolutely determined to cause the break.[71] It is small wonder that men like Waller, Pitt, Cobham, and even Chesterfield often thought they were being duped, when Pelham's own friends also doubted his actions.[72] Several times Bolingbroke had to soothe his allies and beg them to wait.[73] He was almost the only opposition leader to know from personal experience the difficulties of speed in any government alteration. Bolingbroke rightly saw that the united opposition might defeat Pelham on a particular issue, but that it could not win permanently; he would return to office with increased power and without them.[74] They always ended discussions by admitting that Pelham held the whip and could drive as he wished. When the opposition admitted this, Pelham had proof that Carteret could be safely removed. The crisis could be provoked.

Carteret's main strength was the king's favor, and Pelham's was parliamentary support and careful preparation for the rupture. It was really an unequal fight, but men at the time did not realize, until after the crisis, how completely Carteret had been outmaneuvered. The plans for the removal of Carteret were decided in September by Pelham, Newcastle, and Hardwicke. Their first step was to draw up a paper on the state of affairs for the king. Hardwicke phrased the document, and it was put in final form by the three leaders and Harrington. Then it was presented to their friends in the cabinet (Devonshire, Dorset, Grafton, Richmond, Montagu, and the new Argyll), who approved it and promised to support its terms.[75] Newcastle then presented the Remonstrance to the king on October 31.[76]

At the very moment of the need for greatest unity among the Pelhamites, a personal quarrel broke out between Newcastle and Pelham.

They could not reach a private agreement over distribution of money and the eventual inheritance of Newcastle's estates. Pelham's eldest daughter was to marry a cousin, the Earl of Lincoln, and the brothers could not adjust their ideas on settlements.[77] Newcastle called on Hardwicke to support him, and the Chancellor did his best to patch up the quarrel, though it was plain that he believed Pelham to be right.[78] The fight was finally settled as Pelham wished, but Newcastle was angry for a long time at both his brother and his friend. The incident had come very near to destroying the cabinet completely, and only Hardwicke's tact had saved the situation. It was important because it was an example of a state of affairs that recurred several times later. However, of all the brothers' violent personal fights, this was the only one that nearly caused a political split. In spite of Newcastle's threats to resign at this time, he still continued to attend to his political business, and the quarrel did little harm to the plan to remove Carteret.[79]

The Memorial presented to the king included two main provisions: (1) Prussia must be detached from France and reconciled to Austria, and (2) the States General of the Netherlands must be brought to execute its treaties and help Great Britain.[80] These were quite opposed to the war policy of Carteret (now become Earl of Granville), which was based almost entirely on subsidy treaties to gain help for Austria. When Newcastle presented the Memorial, he spoke to the king in its favor. Pelham followed on November 2, when he insisted that George accept the Memorial as a basis for a shift in foreign policy.[81] Pelham met with "sullenness, ill-humour, fear," and opposition on the part of the king, who refused to admit the necessity of reversing his favorite. The king informed Granville of the situation in a short conference immediately followed Pelham's interview. In the next several days Hardwicke and Harrington continued the pressure with personal interviews and urged that the Dutch be forced to join the war.[82] Then the process was continued by the lesser members of the Pelham faction: Dorset, Grafton, Richmond, and Argyll. Only one conclusion can be reached: that this group was determined to apply strong and constant pressure on the king until he gave way and dismissed Granville. Because Pelham had the only extended interview, it must be assumed that he presented the bulk of the arguments of his party, which the others merely seconded. If this assumption is warranted, it is another strong proof that he was recognized as leader of the group.[83]

George II knew that the crisis had arrived and ordered Lord Cholmondeley, the Lord Privy Seal, to send for his father-in-law, Lord Orford. George wanted advice from the "old master politician" before parliament met.[84] Lord Marchmont believed that George was trying to get Orford to persuade the Pelhams to compromise their difficulties and continue in office with Granville.[85] The king desperately wanted to keep Granville in office and could see no other approach as likely to succeed

as support from Pelham's political mentor, Walpole. This move dis-
heartened the members of the opposition at first, but for some unknown
reason they recovered their spirits between the sixth and the eighth of
November. Perhaps they learned that Walpole was too sick to make the
trip. At any rate, on the latter date Bolingbroke was sure that his Tories
were in a position to be assured of some power, and Chesterfield was
prepared to receive a message of alliance from Pelham.[86] George's move
had failed to bring the reconciliation he desired, and Newcastle was
triumphant.[87]

The time from November 10 until November 24, when Granville finally
resigned, was spent in negotiations on the part of various groups to reach
final settlement on reconstruction of the cabinet. On November 10 Newcastle wrote:

> Perhaps Lord Granville may desire to be president, with a garter. I own, I do
> not quite see the necessity of flinging him into a rage of opposition, if we could,
> without it, find means of satisfying Lord Orford, and a certain number of his
> friends; for, without this last, we have no ground to stand on.[88]

Here one can see typical eighteenth-century politics at work, but, more
important, one can also see that the Pelham group knew they had already won and were thinking of the future.

Also on the tenth, Chesterfield and Bolingbroke agreed on their specific demands in preparation for a meeting of Chesterfield and Pelham.[89]
Sometime before November 15, and again on that date, the two held
conferences on the formation of a new ministry. They were apparently
successful in reaching a tentative agreement, for they parted from the
second one with the prospect of meeting a third time as soon as the
resignation had taken place and official decisions could be made.[90] The
stage was set for the public showing, but Granville made one last effort
to save himself on November 20 by offering to form a ministry with the
opposition.[91] Pelham had prepared his ground too well and the opposition was too sure of his success for Granville to break up their alliance.
This must, therefore, be regarded as a final desperate attempt on Granville's part to save his position. Like George's attempt at reconciliation,
it failed.

A few days before Granville's futile contact with the opposition,
George II revealed his intense bitterness toward the ministry in a tirade
against Harrington. During the course of the interview Harrington told
the king to appoint Granville to carry on his work. George furiously replied that Granville could not, for the Pelham faction had allied all the
great lords against him and through their influence would control a majority of the House of Commons.[92] George knew that he was defeated, but
he knew too that he still had the power to make life miserable for the
victors. Lord Orford, several days after the resignation, wrote to the king
suggesting that the Pelhams were seriously worried by his attitude:

I am very sensible, and heartily concern'd for ye great uneasiness, yr Majesty must be under, in ye present circumstances; But it is not in my power, to render your Majesty any service, in the manner you seem to expect and require of me. The present suspence is certain destructive to all your affairs both at home & abroad. For God's sake Sr. give ye proper & necessary support & authority to those, in whose hands you have plac'd your Administration; By that means, I think yr majesties affairs will be carried through, without great difficulty: Any other method, at present, will but increase the impracticability of all business; All new attempts are new confusion. Pray Sr. putt yr. affairs in motion, & you will soon see, who are willing & able to serve you.[93]

George admitted defeat when he asked the Pelhams to write his speech for the opening of parliament. Hardwicke wrote the message, which was then approved by his friends.[94] George accepted it, and the crisis was over except for the formality of resignation, which followed on November 24. On the same day Lord Harrington was appointed Secretary of State for the Northern Department and received the seals from the king.[95]

The simple weight of numbers and power in parliament had forced Granville out of office. Combined with this main reason were the careful preparations of the Old Whigs led by Pelham, the jealousy of Newcastle, the union of opposition Whigs and Hanoverian Tories and their desire for office, Granville's failure to establish a personal following that would have helped him in his time of trouble, and finally Granville's foreign policies, which were unpopular in England because they were expensive and led to no advantageous results. Pelham had taken advantage of all these things to remove his rival from office, yet there is no hint in all the transactions that he did it for anything but the good of the country, as he saw it.

The problem of the resignation was not over with the events of November 24, 1744. There was the preparation of a new cabinet that would satisfy all elements that united to overthrow Granville. On November 24, Chesterfield communicated to Marchmont that he had chosen Ireland for his office for several reasons: it did not involve hard work; it had patronage; it gave entry to the Closet when desired but not too often; it was of cabinet rank; and by this selection he would keep the friendship of the other ministers.[96] On the very day of the crisis, therefore, Chesterfield was prepared to enter the ministry in a definite position. The immediate question facing the unsettled ministry was the meeting of parliament on November 27. To keep everything quiet until the distribution of offices was completed was absolutely necessary. Leaders of all factions cooperated to this end, and the King's Speech was approved without trouble. Practically no other business was transacted until December 22, when parliament adjourned until January 10.[97] All knew that the legislative calm was the cover for political negotiations, which moved slowly.[98] Newcastle caused a certain amount of trouble, for

he felt that Pelham and Harrington would unite to gain their ends whenever he disagreed with one of them.[99] His jealousy was a constant thorn
in the side of any ministry. Everyone moved carefully and tried to avoid
quarrels, but with so many conflicting interests it was natural that it took
weeks to form the new cabinet.

Pelham's plan was to unite, as far as possible, all the groups represented in parliament. He was conciliatory by temperament and was
determined not to have the strong and violent parliamentary opposition
that Robert Walpole and Lord Granville had faced.[100] Chesterfield soon
sent a list of the men whom he, Cobham, and Gower considered necessary
to satisfy the opposition.[101] Newcastle responded two days later with an
invitation to the three to meet with Harrington, Hardwicke, Pelham, and
himself to decide on the offices desired.[102] The opposition leaders—Bedford, Chesterfield, Gower, Pitt, Lyttelton, Cobham, Waller, Dodington,
and Hynde Cotton—were ready with their arguments, and the long
series of talks began.[103] The greatest difficulty was to provide for Pitt. The
king flatly refused to admit him to office, and Pitt could not join
Granville, his bitterest enemy, in opposition. Therefore his friends received posts, and he was promised one as soon as the king could be
brought to agree.[104] Early in the post-resignation period Horace Walpole
wrote the story of the resignation to his friend Horace Mann. He clearly
indicated that Lord Winchelsea, Tweeddale, Bolton, and Cholmondeley
were the only members of the cabinet who did not take part in the
intrigue.[105] Thus, there were only a few cabinet places available to
Pelham to use in negotiating. In fact, the position was so difficult that
Horatio Walpole wrote to his brother, Robert, that the best thing for

Office	Old Cabinet	New Cabinet
Archbishop of Canterbury	Potter	Potter
Lord Chancellor	Hardwicke	Hardwicke
Lord President	Harrington	Dorset
Lord Privy Seal	Cholmondeley	* Gower
Master of the Horse	Richmond	Richmond
Lord Chamberlain	Grafton	Grafton
Lord Steward	Dorset	Devonshire
Lord Lieutenant Ireland	Devonshire	* Chesterfield
Lord Keeper of Scotland	Argyll	Argyll
Secretary of State	Newcastle	Newcastle
Secretary of State	Granville	Harrington
Secretary of State, Scotland	Tweeddale	Tweeddale
Groom of the Stole	Pembroke	Pembroke
First Lord of Admiralty	Winchelsea	* Bedford
First Lord of Treasury and Chancellor of Exchequer	Pelham	Pelham

* Members of the ministry drawn from the opposition.

him to do was to continue his excuse of sickness so as not to have to advise on the filling of the vacancies.[106] The Pelhams realized their difficult position and held a meeting in order to decide on a ratio for distribution of available places among their followers, the Chesterfield Whigs, Cobham Whigs, Independent Whigs, and Hanoverian Tories.[107]

The negotiations dragged on through most of December. The only thing that made the delayed formation of a new government possible was that all sides seemed to call a truce in parliamentary warfare. The best way to understand the results is to examine the personnel of the old and new cabinets.[108] It is not difficult to see that few of the cabinet were from the opposition. A complete picture of the changes can only be seen by examining the noncabinet members of the ministry.[109]

Office	Old Ministers	New Ministers
Admiralty Board	Dr. Lee	* Lord Sandwich
	Mr. Cockburn	* George Grenville
	Sir Charles Hardy	* Lord Vere Beauclerk
	Mr. Philipson	George Anson
Treasury Board	George Compton	Richard Arundel
	Philip Gybbon	* George Lyttelton
Treasurer of Navy	Sir John Rushout	* George Dodington
Cofferer	Lord Sandys	* Edmund Waller
Captain of Pensioners	Lord Bathurst	Lord Hobart
Paymaster of Pensioners	John Hooper	Benjamin Keene
Treasurer of the Chambers	Lord Hobart	* Sir John Cotton
Commissioners of Trade	Benjamin Keene	* Sir John Philips
	Sir Charles Gilmour	* John Pitt
Master of the Mint	Richard Arundel	* William Chetwynd
Master of Buck-Hounds	Ralph Jennison	* Lord Halifax
Vice-Treasurer of Ireland	Viscount Torrington	Viscount Torrington
	Harry Vane	Lord Cholmondeley

* Drawn from the opposition.

It is clear at once where the opposition gained. Pelham kept control of the major offices in the cabinet, but largely turned the lesser offices over to his new allies. He had broken the opposition, for the new ministers were from all sections of the opposition groups. The only really important person missing was William Pitt, though his friends were included. He supported the ministry, however, and through his allies he kept in touch with Pelham.[110] Horatio Walpole summarized the results of the changes as follows:

In short, few are displeased at those that were removed, and as few are pleased with those that are to come in their rooms. The Whigs grumble that there are so many new faces; and the Tories grumble that there are no more of their sort.[111]

In spite of this spirit no organized opposition could develop because almost all the leaders were tied to the ministry. In fact, Pelham himself expected little trouble once the ministry was set, and believed that there would be few changes of policy, only of methods.[112]

The new administration was, however, too optimistic, for they had one great problem—the king. George II was still irate at having had to remove his favorite, Lord Granville. Interviews between the king and various ministers were usually stormy, and measures were accepted by the king with bad grace.[113] The whole ministry was well aware that Granville was playing on the king's anger in secret meetings and attempting to rebuild his position by this means. Pelham, Newcastle, Hardwicke, Harrington, Dorset, Chesterfield, Cobham, Lyttelton, and Pitt were specifically mentioned as exerting all pressure possible to force George to quit these meetings with Granville.[114] They were not able to stop them, but the result of their determined protests was that George did not countenance the possibility of Granville's opposition in parliament.

In January various threats by opposition Tory members of parliament arose because the Whigs' promise to create many Justices of the Peace from their ranks had not been fulfilled. Bolingbroke took up this issue and persuaded the Pelhams to keep their agreement. By April the quarrel was settled to the satisfaction of the Tories, and Granville had lost that chance of gaining strength.[115] There were two other minor debates in parliament—over men and money for the army during the next year.[116] These were more tactical quarrels than anything else, and they were soon settled. On the whole, Horace Walpole was right when he said, "The Parliament is met: one hears of the Tory opposition continuing, but nothing has appeared yet; all is quiet." [117] The only real opposition came from Granville and his very few friends, who were unable to stir up any serious trouble.

In March there was some suggestion that changes might be made in the ministry at the end of the session, but by the end of April all was well and Horace Walpole could say, "There is no kind of News; the Parliament rises on Thursday, and everybody is going out of town." [118] With the departure of the members of parliament in the spring of 1745, the cabinet crisis that had been started a year before was over. Pelham had won and turned out a new cabinet as a finished product—one that was to be the ultimate basis of the government during the next ten years, in spite of changes and alterations. Chesterfield, early in the session of parliament, described the situation very well when he said:

Upon the whole I find things have gone well in the House of Commons. If you encourage those who have behaved well or pretty well this year, without distinction of party, you will have no difficulty next year; the sour Whigs and Tories will both stay in kennel and content themselves with drinking to your confusion, which will not contribute in the least to it. Please Gower and his detachment . . . which will at least break the Tory Party, so as to make the other part of it absolutely inconsiderable.[119]

Pelham followed this line of political policy for ten years, and he was rewarded with an administration that was on the whole safe from the violence of party politics. The old Whig and Tory parties were finally destroyed during these years, and the process that Robert Walpole had speeded along was finished by Henry Pelham in quite a different manner.

One other aspect of the cabinet crisis must be mentioned. On the basis of his leadership of the Old Whigs at this time, Pelham established himself as prime minister. Newcastle and Hardwicke recognized Pelham as their leader, even though the duke often protested against it. The correspondence among the three proves that Pelham guided their decisions. Harrington, Dorset, Devonshire, Argyll, and other Old Whigs did not have the power to influence the Pelhams, and they accepted Pelham's lead. The opposition Whigs under Chesterfield, Bedford, Cobham, and Pitt, and the Tories under Bolingbroke and Gower believed Pelham to be the cabinet leader. It was with Pelham that they negotiated for alliance and office before and after the resignation of Granville. Bolingbroke was an excellent judge of men, and it was unlikely that he would have erred in such an important guess. Lord Orford treated his "pupil" as the leader and supported him steadily. Outsiders like Horace Walpole and Duncan Forbes bear testimony that Pelham was the leader. There can be no doubt that it was Pelham and not Newcastle who directed the entire action against Lord Granville. The final proof of Pelham's recognized leadership was that he ran the policy of England for the next ten years with increasing sureness. He could only have had the ultimate control by putting himself, his brother, and their friends into complete power, for he had little wealth or power in his own person. The event of November 24, 1744, and its results during the next few weeks, was therefore one of the most important political events in the middle of the eighteenth century. It determined policy for many years, and it is to the working out of that policy that one must now turn.

BOOK TWO

Ministerial Establishment under Wartime Conditions

CHAPTER VI

Pelham and Parliament

UNDER ROBERT WALPOLE the House of Commons had become the dominant partner in parliament. It had long been recognized as the financial center of the government, but the House of Lords was its equal in other legislation until Walpole stamped his forceful personality on the government. When Walpole was forced from office, one of the great questions was what would happen regarding the relative position of the two houses. Many outward signs indicated that the Lords would again return to the importance it had held before Sir Robert. Certainly the fact that every traditional cabinet position except one was held by a member of the peerage gave that impression. Lord Granville, the Duke of Newcastle, the Earl of Wilmington, the Earl of Harrington, and other Whig leaders were all in the Lords. Samuel Sandys, the Chancellor of the Exchequer, was the single member of the Commons, and his job required that he sit there. Moreover, it was soon clear that Sandys was unimportant and acted merely as an agent for Granville. In spite of this, a shift of power was not definite, for the Paymaster-General of the Forces was made a member of the cabinet. Henry Pelham held that post, and it became plain that the raising of the stature of the position was a personal one. It was Pelham who sat in the cabinet and also in the Commons. Besides, it was soon evident that Pelham was determined to direct the House of Commons. Nevertheless it was true that between the fall of Walpole and the fall of Granville, the House of Commons slipped from the position of domination it had held under the former man.

There was no definite position recognized by law or tradition as that of leader of the House of Commons. However, men like Henry St. John had been recognized as the spokesmen of the Council in the Commons in the time of Queen Anne. As the voice of the monarch's advisers and dispenser of patronage St. John had become very important in the direction of the Commons. When Robert Walpole rose to this indefinite leadership, he also was the recognized leader of the group called the Cabinet Council. Thus for twenty years the duties were held by one man. The previous discussion of the crisis at the fall of Walpole and during the next two years makes it clear that Walpole, Granville, Newcastle, the king, the Whigs in general, and in fact most Englishmen recognized

65

Pelham as the new leader of the Commons. The part he took in all the legislative activity indicated that he saw himself in such a role.

There were many incidental examples which showed that Pelham had little trouble capturing the vacant leadership. In November 1742, Henry Finch [1] described conferences between himself and Pelham on measures for control of the Commons.[2] At the end of the letter Finch reported an amusing event in the House when Sir John Rushout, newly a member of the Treasury Board, spoke against a ministerial measure and Pelham, assisted by Sir Thomas Winnington, had to exert his authority to cause Rushout to stop his speech. If Pelham was able to stop a man's speech in the Commons, he was really recognized as the leader of the ministry's adherents.

Furthermore, a letter of Pelham's, written at the time of the above incident, shows that he took the duty of leader seriously and tried to keep all parliamentary allies satisfied with his leadership.[3] As leader of the Commons, Pelham was vitally interested in its membership, and he took pains to see that the cabinet's majority was retained. Whenever a seat fell vacant through death, it was his duty to obtain a favorable replacement if at all possible.[4] Another example of the work involved was the desire of Lord Dalkeith to enter the Commons. Because he was the elder son of the Duke of Buccleuch, he could not sit for a Scottish borough, but he was eligible for an English seat. Dalkeith had £1,000 to spend to secure his election, and he swore to support the cabinet. Pelham therefore undertook to get a place for him.[5] Another instance of the same kind was an agreement made by Pelham with the Earl of Marchmont and his brother, Alexander Hume Campbell, in which Pelham agreed to support Hume Campbell's bid in the next election in return for parliamentary support.[6] These are only a few of literally hundreds of similar cases wherein Pelham made deals to secure a safe majority for the government in the Commons.

Another problem facing any leader of the Commons was to insure agreement between the Commons and the Lords, particularly in regard to a bill or resolution. If parliamentary action was to have a significant effect, the two versions of a measure needed to be brought into agreement. Pelham and Lord Hardwicke seem to have been responsible for smoothing out differences in the acts passed by the two houses.[7] In fact, it seems likely that these two, after consultation with Newcastle, effectively rewrote acts whenever there was disagreement between the two houses. Also the preparation of the king's opening and closing speeches, as before noted, were the work of Hardwicke, Pelham, and Newcastle. Though Hardwicke did the actual writing, the three framed the policies to be presented. In the opening speech in 1748, Pelham and Newcastle did more of the actual preparation than ever before.[8] The reason for this variation is unknown, but Hardwicke handed over almost the whole of his work to them. These were regular and recurring problems of any leader of the legislature in England, and Pelham, almost alone in the Commons, did his part in solving them.

In the management of the affairs of the House of Commons, Pelham had profited by Walpole's example. For instance, he never proposed a finance scheme such as Walpole's excise plan of 1733, which had to be abandoned because of the widespread national opposition. Pelham was less dictatorial in his treatment of the House than Walpole, though the charge that he maintained little discipline is not true. His relaxation of discipline, as compared with Walpole's tight hand, was necessary because of the absence of party or personal rule. In order to keep the government alive, Pelham was forced to allow variation of opinion within the many groups of the government represented in the Commons. Yet if a particular issue was important, he had his way.

Pelham made mistakes, just as other parliamentary leaders have done. One of the most obvious miscalculations involved the naval quarrel between Admirals Mathews and Lestock. This fight had caused the British navy to lose the action in the Mediterranean Sea in 1745, and the Commons demanded courts-martial for all involved.[9] Mathews was a member of parliament and an ally of the Pelham government, which tried to remove his name from the list of those to be tried. The House defeated this effort by the large majority of 215 to 78.[10] One member of parliament wrote to a friend:

> This great majority, as it shewed the general sense of the House, was no small mortification to him and his friends, who certainly did not know their strength, or else they had never made this unlucky attempt.[11]

Such errors of judgment and miscalculation of strength were bound to occur in a Commons no more definitely organized than it was in the eighteenth century. Nevertheless, under Pelham's leadership there were no serious revolts against his wishes. There were many attacks by the opposition, especially before 1745, but after that date affairs were relatively peaceful. The great attacks of William Pitt were all made by the end of that year, and one may say that once Pelham and Newcastle were in complete control of the cabinet, things went easily in the Commons.

One very important aspect of control of the House of Commons to any leader was the men available to carry the debates as lieutenants. During the first year Pelham always had Samuel Sandys, but the Chancellor of the Exchequer seemed to take little part in the parliamentary activities. He is seldom mentioned as taking part in any but strictly financial measures. He did, however, bring a group of Whigs from the opposition into the government in 1742, and as leader of this segment he controlled some votes. His promotion to the Lords in 1743 seemed to make no difference in the voting, so he must have been personally unimportant to the running of the Commons. Sir William Yonge, the Secretary at War until 1746, was a holdover from the Walpole regime. He took important parts in many debates and often acted as Pelham's chief lieutenant. Sir John Rushout, a member of the Treasury Board, was another capable speaker, but he was often opposed to Pelham's ideas. Sir Thomas Winnington, member of the Treasury Board until 1742 and Paymaster General from 1743 to 1746, was one of the mainstays of the Whigs during these years. He, perhaps more than any other during this time, might be called a second in command to Pelham. Dudley Ryder, the Attorney-General, was another able man, but he did little in the Commons. William Murray, the Solicitor-General, was one of the most brilliant men in the House of Commons. From the time he entered parliament he remained a steadfast friend and supporter of Pelham. Horace Walpole even commented favorably on his excellence in the Commons.[12] After the removal of Granville, the Cobhamites, represented by George Lyttelton, George Grenville, and eventually William Pitt, joined the Pelham ranks. At the same time that Pitt became Paymaster, in 1746, Henry Fox was promoted from the Treasury Board to Secretary at War. Thus in 1745 and 1746, Pelham gained four excellent speakers, of whom two were good parliamentarians.[13] To these names should be added those of Henry Bilson-Legge, George Dodington, Speaker of the House Arthur Onslow, and Conyers D'Arcy, who gave capable support to Pelham in the House of Commons.

Necessary as many of these men were to the government in the Commons and in executive office, their appointments often provoked trouble. The Duke of Richmond had a personal and family dislike of Fox, and he agreed on Fox's appointment only because Pelham felt Fox was necessary.[14] The Townshend family felt that the promotion of Pitt, Legge, and others in 1746 would destroy Pelham because they were all his enemies.[15] However, none of the dire predictions proved true, and Pelham gained strength from his moves.

A quick glance at this partial list of Pelham's subordinates is sufficient to show that all the Commoners who rose to high office in the 1750's and 1760's (Grenville, Pitt, Fox, Legge, and Murray) were lieutenants to Pelham during the 1740's.[16] There was, then, by 1746 a corps of able men enlisted under the leadership of Pelham in the House of Commons, and as long as he remained alive they followed his direction. The opposition had no leader in the Commons equal to any of these men in ability, and only when Dodington returned to the support of the Prince of Wales did they gain a prominent speaker. The relative ease with which almost all bills were carried through the lower house for the next eight years was ample proof that control of that house was firmly held by Pelham and his subordinates whenever they wished to exert their superiority.

In the last analysis, however, leadership and control of the Commons

rested on the return of members who would loyally support the ministry. The eighteenth-century practice was to elect a parliamentary majority to support the ministry, rather than the modern idea of selecting
a ministry dependent on the majority in the Commons. The securing of
a safe majority in the Commons, therefore, was one of the principal
jobs of any leader.

During the war years, 1739–48, two elections were held under the Sep-
tennial Act. The first, in 1741, so weakened Walpole that he could not
resist attack. The second was held in 1747. It was this election that reflected the sentiment of the electorate regarding the Pelham government in the midst of a losing war. Walpole had lost great prestige in
1741 because he was blamed for the losses to that date. By 1747 the losses
were greater, but still Pelham won. Several developments account for
the changed opinions of the voters. First, many people were tired of
Walpole's domination of the government. Second, Walpole had provoked a large and vocal opposition in and out of parliament. Third,
Walpole was opposed to the war, which was popular in England in spite
of the poor results in 1741. The first two did not apply to Pelham. In
the case of the third the public had swung around to a desire for peace,
which Pelham also wanted. Moreover, and probably very important,
Pelham called for the election before the opposition was ready.

The election of 1747 was one of the few examples in the eighteenth
century of the proroguing of parliament before the law made this necessary. Parliament had another year to run before its seven years were
spent, and the opposition did not expect to have to campaign until the
time expired.[17] Newcastle made it clear to Lord Irwin that the ministers
were aware of their advantage:

> The nation is now in good humour; no incident has yet happened to make
> them otherwise, since the happy extinction of the rebellion; and therefore I
> verily think we cannot now fail of getting a good Whig Parliament. What
> might have been the consequence of putting it off another year, nobody
> can tell.[18]

Charles Yorke, the second son of Lord Hardwicke, wrote to his older
brother:

> I give you joy of the dissolution of the parliament. It is a master-stroke of
> politics. . . . There will be no time now to tamper with Elections: popular
> Question in a Seventh Session will be avoided: The Rebellion recent in men's
> minds: no misfortune as yet in Flanders: a flattering Revolution in Holland.[19]

At the same time Newcastle wrote to the Duke of Cumberland:

> The present Session of Parliament will end, the next week; and, in two, or three
> days after, Writts will be issued, for calling a new one. . . . The King is sure of

having a good parliament chose now, when the Nation is in good Humour
[Anson's sea victory and the defeat of the rebels]; retains a greatful sense of
their late Deliverance . . . and when no foreign Transactions, either of
Peace, or War, has happen'd to blow up, or pervert, the Minds of weak People,
capable of being seduced. There is but one *Place* [Leicester House], where
this measure is openly blamed. . . . The great Objection of all is, that It is to
enable the *Wicked, Tyrannical Pelhams,* to execute, indeed the most wicked
Designs.[20]

It is clear that the technique, which has since become common in English
politics, of catching the opposition off balance was deliberately used by
Pelham in 1747 in order to insure success.[21] The government was right,
and the voters returned a larger majority for the ministry than before.

In addition to the general plan for the elections, Pelham had the duty
of utilizing his power and prestige as leader of the government in the
election campaigns. His first interest was in Sussex, for on the Pelhams'
control in that county rested their national position. Newcastle had long
been recognized as the Whig leader of most of Sussex, and in alliance
with the Duke of Richmond, the Duke of Dorset, and Lord Irwin, he
dominated the entire county.[22] In this capacity Newcastle had long dic-
tated to everyone the political strategy to be pursued, but in the election
of 1747 Pelham rose to a much more important position than he had
ever held. The power was split between the brothers for the first time.
The Duke of Richmond, who acted as the chief agent of the Pelhams,
reflected this change in the case of the Arundel election. In January,
Richmond wrote to Newcastle:

> I wish I could have had your answer about Orme, for he presses most prodi-
> giously to declare & engage the government interest at Arundell for him, & to
> which as I told you before I could not nor would not make any answer without
> you. Had it been a comon house of Commons affairs, I should only have
> troubled Mr. Pelham about it.[23]

In February, he wrote Newcastle, "I have wrote about Arundell affairs
to Mr. Pelham, haveing [*sic*] troubled you enough with this long letter
already." [24] By June he indicated in two letters that his orders were from
Pelham, and that he obeyed the instructions.[25] Pelham clearly increased
his political activity in this election even during the general campaign.
Furthermore, there was a great flurry of correspondence in June between
Newcastle and various Sussex boroughs, all of which indicates Pelham's
direction of the campaigns. He and Newcastle pushed Andrew Stone and
James Pelham as candidates for Hastings.[26] They recommended William
Pitt as candidate for Seaford and achieved his election, which Pitt ac-
knowledged profusely.[27] Pelham was particularly active in the election
of Pitt and personally went to Seaford to direct the Whigs.[28] There is little

indication that Newcastle went to Sussex more than usual during the election year. There is, however, good evidence that the duke left his usual part in the election to Pelham, who was assisted by Richmond and lesser men.

As leader of the House of Commons, Pelham was interested in the results of the election far beyond his own sphere of Sussex. Moreover, as head of the government he was involved in election campaigns and plans all over Great Britain. Extant letters show that Pelham followed the usual eighteenth-century methods to collect votes. He used the Duke of Rutland and his sons, Lady Katherine Pelham's family, to gain his wishes at Newark.[29] He gained the support of the Walpole family in Norfolk, and especially at Yarmouth.[30] He used the Duke of Grafton and his son, Lord Leicester, to win in Suffolk.[31] He collaborated with Lord Irwin to gain the election of Ibbetson and Thornton in York.[32] He promoted George Lyttelton's bid for election at Oakhampton.[33] He made use of Lord Sandwich, who returned from the peace negotiations to campaign.[34] He negotiated with the Duke of Marlborough, through James West, to provide mutually acceptable candidates in areas where Marlborough's interests predominated.[35] And he sought out relatively safe contests in which to place special friends whom he wished to have in Commons.[36]

His moves were not always successful, as the case of William Cayley showed, for Pelham was forced to try three constituencies before Cayley was elected. Lord Fane also noted mistakes that Pelham had made in Berkshire:

> I am just going out of town in order to set right as much as may be in my power the matters in Berkshire, strangely confused, and to the prejudice of the government, by Mr. Pelham's having harkened too much to silly or interested people there. As I took an opportunity of saying all that I judged significant upon this affair, or upon any thing relating to myself, I give your Grace this trouble to avoid you a farther, which you were pleased to promise me to take in speaking to him, that will not be necessary now.[37]

The most useful way for a ministry to gain elections was the method employed by Pelham: bring the local political powers into agreement with the cabinet and use their actions to achieve agreeable results. There can be no doubt that Pelham's careful cultivation of the many Whig leaders and some Tory people during the previous four years explained much of his success at the polls in 1747.

Cultivation of prominent local leaders also reduced the cost of elections to the government. The widespread charges of corruption by contemporaries and later historians are not supported by the facts of the election of 1747. No doubt government money was distributed to some candidates to buy support through dinners or actual purchase of votes. The Treasury boroughs were most open to these accusations, but there remains little correspondence indicating an actual use of money by the government. In fact, there is more proof that this election involved much less cash than previous ones. Pelham said:

> Our Elections have gone beyond expectations; and I will venture to say this Parliament has been chosen with less publick expense on one side, than any former one has been since the Revolution.[38]

There was no reason for Pelham to have told anything but what he believed to be the truth in this letter, and in view of his known economy it would fit his character. There was little chance that money was spent which Pelham did not know about, for a letter from the Earl of Tankerville to Newcastle appealed for funds that Pelham controlled.[39] Tankerville indicated that there was very little chance of getting money unless Pelham approved, and he promised to spend only what was absolutely necessary. The largest amount of money spent in the election undoubtedly came from the individual candidates and their local patrons.

One example was the Cambridgeshire campaign of Philip Yorke, who kept his father informed of his expenses. Yorke proposed that the cheapest way of conducting the campaign would be to "treat the gentlemen electors" and give the common freeholders a guinea if from the Isle of Ely or one-half guinea if from the county.[40] Later he sent an account of expenses to Hardwicke which totaled 2,003 pounds and 11 shillings less 314 pounds, 16 shillings sixpence pledged by a Mr. Jenyns toward the costs.[41] This total was broken down as follows:

tickets on election day	£815
bill at the Rose	245
meetings	136
rent of two chairs	4s–4d

What was done with the remaining 807 pounds, 6 shillings eightpence is unknown. Yorke ended the letter by saying, "I believe it is the cheapest election that has been in Cambridgeshire for many years." Lord Hardwicke responded a few days later:

> I have not of late expected that the Expense of the Election would be much less than You mention, tho' it is a monstrous one for an Election without any Opposition. . . . Some method must be fallen upon to correct it on another occasion.[42]

This, then, was an expensive election, but the two candidates, or their families, bore the cost. The government spent nothing to influence the voters. No one in the eighteenth century considered this expenditure by the candidate in the least corrupt; it was only the expenditure by the government that brought criticism. The Cambridgeshire contest was a good example of the results of Pelham's maneuver to achieve a favorable

Commons at a minimum expense to the government by promoting alliances with people who could afford to finance their own political activity.

Several incidental aspects of the election deserve notice. Elections in Scotland were operated on different rules than in England, and they were notoriously corrupt even for the time. Pelham and Newcastle had no personal influence in Scotland and therefore worked through Scottish officials in Edinburgh, especially Duncan Forbes, the Lord President of the Court of Sessions, and Andrew Mitchell.[43] Because of the fierce personal rivalries in Scotland, the actions of Forbes and Mitchell often provoked opposition from local powers.[44] Yet through their influence and patronage powers, the two were able to gain most of their selections. Hugh Dalrymple (a member of the Earl of Stair's family) protested violently against Pelham's handling of several elections, but in so doing he made it quite clear that Pelham was the power "above" who had the final decision on Scottish elections.[45]

Another incidental question in the election was whether the fighting men in Flanders who had a vote should be permitted to return to England. The war was in a critical state, and men could not well be spared from the front. Many of them apparently requested permission from Cumberland to return to England, but few, if any, of the requests were granted.[46] Pelham seemingly did not press Cumberland to send the men home, as had been done on earlier occasions; at least there are no references to such demands by the Prime Minister. One explanation may be that Pelham felt his friends were sure enough of victory not to interfere in the war effort.

Finally the autumn and the winter brought the usual portion of post-election problems. Some men whom the cabinet wished to have in the Commons had been defeated, and they had to be provided with seats vacated by those who had won two or more elections and could take only one seat. Such seemed to be the case with Lord Dalkeith and Viscount Perceval.[47] It was clearly stated in a letter to Perceval that Pelham was the official applied to and that he had promised that Perceval "shall be taken care off [*sic*] and assisted." There were also contested elections (though not so many as usual) that had to be settled by the new House. Perceval contested the result of his campaign, with government support.[48] John Pitt, a relative of the famous William, who was vocal in the opposition, contested the result in the borough of Wareham and caused considerable trouble.[49] Pelham was forced to take a firm stand against this contest, and he used Fox, Pitt, Lyttelton, and Hume Campbell in the debates—which angered the Prince of Wales.[50]

It is quite plain that Pelham greatly increased the part he played in elections between 1741 and 1747. In the former he was director of Newcastle's interests in Sussex and acted as lieutenant for Walpole in various places in the rest of England. In the latter year he was at least the equal of

Newcastle in Sussex, and he was the director of the campaign throughout all England. This change is one of the most significant proofs of Pelham's leadership of the cabinet. The eighteenth-century Whig politicians were extremely jealous of their power, and they would seldom let an outsider meddle in their local bailiwicks unless he was of great importance to the national government. Pelham constantly mixed in the local elections all through the campaign, and he was accepted by the local Whig magnates.

The result of the election showed the effectiveness of holding it a year early, when foreign and domestic events favored the ministry. The election also showed that someone—it must be presumed Pelham, from the prominent part he played—had managed the campaign with great skill. Though he and other leaders discounted this aspect, it was a pleasant result for them. Of the parliament elected, Pelham wrote, "Our majority is, not withstanding that [less money was spent], much greater, which I can impute to nothing . . . but a zeal for his [the king's] person and Government—a thorough detestation of Jacobitism, and confidence in his administration." [51] Later he wrote to Horatio Walpole, "I think of the parliament as you do. . . . I am sure they will approve of any measures the king's joint administration shall lay before them." [52] Hardwicke likewise testified to the pleasure of the Whigs at their great success.[53] Finally Horatio Walpole wrote that he believed it to be the best "affected" parliament since the Hanoverian succession.[54] The end result of the election was, therefore, proof that the men leading the government were satisfied with their work and their strategy.

Another important part of the parliament was the House of Lords, which was one of the problems of any administration of the time. As noted above, the Lords was extremely important during the period of the Pelhams because it was reasserting its position after its diminution of power under Walpole. During the years that Granville was in alliance with the Pelhams, from 1742 to 1744, the entire political picture was upset. Granville and Newcastle, with their various allies, faced strong but unorganized opposition most of the time. After Granville was ousted by the Pelhams, the opposition was completely disorganized, and it never regained form during the period of the War of the Austrian Succession. All the important segments of the Whigs were represented in the cabinet except that of Granville and his few personal friends. The Hanoverian Tories were also included, and thus the Jacobite Tories were the only outside group. The Prince of Wales had less success among the Lords than among the Commons when he tried to negotiate a party to support himself. It is rather easy, therefore, to see that the policy of Henry Pelham, based on as wide a political alliance as possible, was particularly successful in controlling the House of Lords, even though his leading opponents sat there.

If one examines the cabinet members of the years of Pelham's leadership, one immediately sees that the great Whig lords were included most of the time. They held most of the places on the Privy Council, the Bedchamber, the lord lieutenancies, the keeperships, rangerships, and the wardenships of the royal forests, castles, and palaces. They had, therefore, a vested interest in supporting the Pelham ministry. These men, combined with the twenty-six bishops, made a majority vote in the House of Lords almost sure.[55] The maintenance of this majority was not a serious problem; the real problem was how to direct the majority that the ministry held.

It is, of course, self-evident that Newcastle was the most important member of the cabinet in the Lords. Because he had a fairly free hand in directing the day-by-day business of the Lords, it is difficult to make any direct statement about Henry Pelham's connection with the upper house. He and Newcastle had many meetings during the years, but it is impossible to know whether the questions they discussed dealt with the Lords or not. The indefinite conclusion to be drawn must be that the brothers could and did discuss whatever they wished in secret, and then each carried out the joint decision in the way he saw fit in his own house of parliament. Newcastle proposed this procedure on a more or less formal basis after the dismissal of Granville:

> I am sure, You will not think unreasonable what I now propose: That Every thing, as far as possible, should be first talk'd over, by You, and I; before It is either flung out in the Closet; or communicated to *Any* of our Brethren; I always except the Chancellor, who, I know, is a Third Brother. That We should have no Reserve, either *publick,* or *private,* with Each Other; and that in Our Transactions with the Other Ministers, and Other persons, who may be to be negotiated with, We should always let it be understood, that We speak in the Name of Both, or in the Name of Neither. This Conduct, once establish'd, will grow easy, & natural. . . . In order to make this practicable, I will call, every Morning, as regularly at Your House, as I once did at Sr Robert's. There the Scheme of the Day shall be settled, to be handed out to Others afterwards, as shall be necessary.[56]

It is unfortunate that so much of the actual working of the eighteenth-century government was conducted in this informal manner, for few records were made. Because Pelham and Newcastle were brothers, the ease of communication between them was more complete than between almost any other leaders.[57] Therefore few facts can be stated with finality.

This much can be said: Newcastle had the job of directing government affairs in the House of Lords. Hardwicke was Newcastle's primary lieutenant, and the other cabinet members, like Harrington, Chesterfield, Bedford, and Devonshire, were active aides. The rest of the cabinet and other officeholders supported the duke in his motions. We may also say that to the extent that Pelham was the primary architect of the cabinet in December 1744, and kept it functioning, he was responsible for the majority in the House of Lords.

Contemporaries really made little effort to distinguish between the brothers. Chesterfield told Newcastle that he saw no difference between them when he said, "I beg my compliments to Mr. Pelham. I don't write to him because I have writ [sic] to your Grace; and you know that I insist upon it that whoever writes or speaks to one, writes or speaks to both." [58] He also wrote to Andrew Stone during a quarrel between the brothers, expressing the same view and wishing that they would act less like brothers, because their quarrels caused uneasiness.[59] The last-mentioned letter brings to attention the recurring problem of quarrels between Pelham and Newcastle. Hardwicke spent much time soothing Newcastle and settling the disagreements, and he commented on the woes caused by them.[60] Newcastle also knew that the quarrels hurt the government, but he seldom tried to settle them. Only in the spring of 1748 did the duke seem seriously alarmed at a disagreement.[61] Pelham recognized the seriousness of the arguments and referred to them many times.[62] Other friends were also worried over the various quarrels. Horatio Walpole gave Hardwicke credit for saving the life of the cabinet in one quarrel.[63] The Earl of Marchmont said of the brothers, "They would surely break, if Mr. Pelham did not think it would be the ruin of them both." [64] These disagreements affected Pelham's relationship to legislation in the Lords, but to what extent it is impossible to know.

On the other hand, it would be wrong to overemphasize the effect of the quarrels between Pelham and Newcastle, for they seldom were serious enough to affect the essential measures of the cabinet. Both men drew back from carrying their fights to the point of actually harming the government. Pelham assured Newcastle once that though they differed in "acting," they never differed in the real "matter itself." [65] Another time, during one of their quarrels, the Duchess of Newcastle became sick, and Pelham dropped the quarrel immediately to express his anxiety about her to Newcastle.[66] Newcastle invariably lauded his brother every time a quarrel was settled, and he never held a grudge for long, no matter how angry he had been. He also recognized that Pelham was often right in their disputes.[67] Hardwicke noted that the brothers agreed in all their actions after every quarrel and that their agreement was the basic strength of the cabinet.[68] Hardwicke knew more about the personal relations between the brothers than any other man, and his belief in the real agreement between Pelham and Newcastle remains the best proof that, in spite of apparent differences, the two really worked effectively together.

None of the facts about the disputes between the brothers prove that Pelham had anything to do with the direction of the House of Lords. Rather they do prove that the disputes were not serious and that the brothers kept very close relations over a long period. The fact that they were so close to each other allows one to conclude that whoever led the actual moves in the Lords, the basic policies were decided in conference.

Moreover, except for foreign policy, Pelham had the primary voice in their conferences. Thus it is safe to believe that Pelham exercised some indirect control over the House of Lords.

It is important to remember that Pelham had several ways of influencing the Lords without Newcastle. First, in the case of the election of 1747, Pelham was active in the selection and success of the sixteen Scottish peers. For example, the Earl of March applied to Pelham and the Duke of Argyll before he wrote to Newcastle in order to become one of the sixteen.[69] It would seem that March believed Pelham's support was essential in this affair, which was a House of Lords matter. Also as regards Scotland, Newcastle at least once referred a request of Lord Rothes to Pelham.[70] If Pelham was the minister who was consulted by the Lords, obviously he could influence the various Lords in their parliamentary life. Another time the Duke of Portland applied to Pelham to gain a clerical preferment, even though Newcastle supposedly directed church affairs and was Portland's ostensible leader in the Lords.[70] The explanation must be that Pelham's position as Prime Minister was recognized by the Lords as well as the Commons. In 1746 the Marquis of Rockingham wrote a most telling letter to Pelham:

> It being generally agred some Peers are soon to be promoted to Earldoms, I hope for your Pardon in seconding Ld. Fitzwilliam's Request that he may be one of the Number if there are to be any who are not in particular High Stations: You may remember my desiring Your Favour on this Subject before now, & that I told you I had named it to the King. . . . I will only add that I dare answer for his ever retaining a most Grateful Sence for Your Assistance herein.[72]

This was absolutely a matter for the king and his ministers, and it affected only the House of Lords. The only conclusion possible is that Pelham's position as Prime Minister made him a power in the Lords even to the naming of new peers. Thus Pelham could keep control of the Lords without Newcastle, though it was much easier to work through his titled brother.

CHAPTER VII

Pelham and the Cabinet

℣ THE MOST IMPORTANT part of the government in the eighteenth century was the ministry. There were three parts to any ministry: the cabinet, the noncabinet ministers, and the lesser officials, who may be described as an embryonic civil service. In order to get a complete picture of the executive branch of the government, the relationship of the Privy Council and the Lords Justices to the ministry must be examined. And above all, the disputed title and office of Prime Minister must be seen in its proper place in the practice of the eighteenth century. The main question here is how Henry Pelham and his administration filled the various duties involved in the execution of the government.

By 1744 the recognition of a leader of the cabinet was an accepted fact, though most men avoided the use of the actual term Prime Minister or First Minister. The basic trouble with the Carteret-Pelham-Newcastle cabinet was that there was no single leader, and each member pursued his own ends. Once Granville was removed by the other two men, the troubles of the administration were considerably reduced. Though Newcastle strongly maintained in public that all the ministers were equal, he acted on the principle of leadership. He wished to exert leadership by means of an inner cabinet composed of himself, Pelham, Hardwicke, and the other Secretary of State. Pelham, on the other hand, was quite willing to be First Minister.[1] He worked through the four-man group at the beginning of his office but gradually exerted his personal power in most departments of government. This was clear even before the War of the Austrian Succession was over, and the increase of his power expanded still more rapidly after the war.

Even before the ousting of Granville, the shrewd sister of the Marquis of Rockingham recognized that Pelham had the last word in the ministry, and she advised her brother to work with Pelham, taking care to keep Newcastle from becoming jealous.[2] Pelham's control of the ministers in the day-by-day problems gives added proof of his gradual assumption of power. J. H. Plumb explicitly and O. A. Sherrard, implicitly, in their recent books, give Pelham complete credit for controlling William Pitt during the entire administration, which was no easy task. Walpole and Granville had both stumbled in this effort, and several future ministers were to have the same difficulty with the "terrible" Pitt.[3]

78

In 1746 the Earl of Sandwich expressed Pelham's superiority when he wrote to Newcastle:

> I have great reason to be satisfied with my journey to Woburn. . . . As to my own point with the D. of Bedford he is disposed as I could wish, & will take the resolution in my favour whenever I desire, provided Mr. Pelham consents to it; as by that means the whole difficulty is reduced to that of procuring his approbation, and that there is no other obstacle whatever in the way.[4]

Pelham held the reins to any personnel change within the ministry—one of the absolutely essential requirements of a First Minister. There was, however, one major exception to Pelham's control. In October 1746 Lord Harrington and Newcastle were involved in a serious quarrel over foreign policy, and Harrington suddenly resigned his office. Newcastle visited the king immediately after the resignation, and the two men decided to appoint Lord Chesterfield, without consulting any other person. Pelham learned of the decision within a few hours and was seriously disturbed. He and Harrington agreed almost exactly on the need for peace, while Newcastle wanted to continue the war. Pelham felt that he had been placed in a very awkward position.[5] In spite of this he agreed to the appointment, primarily because he felt that Chesterfield was the next best man for the vacant place.[6] The major problem was Harrington's demand to be Lord Lieutenant of Ireland, a post that had earlier been promised to Dorset. Pelham took this problem in hand and finally arranged for the stubborn Dorset to agree to Harrington's becoming Lord Lieutenant.[7] The entire crisis arose on the spur of the moment and was seized by the king and Newcastle to satisfy themselves. Because George II had joined Newcastle in naming Chesterfield, Pelham could hardly refuse to agree unless he was willing to resign. There had already been one major cabinet crisis in February of that year, and he did not want another to materialize so soon.

Newcastle was the one minister over whom Pelham did not wield almost complete control. The question was not so much whether Pelham could demand and obtain obedience from his brother but rather whether he would do so. It was clear even at the time that Pelham refused positively to force his brother because he did not want to make the duke unhappy. Chesterfield at least three times gave this as Pelham's reason for agreeing to some of Newcastle's plans, and the weight of all incidental testimony supported Chesterfield's view.[8] Thus in regard to the final decision on cabinet problems Pelham could, if he wished, have forced his point of view on the whole government, and sometimes he did so.

In specific questions of policy, such as the dates for proroguing parliament, calling regency meetings, and attending to the daily business routine, Pelham also issued orders, or directed someone else to issue them.[9] He directly intervened in the activities of all departments except

the legal, which issued executive orders. In 1745 when General Churchill
died, the leadership of his regiment of dragoons was widely contested.
Richmond sought the place for General Huske and wrote, "Mr. Pelham
who is a sort of a millitary [sic] man, must know that Huske's preten-
tions are good." [10] In the end Pelham directed that the king should appoint Lord Cobham to the vacancy and give Cobham's regiment of horse
in Ireland to one of the others who sought the dragoons. [11] George II
was jealous of his position as head of the army, and he disliked any
interference from his ministers in that sphere. He refused many requests by officers and ministers but seldom seemed to deny Pelham's
suggestions. [12] In naval affairs the case is more clear cut. Pelham personally intervened in the court-martial of Admiral Mathews and reported
directly to the king instead of using regular navy procedure. [13] He arranged a special committee of the Privy Council, on which he served, to
examine into an affair of Commodore Acton, who had trouble with
privateers. [14] Even more definitely, he vetoed Bedford's selections to
fill vacancies in the fleet and named his own candidates, though Bedford
was First Lord of the Admiralty. [15] Moreover, George Anson kept Pelham
informed of naval affairs throughout the time Bedford was First Lord,
and Pelham replied with orders. [16] Since Anson, though junior to both
Bedford and Sandwich, was the active member of the Admiralty Board,
Pelham kept in very close touch with the navy.

By the end of the war in 1748, Pelham had increased his role in
foreign affairs from a minor one in 1744 to a place second only to the
two Secretaries. He gave Newcastle advice as to what measures to pursue
and prevented many of Newcastle's favorite schemes from taking place. [17]
Pelham's relationship to foreign policy will be discussed more fully later,
so it is sufficient here to note that he wrote and received information
from various foreign envoys, especially Keene and Robinson, as to conditions abroad. [18] These were the very acts that caused Newcastle to break
with Walpole, Townshend, Carteret, Harrington, and Chesterfield, yet
the duke never did more than complain of Pelham's opposition to certain plans. It was no easy task to make the duke accept advice in foreign
affairs. The fact that he did in this instance remains the clearest proof
of family affection and of Newcastle's acceptance of Pelham as First
Minister, despite the duke's tirades on that subject when he was angry
at Pelham.

In financial matters Pelham allowed no other minister to interfere.
He himself passed on such small items as the release of an excise officer
from the usual inspection. [19] In the Treasury Minute Book are the records
of the 509 meetings of the Treasury Board from September 7, 1743,
when Pelham became officially First Lord of the Treasury, until February 27, 1754, which was the last meeting before Pelham's death. The only
exception is the year 1746, for which there are no minutes. Of these 509
meetings Pelham missed only four, and he executed almost all the acts

that were merely approved by his colleagues of the Treasury Board. On one occasion, August 30, 1744, only Pelham and Lord Middlesex attended the Board Meeting.[20] The position of the junior members of the Treasury was the highest of any noncabinet members of the government, but still their job was more or less of a formality. Pelham steadily shifted the members of the Board until he had a group of men who completely agreed with him.[21] Finally, with the end of the war, Pelham began to reexamine the financial structure of the government with a view to reducing the fixed interest rates on the public debt. This was his own prized formula, and he did almost all the work himself.[22] Pelham therefore acted freely in all major departments of the government, and there can be no doubt that these actions are sufficient proof that he was Prime Minister, as the term was understood in the eighteenth century.

In August 1748 Pelham had his first serious sickness. The Duke of Bedford twice wrote to Newcastle in Hanover that Pelham's illness prevented any business' being transacted.[23] It was also true, as Bedford said, that most of the other Lords Justices were absent, but when Pelham was well and present, business was transacted with only one or two other members of the regency. The only conclusion which can be drawn is that no other member of the Lords Justices was willing to take final responsibility for decisions. Richmond expressed great alarm to Newcastle at Pelham's sickness.[24] And John Cleveland, the Secretary to the Admiralty, also expressed similar fears to George Anson.[25] The ministry seemed to be paralyzed, except for routine business, and could not function without Pelham. No more definite proof of his position as Prime Minister seems necessary.

If one examines the cabinet of the time of the Pelhams, it is plain that there were three types of cabinet posts: heads of executive departments, heads of household departments, and inherited or prestige positions. The Archbishop of Canterbury was the one remaining example of the third type. Into the second category fell the Lord Steward, the Lord Chamberlain, the Groom of the Stole, and the Master of the Horse. The Lord Chancellor, First Lord of the Treasury, Chancellor of the Exchequer, First Lord of the Admiralty, Master General of Ordnance, Lord Lieutenant of Ireland, and the two (or three) Secretaries of State made up the first division. The places of the Lord President and Lord Privy Seal were somewhere between the first and second categories, for they were neither heads of great executive departments nor heads of household departments. On the whole they tended to be active wheels in the government and may therefore be put among the first group.

It is, of course, obvious that the real functions of directing the government rested in the hands of the executive departments and that the other officials were used as special advisers to the king. The First Lord of the Treasury had become the coordinator and director of the cabinet and controlled the distribution of money from the Treasury. The

Chancellor of the Exchequer was the money-raising official. The Secretaries of State, who were the voices of the government, issued the official orders and directives, except financial, of the multiple executive. In this capacity they ran foreign affairs and most of the ordinary domestic affairs, including army affairs through the Secretary at War, colonial affairs through the Board of Trade, and Scottish affairs. The First Lord of the Admiralty directed the navy. The Master General of Ordnance controlled the supply and distribution of munitions and arms for the army and defense posts. The Lord Lieutenant of Ireland was responsible for the administration of that dependent kingdom. The Lord Chancellor (with his colleagues, the Lord Chief Justices) was the supreme legal authority of the realm, and he presided over the House of Lords in the interest of the government. Finally, the Lord President was the coordinator between the cabinet and the Privy Council, which was the formal and legal administrative unit. And the Lord Privy Seal was, with the Lord Chancellor, a legal and formal distributor (by means of the Privy Seal) of the king's orders and commands.

The household officials had well-defined duties, which were mostly court functions relating to the monarch. The officers retained little of their earlier power except for their vitally important entree to the ruler. Through this power they were well adapted to persuade the king of the wisdom or folly of the cabinet's decisions. Thus at a time when the king still held the key to the success of any government, they were vital links in a smooth-running administration. The Lord Steward, Lord Chamberlain, Master of the Horse, and Groom of the Stole also provided convenient posts for political allies or valued friends of the clique that ruled the cabinet.[26] The Archbishop of Canterbury remained as a relic out of the past; he lent dignity and the moral standing of the Church of England to the decisions of the cabinet, though in fact he was very seldom consulted or even called to meetings. A last expedient was to appoint cabinet members without office. These men usually were appointed for their political power or knowledge of some specific phase of government.

In examining the Pelham cabinet during the years 1744–54, we may deal briefly with the Archbishop. John Potter was an entirely unexceptional man, and he took practically no share in cabinet matters. Thomas Herring was a much more important man. He was a close friend of Lord Hardwicke, and during the Jacobite Rebellion, as Archbishop of York, he had been one of the few really active defenders of the north. Still in 1748, Pelham could write, "There is nobody in town but the Duke of Bedford, the Archbishop and Lord Harrington, You cannot expect any instruction letters from hence, His Grace don't love much writing, and the other two are not called to give their opinions." [27] Thus even when the Archbishop was one of the Lords Justices, he was largely ignored.

The most active members of the cabinet, other than the First Lord of the Treasury in his capacity as First Minister, were the Secretaries of State, and they deserve the most attention. In this office the Duke of Newcastle must be given primary place, since he dominated the conduct of foreign affairs for twenty-four years. Chesterfield, who was no admirer of Newcastle, has left a fine word picture of the duke:

> The public opinion put him below his level; for though he had no superior parts, or eminent talents, he had a most indefatigable industry, a perseverance, a court craft, and a servile compliance with the will of his sovereign for the time being; which qualities, with only a common share of common sense, will carry a man sooner and more safely through the dark labyrinths of a court than the more shining parts would do without those meaner talents.
>
> He was good natured to a degree of weakness, even to tears, upon the slightest occasions. Exceedingly timorous, both personally and politically, dreading the least innovation, and keeping with a scrupulous timidity, in the beaten track of business as having the safest bottom. . . . From such weaknesses it necessarily follows, that he could have no great ideas, nor elevation of mind. . . .
>
> His ruling, or rather his only, passion was the agitation, the bustle, and the hurry of business, to which he had been accustomed above forty years. . . . He was as jealous of his power as an impotent lover of his mistress, without activity of mind enough to enjoy or exert it, but could not bear a share even in the appearances of it. . . .
>
> He was exceedingly disinterested, very profuse of his own fortune, and abhorring all those means, too often used by persons in his station, either to gratify their avarice, or to supply their prodigality; for he retired from business in the year 1762, above four hundred thousand pounds poorer than when he first engaged in it.
>
> Upon the whole he was a compound of most human weaknesses, but untainted with any vice or crime.[28]

The picture drawn is that of a very human and in many ways likable man. It must be remembered that Chesterfield disagreed in foreign affairs with Newcastle and that therefore the earl found faults where others might find nothing wrong with the duke's foreign policy. There can be no question that Newcastle knew more about certain aspects of foreign affairs than any other Englishman of the mid-eighteenth century. Basically he agreed with most critics that France could be controlled only by an alliance system. He favored Austria, Russia, and some small countries (as did Granville), while his main opponents wanted to reach an agreement with Prussia. This was the chief difference between Newcastle and men like Pelham and Pitt. His methods of subsidies were the same as those earlier employed by Granville and later used by Pitt. His greatest failure as a foreign minister was that he did not rally the best men available to fight the war or negotiate for him. Nor did he understand the art of gaining the popular support of all groups for his measures.[29]

Newcastle's worst fault as a foreign minister was that he expected all other ministers to approve publicly and applaud his measures. In the autumn of 1748 the Peace of Aix-la-Chapelle was finally concluded. Newcastle was irate at Lord Sandwich for his conduct of the negotiations and at Pelham, Hardwicke, Bedford, and others because they agreed with Sandwich more than with him. He sent a shower of letters to Pelham and Hardwicke, which denounced them and the others for not giving him complete support.[30]

Hardwicke reflected the troubled condition within the cabinet when he defended himself and Pelham from Newcastle's charges and tried to explain that the two in London did not reject Newcastle's peace.[31] Pelham's letters to Newcastle at the time indicated that he gave Newcastle a free hand in the negotiation and confined his complaints to personal letters to the duke.[32] In one letter Pelham wrote of his position:

> It is the success of the whole, that will make your character and administration considerable. I told you, in a former letter, that was the touchstone we went by; and that, I thank God, you are now secure in. I could say, if I would, something on my part. I have borne the burden of measures I did not approve of; for God's sake, let me have the comfort of seeing you easy and happy in measures we both approve of.[33]

In letters to Hardwicke, Pelham gave some explicit reasons for his dislike of Newcastle's behavior. In September he wrote:

> I am sorry to see the ill-humour remain towards Lord Sandwich and Mr Bentinck, not from any personal affection to them, but from this reflection, that his Grace will, upon summing up his whole account, have agreed with nobody. We all know he quarrelled with every minister att home he was ever join'd with, if it should be his fate to do the same with everyone he himself has sent abroad, I leave your Lordship to judge of the consequences.[34]

This was a serious accusation, and even though the brothers were having one of their periodic quarrels when it was written, the truth was not to be denied. Newcastle was an extremely poor colleague for any man, for he simply lacked the ability to get along with anyone in the conduct of foreign affairs.

At the end of the peace negotiations Newcastle supported a move by Austria to receive the final payment of its wartime subsidy. This was Pelham's answer:

> I cannot but stand amazed at the impudence of the Court of Vienna, to make a demand of £100,000 of us, as a kind of condition for exchanging the ratifications, is, after their behaviour an instance of assurance beyond example. . . . Nothing shall make me come into it. I see the behaviour of that Court in a very different light from what my Brother does, and I think this very packet proves that I am in the right.[35]

Two weeks later he wrote:

> I don't know whether it is not right that your Lordship should be apprised of my firm resolution to be no ways concern'd in helping the Austrians to the £100,000 they seem to have set their hearts so much upon receiving, and my Brother his upon granting.[36]

Here, then, was a limitation on Newcastle's conduct of foreign affairs, for Pelham effectively blocked what, in fact, was a peacetime subsidy to Austria. Pelham's control of the purse strings gave him a veto on most of the foreign policy. The event also demonstrated Pelham's increased powers, for at the beginning of the ministry Pelham left foreign affairs almost entirely to Newcastle, while in 1748 he was exerting force against the duke's plans.

Newcastle, as a foreign minister, ran against the wall of his brother's opposition to certain measures, and this he could not overcome. During the general discussions among the ministers on the future foreign policy for England following the peace, Pelham wrote of Newcastle's ideas:

> I have read it over twice and consider'd it as well as I am able to think of things of that nature. You may be sure it is not at all agreable [*sic*] to my notions, I mean the new modelling, or negotiating with any of the great Powers att present, further than to assure them we desire Peace and quietness, and that if they will not personaly meddle with us, we do not desire to disturb any of them, but will abide by our Treatys and perform the several engagements we have enter'd into, when ever we are properly and legally call'd upon. Indeed, My Lord, we want rest, and so does all Europe, all this proceeds only from his [Newcastle's] active spirit, he wants to be doing, and the many interested partys he has been lately with [Cumberland, the king, and foreigners], have found out that, and of consequence flatter him into their own measures. He always had a partiality and regard for the late Lord Stanhope, I know he thinks no Minister has ever made a great figure but him in the two reigns; He will therefore imitate him as far as he can, and I doubt, if he is not check'd by somebody, will bring himself, if not his country into the same distress that fertile but well intention'd Lord did before him.[37]

It was Pelham's view, opposed to the previously quoted view of Chesterfield, that Newcastle wanted to be too active in foreign affairs. Since Pelham was an eighteenth-century English isolationist, it is not surprising to find him opposed to Newcastle's efforts in the international field.[38] Though Pelham opposed active participation in European affairs, he had promised—and kept his promise—to support Newcastle during the war.[39] It was only with the peace that Pelham began active opposition to Newcastle's whole policy.

Whatever the success or failure of Newcastle's foreign policy, it must be admitted that he spent a prodigious amount of time and effort to achieve his ends. His correspondence with his own envoys and with foreign governments was enormous. During the war years the diplomacy he pursued was not wrong or illogical, though the over-all strategic planning was. The English lost the war primarily because of poor army commanders, insufficient over-all planning, inefficient supply of weapons of war, and incapable allies. Newcastle was in part responsible for all these, but the entire cabinet was jointly to blame. Walpole had refused to prepare for war in the beginning, and the following governments never caught up with the lack of preparation. Pelham found all the necessary money, and Newcastle was usually successful in supplying allies from the countries available, but inefficiency in high places combined with no definite aim ultimately ruined all prospects.

The domestic duties of the Secretary of State were subordinated to foreign affairs during the war, but even so the vast number of letters that Newcastle wrote on almost every conceivable subject testify to his attention to these matters. There were few troubles in England during the war other than the Jacobite Rebellion, which will be treated separately, so there were no startling events. Life moved slowly along much the same path it had followed since the Restoration. The calmness was somewhat illusory, however, since the government had matters well under control and stopped any serious trouble early.

Though Newcastle was the "eternal" Secretary of State, there were four other men who held the office of his colleague in succession: Lord Harrington and Lord Chesterfield in the Northern Department and the Duke of Bedford and Lord Holdernesse in the Southern Department. Lord Harrington, as William Stanhope, had had good experience as a diplomat during the twenties and had been Secretary of State with Newcastle from 1730 until 1742. He had made way for Lord Granville from 1742 to 1744, then returned to the secretaryship. From 1744 until 1746 the war was dragging on, and Harrington's time was taken up with the daily business of war. He went to Hanover with the king in 1745 and while there had a chance to have a greater say than ever before. Newcastle had been Harrington's sponsor; in fact, the duke had been the source of the earl's power. Newcastle therefore resented Harrington's moves to develop an independent policy in 1745.[40] Harrington had swung to the position of peace as soon as possible, and Newcastle was strongly in favor of continuing the conflict. From that time on, Harrington's position steadily deteriorated, and his resignation was to be expected. It was no surprise, then, when he suddenly quit his post in October 1746. Only the timing was unexpected. Harrington was not an original thinker nor did he initiate any policy, but he realized much earlier than Newcastle that the war was lost and peace was the only safe policy. The Earl of Harrington must be regarded as a loyal lieutenant able to carry out the decisions of others but a man with few positive abilities.

The Earl of Chesterfield followed his cousin in office. When Chesterfield entered office, he made it clear to Newcastle that he supported the war because it was decided on and even supported a subsidy to Russia to achieve victory.[41] Pelham was extremely surprised that Chesterfield accepted office, since it was well known that the earl was strongly opposed to the war.[42] Chesterfield thus entered office with a basic misunderstanding on policy. It clouded his relations with Newcastle during the next eighteen months until his resignation. At first Chesterfield's tact made him acceptable to Newcastle, but tact alone could not overcome the duke's jealousy or the earl's different ideas on policy.[43] Chesterfield understood Newcastle and advised the men in his department to agree to any requests by the duke. He even wrote Sandwich, "There are certain weaknesses that it were weak not to conform to. I have many of my own, but jealousy and suspicion are not of the number."[44] This was Chesterfield's greatest asset as Secretary. He had been a successful ambassador to the Hague several times in the past and was considered the Englishman best able to negotiate with the Dutch as late as January 1745. His intelligence has always been admitted by historians, and certainly he was a good choice for Secretary of State. Yet while in office, though he did much in the regular, day-by-day conduct of affairs, he was allowed little control of final foreign policy.[45]

By July 1747 Chesterfield was aware that Newcastle was scheming to remove him from office. Newcastle was jealous of him, and this was the basis of the whole difficulty. Chesterfield wrote to his old friend, Solomon Dayrolles:

> Sandwich I know has instructions from the Duke of Newcastle to watch you carefully; he goes back much puzzled between his Grace and me; he would be well with both, and sees that it is impossible. The Duke of Newcastle has, I believe, shown him my place *en perspective,* which possibly it may not be in his Grace's power to dispose of.[46]

Newcastle continued his schemes until February 1748, when Chesterfield seized on an insignificant slight and resigned. The earl retired completely from politics and only occasionally joined his voice in the Lords with the Pelhams. Sir Richard Lodge summed up Chesterfield's position concisely when he said:

> Newcastle was obviously his [Chesterfield's] inferior in intellectual power, but he had far more persistence. Timidity at times made him appear to vacillate, but he rarely made any substantial change in his aims. When he had decided on a particular course of action, he sought by all possible methods to follow it, and, as the querulous member of a family so often does, he usually got his own way.[47]

Chesterfield was not sufficiently capable as a politician to beat Newcastle and force his foreign policy on that wily politician.

The third colleague of Newcastle was the Duke of Bedford. There can be no doubt that Bedford was the least able of any of the Secretaries. From the beginning of his four-year term of office, Bedford was criticized for lack of attention to the duties of his office and for spending too much time at his home, Woburn Abbey.[48] He seldom spent more than three days a week in London, and no one could administer an important office on such a part-time basis. However, it is only fair to Bedford to recognize that the Pelhams did not permit him an equal share in important matters. He was called upon to approve decisions, but only part of the time was he requested to help in making those decisions.[49] Bedford had no special background to qualify him as a foreign minister, except four years as First Lord of the Admiralty, and he never showed any special ability as an administrator to warrant his position. In fact, the reverse was more nearly true. He must be considered one of the poorest of the cabinet officers of the Pelham administration, for his only assets were great wealth, social position, and political influence.

Finally, the last colleague of Newcastle was the Earl of Holdernesse, a young and inexperienced man. He was appointed merely to satisfy Newcastle's wishes and had few qualifications for the office. In the end, however, he turned out to be the most useful of all the men who were joined with Newcastle. This was not because of his ability but rather because he made no effort to direct his department and allowed Newcastle full sway. At long last the duke had found the ideal "junior" Secretary, and harmony returned to the divided office. There was the practical view that the geographical division of power between the two Secretaries was completely out of date by the mid-eighteenth century; one man really had to direct the whole of foreign policy. In this sense the hard-working subordinate was more necessary than an equal Secretary. It was the inefficient and irregular system Newcastle used that foreshadowed the later reorganization of the office of Secretary of State.

Besides the two main Secretaries of State, there was a third Secretary of State for Scotland until the spring of 1745. The office had been re-created when Walpole fell in 1742 and was given to the Marquis of Tweeddale, an ally of Granville. He was quite undistinguished, but he led a group of Scots who were opposed to the Duke of Argyll. The Pelhams retained him in office for about five months after the ousting of Granville. Then he was removed, though he did not join the opposition as did his erstwhile leader. Tweeddale was given little power when a minister, but he was made one of the Lords Justices in 1743 and 1745, and he kept the latter appointment after he was removed from office.[50] Scottish affairs were handled through his office, but the officials in Scotland were friends of the Pelhams, and secret correspondence continued between them. Even in ordinary business Newcastle or Pelham usually had a part in the decisions.[51] When the Jacobite Rebellion broke out in the summer of 1745, Henry Fox blamed Tweeddale in particular and the Scots in general for their unpreparedness. This was not fair of Fox, but it was justified to the extent that Tweeddale had not taken efficient note of events in Scotland.[52] Argyll, Forbes, and other Scottish officials were also to blame for the surprise, but Tweeddale as the official leader of Scotland for three years must be censured, even though he was out of control at the moment of the rebellion.

The office of Lord High Chancellor was the next most important because of the personal relationships of Hardwicke, Pelham, and Newcastle. All authorities agree that Hardwicke was one of the most capable of all English Chancellors, and he administered his legal duties with great ability.[53] However, from the point of view of the administration, Hardwicke's most important function was that of adviser and confidant of the Pelhams. In this capacity he was a conservative force that tried to avoid all upset. As a greatly respected legal authority he was able to perform a steadying influence many times. Few acts may be traced to him directly, but few acts were taken without his agreement and advice.

One of Hardwicke's prime duties was to draw up statements of policy, especially the king's speeches, for the cabinet. He always consulted the Pelhams, and even during the period when Granville was in the cabinet this duty was delegated to the Chancellor.[54] Another aspect of his duty was the prorogation of parliament. As presiding officer of the House of Lords, he could control the meeting and business of that house, and as one of the "inner cabinet" he knew the desires of the group that controlled the government. Hardwicke and Pelham, therefore, determined the course of the meeting of the legislature by their knowledge of their respective houses. They proposed the dates for meeting and adjournment; these were then made known to Newcastle and one or two others, who usually agreed to the suggestion.[55] There were few other things done that can be definitely attributed to Hardwicke, but his presence was felt indirectly in most affairs.

Probably the next most important office was that of the First Lord of the Admiralty. During this period it was held by Bedford, the Earl of Sandwich, and George Anson. Bedford gained the office in the general upheaval after the resignation of Granville. The Pelhams agreed to Bedford solely because of his political power, not for any great ability.[56] While the little duke held this office he was accused of spending too much time at Woburn just as he was later when Secretary of State.[57] In reality Bedford cared little for the work of major political office and allowed his decisions to be made by his favorite friend, the Earl of Sandwich. Sandwich spent a good deal of time arranging the Admiralty Board so that he could dominate its proceedings.[58] Bedford's greatest effort was to achieve the desires of his friend. The day-by-day conduct of naval affairs was left in the capable hands of Admiral Anson, a son-in-law of Lord Hardwicke and a favorite of the Pelhams.[59] He had been one of the few successful naval commanders during the war, and he was a great friend of the Earl of Sandwich.[60] Therefore he had the power, connections, and knowledge necessary to run the Admiralty, and the increasing efficiency of the navy at the end of the war was Anson's contribution, not that of the politicians. Bedford deserved little credit for his personal directions but deserved praise for allowing Anson a free hand. Marchmont's testimony that Bedford ran the Admiralty alone cannot be accepted, and the final evaluation must be that the duke was not much better as First Lord of the Admiralty than he was to be as Secretary of State.[61]

When Bedford was promoted to the secretaryship, Lord Sandwich became First Lord of the Admiralty. This occurred in the spring of 1748, and Sandwich was abroad until autumn on his diplomatic mission. Anson continued to direct the navy during the period, and very few changes took place. When Sandwich returned, he spent more time in general political intrigue than as head of Admiralty. Therefore Anson continued in practical control, and when Sandwich was finally removed by the Pelhams in 1751, he took control officially. His policies of revitalizing the navy and seeking younger commanders were more openly pursued. His success was shown only during the Seven Years War, but this marked him as one of the best appointments made by the Pelhams.

One of the most coveted offices in the cabinet was that of Lord Lieutenant of Ireland. It was not an important office in England, but it carried great prestige and had great independence and patronage in Ireland. From the fall of Granville until 1754 the position was held by four men: the Duke of Devonshire, the Earl of Chesterfield, the Earl of Harrington, and the Duke of Dorset. Devonshire was a holdover from earlier days who remained Lord Lieutenant until the summer of 1745, when Chesterfield returned from the Hague to assume the duties. Devonshire had been a successful administrator, though unspectacular. From the view of the cabinet, he was a "safe" man who brought the powerful Cavendish strength to the cabinet, and he was shifted to the less important post of Lord Steward upon Chesterfield's arrival.

Chesterfield was one of the best Lord Lieutenants of the eighteenth century, but he retained the position for only slightly more than a year. He had taken it because it appealed to him and occasioned no quarrel with the Pelhams, his new political allies.[62] His administration was characterized by sympathy for the Irish and peaceful enactment by the Irish parliament of the laws desired by the English government.[63] This was no easy task, and when compared with the records of other Lord Lieutenants of the eighteenth century, especially the Duke of Dorset, it was a major triumph. According to Horace Walpole, Chesterfield and the Pelhams argued over the various policies to be pursued, but the end results were satisfactory to all.[64] At all events Ireland lost one of its most capable officials when Chesterfield resigned to become Secretary of State.

In February 1746, upon Harrington's resignation as Secretary of State, there was a serious quarrel between him and the Duke of Dorset over the Irish position. Newcastle, Hardwicke, and Andrew Stone exerted great pressure on Dorset to give up the reversion of the office to Harrington.[65] Pelham insisted to the cabinet that the Lord Lieutenancy must be given to Harrington, and in the end Dorset gave in unwillingly.[66] Lord Gower and the Duke of Argyll were also strongly in favor of Harrington, and they supported Pelham in his insistence.[67] Lord Harrington did little except to keep peace between the parliament of Ireland and the cabinet. There were no important crises or arguments, and that state of affairs was really all an eighteenth-century English government required. Harrington liked the post and was angry when he was removed in 1751, but his rule did little for Ireland or the Irish. On the whole it was a mediocre administration.

In 1751 the Duke of Dorset finally attained his ambition and became Lord Lieutenant. His term was one of the worst of the eighteenth century, and the crisis that occurred will be discussed elsewhere. It is sufficient to indicate here that Dorset was an utter failure.

During the entire period of the war the office of Master-General of Ordnance was held by the Duke of Montagu. He was probably the most incapable cabinet member of the whole Pelham period. He followed the laws strictly and allowed no modification to suit individual circumtances. He refused to delegate authority to his subordinates, and he changed no rules or regulations that had become outdated. On the credit side must be listed the fact that he took his duties seriously, even though he interpreted them in the narrowest sense possible. He went on inspection trips to many garrisons and saw for himself their condition. Sometimes he recommended steps to be taken, but his slowness and refusal to take the initiative in any positive action always spoiled his recommendations. In 1744 Montagu went on an inspection of the northern area. He found Scarborough in a dreadful state of defense and ordered its repair, but he found Berwick, a much more important garrison, in far worse condition and refused to order its improvement until specifically ordered to do so by the Lords Justices.[68] This attitude was indefensible in view of the earlier fears of a French invasion and the unrest in Scotland. When the Jacobite Rebellion broke out, Henry Fox blamed Tweeddale and the Scots, but Montagu, responsible for forts and munitions, and he himself, as Secretary at War, were equally responsible. It is hard today to imagine a person more out of place in important office than the Duke of Montagu. After his death the post remained vacant for some time and then was filled by persons not called to the cabinet.

Lord Gower held the post of Lord Privy Seal from 1744 until after the death of Pelham. The duties it carried were indefinite except to care for and affix the Privy Seal when required. Gower entered the Pelham coalition government as a leader of one group of Tories, but he soon became more Court Party than Tory and lost many of his followers.

Nevertheless he remained one of the staunchest allies of the Pelhams and wielded great influence in their councils. On the peace negotiations Pelham wrote to Hardwicke that he sought the advice of Gower and Dorset.[69] Later the same year someone, probably Andrew Stone, wrote to Chesterfield that a political move against the brothers was afoot but that they continued to lead policy, strongly backed by Hardwicke, Harrington, Gower, and Bedford.[70] These are merely two examples of many which indicate that Pelham and Gower worked together as long as the former lived. The office of Privy Seal was not difficult, and almost anyone could perform its functions; the critical question about any holder of that office was how well he could perform his unofficial duties. Gower gave advice, contributed political strength, and remained loyal throughout the life of the administration. These were the important requirements of his post, and he fulfilled them well.

The remaining active executive office was that of Lord President of the Council, held by the Duke of Dorset from 1745 until 1751. Dorset performed his duties during the war with competence. As the presiding officer of the Privy Council he had little to do but present the business that the cabinet had prepared for decision. His greatest responsibility was to attend the meetings and be prepared to obtain the Privy Council approval if no more important cabinet members were present. During these years Dorset missed only thirteen sessions, and since these were all attended by one or more of the leading cabinet ministers—Pelham, Newcastle, Hardwicke, Harrington, or Devonshire—there could have been little trouble caused by his absences. Of the Committee of Plantation Appeals, Dorset missed only ten meetings during the war years, and all these were attended by at least one of the Chief Justices, who were the important persons at such meetings. Two of the meetings he missed were attended by Bedford as Secretary of State and Lord Edgcumbe, who was a loyal lieutenant of the Pelhams. Again, little harm could have resulted from Dorset's absence. He missed only one meeting of the Committee on Irish Bills, and Hardwicke attended that. He missed another meeting of what was called simply "A Committee," but Pelham, Newcastle, and Hardwicke were all present. During the same period Dorset also missed six sessions of the Lords Justices with the Privy Council, but this was the least serious defection of all because several important cabinet members were always there, and permission was granted for his absences.[71] Beyond this regular duty as the link between the cabinet and the Privy Council, Dorset was consulted by the leading ministers and apparently satisfied their demands.[72] Thus Dorset may be regarded as a fairly efficient lieutenant when responsibility and initiative were not necessary to his position. However, he was a troublesome ally if he thought his rights were endangered, as his stubborn fight with Harrington over the Irish Lieutenancy showed. His lack of ability was not to appear until he became Lord Lieutenant of Ireland in 1751.

For most of the administration the four men who held the important household offices that gave cabinet rank were all men of great prestige and political power. The Duke of Devonshire was the greatest of the Whig oligarchs and a man of rather solid common sense. He performed his duties as Lord Steward in a way pleasing to George II and gave loyal support and advice to the cabinet, though he was never particularly prominent during the Pelham administration and finally resigned. The Duke of Marlborough, who succeeded him, was so nearly a carbon copy that an observer would hardly notice the change. The Duke of Grafton (a grandson of Charles II) had long been an ally of Walpole and Newcastle.[73] He used his political power, especially in Suffolk, on behalf of the ministers and exerted important influence on the king. He had been Lord Chamberlain since 1724, and though his health began to decline by the end of the war, the Pelhams considered him one of their most important advisers, and he retained his post until after Pelham's death. The Earl of Pembroke, Groom of the Stole, was the least active member of the cabinet. He was probably the personal choice of George II, and he did little but approve the actions of the leaders.[74] His successor, the Earl of Albemarle, was likewise the king's choice. His main virtue was an ability to persuade George II of the wisdom of cabinet decisions. And last, the Duke of Richmond (another grandson of Charles II) was Master of the Horse. This position was quite unimportant to the government, but the Duke of Richmond was extremely important. Both Pelham and Newcastle considered him one of their best friends. They were political allies in Sussex, and Richmond was usually consulted on important matters by the Pelhams.[75] He was not a brilliant man, but he was shrewd and made sound judgments on political and government matters. He strongly advised Newcastle against appointing Bedford as Secretary of State because he felt that Bedford would not be satisfactory.[76] He recommended Fox or Robinson as far better choices but agreed to Bedford because Newcastle wanted him and especially because Pelham refused to accept anyone who was a member of the House of Commons.[77] Richmond was the one member of the cabinet other than Pelham who freely disagreed with Newcastle and told the Secretary when he was wrong. In spite of Richmond's refusal to accept Newcastle without question, he was the one man whom Newcastle always treated as a trusted friend. Richmond thus was an extremely useful member of this particular cabinet, for he was able to speak his mind on any issue and still not upset Newcastle. On his death in 1750, the Marquis of Hartington, son of Devonshire, was appointed. He had no power while Pelham lived, and he was named solely to retain the active support of the Cavendish family.

Finally there were two members, or semimembers, of the cabinet who held no office, the Earl of Bath and the Duke of Argyll. Bath retained his place after the fall of Lord Granville until February 1746. He did practically nothing and was called less and less often. After the crisis of the four-day ministry, Bath was removed altogether. On the other hand, Archibald, Duke of Argyll, was an extremely important link in the chain. He held the office of Keeper of the Great Seal of Scotland, he was an extra Lord of the Sessions, and he was the Lord Justice General—all these being jobs in the Scottish government. As Earl of Ilay, Argyll had long been a political ally and confidant of Walpole and the Pelhams, and he controlled the government of Scotland for both administrations.[78] Since he had no official duties in the cabinet, Argyll's major duty was to advise the cabinet on any matter but especially on Scottish affairs. He maintained the political control of the cabinet over Scotland, but he was not of much use during the rebellion. He knew unrest was afoot but could not prevent it. Nevertheless Argyll was one of the most useful and reliable members of the cabinet to the Pelhams, even if he failed in time of crisis.

This, then, was the cabinet of Henry Pelham during the years 1744–54. It was not a brilliant cabinet at any time, but neither was it worse than the average eighteenth-century cabinet. It had more political power and prestige than most, which was advantageous in the eighteenth century. And it contained several good men who knew their departments and how to manage them. It controlled parliament well, and this was more than most were able to do. The most peculiar aspect of it to our modern minds is that all members except Pelham were Lords, which made it unbalanced and conservative. Yet in the eighteenth century this was a virtue.

CHAPTER VIII

Pelham and the General Administration

༜ BELOW THE RANK of cabinet ministers were many members of the government who held important positions. A brief comment on some of these officials will make clear their importance. One of the most prominent of the secondary offices was that of Paymaster-General of the Forces. Of itself the job was not important, but for many years the practice of placing favorite young followers of the cabinet in it gave it great prestige. Robert Walpole, the Earl of Wilmington, and Henry Pelham had all held the post, and when Pelham became First Lord of the Treasury it was given to Sir Thomas Winnington, who was one of Pelham's main assistants in the House of Commons. In May 1746, after Winnington's death, the position was given to William Pitt to satisfy his demand for an important office. Pitt administered the office through subordinates, as was the custom, but put his parliamentary talents at the service of the cabinet.[1] Since this was the aim of Pelham and the cabinet, they were well satisfied with Pitt's conduct.

The Secretary at War was another of these ministerial posts. The office was held by Sir William Yonge from 1735 until his health collapsed in 1746. Yonge directed the office efficiently but was particularly useful to Walpole and Pelham as a prominent lieutenant in the House of Commons. In May 1746 Henry Fox assumed the duties of the War office. Fox was a useful parliamentary debater, but he was not an efficient administrator. He tried to shift blame for errors onto others, as his attitude toward Tweeddale and the rebellion indicated. Moreover, he often had to be pushed to execute orders in connection with troops for the war.[2] On the whole, Fox did not make a good departmental executive. While he was in this office he schemed to attain greater power, as the following letter shows:

I think Mr. Fox, whose ability and credit in the House of Commons are great, will, in my private opinion, push both the brothers (Duke of Newcastle and Pelham) whenever he sees a fair opportunity, for he does not want [lack] ambition, nor any qualities that are necessary to raise a man in this country to the height of power.[3]

Sandwich replied to the above letter with a very shrewd observation about Fox:

> I agree with you in what you say about this gentleman, that he does not want ambition or any qualities to raise a man in our government; but that is not enough, as I am sure he wants many qualities necessary to maintain himself after his rise, so that it would be much more easy for him to pull down than to build.[4]

The future proved Sandwich to be quite correct. Fox was not an easy companion or a help in his department.

The Treasurer of the Navy was another office of importance connected with the armed forces. The Treasurer, as the Paymaster did for the army, controlled the naval funds. In 1744 the place was held by Sir John Rushout, who was replaced on the fall of Granville by George Bubb Dodington, one of the most untrustworthy of eighteenth-century politicians.[5] Dodington took office as one of the Broad-Bottom against Granville. His appointment pleased the opposition, but he used the post purely for his personal advancement.[6] He was a clever, if shifty, politician but nothing more. No cabinet could ever be sure how long he would remain in office. When he resigned in 1748 it was no loss to the government.

The position of the First Commissioner of the Board of Trade was gradually increasing in importance. The First Lord of Trade for several years was Lord Monson, a relative of the Pelhams and one of the poorest officials retained by the brothers from the Walpole regime. Monson was responsible for much of the delay and inefficiency in relations with the colonies; in fact, the Earl of Morton especially commented on Monson's slowness when he applied to succeed to the office.[7] Pelham regarded the office as important and wrote to Newcastle at Monson's death that the choice of a successor was "pretty" material.[8] Bedford suggested the final adjustment, which settled on the Earl of Halifax as the new First Lord of Trade.[9] Halifax was a definite improvement over Monson, and he showed the interest necessary to improve the administration of colonial affairs.

The promotion of Halifax to the Board of Trade was made difficult by the Duke of Leeds, Newcastle's brother-in-law, who demanded an important office. In the end he accepted Halifax's old job of Chief Justice in Eyre South of the Trent.[10] The two Chief Justices in Eyre (North and South of the Trent) were positions secondary to execution of justice and government orders. During Halifax's tenure of one of these posts, he had caused a serious crisis within the cabinet by threatening to resign. His friends Gower, Bedford, Sandwich, and Chesterfield demanded that the Pelhams agree to the requests of Halifax.[11] The importance of the posts was further shown by such men as the Dukes of Ancaster, Somerset, and Leeds, the Earls of Cardigan and Halifax, and Viscount Cornwallis, who were willing to accept the offices for the prestige they carried. The government, therefore, used them as rewards for members of the nobility who were politically helpful to the cabinet.

Another office used by the cabinet to reward friends or gain political allies was that of Vice-Treasurer of Ireland. For some time the office had been split between two men, each of whom was known as a Joint Vice-Treasurer. Viscount Torrington and Henry Vane held the positions until the removal of Granville, when William Pitt was given Vane's post as his share in the new government. The office involved no effort from its holder, for deputies did all the work. In fact the holders did not even need to go to Ireland, and many of them, including Pitt, did not.[12] There was really no question of performing the duties well, since the main duty was to draw a salary and support the cabinet in parliament. This Pitt and Torrington did.

Lord Edgcumbe occupied the post of Chancellor of the Duchy of Lancaster, which was another of the secondary places of some importance. In this capacity he was an administrator of the duchy and a judge in the court of the duchy. Therefore he was a link in the involved chain by which the laws were carried into effect. Edgcumbe was sufficiently regular in his work so that, though Pelham wished to switch him to another position, it was agreed to leave him in the duchy when he expressed a desire to remain.[13]

Beside these positions there were several others of importance at the time. The Master of the Rolls, William Fortescue, was custodian of the official records. William Finch, the Vice-Chamberlain, was the person who had the most frequent, private relationship with the king, and he influenced George II against many of the policies of the Pelhams.[14] The Treasurer of the Chamber was another post used for political negotiation, and its duties were performed by subordinates. During this period John Hobart, Sir John Hynde Cotton, and Richard Arundel held the post in turn, and the first and third used it as a step to better things. The Earl of Fitzwalter, as Treasurer of the Household, and Lord Sandys, Edmund Waller, and the Earl of Lincoln, as successive Cofferers of the Household, controlled the distribution of royal money for the personal living of the king. Neither was a difficult post, and both carried prestige because of closeness to the monarch. Sir Conyers D'Arcy, who was Comptroller of the Household during almost the entire Pelham administration, was extremely capable at the financial duties involved. Moreover, he was a shrewd and loyal friend of Pelham. And finally in this class of officials belonged the Master of the Wardrobe, the Duke of Montagu before 1746 and Sir Thomas Robinson afterward, whose duties were confined to the personal care of the king. The common denominator of all these posts was membership in the Privy Council. Almost every man who occupied them was made a Councillor, whether he was a member of the aristocracy or not.[15] The membership on the Privy Council that these offices usually entailed helps to explain why certain choices were made, for the cabinet was thereby guarded against difficulties in the Council.

Besides these officials there were five legal figures who were important to the cabinet: Chief Justice of the King's Bench, Sir William Lee; Chief Justice of the Court of Common Pleas, Sir John Wiles; Chief Baron of the Court of the Exchequer, Sir Thomas Parker; Attorney-General, Sir Dudley Ryder; and Solicitor-General, William Murray. The titles of the judges make clear their duties in the courts, and as members of the Privy Council they, with the Lord Chancellor, gave the necessary legal rulings on orders. The two law officials, Ryder and Murray, were extremely important to the cabinet. They were the principal legal advisers on almost all matters. One or both of them were called to pass judgment on the legality of proposed bills and orders. Ryder was of average competence, but Murray (the future Lord Mansfield) was one of the best legal minds in English history. Moreover, Murray was an extremely able House of Commons man.[16] The law, therefore, as well as the secondary ministers, was an important key to the cabinet's control of the whole machinery of the government.

Beneath the heads of the departments there were a number of vital secretaries and undersecretaries. These posts are quite interesting, for during the middle of the eighteenth century they were developing into a true system of civil service. Moreover, certain of the officials who held them were men who actually made many of the important decisions and directed the policies decided by their superiors in the cabinet. Among these posts two of the most important were the Secretary of the Chancellor of the Exchequer and the two Joint Secretaries of the Treasury. The Secretary of the Chancellor of the Exchequer was Henry Legge, until he became a member of the Treasury Board in 1746, and then James West. This was the post in which much of the actual work of the Exchequer was done, and West became a regular avenue through which Pelham ran the department. Men applied to West to get government positions in the Exchequer, and he aided Pelham in decisions on the many applications.[17] Even more important, West was a dispenser of the Secret Service funds. At least twice in 1747 the king ordered payments to West for this purpose: in June £10,000 and in September £6,000.[18] Whether these grants were made to West as a Secretary of the Chancellor of the Exchequer or as one of the Joint Secretaries of the Treasury is unimportant. In either sense West was extremely important to the government. The Joint Secretaries of the Treasury during this time were John Scrope and James West. Scrope was appointed to the office on January 28, 1724, and retained it until his death in 1752. West was appointed in 1741 and remained in office until 1762, when he retired on a pension. Scrope held office under Walpole, Wilmington, and Pelham—which was not hard to understand because all three belonged to the same political group—but West served under them and continued under

Devonshire who led another group. This is clear proof that the political quarrels of Newcastle, Pitt, and Fox affected the Secretaries to a very slight degree. They did not regard themselves as political appointees or they would have resigned or been removed in 1742 or 1756. This is one of the fundamental bases upon which a civil service can be constructed. Scrope often was a recipient of Secret Service funds. In 1747 he received £6,000 and £5,000 twice, and in 1748 he received £6,000 twice.[19] Since Newcastle was the principal person receiving Secret Service money, Scrope and West must have acted as Pelham's avenue for the distribution of money. As such they were very important to Pelham's control of the government, and their long experience was essential to the smooth running of the department he headed.[20]

Both Scrope and West were members of parliament; Scrope for Lyme Regis (1734–52) and West for St. Albans (1741–68). They were able, therefore, to support Pelham in the House of Commons. Though there is no evidence that Scrope ever did anything but vote, West was often employed on parliamentary matters as a patronage official.[21] He also, as Recorder of Poole (1746–72), was able to influence elections in that place as well as his own St. Albans. During these years Pelham relied on Nicholas Hardinge as his primary adviser on matters in the House of Commons. Hardinge was the man who succeeded Scrope in 1752 as one of the Joint Secretaries, but he still retained his position of parliamentary adviser. Thus there was developing, alongside the growth of the civil service spirit, the idea that the Treasury aides were useful Commons aides.

One other Treasury official, the Solicitor to the Treasury, appeared as an important person during the tenure of Henry Pelham. Whether it was the legal training of John Sharpe or his personal relationship with Pelham that made him important is not now clear, but he was a significant element in the conduct of the department. Legal claims against the Treasury naturally passed through his hands, but other large payments were also made through his office. For example, in 1747 and 1748 some kind of infection killed large numbers of cattle in England, and Sharpe was authorized to pay out at least £105,000 at various times to compensate for the losses.[22] The fact that this was a huge sum of money to pass through any one man's hands in the eighteenth century indicated that John Sharpe was considered an important member of the government staff. It also showed that Pelham was willing to delegate large amounts of the routine Treasury work to his subordinates.

The most important positions other than the Secretaries of the Treasury were the Undersecretaries of State. During the Pelham administration several men held these posts, but Andrew Stone was by far the most notable. Stone had begun his political life as a private secretary to Newcastle, but he soon became a very intimate friend and complete confidant. He became Undersecretary of the Southern Department in 1734 and

shifted to the same position in the Northern Department in 1748 with
Newcastle. Even after 1751, when he became Sub-Governor to the Prince
of Wales (George III), he remained Newcastle's trusted adviser. The
two men were so close that it is often impossible to guess which one
framed the policies of the State Department. Stone was the admirable
type of servant who performs his duties intelligently and without display.
Not only was he the principal adviser of Newcastle, but he was also a
firm friend of Henry Pelham. There are many letters from Pelham which
indicate that Stone was highly respected and one of the main supports
that helped hold the brothers together during their many quarrels.[23]
Other men understood Stone's power, and envoys applied to him almost
as often as to Newcastle for instructions, money, or an infinite variety of
other things.[24] One example of the Pelhams' complete trust in Stone and
his ability took place in 1748 when Stone alone accompanied the king to
Hanover to act in control of business until Newcastle could arrive. No
other subordinate ever received such a mark of importance from ranking
ministers in the mid-eighteenth century, and very seldom at any other
time. Later in 1748 Pelham urged that Stone be sent as envoy to Paris
on the conclusion of the peace, saying that he was the best man available.[25] No doubt Stone's personal relationships with the Pelhams accounted for most of his great influence, but his office gave him some
power and the position to exert it. It is important that Stone never really
tried to obtain a ministerial post (which he might have got from Newcastle) but was content to remain Undersecretary.

Edward Weston, Thomas Ramsden, Richard Aldworth, Claudius
Amyand, William Chetwynd, and Hugh Valence Jones were all important officials who were Undersecretaries at one time or another. Weston
had been Harrington's primary prop, and he followed the earl to Ireland
in 1746, where he became Chief Secretary. He had been a loyal lieutenant to Townshend, Harrington, and Granville, and he demonstrated the
development of the continuity of the undergrades at the time. Ramsden,
Amyand, and Jones were especially important because they were friends
of the ministers. There were some lesser men who held undersecretary-
ships—John Potter, Richard Pottinger, John Balaquier, and James Wal-
lace—but none of them held office for a long time. Finally the Secretaries
of the Lords Justices were inevitably selected from the Undersecretaries of
State.[26] This practice was extremely important, for these secretaries were
the men who planned the work of the Lords Justices. Thus in an indirect way the Undersecretaries of State were in a position to influence
the entire action of the government. Certainly they held vital posts.

Outside the Treasury and the State offices were two important secretaryships: the Secretary of the Admiralty and the Secretary of the Lord
High Chancellor. The Admiralty post was divided into two parts: a Secretary and a Deputy-Secretary (sometimes both were called Secretaries),
but the distinction seemed more one of prestige than of power. Thomas

Corbett, Secretary from 1742 to 1751, and John Cleveland, Undersecretary from 1742 to 1748 and Secretary from 1748 to 1754, both issued orders and carried on correspondence. Cleveland seemed the more active of the two, and he understood the workings of the Admiralty. Change of personnel in the Admiralty Board had no effect on these men; they performed their duties without comment whether Winchelsea, Bedford, Sandwich, or Anson was head of the Board. Here is one of the most definite examples of the fact that office positions of importance were not considered political posts but rather as career service to the king.

The office of Secretary to the Lord Chancellor was held throughout the Pelham administration by Hutton Perkins.[27] Lord Hardwicke left many papers, mostly on official business, which indicate that Perkins was in rather complete control of the office work of the Chancery. In this capacity as well as that of a friend, Perkins was able to influence Hardwicke to a considerable extent.

Other offices of the lower ranks were important administrative units. There was a Stamp Office, whose Commissioners were responsible for that form of excise revenue. The work was not heavy, and the posts were usually used as rewards for good service in some other capacity on the part of the appointees. This was true of the Board in 1746, when Richard Shelley, John Barnard, John Plumptre, and William Blake were the members.[28] The Board of Works had supervision of government building and repairs. Its members were both political appointees and what appear to have been career men.[29] Henry Finch was the only completely political appointment in 1746. On the other hand, the First Commissioner of Police was definitely a political job, and in 1747 the Earl of Marchmont was appointed for political reasons alone.[30] The same political dominance controlled the office of Comptroller of the Customs and Subsidies of the Port of London. Lord Bolingbroke's father had purchased it for two lives for £4,000, and in 1748 Pelham obtained it for the lives of his son-in-law, the Earl of Lincoln, and his grandson, Lord Clinton.[31] Both of these posts should have been administered by experts, but both were sinecures, with the work left to subordinates. Again the transition to a civil service is demonstrated, for these offices were still operating under the old patronage system, while others had advanced to a stage much nearer that of career posts.

The diplomatic service was likewise split between career men and patronage appointees. But even the career men looked forward to rewards for their service. In 1746 Robert Trevor, envoy at the Hague, negotiated with Pelham to be relieved. Pelham finally arranged the retirement, and Trevor received the post of a Commissioner of the Revenue of Ireland.[32] The same was true in 1748 of Sir Thomas Robinson, who finally achieved his retirement in 1750. Pelham appointed him a member of the Board of Trade and gave him a seat in parliament.[33] These two men had given long years to the service of England abroad and may truly be called career men. Nevertheless Robinson became a politician after 1748, and Trevor became a patronage official. The regular officials of the government were thus split in almost all fields between the civil servants and the patronage men, with a very indefinite boundary between them.

The Privy Council of the mid-eighteenth century was a collection of many different types of men. The two sons of George II were members, but the Prince of Wales did not attend sessions during the administration because of his quarrel with his father and his leadership among the opposition. The Duke of Cumberland was recorded as present at four meetings in 1742 and 1743, but for the rest of the war he did not attend sessions even though he commanded the English armies.[34] Neither could, therefore, be considered active members. The clergy was represented by the Archbishops of Canterbury and York and the Bishop of London. Of these churchmen, the Archbishop of Canterbury was the only active attendant, and he usually joined only the full formal sessions to which the king or the Lords Justices came. The members of the cabinet for the time being were always Privy Councillors, and many of them retained their places even after leaving the cabinet. The lesser ministers and the two Chief Justices were sworn to the Privy Council when they received office but were removed when they left office. These last two groups were the most important members of the Council, but the next less important groups were the most interesting. One of these was composed of prominent and powerful members of the Lords, and the other was made up of a few important members of the Commons. The lords were chosen for their position of prestige or because the cabinet relied on them to insure a safe majority in the Privy Council. Usually three or four of them attended the committee meetings under the leadership of one of the cabinet members, generally the Lord President, and thus they were the men who voted most frequently on the decisions brought before the Privy Council. During the years when they were members of the Privy Council, Lords Grantham, Fitzwalter, Delaware, Cornwallis, Edgcumbe, and Abercorn were most active in Council business.[35] None of them achieved cabinet status under Henry Pelham, yet they were loyal to the cabinet and did regular work that the more important ministers had no time to do.

The last group was made up of individuals who were appointed for some special talent. The Speaker of the House of Commons, Sir Arthur Onslow, was one of these, for obvious reasons. Sir John Norris, Field Marshal Wade, and General Sir John Ligonier were members consulted at various times for naval or military advice. Horatio Walpole the elder remained from the days of Sir Robert, because Henry Pelham respected his advice. Sir Paul Methuen and Stephen Poyntz were old diplomats who were probably kept to give information on foreign countries. Finally, Sir Robert Sutton and Sir George Lee were members, the first because he was Pelham's nephew and for no other reason, and the latter as representative of the Princess of Wales after 1752. These men did not attend with any regularity and, except for Sir George Lee, did very little committee work. The most interesting thing about them was that they were not removed from their places as were the men who were ministers when they left office, or the lords when they disagreed with the cabinet. They were considered experts and therefore entitled to remain as advisers to the political appointees.

The Privy Council had its own staff of clerks who kept records and transcribed orders. The clerkships were not political positions, though several clerks were appointed originally for political reasons.[36]

Finally, the Lords Justices as a joint regency cannot be ignored. When George II went to Hanover they performed the legal functions of the king, though George retained the right to conduct any business he wished from across the channel. In practice this meant that the king and the minister in attendance directed foreign policy and the army, while the Lords Justices directed domestic policy. In 1743 every member of the regency was a member of the cabinet.[37] In 1745 Bolton, Tweeddale, Stair, and Cobham were members of the regency in addition to the cabinet.[38] In 1748 Lord Cobham was added to the cabinet to form the regency.[39] In 1750 and 1752 only cabinet members were named. In practice, therefore, the cabinet became the regent—the only common-sense approach to the problem when the heir to the throne, the obvious choice for individual regent, was a leader of the political opposition to the cabinet. The few extra members of the regency were in agreement with the cabinet when chosen and hardly appeared to contradict the fact that all power was placed in the hands of the Whigs who dominated the cabinet.

The procedure of the Lords Justices was to meet twice a week and to attend full meetings of the Privy Council. On the whole they followed their schedule closely, and a majority of members were present. The leaders of the cabinet usually met beforehand and decided on the questions to be discussed, but others could also bring up problems. Probably at no other time in the eighteenth century did the cabinet control domestic matters so completely as during the trips of George II to Hanover between 1737 and 1760.[40] The Lords Justices were, therefore, one of the many illustrations of the growing control of the cabinet over the monarch. By nature they were a temporary body, but this was one of the means by which the cabinet developed its leadership of the entire government.

This, then, completed the government of the Pelham period: Commons, Lords, officials, Privy Council, and Lords Justices, with all of whom Henry Pelham had to deal. Within the limits set by the structure, he had to lead the government to a consistent policy toward the war and later through a disturbed period of peace. The structure did not radically change for many years, and every minister who ever pretended to be First had to face the problems created by its various units. The people who made up this government for Pelham have been seen on several levels. They were not all good or efficient, but they were typical of the time in England. It was on their shoulders that the final success or failure of the ministry depended. To know how well they succeeded, one must turn to an examination of some of the policies and their results. To know how well Pelham succeeded, one must see what share he had in carrying out the policies and how he controlled the other officials.

CHAPTER IX

Financial Problems of the War

℘ PELHAM, as First Lord of the Treasury and Chancellor of the Exchequer, was responsible for raising the money necessary to finance the war after 1743. On June 27, 1742, William Pulteney wrote an extremely optimistic letter on the financial condition of the British government:

> I am very well assured that nothing astonished and struck France so much, as England's being able to raise upwards of six millions this year, with so much ease. If this cast a damp on our Enemys, it cannot fail being a great encouragement to our friends, & must have the best effect when generally known.[1]

If this was a true picture of the fiscal situation, and there is no reason to think otherwise, the first two and a half years of the war were financed with little trouble. However, the longer the war dragged on, the more difficult it became to find sources from which desirable loans could be made. Therefore by the time Pelham became responsible for finances, it was not easy to find new revenue.[2] Pelham voiced his troubles at the Treasury to Robert Trevor:

> I wish it was in my power to keep touch with you all, but when I came into the Treasury I found a vast arrear and the expenses have increased, and the revenue diminished ever since, this I hope will plead my excuse.[3]

As a result of the increasingly difficult money market, Pelham spent much of his energy trying to find ways to cut expenses. He understood that the war was expensive and the costs were necessary, but he constantly urged economy whenever possible. Economy was a constant theme of his correspondence from 1743 until 1748. While still Paymaster, Pelham wrote to the Earl of Stair:

> Forgive me, my Dear Lord, that I presume to recommend economy, as far as it is consistent with the service, I understand the extraordinarys of the Warr will amount to a very great sum, such a one as this country is not yet acquainted with; I know the difference of an Army marching through a country where they are to pay for every thing, and where they live upon free quarter. But there is no making the Gentlemen of the House of Commons understand that, precedent is all they go by, and from that they determine without con-

sidering circumstances. I ask pardon for this liberty, it proceeds from a desire
to keep every thing att home quiet, in order the better to support success
abroad.[4]

In the next years he wrote, "The expense this country is now at, is
immense, and if no fruit is found from it this year, nor expectation of
reaping any next, who can promise for success another session of Parliament." [5] For 1745 the indications are that money was very tight. Pelham
had difficulty producing the money necessary to pay some of the ordinary
costs of government and the interest rates were high.[6] In 1746 George
Grenville wrote:

> Perhaps my real compassion for the many unfortunate people that are affected
> by it [deficiencies of the Civil List] may incline me to wish it more than the
> other exigencies of the government will allow of: this consideration has with-
> held me upon saying any thing on this subject to Mr. Pelham, who I see labours
> under so many difficulties to get the money for the service of this year, that I
> cannot think of increasing them by any representation of mine, except upon
> the utmost necessity.[7]

By 1747 Pelham was insisting that there was no money to continue
fighting and the war must be stopped. He even told the Duke of Cumberland that England had no prospect of getting more troops and if they
were obtainable there would be no money to pay them.[8] In March 1748
Newcastle admitted that money was a serious problem:

> I will speak to my Brother [about a loan to the Dutch]; But Money is so
> scarce, that It cannot be got at any Rate, or for any Service. The Duke of Bed-
> ford, and I, press extremely for the Money for Genoa; Hitherto We have not
> prevailed, Tho' I rather think, It will be acquiesced in at last.[9]

And finally, at the end of the year, Pelham congratulated Newcastle on
the conclusion of the Peace Conference:

> every day convinces us of the great service you have done your Country by put-
> ting an end to the war in so honorable a manner. The want of money is such,
> that the stocks fall even tho' the Peace is confirmed, I have enquired into the
> causes of it, and most reasonable men think it is the demand of some to employ
> in trade, and others, who have borrowed att a considerable interest to make
> their payments in the publick subscriptions, are now forc'd to sell to make good
> those engagements. But one and all agree, that there is not Specie sufficient in
> the Kingdom to circulate the interest of that vast Capital which we have cre-
> ated in the Publick funds, to pay the rents of those lands of England, and to
> employ in the trade which now every one is venturing his small fortune in.[10]

The clear implication of all the statements is that neither parliament nor
the money market was prepared to grant money to the war without

considerable political pressure or high interest rates. It was not easy, therefore, to be the minister responsible for finances.

On the other hand, Philip Yorke noted that the Commons almost always passed Pelham's proposals, though usually only after a fight.[11] Yorke ended his diary entry for one day by saying that Pelham's reputation for honesty and integrity had much to do with getting the bills passed and that the Commons would not have passed them for any other man. Horace Walpole the younger, after some typical sarcasm, agreed that Pelham got his measures passed by safe margins in spite of opposition.[12] The key to the financial troubles lay in finding sources from which sufficient money could be borrowed at moderate interest rates.

William Pitt, during the Seven Years War, summarized the costs of the two previous wars. He estimated that the War of the Spanish Succession on the continent cost £20,000,000 and increased the debt £47,000,000 in eleven years. He estimated that the War of the Austrian Succession increased the debt £30,000,000 and cost nine years' extra tax on land and money from the sinking fund.[13] The interesting figures are the two debts. The war fought under Pelham was cheaper to the future, for his debt averaged £3,333,333 a year, and the earlier one averaged £4,272,727 a year. It was, however, not easy to raise three and one third million a year to finance a losing war. Pitt noted the fact that the earlier war was a winning one and the latter a losing one, and this he believed offset the greater cost.[14]

Among the Treasury Papers there is one called a "State of the National Debt, December 31, 1739, to December 31, 1745." [15] This paper lists the national debt as follows:

December 31, 1739	£46,129,946– 3–5¼
December 31, 1740	45,943,946– 3–5¼
December 31, 1741	46,956,046– 3–5¼
December 31, 1742	48,915,047–16–9¼
December 31, 1743	51,043,347–16–7¼
December 31, 1744	53,679,247–16–9¼
December 31, 1745	56,795,447–16–9¼

The last three years are not included, but the list makes it clear that the costs of the war rose steadily each year after 1740 and that each year a larger amount was borrowed to pay for it. The increase in the debt is much below Pitt's average, but if the same rate of increase was maintained for the last three years, the debt would have approached £20,000,-000. Whether Pitt included figures other than those of the national debt is unknown, so it is impossible to account for the difference. At any rate, the important fact is that Pelham raised large sums (for the time) by borrowing to pay for the war. Pelham gained and preserved the confidence of the money market in order to gain the necessary funds, and this was one of his greatest services to the country. The steady increase of the costs also explained his growing opposition to the war.

Among the Treasury Papers there also remains a summary of the net revenue of the Exchequer from six sources.[16] This indicates that there was a decline in revenue from these six sources from 1738 to 1745. The revenue from the Post Office, licenses for wine, hackney coaches, and chairs rose in 1739 and then rather steadily declined. The income from Hawkers and Pedlers declined from 1738 on, except for the year 1744 when a fairly sharp rise took place. And finally, the duties on stamps and salt, though declining slightly, remained almost constant until 1745. The total revenues from these sources declined from £380,298–5s–11d to £361,003–10s–11½d, a loss of £19,294–14s–11½d (roughly 5 per cent) was recorded. Even this relatively small drop was extremely important at a time when expenses were constantly rising. The loss of established income was one of the serious financial problems faced by Henry Pelham, and he had to find new revenue not only to meet new expenses but to replace the decline in the old income.

Various methods were employed by the Treasury to increase revenue by parliamentary action. All the usual expedients were employed; in fact, the schemes were so numerous that it is impossible to do more than take samples of the actions. The year 1744 was the first in which Pelham had complete control of the Treasury. Thus his plans at that time formed the basis for his future actions. Moreover, those plans provoked considerable opposition, and the details of the plans are more complete than for other years.

Pelham's first step was to propose in the Committee of Supply that the cabinet accept the East India Company's offer of a million pounds toward the current service of the year.[17] After a fight, Pelham won and had the cash at hand necessary to run the government. His problem, then, was to raise the money to repay the loan and its interest. His plan of a two-shilling, sixpence tax on muscovado (West Indian) sugar was presented to the Committee of Ways and Means, where strong opposition, led by Sir John Barnard, occurred.[18] Barnard demanded that the past surpluses of the Gin Bill and a new duty on spirits be used to raise the money.[19] Pitt and his friends also opposed Pelham, for they wanted the money raised by a tax on foreign linen.[20] Lord Limerick proposed one-penny-per-yard tax on linens, and Pelham strongly objected. The Scots supported Limerick, and the report of Pelham was recommitted.[21] On this defeat Pelham adopted Barnard's scheme for the use of the previous year's Gin Bill surplus and a halfpenny-per-yard tax on linen. At the vote, Pitt and Hume Campbell supported Pelham, but Barnard and Limerick still opposed.[22] The government won, but agreed to delay the linen duty clause until a commission to investigate the subject had reported.[23] It is obvious that from the beginning Pelham was unable to get parliamentary support for extra taxes, especially when he wished to tax the strong West

Indies lobby. As a result little new revenue was raised by taxes during the year, and the surplus income from earlier taxes, which should have been available for unexpected costs, was used up in the regular budget. It was not a happy solution, but Pelham made the most of a bad situation and obtained the revenue necessary to finance the war for another year.

There was little trouble over finance bills in 1745, but in 1746 opposition rose again. By January 1746 income from licenses and duties on spirits, glass, liquor, and wine were £76,325–4s–2d short of paying the statutory charges on these excises.[24] There can be little doubt that the increase of smuggling, which greatly worried the cabinet, accounted for part of this loss, but it meant that more new revenue was needed.[25] Again Barnard led the attack on Pelham's plans for raising the money. The debate got underway after the cabinet crisis of February 10–14, and Pelham owed much of his victory on the bills to his earlier political victory. His plan to borrow the money was carried by

> above 100 majority, though not so cheap for the nation as another scheme offered by Sir John Barnard, but it was not sure that the moneyed men of the city, who were to support this last, were able to raise the money proposed; whereas those who engaged with Mr. Pelham were sure men.[26]

Sir Benjamin Keene reported a similar version of the debates,[27] so it seems plain that Pelham's prestige in financial circles had risen during the past two years to the point where he could control the money of the majority of the bankers. Parliament recognized this vital fact, and Pelham had very little trouble with that body on financial matters after this debate. The finances of the country were taken care of for another year, but by borrowing instead of taxation. Parliament was willing to approve money for the war as long as it was not asked to increase the tax load. This accounted for the rise of the national debt as the war dragged on, and especially accounted for the rate of increase each year.

Finally, the revenue question for 1747 showed that there was another reason for the smooth passage of money bills. Philip Yorke wrote to his brother as follows:

> Mr. Pelham opened ye Supply on Friday last in a very able manner; We must raise this year for the public Service between 8 & 9 Million, an immense sum indeed, as the Speaker tells the King every Session. . . . Sr. J. Barnard & Mr. P. had settled the Matter in concert, so that the money is borrowed at a cheap rate, & the Loan was filled in 3 days, & a great deal more subscribed than was wanted.[28]

Without Barnard to lead the opposition in the Commons, Pelham's plans were accepted with little question. It was also during 1746 that Pelham reintroduced a national lottery to raise money.[29] The lottery could not finance the war, but it did provide extra money without raising opposition. By the end of 1746 it may be said that Pelham had developed his wartime financial policy: small tax increases where opposition was weak, borrowing from his friends of the London money market after carefully working out his plan with leaders of the opposition, and any extra money schemes that, like the lottery, seemed workable. It was not a strong policy, but in Pelham's hands it worked, and he always obtained the necessary money for the war.[30]

The expenses of the war itself may be divided into five main categories: army, navy, secret service, subsidies, and diplomacy. Of these the army and navy were the greatest charges on the public purse. According to Newcastle, the army pay for seven years totaled roughly £10,500,000 for slightly over 400,000 men:[31]

Year	Troops Stationed in Britain, Colonies, and Flanders	Total Pay
1742	51,402	£ 1,345,855–12s– 7½d
1743	51,696 *	1,397,078–11 – 5½
1744	52,358	1,435,785– 8 – 8
1745	56,611	1,572,163– 8 –10½
1746	64,256	1,641,541–12 – 8½
1747	63,253	1,571,967–18 – 3½
1748	64,966	1,617,411– 9 –10¾
Total	404,542	£10,581,804– 2s– 6¼d

* Corrected from 51,698

The payment of this large sum was handled by the Paymaster's Office and involved several problems. A deputy Paymaster-General stationed in Flanders, was the official in charge of the money for the troops on the continent.[32] His principal problem was that of exchange and the cost of exchanging money so that he could pay the army.[33] It was an involved process and accounted for much of the delay in paying troops. There was also the problem of insufficient authority for money issued by the Paymaster of the Forces. In 1743 Pelham was relieved of responsibility for the money spent on authority of the Secretary at War by means of a special warrant.[34] Again in 1744, £50,000 was issued to Pelham by the Treasury to make up extraordinary expenses. At the same time a special Privy Seal warrant was issued that allowed all his payments which had any sort of reasonable acquittances, even if they did not have proper authority.[35] At the end of 1744 another warrant was issued to allow Pelham's accounts to be signed only by General Wentworth.[36] And in 1746 Pitt had to receive such a special warrant to cover some of his payments.[37] Thus it is clear that the Paymaster-General was attacked from both sides: by the troops for pay at reasonable rates and by the auditors, whose regulations allowed for no flexibility in the audits. It is also plain that special warrants were the loophole through which large sums could pass for any purpose. Pelham as Paymaster was helped by these special warrants, and as Prime Minister he helped others by this means. It was an inefficient method of payment that kept the Secretary at War from spending money and made the Paymaster-General, because of an over-rigid account system, find loopholes to allow payment of necessary money. It was also slow. For example, when General Cope needed money quickly in Scotland, he had to get Treasury approval to take the money from the Scottish Collector of Land Tax, which would then be repaid by the Paymaster.[38] All the offices involved, as well as the Secretary of State and the Secretary at War, had to be informed and issue proper orders before Cope got the money he needed to fight the rebellion.

At the end of the war Pelham was much concerned with the expense of the army. He wished to reduce its size and effect various operating economies.[39] Pelham went into the problem with the Duke of Cumberland, and the two compromised on the size.[40] Little, however, was achieved in reducing the running expenses of the army, and nothing was done to improve the efficiency of the methods of getting money to the army. That had to await a general overhaul of the entire government.

The navy got an even larger share of the money spent by the government than the army. Newcastle has recorded the money granted and men voted for the navy for the entire war. Almost £24,000,000 was granted and 367,000 men were voted.[41] The Treasurer of the Navy distributed the funds, but the Admiralty Board had control over his actions such as the Secretary at War never held over the Paymaster-General. Therefore, the navy operated more nearly as a unit than did the army. In spite of the very large grants to the navy, by 1746 there was a large naval debt. This was one of the serious problems of the later stages of the war, and Pelham had to spend much time in trying to solve it. Henry Legge wrote:

I dare say it will appear that the cause is not owing to mal-administration, but to that which occasions all our other debts—a larger plan of war than we have money to make good. When this is the case, and yet the plan cannot be contracted without submitting to France, I should hope the next consideration . . . will be to find some expedient for easing that most intolerable burthen— *the debt of the navy.*

Mr. Pelham, who sees and feels the weight of it, has had it much in his consideration, and, I believe, has thought of the only expedient which can have any considerable effect; which is, to get a part of it taken into the S[outh] S[ea] Company by way of increase to their capital, as has been practiced heretofore. But this is a secret I should not dare to tell to any man living but yourself. For as it cannot be put in execution till after the supplies of the year are raised, or beyond all doubt, so neither should it be suspected, or get the least wind, for fear of any bad effect it may have upon the raising of these supplies.[42]

Three days later George Grenville indicated that Pelham did not want to borrow the money to pay a part of the navy debt from the open market because he was afraid this would drive up the interest rates on the regular loans.[43] Thus the South Sea Company seemed the only source of funds for relieving the debt. The funding of this naval debt solved the problem at the time, but the Admiralty was always short of money until the end of the war.[44]

In the early years of the war another expense was charged to secret service. While Lord Stair was in command of the armies in Flanders, he was granted money for this purpose.[45] Though there are no records left of similar grants to the Duke of Cumberland, it is fairly certain that such grants were made. While the king was on the continent he also had funds at his disposal for the purpose of the secret service.[46] The total amount of money spent on the wartime secret service will remain a secret unless, or until, the papers of Henry Pelham are rediscovered, for the amounts were only occasionally recorded elsewhere than in his private papers.[47] The indications are, however, that substantial sums were spent in this fashion.

During the entire period of the continental war, England paid subsidies to various states for their participation in the war or for the hire of troops. One abstract prepared for Newcastle gave the total of £6,950,253–0s–3½d as being paid by England to seven states, and these did not include the payments made to the Dutch or the Scandinavian countries.[48] The policy of subsidies was the common method used under Granville, Newcastle, and Pitt—most extensively under Granville—as it was in all countries.

In July, 1743, Granville wrote privately to Newcastle:

> In addition to my public Letter of this date, I beg leave to acquaint Your Grace, that His Majesty thinks the Gaining of the Emperor, or even keeping Him in Suspence, of Such Importance, that though He will make no Stipulations without the combined Sense of His Servants, nor engage absolutely to pay 300m. Crowns; Yet His Majesty thinks it proper, that the Affair should not, in this great Crisis, fall at once to pieces; And therefore thinks it proper to hazard 100m. Crowns under which a warrant is signed according to the Form which Mr. Pelham and I agreed upon. If the Emperor accepts it, as I believe He will, we may insensibly carry Him into all our Measures; and then as more Money will be stipulated for publickly Account; And if He does not accept it, it shall be cancell'd, & never heard of.[49]

If the methods that this letter indicates were common practice, there is no way of knowing the amounts paid in subsidies, for some of those payments would be recorded in the secret service records. However, it seems a reasonable assumption that such payments were the exception and therefore that most subsidies were acted on in the usual fashion by parliament. If secret service funds were commonly used, the entire quarrel over the payment of the Hanoverian troops could have been avoided, and it surely would have been.

In 1743 Granville wished to deal with Hungary through a negotiated convention that covered many subjects, but Hardwicke, Harrington, Dorset, Grafton, Richmond, Montagu, Newcastle, and Pelham refused to agree, and they urged a £300,000 subsidy instead. They won the argument, and the subsidy was given, but the entire debate illustrated the fact that all factions of the government believed in the usefulness of subsidies.[50] In 1744 the policy of granting small subsidies to various nations for special purposes was added to the large general subsidies.[51] In 1745 the debates on subsidies passed with little opposition, principally because Granville's men were too weak in the Commons and because Chesterfield and Pelham prepared carefully in advance.[52] It was also the year in which Pelham began to complain of the expense of subsidies, as the following letter indicates:

> where will this end? we are to pay Princes for the liberty of defending their own countries, we are to complement others for taking our money for their troops, to be employed for purposes which they profess themselves friends to, and above all, we are to dismantle our own country and render its defence precarious, because our allies cannot, or will not put their fortresses in a condition to be defended in a regular way.[53]

At this point Pelham began to be discouraged, and it was the cost of subsidies that made him most eager to end the war. The events of the earlier years were largely repeated in 1746. Money was granted to pay part of the Dutch cost of artillery in Flanders, and subsidies passed with little difficulty.[54] This year Pelham was more explicit on subsidies, for he told Sir Thomas Robinson that though he had got the subsidy there was very little left in the Treasury and extra demands by foreign governments had little chance of passage.[55] Moreover, he doubted that money would buy success. By 1748 Pelham refused to approve loans to the Dutch, and Newcastle was forced to cut his foreign plans for subsidies to Genoa, Cologne, and Hungary.[56] The only subsidy Pelham paid with any show of willingness was that of £50,000 to Russia, which had been contracted two years before.[57]

A final blow to Pelham's economy drive came when Austria demanded the final £100,000 of the subsidy after the war was over. Pelham strongly opposed payment and flatly refused, even though the Austrians were angered by his act.[58] He even directly opposed the king's wishes on the issue, and George accepted the opposition as final.[59] The exchange of letters over this issue made it perfectly clear that Pelham alone controlled the money and that by the end of the war his control of the purse determined the steps to be taken in foreign policy.

There were various other expenses involved in the war. Envoys sent to negotiate issues of the war had to be paid.[60] These were not usually heavy costs but were usually late in payment because of shortness of money or the involved method of getting grants through the proper channels.[61] Small amounts were also necessary to maintain forts and settlements in Africa against the enemy.[62] The peace negotiations also required money, and Pelham was insistent that Sandwich and Robinson, the envoys, receive the money necessary to maintain the prestige of England, even though the sum available was exceedingly low.[63] Pelham did send ample money to the ambassadors, though some of what they spent from their own pockets was not repaid until they returned to England. Thus in small things as well as large Pelham provided the necessary money to fight the war despite the fact that he increasingly opposed it as unsuccessful and therefore a waste. The war was not lost for lack of money.

Pelham's last move in wartime finance was to plan a financial policy which would reduce the expense of the government and gradually retire the national debt.[64] It is not surprising that a Treasury official should plan such a move, but it is surprising that Pelham was able to do a large part of what he planned within a very few years. It is further proof of his very strong position within the cabinet and the Court that everyone, even the Duke of Cumberland, agreed with his plans. There was no opposition to the plan, which in part accounted for the success. Thus Pelham appears clearly to have been an excellent financier, for even the admittedly very able Sir Robert Walpole was unsuccessful in such an attempt. The fact that it could be accomplished at the end of the five war years during which Pelham had been in control showed the basically strong financial nature of the English economy.

CHAPTER X

Foreign Policy, 1743–1748

THE WAR

℘ IN 1743, when Pelham actually took over direction of a large part of the government, the war dominated almost the entire field of foreign relations. The victory at Dettingen at the beginning of the season made it seem that a prosperous campaign was ahead, but the victory was never followed up, and the entire campaign dwindled to nothing. Granville, who reported the result of the battle of Dettingen in a bald statement to Newcastle, was interested in the diplomatic aspects of the war and paid little attention to the military except to block the moves of Stair, the nominal commander.[1] These moves led to Stair's resignation, even though Granville had not worked to replace him.[2] By July, Granville was deep in negotiations with Hungary at Hanau.[3] His conduct of these negotiations irritated the ministers in London, and they objected to the terms.[4] Granville paid scant heed to the objections and signed the Treaty of Worms early in September.[5] This, then, was the condition of the British military and diplomatic effort in the year 1743, which had begun with prospects of success.

January 1744 opened with a particularly violent political debate over the employment of Hanoverian troops for the coming campaign.[6] The government won the vote finally, but politics-as-usual was the keynote of the parliamentary approach to the war. By the end of the month, however, the war took on a more dangerous aspect: the English won a naval engagement from the French, which showed that the enemy was operating in waters the English controlled.[7] A few days later the French fleet was observed off the English coast, and a panic fear of invasion swept London and the southern shires.[8] Admiral Norris was sent to the Downs to get the English fleet ready to meet the French and prevent a landing.[9] His orders indicate that the government did not know whether to expect a true invastion or a sweep to the Mediterranean.[10] All kinds of rumors about French intentions arrived from the continent, but all were unconfirmed, and they only added to the confusion.[11] The Earl of Stair was appointed commander of all forces in South Britain to meet the eventuality of a landing.[12] The great fear of the government was caused by the few English troops (7,000 at most) available for defense and the dreaded bogey of Jacobitism, and those troops were ordered to the defense of

London, leaving other areas open.[13] At the end of February, Pelham and Newcastle laid all papers on the invasion before parliament and received almost unanimous support.[14] And finally, at the same time came the report, always dreaded by the Whigs, that the Pretender's elder son, Charles Edward, was with the French fleet.[15] The entire affair ended with only one concrete result: France declared war on England, and the English replied with a like move.[16] England seized all French property in English ports and all Frenchmen on their boats, and declared an embargo on all French ships. These acts made little practical difference to the war, since both countries had been fighting as auxiliaries of the German powers. The fear of French invasion continued throughout the year, and the whole episode was a prelude to things to come.

The legal extension of the war between France and Britain necessitated a tighter organization of the war effort. The Treasury led a move to revoke parts of the Navigation Acts and thereby made importation of necessary supplies easier.[17] Whether the increased vigor of the war was related to Pelham's greater activity, it is impossible now to know, but it was at this time that he took a much more active part in the direction of the war. This was particularly true in Anglo-Dutch relations, for Robert Trevor, envoy at the Hague, and Pelham kept up a secret correspondence on Dutch affairs.[18] The general conclusion Pelham drew from Trevor's reports was that the Dutch neither would nor could support their share of the war.[19] As a result Pelham was constantly opposed to any reliance on Dutch help in fighting the war, and in the last years of the war this fact accounted for his differences of opinion with Newcastle on continuing the war in the hope that the new stadtholder would support Britain and Austria. Marshal Wade bombarded Pelham with requests, memorials, and troublesome letters that sought ever-increasing favors and amounts of money for the army.[20] Then, too, the Secretaries of State included Pelham in the secret negotiations with Austria.[21] Thus it is clear that Pelham was involved in the conduct of relations with the Dutch, the Austrians, and the army. He expressed his position and that of his followers when, after Granville's removal from office, he wrote:

> This only I can assure you; it will make no difference, as to the support of the true interest of the court where you are. We may not promise so much; but we will perform what we do promise.[22]

The year 1744 may be taken as the year in which Pelham tightened his hold on foreign affairs as well as all other matters; the dismissal of Granville was the climax.

An interesting side light in the realm of foreign affairs was the role of Lord Hardwicke. He acted as the mouthpiece of the Pelham faction whenever the brothers were away from London.[23] He often served them by taking Goerge's criticism when decisions went against the monarch's wishes.[24] There is also a letter which indicates that Hardwicke was the channel through which Bolingbroke communicated his secret information and advice to the cabinet.[25] It may be said, therefore, that responsibility for the various war policies spread from one man, Granville, to four men—Newcastle, Harrington, Pelham, and Hardwicke—during 1744. No new policies were advanced, but the basis of a war policy in line with domestic decisions was laid. Pelham never shifted from this basis and in fact steadily increased the interrelationships.

The year 1745 opened with the usual fight in the Commons over the size of the army. Pelham led the debate, supported by Pitt and Watkin Williams for the first time, and won approval for 28,000 men in Flanders by arguing that since the country was at war, the war must be won.[26] This was certainly a pessimistic approach, but it did face the facts. The campaign of the summer fully reflected Pelham's pessimism, for the allied armies steadily lost ground in the Low Countries. From May until October the Duke of Cumberland had nothing but defeats to report. The worst news was the surrender of Ostend, which laid most of Flanders open to the French.[27] Cumberland's constant wail in all his letters was that the Dutch had no will to fight and were not bearing their agreed share of the burden of the war. By the end of the year Chesterfield told Newcastle that Britain had lost the war and that the cabinet should face that fact and make the best peace possible.[28] The earl was right, but it took three years for all parties to accept this assessment.

Pelham, as Prime Minister, retained a share of control over the army, and early in 1745 he soothed relations between the king and Stair so that the latter could assume the command of the army in England. He also presented Field Marshal Wade to the king as the cabinet's choice of a commander in Flanders and thus made George's approval necessary if the king wished to keep his ministry. He intervened in a quarrel between Cumberland and the Prince of Waldeck, the Dutch commander, by using Edward Weston as a mediator to insist on settlement of the dispute.[29]

In July the French captured Ghent, and in August Ostend fell to the invaders. In the time between these two losses the English naval defense was overhauled. The cabinet wanted Admiral Vernon appointed to command the defensive fleet, but Admiral Norris objected. It was not until the beginning of August that George approved of Vernon.[30] The final siege of Ostend filled the English government with disgust at the Austrians and led to a move to withdraw all British troops, which was bitterly opposed by Cumberland. The troops were not withdrawn immediately, but extensive naval preparations were made to evacuate them when necessary.[31] Matters were complicated by Charles Edward's invasion of Scotland, which upset all calculations of the government. Serious reports of a prospective French invasion of England came throughout July and August as support for the Jacobites, and it was the fear of invasion that caused a near panic among the British leaders.[32] Many of the moves of the cabinet in the face of the rebellion can be explained only by the possibility of a strong invasion of southern England. The one bright spot in the otherwise gloomy picture of the summer military campaign was the capture of Louisburg by Commodore Warren, Governor Shirley, General Pepperel, and the New England colonists.[33] One other modified success was the effectiveness with which the British fleet patrolled the seas, forestalling any major naval clash, though the French-Spanish navies were able to move at various times.[34] By late 1745 the British were in retreat—but an organized retreat that allowed counterattacks at various times.

While the military campaign was being planned and executed, the cabinet was active in the diplomatic field. Chesterfield was sent to the Hague to negotiate for greater Dutch help. While he was there he corresponded with Newcastle and Pelham privately and sent only official records to Harrington, his senior officer. That Pelham was sent separate reports, now lost, is clear from Newcastle's letters, and the existence of such reports indicated that Pelham was taking a definite place in the diplomatic policy of England.[35] When Chesterfield returned home, a meeting was held by Newcastle, Pelham, Hardwicke, and Chesterfield to discuss foreign affairs and advise Harrington and the king, who were in Europe. Again Pelham took a hand in the formulation of foreign policy. These affairs were certainly not left to Newcastle alone; Pelham's active participation was continued through the year, at least as far as the Dutch were concerned. He kept up his correspondence with Trevor, which gave him private information on the Dutch.[36] Though there are no other examples of such continued correspondence with other envoys, there are scattered letters to Sir Thomas Robinson at Vienna and Sir Benjamin Keene at Lisbon, and it is reasonable to guess that Pelham had secret reports from at least these two friends. The most reasonable assumption is that Pelham made definite efforts to be informed on foreign affairs in order to take his part in making foreign policy.

There is one interesting side light in the diplomatic history of 1745 that has been noted by some historians but has not been given sufficient emphasis: the desire for an alliance with Prussia.[37] Disgust with Austria was growing, and all cabinet members agreed that the Austro-Saxon alliance could not defeat Prussia. Therefore in that year the English cabinet tried to negotiate a peace between Austria and Prussia. Horatio Walpole promoted such an accord as being sensible, and Newcastle told Hardwicke that Pelham approved, though he was dubious of success.[38] The one great obstacle to such an alliance was the king, who hated his nephew, Frederick II. When the Treaty of Hanover was signed on August 15, the king was angry with the Pelhams.[39] The positive result of the treaty was the election of Francis I as emperor, but the Austrians refused to ratify it, and the war went on. By the end of the year Earl Fitzwilliam probably expressed the feeling of the English leaders when he wrote:

> This Morning an Express arrived with the News that the King of Prussia has drove that damn'd Beech the Empress before him, which I am most heartily glad of, for her curs'd Obstinacy, in not accepting reasonable Terms, when they were offer'd her.[40]

Thus in 1745 the ground was laid for the diplomatic revolution of a few years later. Many Englishmen were ready to abandon Austria, and there are very strong indications that Pelham was the leader of the group that desired the change. There was no real revolution, for the shift of alliance was actively desired by some people for at least ten years before it occurred.

Incidental letters make it plain that the cabinet was prepared to make a general peace with France if acceptable terms could have been reached. Pelham and Chesterfield seemed to have been the most active in the plans, and Trevor at the Hague was to be the agent of negotiation.[41] The early plans came to nothing because neither side was completely defeated, but the move for peace had started. French schemes at Rome with the Jacobites, the rebellion in England, and the political schemes of Granville kept the cabinet from pushing the peace plan too far, for George II was opposed to it.[42] The French had the greater military success and did not want to give it up for nothing; therefore the peace negotiations collapsed. Nevertheless by the end of 1745 peace was in the air, and Henry Pelham was becoming more and more eager to achieve it.

The year 1746 opened with a series of problems dealing with the supply of troops in Flanders, the treatment of prisoners of war, and the preparations for defending the coasts by means of forts.[43] In the first two it is plain that Pelham was an essential man in executing the action, but apparently he had nothing to do with the last problem. At the very least it can be said that Pelham had a large part in the execution of the war except for the actual fighting of the battles.

The military position in Flanders had been gloomy in late 1745, but by February 1746 it had become desperate. Brussels fell to the French, and the position of the Dutch was almost impossible. Throughout the winter and spring, reports were current that they were to make peace with the French in some manner.[44] Pelham was sure that nothing could be done: "We must pray for better times, though we cannot expect those prayers will be heard; for in truth we do not deserve them." The leaders of the cabinet had agreed to hire Hanoverian troops to bolster the British army in April, but even these mercenaries did not help the military position.[45] During the summer little was accomplished, as indicated by Peregrine Furze, Secretary to the Paymaster, who wrote:

> Mr. Pelham directs me to Acquaint you, that the Armys in Flanders are so near, that there may be an Action; if both are equally inclin'd to it: But in his private Opinion the French will rather avoid it, as they have a probability of doing their Business without it.[46]

The French had every advantage. In October they captured Namur after a token resistance by the Dutch, and the allies fell back toward Maestricht. On the eleventh the French won a victory at Roucoux, and the allies were forced back on Maestricht. However, the French losses were severe, and they were unable to follow up the battle.[47] By the end of the year all the Austrian Netherlands was in French hands.

The military situation in Saxony was little better, for the Austrians were losing ground there to Frederick the Great. The English government concluded from the reports that no relief could come from that front. The only good news seemed to come from Italy, where the Austrians and Sardinians were preparing to attack southern France. They were sure of success, if the British navy would protect the Mediterranean Sea lanes.[48] But their hopes were to be unfulfilled, for though Admiral Byng sailed to the Mediterranean, the attack on southern France failed to materialize. Thus on all military fronts the allies were defeated, and 1746 remained the most disastrous year of the war.

Diplomatically the year was somewhat more successful, after the early chaos caused by the resignation of the Pelhams. Only Robinson, of all the envoys, seemed informed of the reasons for the resignations and the results, and his letters reveal confusion sufficient to have upset the normal conduct of affairs.[49] At both the beginning and the end of the year the cabinet tried unsuccessfully to detach Denmark from its French subsidy alliance. Harrington and Chesterfield were unable to bring Denmark to desert France, but they were able to prevent active Danish participation on the French side.[50] During the summer Philip V of Spain died, and the English cabinet tried to exploit this event as far as possible. Led by Pelham, they hoped that affairs in Italy could be settled, for Elizabeth Farnese's sons could all be provided with suitable lands from the Spanish possessions there. They also hoped that Spain could be detached from the French alliance, since Ferdinand VI was not so pro-French as his father.[51] Spain did not desert her alliance, but her contribution to the war decreased, and harmony between France and Spain was weakened.

The greatest English success came at the end of the year, when Russia finally agreed to send 10,000 troops to aid the Austrians in return for an English subsidy.[52] In the long run the negotiations were of little use, for the war was almost over before the Russians could arrive at the front. The move did, however, check Sweden from joining France and may have helped persuade the French to make peace. The diplomacy was not a brilliant success, but the balance was slightly in the allied favor. Here was some compensation for the military failure. Pelham's part in the actual direction was small, but he had been quick to see the advantages to be gained by the Spanish changes, and he urged the others to use them. He had also found the resources to pay a new subsidy to Russia and approved its use.

On the whole Pelham was definitely against the war in 1746 and said he wanted to make peace. He believed only disaster lay ahead if the war continued, but he approved continuation of the fighting by all means while diplomatic pressure was being exerted for peace. Horatio Walpole, who completely agreed with him, even hinted that Newcastle approved the war because of jealousy of his brother who, he knew, wanted peace.[53] It is worthy of note that Pelham's predictions came true and nothing was gained by continuing the war two years longer. Pelham had become a good, though pessimistic, judge of how far to push an issue in foreign affairs, as he had long been in domestic affairs.

Early in January 1747 the English government worked further along the path of diplomatic negotiation to persuade the allies of France to desert the French. Chesterfield, with the backing of Pelham, Hardwicke, and Newcastle, prepared a draft of instructions for negotiations with Prussia.[54] The four men had great hopes that George II would give up his hatred of his Prussian nephew, Frederick the Great, and approve the measure, for they felt that only in this way could France be defeated. It was another demonstration of the fact that the diplomatic revolution of 1756 was no revolution but the final step in a policy that had been growing for many years. At the same time Newcastle moved to send Benjamin Keene to Madrid in order to take advantage of any "favourable occasion that may offer." [55] The English leaders were all working toward peace or a reduction of the war.

The actual military campaign for the year was bogged down in uncertainty. During the winter, plans were actively discussed for action in North America. Admiral Warren went so far in his planning as to recommend a program of land, free of quitrents, to encourage settlement of Nova Scotia and make its defense easier. But, as in the case of European plans, confusion of purpose and disagreement among officials brought these plans to nothing. Pelham took a direct part in them, but he was not able to coordinate them.[56]

The army on the continent was in a bad position from the start of the military season. It had been driven back to the borders of the Dutch lands the previous year, and the Dutch armies were weak. The only bright spot was the sudden revolution at the Hague, which made the Prince of Orange stadtholder of all seven Dutch states and thus installed a pro-British government in firm control. Even this, however, was not an unmixed blessing, for the new stadtholder was determined to continue the war to enhance his position among the Dutch.[57] This military ardor of the new Dutch government made the task of achieving a peace more difficult, for there was no accompanying increase in Dutch military effort. The land front in Flanders was impossible to maintain, and the siege of Bergen-op-Zoom carried the fate of the whole campaign. The British government, to keep its Dutch alliance, was forced to increase its armies in Flanders by means of the hated Hanoverian troops and by sending two regiments from Scotland.[58]

The people of England were almost desperate on the subject of peace. One bishop wrote, "For God's sake when shall we have done fighting for a desperate game, with Flanders gone, Zealand going, and the King of Sardinia retired to defend his frontier? and yet we are amusing ourselves with, I know not what, Imaginary advantages." [59] Even the Duke of Cumberland, the most outspoken partisan of the war, said:

> I am sorry to say, that I am convinced every Day, of the melancholy Consideration, that we must actually reckon upon the Dutch Troops as Nothing; & unfortunately the greatest part of those Corps, that are employ'd in the Defence of Dutch Brabant, are Dutch. Things being in that Condition it wou'd be very rash in me to answer for any Thing which must, in some Measure, depend upon them. [60]

The peacemakers had to take a definite stand and end such an intolerable situation.

In January 1747, Britain had acceded to the treaty between Austria and Russia and then became involved in a subsidy treaty with Russia. The negotiation of this treaty rested in the hands of Chesterfield, Newcastle, Pelham, and Hardwicke. In April, Pelham gave up his vacation to return to London to discuss the treaty and foreign affairs in general. In this and all later discussions Pelham demanded peace as soon as possible. Newcastle, Cumberland, Chesterfield, Bedford, and Horatio Walpole knew Pelham's position, and all believed his stand made peace necessary and more likely. [61] At the beginning of the war, Newcastle, Cumberland, and Bedford would have paid little attention to the demands of Pelham in foreign affairs, and the care now taken to meet his objections showed better than anything else the increase of Pelham's power. Certainly three years earlier Pelham would not have connived against his brother in the conduct of foreign policy as he did, at least tacitly, with Chesterfield. This occurred when the latter used Dayrolles in the Hague as a spy on Lord Sandwich and on the Prince of Orange to prevent any secret negotiations with Newcastle and George II to continue the war. [62] Moreover, Chesterfield and Pelham drew up a peace treaty to serve as a basis of negotiation, and then presented it for the approval of Newcastle and Hardwicke. [63] Earlier Newcastle would have strenuously objected to any such move. During the autumn Pelham sat in on the secret conferences with Wall, the Spanish agent, and again showed his importance by the very fact of his presence, for Newcastle would formerly have conducted the sessions alone. [64] Nothing could be stronger proof that during the three years following the removal of Granville from the cabinet, Pelham had become not only its titular leader but its dominating force. He was never ready to insist on complete authority, as Walpole had done, but the fact that he took a greater share in foreign affairs showed he was gradually being accepted as the final voice in any decision, even by the Duke of Newcastle.

The last year of the war opened with Pelham's continuing demands for peace. When Chesterfield resigned office in February, he did so because Newcastle's peace policy was devious. This is clear in spite of the official excuse. The earl defended his resignation in a pamphlet, and in defending himself he said that Pelham "unwillingly submitted to, and often protested against," Newcastle's policies. Moreover, the new Secretary of State, the Duke of Bedford, hastened to assure Pelham that he was convinced of the impossibility of carrying on the war. By June, Pelham wrote to Newcastle denouncing delay in the treaty and ordering his brother to hurry the peace.[65] Until the final signing Pelham continued to maintain his stand.

Pelham's position was fully justified by the military events of the spring. Cumberland's army was weak at the beginning of the campaign, and not even the prospect of the loss of Maestricht brought Dutch help for the army.[66] Newcastle admitted on April 1 that the war could not go on,

> Your Royal Highness will easily imagine, how much the continuance of the bad accounts from abroad, affects us here; and if I may presume to mention myself, how mortifying it is to me, to hear, every day, the prophecies of those fulfilled, who, I thought, were prejudiced by their passions and views; and to see those measures, which were most sincerely and honestly advised, blamed and traduced, as wild, ignorant, and calculated for selfish ends. My lord Chesterfield has the happiness to be thought to have foreseen, and to have been willing to prevent, had it been in his power.[67]

In his personal way, Newcastle had exactly described the situation except that he should have added Pelham to Chesterfield. Cumberland and Newcastle were particularly fearful that Pelham would cut down on money for the campaign and thereby effectively put an end to any military moves.[68] The First Lord of the Treasury never went to that extreme, but it was his ultimate threat, and he must have hinted at it to enforce his demand for peace.

Military affairs were not alone in their misfortune during 1748; diplomatic negotiations for the campaign fared no better. The negotiations with Prussia started badly, for the cabinet could not decide whom to send to Berlin to replace Henry Legge. Newcastle was strongly opposed to Legge's continuing as envoy to the King of Prussia and blamed him for the failure. Pelham supported Legge but believed that the mission had failed and the envoy should return home.[69] In the end the negotiations failed completely, and Legge returned home leaving a resumption of the projected treaty until the Seven Years War loomed. Thus one of Pelham's best diplomatic plans failed. There is ample evidence that he was consulted on all the diplomatic steps of the year. Bedford, Hardwicke, Cumberland, and the other ministers acted in all ways with this point in mind. Pelham usually supported peace, and this often provoked a quarrel with Newcastle. The principal reason for the disagreements was that

George II and Newcastle were in Hanover pursuing one policy while the cabinet in London was pursuing another. Generally Pelham had to voice the cabinet's opinion because Bedford spent most of his time at Woburn Abbey. On the whole Bedford and Hardwicke agreed with Pelham's dispatches, and this gave his views a strength that Newcastle was forced to recognize.[70] Often Newcastle accepted Pelham's directions, and by the time peace was signed the duke laid out his future plans for his brother's approval. There could be no objection to Newcastle's plan, and Pelham agreed to it with the remark that public expense must be reduced.[71] Hence, Pelham ended the war on the economic note that was to be the guiding principle for most of the rest of his administration.

THE PEACE NEGOTIATIONS

The first serious steps to achieve a peace were taken in the spring of 1746. By May secret dispatches revealed that the French would make peace on what Andrew Stone considered moderate terms. Robert Trevor, at the Hague, was to be the English delegate in the secret negotiations, and from the beginning Chesterfield indicated to him that the French terms would have to be accepted.[72] The cabinet leaders could not, however, agree on counterproposals to be sent to him. Pelham, Harrington, and Chesterfield wanted to accept the French terms with only a qualification on the Dunkirk clauses. Newcastle and Hardwicke, who had the approval of the king, wanted to send different proposals and then negotiate.[73] Newcastle further complicated matters by telling Austria about the secret correspondence, over the objections of Pelham, Harrington, and Chesterfield. Pelham felt that Newcastle did this because Austria was strongly opposed to any negotiation and would make any conclusion of the war impossible. In the end Lord Sandwich was named British plenipotentiary to a secret conference at Breda. At first Pelham felt Sandwich was chosen because he opposed the return of Cape Breton and this would prevent peace.[74] Newcastle was pleased with Sandwich, for he thought that the earl would follow orders. Pelham was pessimistic of favorable results, for he found Sandwich too exacting in his demands. By the end of October Pelham was angry at Newcastle for the instructions sent to Sandwich.[75] The unfortunate part of the affair was that Harrington had the authority to send orders to Sandwich, and he had done so in line with the views of Pelham and Chesterfield. When Harrington finally learned of Newcastle's correspondence, he was angry and was kept from a public quarrel only by Pelham's efforts. Thus the fall plans dragged on without a conclusion, and the delay laid the basis for Lord Harrington's resignation.

The opening months of 1747 were more promising for peace than any previous time. The new queen of Spain was pro-British and wanted peace if some kind of establishment could be found to keep Don Philip in Italy, so that she could dominate the Spanish court. Maria Theresa was somewhat more inclined to peace because her finances were completely exhausted. And last, the allied troops won a small victory in the Netherlands and the Sardinians a more substantial one in Italy.[76] The hopes of the British government were considerably supported when Marshal Saxe, the French commander, started moves for peace through General Ligonier, who had been captured. Pelham observed that even though peace seemed likely, the cabinet must prepare for a continuation of the war. He believed parliament would support either war or peace if it was seen that everything possible had been done to achieve peace.[77] Cumberland opposed any peace and tried to convince Newcastle and Pelham that Marshal Saxe was insincere in his proposals. When Bergen-op-Zoom was taken by the French in September, even honest men like Admiral Anson believed that Saxe had merely tricked the British to hold the allied war efforts down. However, the cabinet, led by Pelham and Newcastle, continued to negotiate. The brothers, supported by Chesterfield, agreed to accept the French plan for a treaty, and George II was willing to lay it before the Council.[78] There were few advances in the diplomatic field for the rest of the year, and 1748 began with the war still active, though all parties were ready to quit.

There were numerous incidental reasons why it was difficult to negotiate the peace. First, Prussia had to be kept quiet so that France would not expect support from that source. Second, the directors of the South Sea Company demanded that the Asiento Treaty and the trade ships of the Treaty of Utrecht be retained in any new treaty on the same basis. This was particularly difficult because Newcastle could not force Spain, as the ally of France, to accept such a clause, nor could he directly oppose such a powerful group within England. Third, King George announced that he was going to Hanover during the summer in spite of the fact that almost every government official, including Cumberland, opposed the trip. Newcastle was particularly afraid of Pelham's reaction to the trip, and indeed the First Lord was angry and outspoken against Newcastle's journey with the king. It was quite clear even then that Pelham was afraid that when his brother and the king got to Hanover alone, they would negotiate secretly and perhaps ruin the chance of peace. And fourth, Pelham was very indefinite about whether he would make money available to fight on during the negotiations. Newcastle, Hardwicke, and Bedford all tried to get him to commit himself, but he refused. These were all matters that had to be remembered by the English envoy and made his task more difficult.[79]

On the positive side, the French government threw out new hints for negotiations on a somewhat more moderate basis than those of Marshal Saxe, and George II was anxious to accept them. Also the Duke of Cumberland was thoroughly disgusted with the conduct of the Dutch and Austrians, and he who had long been the strongest advocate of war was now ready for peace. With the entire government united for negotiation, the envoy was assured of support.[80]

One of the great stumbling blocks Lord Sandwich faced in the negotiation was the refusal of the French to accept inspection of the port of Dunkirk, though they agreed to destroy all fortifications.[81] The English were eventually forced to accept the French position because Maestricht was besieged without possibility of relief and if it capitulated, all Holland would lie open. On the basis of this final decision of the cabinet, Lord Sandwich was authorized to sign an agreement with the French without England's allies. Once the decision was reached, Pelham began to prepare for the political repercussions; he knew there would be serious criticism, which he wanted to meet.

> I should hope you would consider well the letter you write to Lord Sandwich; for tho' I am convinced the measure is right, and absolutely necessary; yet I see plainly, do what you will, enquirys will be made next year, and therefore, when these orders are given, I should take care to show what were the reasons which induc'd the King not to close the last year which in truth were the representations from every quarter of *your* correspondence, and which have all failed. . . . Peace is what I want both for the sake of the King my country and myself; Peace will be had, I heartily wish it may be no worse than what is represented in your paper; if so, I am sure it is to be defended.[82]

The final steps in signing the preliminaries were taken during April, and Cumberland kept Pelham informed of the negotiations.[83] In the last of these letters Cumberland expressed the opinion that Pelham had been right in demanding peace and, more important, that Pelham was the minister upon whom the burden of carrying the peace through would fall.

> I hope that what has been done there [Aix], agrees with your sentiments. I am convinced, those that undertook it, meant for the best; and you will, I dare say, from the same principles, that made you think those pacific measures necessary, endeavour to support those persons, who gave up their former opinion, on conviction, to your way of thinking. . . . as every one has their difficulties in this crisis, so I am persuaded your brother is not without his. He will have frequent occasion for your assistance and advice in his future conduct. . . . I know you well enough to be convinced, that you will most readily and sincerely give it him.

Thus, in peace, even opponents turned to Pelham to direct the government.

Pelham was delighted that the preliminaries of peace were signed, no matter how humiliating. The main points were these:

1. France was to give up all conquests in the Netherlands.
2. England was to return Cape Breton.
3. Austria was to cede Silesia and Glatz to Prussia.
4. Austria was to cede Parma and Placentia to Don Philip.
5. Sardinia was to receive part of the Milanese lands.[84]

Sandwich announced the signing of the agreement on May 1 (April 20), 1748, and five days later wrote a letter of justification to Newcastle.[85] Everyone in England was pleased with the result except Newcastle, who felt that Sandwich had gone beyond his instructions in agreeing to the terms without word from London. This quarrel was to be the source of much trouble during the summer while the definitive treaty was being drawn up—so much so that peace was seriously threatened.

By the end of May the prospect of peace seemed so close that Pelham took a fortnight holiday and Newcastle left London to join the king in Hanover. When Pelham returned, he urged Newcastle: "push your definitive treaty as fast as you can; leave all little objects to future negotiation." [86] In order to prevent any untoward incidents from disrupting negotiations, the cabinet ordered Byng to restrict his naval activities during the last six weeks of the three-month period of hostilities.[87] Pelham, Hardwicke, and Bedford also were prompt to meet and answer any requests from Newcastle concerning the peace. They released all French prisoners during the summer so that no issue could arise from that source to endanger the peace. And Pelham strongly approved of Sir Thomas Robinson's taking part in the negotiations with Lord Sandwich in spite of the added cost, because he felt Robinson's experience would help speed peace.[88] Thus the ministers in London, under Pelham's leadership, did all they could to promote the peace.

The most difficult problem of the entire negotiation was to gain Austrian approval of the treaty. Austria, as the only real loser in the war, was not reconciled to her losses, especially Silesia, and resented the secrecy with which the British had started the negotiation. Therefore Count Kaunitz, the Austrian envoy, refused to agree to the treaty in any stage of the negotiation. This in turn split the British cabinet, for Newcastle and George II were insistent that Austria must agree before the English would sign. Pelham, Hardwicke, Bedford, Gower, and Dorset just as strongly supported Sandwich's position that England should go ahead and sign, for then Austria would be forced to agree.[89] The quarrel continued throughout the summer and autumn, and had an important effect on future political events, for Newcastle never forgave Sandwich for not following his orders explicitly. It also produced another of the periodic quarrels between the brothers; Newcastle's feelings were hurt, and he blamed Pelham. The final peace, however, solved this disagreement.[90] In the end, Sandwich and the Dutch signed the treaty with France on October 7/18, 1748. As Pelham had believed, Austria and Spain agreed to the terms a few days later, and Sardinia finally acceded.[91] Britain escaped any real losses. Louisburg was restored to France; the Asiento Treaty was revived for four more years; the Protestant Succession was guaranteed by France; the Netherlands were saved from France; and, most humiliating, two English hostages were demanded by the French.[92] It was the best peace possible in the circumstances.

From the end of September, when the peace was clearly near, the leading cabinet members agreed to all proposals and urged that Newcastle push the peace as fast as possible. The only clause over which they haggled was the secret one which promised that the English would send two hostages for the carrying out of the terms, and they eventually accepted this after a change of wording. Even Lord Cobham, who had been critical of the entire affair, approved the conclusion. Pelham was, of course, immensely pleased that the war was over and was eager to get on to the peacetime problems that had been so long delayed. He quickly set to work to dispose of the touchy question of the hostages, regulate peace in India, and establish the numerous commissions to settle particular points left by the general terms of peace.[93]

During the autumn there were many references to Pelham's great financial problems. While pleased with the peace, he noted that if it had been made in the spring, the debt would have been a million pounds less. Previously he had said that he could not promise success in raising money for another year and that therefore peace had to be made. He had had reason to worry, for even the House of Lords was against continuation of the war, and without its support a supply bill had little chance of passage in the Commons. He also claimed that his source of revenue from the London bankers was declining and little money could come from that source as long as the war lasted. Stocks in general declined until word of peace, then went up. Pelham was not only pestered for £100,000 by the Austrians, but petty princes like the Duke of Wolfenbuttel demanded their subsidies even after the fighting was over. When Hardwicke said, "You know his [Pelham's] burthen is the expense, and his great aim is to lighten that, as far as can possibly be done consistent with security," the Lord Chancellor hit at the heart of the problem as far as Pelham was concerned. He was more interested in the financial reconstruction than in the war. Thus when Newcastle appeared satisfied with the peace, Pelham turned immediately to retrenchment. Finally even Newcastle was swept unwillingly into the economy group by the efforts of his brother. Pelham had his way, the peace was signed, and Pelham called for reduction of expenses and a reassessment of taxes.[94]

After the peace, one great problem connected with the war remained to be settled: how to dispose of the army. As early as the beginning of September it had been agreed that the reduction of the size and cost of the army was to be decided by Pelham and Cumberland.[95] They were to have complete control of the policy to be followed, and no other minister was to be consulted except for advice. Pelham was clearly aware of the unsettled state of international affairs, and, though he wanted to save all the money possible, he wrote:

I hear so bad an opinion of the strength and ability of those Powers abroad, who call themselves our friends; and I know the sentiments of those who must direct our forreign affairs too well, to think we shall long keep well with France; and therefore we must have an army, within call att least, to protect us from any suddain attempt of our Enemys, let us have it upon as cheap a foot as we can; for the necessary expenses must be very great.[96]

This remained Pelham's position during the conferences with Cumberland, and it was not unreasonable. Cumberland, however, wanted to retain as many men as possible in the army because it would enhance his personal importance. It took the two men one month to agree on the size of the army, and Pelham, to gain Cumberland's approval, had to make special arrangements to station a large number of troops in Ireland and charge them to the Irish establishment.[97] The final decision was to keep 18,000 men in England and Scotland, and to send 12,000 to Ireland.

The problem seemed settled, but by the end of October it appeared again. The question was when were the armies to be sent home from Flanders and the reductions started. Pelham insisted that the troops should leave Flanders immediately after the signatures were put on the treaty. Basically Hardwicke and the rest of the ministers in London agreed with him, and they protested against any delay.[98] Pelham also remembered to suggest tactfully that George II send his Hanoverian troops home and notify the other hired troops that their payments would cease. Newcastle took a middle position between Pelham, who wanted quick reduction, and Cumberland, who wanted delay. Newcastle was quite realistic, and he finally told Cumberland that the king approved Pelham's plan, so there was nothing to do but comply. Pelham won the dispute, but he added a final blow by sending the transports to return the troops as soon as the peace was signed and by ordering the Secretary at War to prepare the reduction orders.[99] He took no chance that Newcastle and Cumberland would persuade the king to retain the men in Flanders, and by so doing he won a complete decision over the Duke of Cumberland. With this proof that he was the power of the administration, Pelham ended the war.

CHAPTER XI

Domestic Affairs, 1743–1748

PATRONAGE

✣ IN DOMESTIC POLICY Pelham had little direct part during 1743 except in the House of Commons. The day-by-day matters of government were conducted by Granville and Newcastle with the Lords Justices' approval when the king was out of England. The war was the main concern of the cabinet, and other affairs were subordinated to it. However, the ministers were sufficiently interested in maintaining the smooth flow of government so that they and the king attended quickly to petitions and legal cases.[1] The king retained a firm hold on ecclesiastical matters even while out of England, and he directed Newcastle on promotions among the bishops when the bishopric of Worcester became vacant.[2] Other affairs followed their normal course, with the lesser officials directing them. The one crisis came with the uncertainty following Wilmington's death. This was the single event in which Pelham played an active role.[3]

The political crisis of 1744 absorbed most of the energies of the politicians throughout the year, and Pelham was in the thick of this fight. During the year, therefore, little activity came from the domestic front except the usual maintenance of law and order. Libel, rioting, robbery, and cursing the king were violations that called frequently for legal action by the cabinet, and Pelham was involved in most of the decisions.[4] The great activity other than the war and politics was patronage. The Pelhams were tightening their power, and patronage was the one sure way of establishing their control. The most important grant was one engineered by Pelham—£4,000 for Walpole.[5] The king had promised it in 1742, but Granville had prevented it for two years. Pelham finally paid his debt to his mentor, and in spite of young Horace Walpole's bitter remarks, he paid it as soon as was practicable.

The usual patronage requests were for ecclesiastical, political, military, and naval posts. Pelham's support was sought by all levels of society, but the requests from the nobility received his most prompt attention.[6] However, he responded as well as he could to all of them.

The first half of 1745 was politically calm after the storm of 1744, but the outbreak of the rebellion in midsummer completely changed matters and overshadowed all other business. A later chapter will discuss the

130

Stuart revolt, so it is only necessary to note it here. All contemporaries
conceded that Pelham's leadership accounted for the calm; in fact, his
calmness was becoming his best known and most appreciated attribute.[7]
Again, patronage and personal favors were the greatest problems in the
regular conduct of the government, and this year Pelham was constantly
asked to arrange these matters.

The requests for positions and favors increased in 1746, even though
the Pelhams had been settled in power for two years and their allies had
been rewarded. Patronage was a snowball that grew bigger and bigger.
The political system of the eighteenth century made the answering of
such demands almost essential. With the political parties broken up and
many splinter groups maneuvering for position, the Prime Minister was
forced to seek his parliamentary support through personal favors of one
form or another. The personal appeals to Pelham continued to come
from all classes of people, from great lords like Chesterfield and Argyll to
the simple residents of Hastings; from relatives and close friends to
ambitious citizens; from military men and ecclesiastics to men seeking
the minor Treasury offices at his disposal. The stream was unending, and
the labor of working out the applications was the most wearing of any
of the major offices. In October Pelham expressed his weariness to Andrew Stone:

> I am just going to the Play, and as I suppose you have nothing particular to
> say to me excepting what concerns Mr. Sergison [a Sussex politician], I con-
> clude you don't think it so material, as to put off any little entertainment I
> have proposed to myself. I will certainly attend His Grace to morrow at the
> hour appointed.[8]

Newcastle was the only eighteenth-century politician who never tired of
the patronage problem and never tried to get away from it.

The election of 1747 colored all patronage and domestic problems
during that year. The old parliament had been firmly under the control
of the Pelhams and their friends, and the new election was called a year
early to catch the opposition off guard. In this move the government was
quite successful, for it gained an even greater majority. The Duke of
Richmond demonstrated the essential election method when he wrote,
"I can't finish my letter without a bitt of Sussex polliticks, viz: that I
have (by operation) gott the Corporation of Arundell fill'd up with four
of my friends, by which I shall have it sure for the future." [9]

The type of requests for jobs was different than in earlier years. Almost
all the favors were requested by middle-class men—in other words, men
who had a vote for the House of Commons. This, contrary to all statements of cash dealings, was the real way in which an eighteenth-century
government controlled its electorate. The bulk of requests to Pelham
were for jobs under the Treasury in either customs and port offices or tax
collections. Over these posts Pelham had complete control.[10] However,

the demands were so frequent and so great that he was forced to reject many. Even such prominent people as the Lord President of the Sessions and Lord Berkeley were denied requests. Newcastle was likewise beset by requests, and often the brothers were petitioned together. Whenever money was involved, Pelham had to approve the request, and this meant that no matter which other minister received the petition, Pelham had to agree. For example, when George Stone, Archbishop of Armagh, requested an office for an Irish friend, and Lord Sandwich and Admiral Anson asked help for an office in Huntingdonshire, their own area, Pelham had to approve.[11] In May and June considerable time was devoted to the single problem of the election of the Scottish peers. The government arranged the list of sixteen names, which were duly elected.[12] This always involved particular care, especially if the old sixteen were not to be reelected. The important thing was to satisfy the Scots. For instance, Lord Marchmont caused considerable trouble through his brother, Hume Campbell, who carried some weight in the House of Commons.[13] This type of problem caused the cabinet leaders hours of work, for all family connections and friends of a man had to be satisfied before the prospective election could take place.

During the year the war ended, a distinctly new note crept into the petitions: Pelham was addressed in almost all the important requests, even those that would previously have been in Newcastle's sphere. It was quite natural that the patronage distribution of the Treasury should go through his hands, and the one example of the vacant Clerkship of the Pells shows how time consuming the work of his own department was.[14] This clerkship was one of the more valuable posts of the Treasury, and Pelham was beset by many requests for it. He almost gave up trying to settle this particular appointment, as the following letter to Newcastle indicates:

> I am plagued out of my life for this place. . . . I wish therefore, if the king does not approve of Arundel [Pelham's choice], that you would send me word, H[is] M[ajesty] will not give it for life, which will still most of these Gentlemen, and get me rid of much trouble.[15]

In spite of the fact that Pelham had always disclaimed influence in ecclesiastical patronage and referred such matters to Newcastle, in 1748 at least eight such appeals were sent directly to him. In these cases he made the decisions, sometimes without consulting Newcastle.[16] Some of these were as important as the bishoprics of London, Bristol, and Landaff. Occasionally legal patronage was distributed by Pelham, as when the Grenvilles and Chief Justice Willes quarreled over a Buckinghamshire assize place.[17] Pitt, Chesterfield, Lyttelton, Marchmont, and other important personages directed personal requests to Pelham, for they plainly regarded him as the key dispenser of patronage.[18] And finally he received a large number of requests from ordinary citizens and merchants. All these patronage requests are added proof that with the end of the war Pelham was recognized as the most important member of the government—in fact the Prime Minister.

COLONIAL AFFAIRS

The period of the eighteenth century before the ministry of William Pitt the elder is usually considered to have been marked by indifference to colonial matters. It was certainly true that Robert Walpole had little interest in affairs of the colonies, but during his administration such legislation as the Molasses Act was put on the statute books. Lord Granville had little interest in anything other than European diplomacy. And Henry Pelham had almost no experience in colonial matters when he came to office. The Duke of Newcastle was the minister charged with responsibility for colonial affairs from 1724 until 1748, but his temperament and the pressure of more immediate problems kept him from giving the necessary time to the colonies. However, the neglect was not so extensive under the Pelhams as has sometimes been indicated.

Probably the administrative system devised for colonial control was the basic cause for neglect throughout the first six decades of the eighteenth century. Since the colonies were governed through the Board of Trade, that Board and especially its president were extremely important officials to the colonies. However, the President of the Board of Trade was a very unimportant minister in England. He could execute no orders himself. He could only carry colonial requests to the Secretary of State for the Southern Department for action. Thus no matter how interested in colonial affairs he might be, he could do little if the Secretary, who often knew nothing of the subject, was not persuaded by his facts and pleas. During the years 1742–48, the office of President of the Board of Trade was held by a most incompetent man, Lord Monson, whose sole claim to office was that he was a distant relative of the Pelhams. This accounted in large part for the inefficiency of colonial direction. Monson's death in 1748 began a series of events that reawakened the English government to North America and eventually led to the American Revolution.

During the war the Privy Council was the official body that ruled on actual colonial policy. However, the most direct work was done by the Committee of Plantation Appeals and the Committee of Plantation Affairs. The personnel of these two committees was never set, except that the President of the Board of Trade was almost always present, and often either the Lord President of the Council or a Secretary of State. When the committee sat to hear legal appeals, one of the law officers was usually present. Beyond this, the membership was small and irregular, the most common number being three. The complaint has generally been made that appeals by colonials were handled very slowly. Certainly the English government never rushed answers to the colonies, but the Committee of Plantation Appeals generally decided quickly once a matter was brought to its attention. Yet though the committee was not to blame for the slowness, Lord Monson often was guilty of delay in placing matters before the committee.[19] During the six years 1743–1748, the committee met eighty-three times to deal with purely colonial matters.[20] In other words, it averaged a meeting a month to decide on appeals and other matters—with no meetings recorded for the months of August, September, and October. That was not an indifferent record, especially when eighteenth-century transportation, the pressure of the European war, and an inefficient man presiding at the Board of Trade are taken into account In fact, when Monson died and the war was over, the time devoted to these meetings was considerably increased. The great criticism against the Pelhams, as far as it concerns this aspect of the colonial problem, should be that they kept Monson in his position when his incompetence was clear to all.

Until 1748, Pelham was not important personally in colonial matters, and relatively few demands were made upon him in this field. There are examples, however, which indicate that he was often appealed to as a last resort, especially if money was involved. A certain Alexander Heron got Lord Orford to use his influence with Pelham to make up Heron's losses while in Georgia.[21] This was the type of appeal that went to Pelham. Another man, Alexander Cuming, proposed to Pelham a scheme for the creation of £140,000 of Carolina currency and a provincial bank to circulate paper money, in order to improve the financial situation in that colony.[22] Pelham shifted this appeal to Newcastle, and it seems to have been dropped. The interesting thing about this proposal was that Pelham passed it on for further consideration by the department administering colonial matters. At other times charges of corruption in money matters were presented against Governors Shirley, Dinwiddie, and Grenville from places as far apart as Massachusetts and the Barbados.[23] Besides these financial questions Pelham was pressed to support Jonathan Belcher in 1746 as Governor of South Carolina, the sole reason being that Belcher was also from Sussex.[24] Pelham's one definite move on his own initiative was to organize a new office to care for correspondence from Nova Scotia, Cape Breton, and Newfoundland, and he ordered the moves establishing it.[25] This action was an example of Pelham's efforts to make the government function more efficiently. Three years later, in 1748, he was to try again, on a broader scale, to improve colonial administration.

During these early years of the Pelham ministry, it was natural that the primary interest of the cabinet was in the defense of the colonies and in any possibilities for development on the west side of the Atlantic. The Treasury Board under the direction of Pelham decided upon most of the defense measures and occasionally approved the movement of troops in the New World.[26] The Caribbean area was of vital interest to most of the cabinet, and naval plans and the Mosquito Shore (Honduras coast) were constant topics of discussion by the cabinet and the Privy Council.[27] Pelham has left no record of personal participation, but it is impossible to imagine such arrangements being discussed unless the head of the Treasury approved. Therefore it would seem a fair assumption that he had a voice in these colonial naval matters. Finally, at the end of the war the question of French evacuation of the islands of St. Lucia, St. Vincent, and Dominica was a source of trouble between France and England. The cabinet several times had to issue direct orders on this subject and push negotiations with France.[28] While this was mainly the business of the Secretaries of State, Pelham obviously approved any decisions made.

The most ambitious war plan of the cabinet took shape in 1746 on a suggestion by Bedford. It was a scheme for the invasion of French settlements in North America. Bedford's idea was adopted by Newcastle, approved by the king, and then turned over to Bedford, Montagu, Marshal Wade, and Lieutenant General St. Clair for execution.[29] The committee set to work to determine the number of troops and amount of stores necessary for a successful campaign. They especially asked Newcastle to arrange with the local authorities in America and to get help from the Indians.[30] Seven days later, on April 6, the plan was determined, and all members of the government were busy putting it into effect.[31] This speed was almost unknown in eighteenth-century war efforts, and it goes far toward proving that the Pelham cabinet could move rapidly and efficiently when sufficiently inspired. There is little doubt that the confidence gained by the defeat of the Jacobite rebellion was carried into this effort. Newcastle was greatly pleased, for he saw the campaign as a political triumph in the House of Commons as well as a military victory that could offset continental losses.[32] Admiral Anson was active in preparing the fleet for America and arranging for naval defense at home while it was away.[33] He no doubt provided much of the energy and knowledge that made the speed of the preparations possible. William Pitt enthusiastically supported the campaign, which in many ways was a forerunner of his own Canadian campaign in the Seven Years War.[34] Despite all the speed, it was August before the expedition was ready. That was too late to launch a campaign against Canada; by the time the fleet had crossed the ocean the autumn would be well advanced. Pelham entered the planning at this time, on August 21, and advised delay until the next spring.[35] By the end of August the delay was decided upon, and a new plan was hatched to use the fleet for attack against the coast of France during the fall, so that it would not lie idle. Hardwicke and Newcastle were very favorable to the new arrangements, for they saw the double use to be made of the fleet.[36] Pelham was much more realistic. Though he had urged delay with regard to America, he said, "I don't expect much from an expedition when neither of the Commanders will give an opinion and when no direct object is fix'd upon, but the whole left to them being men, who say they know nothing of the matter." [37] The abrupt shift ruined any prospect of an American success, for, as Pelham feared, the attack on the French coast was a fiasco. Earl Fitzwilliam wrote:

> Sinclair and Lestock's Expedition is come to nothing, which I always expected, they are comeing home again, and We shall be laugh'd at by all Europe fore having shew'd our Teeth without being able to bite.[38]

Thus a season's excellent preparations went for nothing, and England was nearer defeat then ever.

There is a clue to why Pelham was not more active in the military preparations in a letter to George Grenville from Bedford, who indicated that Pelham was laboring under great "distress" in the conduct of the government's regular departments.[39] In other words, Pelham was able to spare only brief periods to the colonial enterprise because most of the ordinary duties of administration and legislation fell on him. Hence it was to his credit that he saw the impracticability of the coastal attack on France and advised against it. He alone of the principal cabinet members saw that a fleet and army planned for Canada could not be successful on the French coast. Even Hardwicke, that eminently practical man, missed the plain military facts.

With the death of Lord Monson, President of the Board of Trade, in the summer of 1748, the way was cleared for a major change in the conduct of colonial matters. The government in England had been aware that something needed to be done, but the inertia of officials with long tenure in office had prevented any active reorganization. With Monson's death the chance came to try a substitute for reorganization— to appoint an efficient man to the vacant office and let him function more freely. The Earl of Morton sensed this necessity; in his application to Newcastle and Pelham he stressed his promise to attend strictly to the business of the office and finish work promptly.[40] Newcastle did not wish to increase the power of the office, for it would decrease his own. He also was seeking a prestige position for his relative, the Duke of Leeds; therefore he advocated this favorite rather than someone who could do the job well. Pelham was strongly opposed to Leeds, and matters were at an impasse until the Duke of Bedford suggested a solution:

> I have talked with Mr. Pelham about the vacancy in the Board of Trade. . . . I think both your Grace's and Mr. Pelham's idea is . . . that it would be highly improper, considering the present situation of things, to have a non-efficient man at the head of that Board, and therefore I must take the liberty to differ from you in the arrangement you have proposed to Mr. Pelham, in

order to make room for the Duke of Leeds to come into a post suitable to his quality. . . . I will now mention an idea . . . and that is, if Lord Halifax could be prevailed upon to exchange from what he now has to the Board of Trade (for which I should think him perfectly well qualified), the Duke of Leeds might succeed him as Chief Justice in Eyre.[41]

This was one of the most practical solutions possible, and Pelham readily adopted it. Newcastle finally agreed, and the king approved. Early in September, therefore, Bedford, in the name of the cabinet, offered Halifax the position.[42] Halifax accepted with certain financial reservations, the resolving of which was left to Pelham.[43] It was a good choice, for Halifax was young, capable, and interested in the position.

With this appointment the Pelhams opened a new period in colonial rule. Halifax's ideas, changes, and political importance produced a new official attitude toward the colonies. The change was to show itself in full force during the 1760's, when British authority tried to enforce an organized government on the colonies. Halifax eagerly set to work to direct colonial affairs and make them conform to the central government. This was the most important single move that the Pelham ministry made in colonial matters, and it ultimately led to the American Revolution.

IRISH PROBLEMS

Though colonial affairs were considered important during the war, Ireland caused more worry among military men. However, much less was done to solve Irish problems. The extablished rule of Ireland by the Lord Lieutenant and the Irish parliament in Dublin continued its placid course, with all its old inequities. No one thought to question the complete domination of Ireland by English interests. The one exception to this general political control was the growing independence of Henry Boyle, Speaker of the Irish House of Commons. To be sure, he used his independence primarily for selfish interest, but at least he led a small group of Irishmen against the English. The actions of Boyle were to lead to important problems in the following years.

Lord Chesterfield and Lord Harrington were fairly successful in keeping political peace in Ireland during the war while they were Lord Lieutenants. They obtained Irish support for financial and military demands made by London, and this was all the English cabinet really was interested in achieving. Among the Irish, disagreement over the extent to which they should support England in the war was expressed as follows:

An Expression of my Lord Egmont's in Letter to Mr. Purcell viz. That every Body knows that Ireland after the first Year will be rather a Gainer than a Loser by the French War has found different Advocates for and ag[ain]st the question.[44]

As long as the Irish were divided on the issue, England gained her ends, for no united front could be formed.

Irish ecclesiastical appointments were kept firmly in the hands of the English government, for the twenty-six English bishoprics were not enough to reward deserving English churchmen. As a result the Irish bishoprics were usually held by Englishmen. Moreover, these ecclesiastical offices were used by the English government to enforce English ideas and laws. Under the Pelhams this was particularly true of George Stone, Archbishop of Armagh and Primate of All Ireland. Archbishop Stone was the brother of Andrew Stone, Newcastle's confidential secretary and friend, and he functioned as a major arm of the Irish government. He kept in close touch with Pelham and sent him secret reports on affairs in Ireland.[45] Pelham and Newcastle also were regularly informed of Irish affairs by whoever was the Lord Lieutenant at the moment and by the Lords Justices of Ireland.[46] Chesterfield worked especially close to the brothers while he was in the office of Lord Lieutenant. It is safe to say that the Pelhams were well informed on Irish matters, but they were interested only in what could be got from Ireland for British interests.

The records of the Privy Council bear out this estimate, for in the five years from 1744 through 1748 only nineteen special meetings of the Council Committee were held to consider Irish bills. Since eight of these occurred during 1748, there were about three meetings annually.[47] Thus in spite of the fact that the Council had to approve Irish legislation, much less attention was paid to Ireland than to the American colonies. Because the Council meetings on Irish affairs were poorly attended, the Lord President, one of the judges, and one or two others usually made the decisions. The fact that the Lord Lieutenant was a close political ally of the Pelhams accounted for some of the lack of attention by the cabinet. Chesterfield or Harrington, as a member of the British cabinet, was expected to see that English interests were carried out. However, a large share of the lack of interest must be assigned to indifference on the part of the Pelhams, as long as no serious crisis developed. Luckily none occurred during the war.

CHAPTER XII

Wartime Politics, 1745–1748

♄ THE YEAR 1745 opened with the newly reorganized cabinet in firm control. Lord Granville had not recovered from his defeat and removal from office the preceding November, and all prospects seemed to point to a time of political peace for Henry Pelham. Such, however, was not to be the case. George II had not been pleased with the removal of Granville, though he had accepted the situation and the reorganized cabinet that followed. He still refused to admit William Pitt to important office, and Pitt continued his campaign for recognition and voiced his opposition in the House of Commons. Pelham had long been in favor of adding Pitt to the ministry, and during 1745 he pressed the king to accept the brilliant orator.[1] Thus, George was irritated by Pelham and dissatisfied with his administration.

The Jacobite rebellion, beginning in the summer, had an immediate effect on the king. First, it made him fear for his crown, so he supported his cabinet in all its actions. Second, the success of the rebellion made him listen to Granville's protests against the cabinet. The remnants of the opposition in parliament made the most of the unsuccessful government attempts put down the rebels. When parliament met in the autumn, Pitt returned to the attack and opposed almost all measures taken by the cabinet to handle the Scots as too little, too late, inefficient, or tending to put unnecessary power in the hands of the cabinet.[2] Granville secretly used the rebellion, Pitt, the cabinet's attitude, and George's favor to promote his position with the king and undermine Pelham and the Duke of Newcastle.

In September Chesterfield wrote to Newcastle, "The Danger at home, strengthens you too, and must produce compliance on one side, but not on yours. I think you have the Domestick game in your hands, though by no means the foreign one, as Lord Granville has the impudence to say." [3] This was Chesterfield's position throughout the crisis: The Pelhams should insist that the issue of Granville be settled with the king, for they could not lose. Lord Hardwicke recognized the same strength of the Pelhams and declared that Granville could not replace them.[4] And there is considerable proof that the merchants and bankers agreed to support the existing government.[5] On the last day of September Chesterfield wrote:

139

I have long entertain'd, that those two Brothers have the Game in their hands. How can somebody help himself, if he can't get others, as I am persuaded he can't, to under take the Administration? The present publick situation of affairs, and private distress in the Closet; should in my humble opinion be made the proper use of, and immediately. . . . The two Brothers can never expect favour but they have strength, and should enjoy it without loss of time; they have friends who will stand or fall with 'em, and if they will give the law, I am convinc'd they may. . . . If a publick Brand be not put upon Ld. Granville and his adherents before the meeting of Parliament; they will have the strength before the ending of it. . . . There is a Moment in all affairs, This is it in my opinion; for the Brothers to secure themselves, their friends, and the Publick. The[y] can't fall now, if they will stand.[6]

Three weeks later he wrote to Newcastle, while reinforcements were arriving in England, "Look to your selves in the Closet, before the appearances of danger are quite remov'd" [7] For once, therefore, Newcastle was slower than other men to recognize a political situation that could be used to his advantage.

The Earl of Harrington applied the first direct pressure on the king to choose between Granville and the ministers. He, Pelham, and Newcastle agreed that this was the only course of action possible, and they called a meeting, attended also by Bedford, Gower, and Hardwicke, to decide on exact steps to be taken.[8] During the time required for those six men to determine their course of action, the king became steadily more angry with his ministers. Newcastle wrote to his good friend Richmond:

The Closet grows worse than ever. We are now come to bad language; *Incapacity* to my Brother, Spectator of other people's policy and measures, and yesterday *Pitifull Fellows*.[9]

By November, however, the Pelhams got their chance to force the issue whenever they were ready. The party of the Prince of Wales, which meant primarily Lord Cobham and Pitt, hinted they were prepared to settle their quarrels with the Pelhams if only Granville were completely ignored. Pelham and Pitt held a private meeting and ironed out their differences. Then a grand strategy meeting, attended by Pelham, Hardwicke, Harrington, Newcastle, Pitt, Cobham, Gower, and Bedford, was held.[10] The three issues discussed were the extension of a place bill to army officers below the rank of lieutenant colonel and naval officers below captain; removal of all Granville's friends from the Court, especially the Finches; and a change of foreign policy to concentrate on the naval war. The first two were easily agreed upon, but the last caused a breakdown in negotiations. The ministers decided to scrape along for the time being. Pitt therefore returned to the attack in Commons, and the opposition thought Pelham was sure to fall. They forgot that only one issue separated the Pelhams and the Cobhamites, and Pelham could insure Cobham's support whenever he gave in or compromised on it.

Lord Chesterfield, the Lord Lieutenant of Ireland, undertook to re-establish negotiations. He urged the Pelhams to find jobs for the Cobhamites and use the prospect of place to obtain settlement of the stubborn point.[11] On the Cobham side, George Lyttelton was eager to reach agreement even if Pitt remained obstinate.[12] The basis for agreement was present. In December, Chesterfield wrote to Gower, who had a foot in both camps:

> By all that the Pelhams have writt me, I am convinc'd they had a sincere desire to form an Administration upon a Tolerable Plan, though possibly not so extensive a one, as even their own interests requir'd; Pitt, I know was one of the principal parts of their Plan, together with our Connection, and I did not doubt but this arrangement better or worse, would be made, by the meeting of the Parliament.[13]

He went on to criticize Pitt's position and to note that previously he had urged Pelham to make a deal with Pitt if he proved to be reasonable in his demands or, if these were excessive, to strip him of all his friends. His final remark was that he would support Pelham as long as Gower did. Chesterfield clearly hoped that Gower would spread the word to the Cobhamites, and if that failed he would continue in his present course of action. The latter was certainly trying to reestablish negotiations so that the Granville problem could be solved.

The Christmas recess of parliament stopped the political maneuvers for a while, but the new year found the cabinet entrenched against the Granville attack. Bedford, Gower, and Chesterfield assured the Pelhams that they would remain in the government even if Pitt and the Cobhamites refused to join. Then Granville made a tactical error: he promised George II that he would not join the official opposition even if the Prince of Wales did.[14] That move gave Pelham room to negotiate, for he no longer needed to worry about a united opposition. Chesterfield wrote him a last bit of advice about Pitt. He suggested that if Pitt remained stubborn Pelham should make the most of it with the king and ignore him, for Pitt would hold no grudge. "He has neither love, nor hatred in his temper, and those who are worst with him today, are as likely, as those who are the best, to be well with him to morrow." [15] By the middle of January the general decision of the cabinet had been made. The first notice that the Pelhams were prepared to force the king's hand was the removal of Sir John Hynde Cotton from the post of Treasurer of the Chamber.[16] Cotton was not a friend of Granville, but he was a Tory who was possibly a weak member of the ministry. The cabinet was clearly closing ranks.

According to Hardwicke, the cabinet made its final decision to resign on February 8, 1746, at a secret evening meeting.[17] On February 9 the cabinet reduced its demand that Pitt be made Secretary at War. Lord Bath had an interview with the king and persuaded him not to allow Pitt the office. When the cabinet reduced its demand from a specific post to a demand

for an important post, Bath prevented that also.[18] In reality it was plain
that the cabinet had made the Pitt appointment an excuse to force George
II to make a move. Its members resigned not primarily because of Pitt
but for three positive reasons: First, they feared the king would remove
them from office once the budget and supply had been passed. Second,
they wanted to remove all Lord Granville's influence. Third, the Jacobite
threat still existed—a strong factor in their favor that would be gone in a
few months.[19] On February 10 the amazing resignations began with Lord
Harrington and Newcastle. On February 11 Pelham and all the Treasury
Board except Lord Middlesex resigned, followed by Bedford and all the
Navy Board except Lord Archibald Hamilton. Later in the day Lord
Gower, the Lord Privy Seal, and Lord Pembroke, the Groom of the Stole,
joined their leaders. The Dukes of Devonshire (Lord Steward), Grafton
(Lord Chamberlain), and Richmond (Master of the Horse), Lord
Hardwicke (Lord Chancellor), and Thomas Winnington (Paymaster-
General) all prepared to resign as soon as possible. Chesterfield wrote,
upon receiving the news, that he would return and join the exodus of
ministers. And finally the Duke of Dorset (Lord President) and Henry
Fox (Secretary at War) indicated that they would also resign.[20] The confusion was complete; nothing like this had ever happened before. Benjamin Keene wrote to de Castres in Lisbon describing the scene as one of
complete public amazement.[21] When the resignations of the leaders became sure, those of the lesser public officials followed, to form a movement that fell like a veritable avalanche on the king. The Earl of Malton
(soon to become the Marquis of Rockingham) wrote:

> The whole Whig Corp[s] are throwing up their places tis needless to tell
> names for those that have not yet done it, will one after another as fast as pos-
> sible, I hope to get rid of my Lieutenancy in the Crowd.[22]

When men like Lords Lothian and Albemarle offered their support to the
Pelhams and volunteered to join the parade, the pressure on the king was
impossible for him to withstand.[23]

Immediately on the resignations of Newcastle and Harrington, George
II sent for Earl Granville and entrusted him with both offices until a
colleague could be found. When Pelham, Bedford, and Gower resigned,
Bath, the Earl of Winchelsea, and the Earl of Carlisle were appointed to
the respective offices. But further resignations continued for which there
were no immediate replacements. A second weakness of Granville was the
House of Commons. There he could find no leader more capable than Sir
John Rushout, and the Pelhams still controlled the majority.[24] Also very
important was the fact that the new ministers were unable to get any
money from the financial interests in London.[25] On February 13 Lord
Marchmont noted in his diary that Viscount Bolingbroke told him that
Bath had resigned because there was no hope.[26] Actually Granville and
Bath knew they were beaten on the twelfth, for

The King Sent a Messenger this afternoon to Mr. Pelham, by Mr. Winnington, to let him know that His Majesty was determined to accept no more Resignations, & intimating that he would have his old Servants return back & accept their places. That he expected an Answer to morrow morning.[27]

Granville and Bath became the butt of many jokes when the Pelhams returned in force on the fourteenth.[28] Granville took the fiasco in good humor and admitted that he had been mad to try to upset the Pelhams, but he claimed he would do it again. Nothing, perhaps, was more typical of Granville's attitude toward governing than his impossible direction of the cabinet crisis of February 1746.

There was a very serious significance to the organized cabinet resignation and Granville's failure to replace it. First, it meant, in the eyes of contemporaries, that Granville, Bath, Winchelsea, Carlisle, and Bathurst faced the prospect of lifelong opposition, since the Pelhams' strength was much increased after their recall.[29] Second, it was one of the most important steps in the formation of cabinet solidarity, which was to be of great influence in the later development of parliamentary democracy in Britain. It showed future prime ministers one more way to exert pressure on the Crown for the attainment of desired policies. Granville himself put his finger on this point when he said, "My Lord [Hardwicke], you and your friends have done a thing not known before in any Country; deserting the K[ing] by Troops, in a dangerous Crisis. What can this mean? I could raise a flame upon it, but I won't." [30] And third, it revealed that though Pelham regarded himself as a friend of the king, he regarded himself even more as head of a ministry whose primary responsibility was to govern according to the decisions of parliament. This is not far from the belief that the cabinet and ministers are responsible only to parliament. In this sense Pelham contributed more to the institution of the cabinet than did Sir Robert Walpole.

Granville's reputation as a quixotic individual and as a European schemer did great damage to his cause in the Commons and in London, and Pelham's dependable reputation was one of his greatest strengths in this contest for office and power.

When it was known that Mr. Henry Pelham had given up his place, 192 members went to his levee to compliment him, and the City of London determined to advance no money, crying out, "If no Pelham, no money." [31]

According to Charles Yorke, second son of the Chancellor, public credit sank on the day Pelham resigned, and there was a run on the Bank; furthermore, the London bankers and merchants withdrew their promised subscription for £2,500,000. As soon as the Pelhams returned to office, the contract for the money was renewed in the financial circles of London.[32] Since no eighteenth-century political figure was strong enough to organize London wealth for political ends, the only conclusion is that Pelham, by long effort and faithful attendance to the Londoners' wishes, had so gained their favor that they came voluntarily to his political aid. That was no small compliment to the skill of Pelham in both political and financial fields.

On February 13 a secret meeting of the Pelhamites was held at the home of the Duke of Dorset, where they formulated the terms on which they would return to the cabinet.

That, out of Duty to the King, & Regard to the Public, It is apprehended that His Majesty's late Servants cannot return into his Service, without being honour'd with that degree of Authority, Confidence, & Credit from His Majesty, which the Ministers of the Crown have usually enjoy'd in this Country, & which is absolutely necessary for carrying on his Service.

That His Majesty will be pleas'd entirely to withdraw his confidence & countenance from those Persons, who of late have, behind the Curtain, suggested private Councills, with ye View of creating difficulties to his Servants, who are responsible for every thing, whilst Those Persons are responsible for nothing.

That His Majesty will be pleased to demonstrate his Conviction of mind that Those Persons have deceiv'd or misled Him by representing that they had sufficient Credit & Interest in the Nation to support & carry on the public affairs, & that he finds They are not able to do it.

That in order to these Ends, His Majesty will be pleas'd to remove [Granville's followers]. . . .

That He will be graciously pleased to perfect the Scheme lately humbly propos'd to Him for bringing Mr Pitt into some honourable Employment, & also the other persons formerly nam'd with him.

That His Majesty will be pleased to dispose of the vacant Garters in such manner, as to strengthen, & give a public mark of his Satisfaction in, his Administration.

That, as to foreign affairs, His Majesty will be pleased not to require more from His Servants than to support the Plan, which He has already approved.[33]

The Pelhams therefore came back without any qualification, and stronger than ever. They wasted no time, for by February 18 they had removed Granville's friends from their offices. The Duke of Bolton, the Earl of Bath, Lord Berkeley of Stratton, Lord Archibald Hamilton, Mr. Bladen, and Mr. Boone were quickly ousted.[34] They had intended to remove William Finch, Vice-Chamberlain, and his brother, but the king begged as a personal favor that they be left, and the Pelhams agreed in order to keep the king from becoming further alienated.

In the places of these men, William Pitt and several lesser men were brought into the ministry. Pitt was made one of the Joint Vice-Treasurers of Ireland, which was an honorary post with no active duties. The Pelhams promised to obtain an important post for him as soon as they could, and on this basis he was satisfied.[35] Chesterfield was triumphant at the return of the Pelhams, and he urged that all Granville's friends be made examples, for "every body now sees and knows, that you have the power; let them see and know too, that you will use it." [36] The Lord Lieutenant of Ireland also very privately advised Pelham and Newcastle to watch the Old Whigs and the Cobham Whigs, for they were jealous of each other. His recommendation was to increase Gower's power and add a few Tories as a balance, gain Lady Yarmouth for secret power over the king by an Irish pension, and again to get the Finch brothers out of the Bedchamber. [37] During the next months all these suggestions were carried out except the last, for William Finch remained in his post until Pelham's death. However, Pelham and his brother had won their last joint political fight, and the rest of Pelham's life was free from serious political trouble. The last attempt at organized opposition to replace him had been smashed.

For the next three years there was little opposition in either house of parliament except by individuals. In March 1746 Pelham's plan for supplies was carried by a majority of more than 100, even though Barnard's plan was cheaper. Only the followers of the Prince of Wales and Lord Bath voted against Pelham. [38] In June, Lord Lonsdale offered a resolution against sending troops to Flanders again, but he was defeated. [39] In both cases Granville's friends voted for the government, and more than anything else this showed that opposition was impossible. In 1747 the newly elected parliament was greeted by Pelham as "a good one. If we do not furnish matter against ourselves, I have not the least apprehension of any thing they can furnish, to hurt us." [40] The eldest son of the Chancellor estimated that the Court held 148 votes against the combined opposition of 116 Tories and 41 friends of the Prince of Wales. [41] The unconnected members more than made up a definite majority for the Court, with whom they usually voted; furthermore, the two opposing groups seldom voted together. At the end of the year Bishop Sherlock said, "There seems to be a Stagnation in politicks. The Opposition (if such there be) is Silent, & waits for Events." [42] Horace Walpole the younger noted the same success of the cabinet in 1748. [43] That year the Prince of Wales attempted to organize an opposition party, which made little headway. [44] The one effective member of the Prince's group was the Earl of Egmont, who thundered against the conduct of the war and the peace and anything else that seemed a likely issue. [45] However, he failed to raise any support, and the opposition of the Prince continued unimportant through the year. Bolingbroke summed up the situation rather well when he wrote to thank Pelham for gaining a favor for him; he indicated Pelham was in such complete control of events that only through his agency could anything be accomplished. [46] And Richard Glover, an opposition member of the House of Commons, wrote, "Our peculiar disappointments were owing to ourselves, wanting both Statesmen and Commanders, economy, discipline, and conduct." [47] The opposition was obviously plagued by incapacity, which people of all shades of opinion could see.

The only serious political trouble for Pelham came from within the ministry. The experience of the past suggested that Pitt might be a source of trouble, but this was not so. In May 1746, Sir Thomas Winnington died, and William Pitt was promoted to the vacant post of Paymaster-General of the Forces. Though it was not so active a post as that of Secretary at War, it was an important place and satisfied him. The first real jolt was Harrington's resignation in the autumn, but this was worked out by the arrangement for Harrington to trade positions with his cousin, the Earl of Chesterfield. The resignation was provoked by Newcastle's interference with the Northern Department and disregard of a policy seeking peace. Since Chesterfield was even more active in seeking an end to the war, his acceptance of office surprised many people. Chesterfield himself was probably surprised at the offer, for within a few months he was complaining of the lack of attention to his ideas and suggestions.[48] Occasionally Chesterfield's relations with Newcastle seemed to improve, but they always reverted to dissatisfaction.[49] Finally, on February 6, 1748, Chesterfield suddenly resigned. Pelham was angered at Newcastle for not being able to keep any partner in the secretaryship. Pelham had been pleased with Chesterfield and was afraid that his resignation would cause trouble in the House of Commons. Newcastle knew his brother's feelings and tried to defend himself by getting support in naming a successor from other cabinet members.[50] When Bedford was named to the Southern Department on February 12, Newcastle shifted to the Northern, but the duke never completely reconciled Pelham to the change.[51] In Chesterfield's *An Apology for a Late Resignation,* written to defend his action, he laid the blame for his resignation directly on Newcastle's conduct of the war.[52] However, the earl promised Pelham that he would not go into the opposition but would support the government.[53] In return, Pelham proved his friendship by keeping friends of Chesterfield, like Solomon Dayrolles, in their offices.[54] All these main cabinet crises were overcome, and the cabinet went on.

Minor arguments constantly disturbed the steady direction of the ministry, for every one of the groups represented in it tried to increase its share of power. The Duke of Montagu threatened to withdraw his support over an insignificant issue of promotion in the army.[55] The Earl of Marchmont demanded promotion in the government, but Pelham's friendship for the Duke of Argyll killed any chance of Marchmont's success because of the long-standing feud between the two Scots.[56] Lord Sandwich constantly stirred up trouble by his desire to be a Secretary of State, which was bitterly opposed by Newcastle after the negotiations at Aix.[57] No final solution was reached until Sandwich was made First Lord of the Admiralty at the same time that Bedford became Secretary. Other minor members of the ministry, like James Oswald, resigned or made impossible requests for favors, which had to be rejected.[58] Only one member of the

cabinet, Lord Gower, made no calls on Pelham, and it was from this period at the end of the war that Pelham became a firm friend of the one-
time Tory leader.[59] A multitude of little matters made direction of an
eighteenth-century government difficult, and the success of a politician
was dependent on the handling of them. No minister from Pelham to
Lord North was successful, and the failures help to explain the instability
of the intervening cabinets. The collapse of the parties made any other
methods impossible.

Last, notice must be given to the long quarrel between Pelham and
Newcastle during 1747 and 1748. After the successful elections, Pelham
became more and more critical of the continuing war. The resignation of
Chesterfield added fuel to the glowing embers, and the final peace made
the question of alliances still more prominent. At one point Pelham and
Newcastle conversed only through their intermediary, Andrew Stone,
lest a public quarrel ruin the political future of both.[60] At various times
Pelham tried to compromise his and his brother's views on the war, but
Newcastle's jealousy prevented any agreement.[61] At the end of 1748, Pelham's campaign to reduce expenses upset Newcastle's foreign policy.
Newcastle insisted that alliances must come first, no matter how worthy
the economy plan, and this attitude made the quarrel almost as intense
as it had been the year before.[62] In spite of all the internal bickering and
quarreling, however, Newcastle as well as Pelham realized that they had
to agree outwardly. Their basic affection for each other and their sense
of political interest overcame their problems. The ministry went merrily
on, to the amazement of each individual and group opposed to it. It entered the postwar period strengthened perhaps by the knowledge that it
could outlast any trouble. It also entered 1749 with a leader who had
gradually assumed control and exercised it whenever he felt it was necessary. Pelham certainly ended the period of the war a more outstanding
man than he had been at the beginning or in 1744, when he had openly
assumed leadership.

The essential strength of the ministry during the years after 1746 rested
on the complete victory that Pelham achieved in the cabinet crisis of
February 1746. The joint resignations at that time are usually considered
important only as one precedent in the development of cabinet solidarity.
This is, of course, correct; yet they are probably more important in the
history of the eighteenth century as the method by which Pelham fastened
himself firmly in the position of leadership of the Whigs. His leadership
was essential to the maintenance of any semblance of a Whig government,
as is perfectly clear from the disintegration of the ministry following his
death. The cabinet crisis and Pelham's leadership of the government in
that crisis were responsible, therefore, for the politically peaceful years
that followed and also for the delay of complete Whig fragmentation
until the 1760's. This was undoubtedly much more important to the

eighteenth century than any precedents established for the future. A clear understanding of this event in the light of how it affected the people of the day is essential to the interpretation of subsequent political developments. No amount of establishing precedents for modern times can do that.

CHAPTER XIII

The Jacobite Rebellion, 1745–1746

❧ AFTER THE FAILURE of the Jacobite rebellion of 1715, the friends of the exiled Stuarts remained quiet for many years. For most of that time Sir Robert Walpole was First Minister in fact, if not in name. Under his leadership the Whig lords made political capital out of the public fear of a second attempt by the Stuarts to regain the Crown. Walpole also used this fear as justification for his isolationist foreign policy for twenty years, even though many Whigs like Carteret, Newcastle, Cobham, and Chesterfield saw with increasing clarity the diplomatic defeats England suffered during the 1730's. No doubt much was gained by the years of peace, but when war finally struck in 1739, England paid the price of having ignored the cultivation of allies. Neither had Walpole succeeded in removing the possibility of trouble from the Jacobites; he had merely delayed it until he was out of office. England's weakness and semi-isolation during the War of the Austrian Succession gave the friends of the Stuarts a better opportunity than they could have had at any earlier time. Even the Austrian allies were not strongly opposed to the Catholic exiles.

By the beginning of 1743 Jacobite propaganda was being openly distributed in England. Three letters—one signed "Ireland," another "Scotland," and the last "England"—appeared and proclaimed the virtues of "Charles St. George, Esq.," which was the euphemism for the Young Pretender.[1] By 1744 the propaganda had changed to rumors, disquieting reports that Prince Charles was ready to invade England. This idea was more easily believed because the fear of an active French invasion was very strong, and it was thought that the Young Pretender would be supported by them. At the end of January, Carteret sent official word to Trevor that the young Stuart had left Rome for France, and Trevor was ordered to demand 6,000 troops from the Dutch to fulfill their treaty obligations.[2] Reports arrived in London from Dunkirk and Scotland giving details about the preparations of the Jacobites.[3] Duncan Forbes, Lord President of the Sessions, and the Marquis of Tweeddale, Secretary of State for Scotland, were the principal government men who executed the orders of the cabinet in Scotland. They were, however, only two of the funnels of information available to the cabinet, which relied heavily on continental reports.

The government acted to remove any danger of help being given a

149

Stuart or of French invasion of England. The measures taken were severe and often senseless. All arms belonging to "Papists, Non Jurors, or other Persons judged dangerous to the Peace" were ordered seized. And all horses were ordered confiscated from Roman Catholics, even from old men of eighty years. Somewhat more useful was the arrest of Lord Barrymore, who was a potential leader of a revolt, but the charge of high treason was quite dubious. The suspension of habeas corpus for two months was a definite infringement on the rights of Englishmen, but it was passed by an almost unanimous vote in the Commons.[4] More sensible was the bill to make it treason to correspond with the Pretender's sons; this was sponsored in the Lords by Hardwicke and passed without division. In the Commons there was some opposition, but the bill was a legal answer to the possible threat. Perhaps the most useful moves were the attempts to form new Highland regiments that would be loyal to George II and the distribution of some arms to loyal Scots.[5] The plan of the Duke of Argyll and Pelham, if it had been carried out completely, might have prevented further trouble, but too many people objected to the power it gave the Duke of Argyll. As the threatened French invasion grew less likely during the year, the cabinet relaxed its activity and interest. By the end of the summer the government decided the danger was over. The high excitement about the invasion in early 1744, and the gradual end of Jacobite activity in Europe during the latter part of the year, had much to do with the complacent attitude of the Pelhams when similar threats developed in 1745. The danger, once met by half measures, did not again seem really serious to the government until too late. At all events it was fear of a French invasion that disturbed the cabinet, and this fear repeated itself again in 1745.

It was not until March of the new year that word began to be whispered through Europe that the "young Chevalier" was preparing an attempt on Scotland.[6] The English feared that the British-Irish troops in the service of France would follow him. The Scottish chiefs were upset at the rumors, for they feared all "worthless" men would join the Stuarts, and they urged a few small ships to guard the coast to prevent a landing. The government in London tried to discover the truth of the rumors by employing European spies and informers. Few practical results came from the spying, and little news of Prince Charles was learned even as late as June. More information about secret moves was learned in Britain itself.[7] However, no definite evidence was gained except that money was arriving in England to finance Jacobite preparations for an invasion, and this did not seriously alarm the cabinet.

On July 24, 1745, Harrington sent the first official word from Hanover that an invasion of Britain was afoot. Six days later the cabinet officially took notice of the sailing of Charles Edward from France and issued various orders for defense. On August 1, Newcastle wrote to the Duke of Argyll that a French invasion was imminent and expressed a great fear of the prospect.[8] This fear dominated the thoughts of the London government for the next four months. Tweeddale sent orders to Sir John Cope to prepare the defenses of Scotland, 5,000 men were ordered to Edinburgh Castle, and arms were prepared for shipment to Scotland. Political opponents blamed the Pelhams for having no ready defense, though almost the entire English armed force was in Flanders and could not be returned promptly.[9] There was actually no army with which to defend Britain until Cumberland could return. The only possible move was to delay any action. The government could have been more active at first, but it would have made little difference.

Official and public notice of the rebellion was given by the issuance of a proclamation calling on the people to seize the son of the pretender and offering a reward of £30,000 for his capture. The proclamation was signed by the Lords Justices who were in London on August 1: the Archbishop of Canterbury, Hardwicke, Dorset, Gower, Devonshire, Bolton, Newcastle, Tweeddale, Bedford, Grafton, Stair, and Henry Pelham.[10] These were the men responsible for the early measures taken to defeat the rebellion, and on them has fallen the majority of blame for the ineffectiveness of these measures in the first months. Since the Pelhams were the leaders of the cabinet, they have received the greatest share of that blame. The facts do not bear out the accusations as usually presented.

Charles Edward began his organized campaign soon after his landing, but he moved slowly while he waited for recruits. By the end of the month he felt himslef strong enough to issue a counterproclamation offering £30,000 reward for the capture of the "Elector of Hanover." Throughout the next three months the Young Pretender issued proclamations and orders as if he were the actual ruler and undertook to run a government in the areas his army controlled.[11] Because of the disrupted communications and the general chaos in northern England and Scotland, these papers were often days old before London knew of them. It was exceedingly difficult for the cabinet to keep up with the Stuarts' movements, especially in the early days of the rebellion. No one in London was sure of the state of affairs in Scotland.

Duncan Forbes, one of the shrewdest men in Scotland, could write to Pelham on August 2 that there was no preparation for a rebellion and that if Charles Edward landed he would receive no help. On the eighth Forbes repeated his doubts of an actual rebellion to the Marquis of Tweeddale, because any possibility of success had been destroyed in 1715. Forbes was not alone in his beliefs, for as late as the thirteenth the Earl of Loudoun, at General Cope's headquarters, still knew nothing of the prince's landing.[12] London did receive various anonymous reports, and Hardwicke wrote to his son's father-in-law, Lord Glenorchy, to get trustworthy information.[13]

Matters were further complicated by the personal rivalry and dislike between Tweeddale and Argyll. Tweeddale tried to keep all power over

Scotland in his own hands, and Argyll was too strong in Scotland to admit Tweeddale's claims. As a result, when reports did arrive from Scotland there was almost certain to be a quarrel between these two men as to what should be done. In September the Earl of Marchmont and the Duke of Montrose offered their services to the king, but the rivalry of Tweeddale and Argyll made action impossible.[14] They were finally forced to approach Lord Gower and make their offer directly through him. The situation was extremely unfortunate because no one was functioning as Secretary of State for Scotland, and the rebellion rolled along.

Added to the confusion was a further element. Tweeddale was the last important member of the Granville faction left in the government, and Granville was busy planning his return to power. The earl made use of the rebellion to advance his own political ends, and he supported Tweeddale when the marquis said there was nothing serious about the rebellion. Since Granville again had the king's ear, he was able to instill that idea in George II. This only made the life of the cabinet leaders more difficult and eventually led to the four-day cabinet of February 1746. Thus bad communications, no troops, personal feuds, and political ambitions all combined more or less to paralyze the cabinet in the first weeks of the revolt.

The basic cause of the confusion, which made all the above causes possible, was the position of the French army. All the fears of the previous year were revived with added force, for Ostend was besieged and near collapse, and that port would give the French an excellent place from which to launch an invasion. When Trevor sent word that 6,000 Spanish troops were shifted to Ferrol, where a squadron of warships lay, it seemed certain that a well-coordinated plan of invasion was being prepared.[15] After Ostend fell to the French, another difficulty presented itself, Cumberland opposed returning any of his troops to England and had to be ordered explicitly before he would do so. Cumberland's attitude thus explains much of the anxiety about troops, for unless he returned some men there was practically no army available. Pelham wrote, "I am not so apprehensive of the strength or zeal of the enemy Jacobites, as I am fearful of the inability or languidness, of our friends," but Newcastle expressed the more common attitude—fear of France, not of the Pretender.[16] Again Pelham made a sound estimate of the situation in spite of all excitement, and he maintained the calm necessary to meet the prospect of invasion.

In September Henry Fox wrote that a fleet of warships and thirty transports had been collected by the French at Dunkirk and nothing had been learned of the Ferrol or Brest squadrons. He bitterly denounced Tweeddale, Argyll, and the Duke of Athol for deserting Scotland in the face of the Pretender. He ended by saying, "England . . . is for the first comer; and if you can tell whether the six thousand Dutch and the ten battalions of English, or five thousand French or Spanish, will be here first, you will know our fate." [17] On the tenth Pelham expressed his feelings about the rebels to Robert Trevor:

> I heartily wish the troops were arrived both Dutch & English, for though I look upon these Highland rebels as a sort of rabble, yet if there is no force to oppose 'em, they may come in time to be considerable. We have scarce any regular troops in the country.[18]

There were also many expressions of contempt toward the rebellion by different classes of people. The panic of Newcastle and Henry Fox and the indifference of Granville and Tweeddale were not typical. Pelham remained worried but calm, and there was no great outcry from Londoners or politicians during the month of September. When the Dutch reinforcements arrived, toward the end of the month, confidence became even greater. Fox expressed relief in spite of the rebel advance in Scotland, and Newcastle said that the prospect of French invasion was the greatest danger left.[19] At the end of the initial stage of the rebellion, therefore, the cabinet members felt they had the matter well under control. It was only in the second stage, when the rebels won some surprising victories, that confidence was lost, and only then did the government even equate the danger from Charles Edward with that from a French invasion.

Meanwhile Sir John Cope was trying to organize the feeble defenses that existed in Scotland, but he was hampered by lack of money and the rivalries of local lords. Lord Tankerville, from northern England, wrote that the common people of Scotland were favorable to the Jacobites and that the fears of the Scottish nobles prevented any action being taken. Other reports confirmed Tankerville and suggested that the disaffection was spreading into northern England.[20] These reports finally caused direct action aganst the rebels in spite of the fact that adequate resources were not available. An Order in Council was issued to the Lords Lieutenant of the counties to seize all arms from "Papists, non-jurors, & other dangerous people." Cumberland finally agreed to return home with troops. Two Irish regiments were ordered to stand prepared to cross to Chester if necessary, and Dutch troops were sent north as soon as they landed in England.[21] These measures were, naturally, too late, and the rebels' complete victory at Prestonpans finally revealed the dangerous situation to everyone. Newcastle's letter to Cumberland on September 25 described the first reaction to the defeat as follows:

> now there is no army between Scotland and London. The Pretender, having entirely got possession of the whole kingdom of Scotland . . . and Sir John Cope being most thoroughly defeated . . . will, I hope, justify the early fears and humble application of your Royal Highness's faithful servants here, for a considerable reinforcement from your army. . . .
>
> if the rebels should increase, as may very well happen, or should France, who

has set this young gentleman to work, support him . . . we have no way to save this country but by farther reinforcements from your Royal Highness's army.[22]

The danger could no longer be considered unimportant, and to defeat the Pretender chances had to be taken on the possibility of a French invasion.

The cabinet relied on three men—Cope, Argyll, and Duncan Forbes —to put down the rebellion in this early stage, but they failed. Cope's military efforts collapsed at Prestonpans because he had insufficient troops and had not organized them efficiently. Argyll proved a weak reed upon which to build noble opposition to the Jacobites, for he had antagonized most of the other lords and had left for London as soon as the rebels became dangerous.[23] Duncan Forbes, an extremely cautious man, moved carefully to preserve his own property. However, the greatest obstacle to the organization of a defense was lack of money. At first Tweeddale urged Forbes to spend his own money, and Pelham promised to repay him as soon as the money could be brought north. But it was, of course, impossible for any individual to finance the defense. In September the Barons of the Exchequer in Scotland were ordered to make money available to Cope from the customs and excises collected in Scotland. This revenue was good only as long as Cope controlled the ports of Scotland. Then Forbes was told that he should take money from any source and that Pelham would repay it. When the rebels approached Edinburgh, Forbes was isolated in the north of Scotland without hope of money unless a connection could be established by sea with London. This he pleaded for, but little was done to relieve him for several months.[24] The whole financial management in Scotland was in confusion throughout the rebellion, which accounts for much of the ineffectiveness of the Scottish local officials.

Another move suggested by the Scots was to organize local troops under the command of loyal Scottish lords. Forbes strongly advocated this measure, but Tweeddale resisted it. Then Forbes tried to enlist Harrington's support for the move, since Tweeddale refused. Other Scottish lords, led by the Earl of Stair, the Duke of Montrose, and the Earl of Marchmont, gained Pelham's approval, upon which Tweeddale gave up blocking the plan.[25] It failed, however, because Oswald Campbell, a member of the northern nobility, attacked the government on another issue in the Commons. As a result, Bolingbroke recommended that Marchmont and the others give up the plan lest they be accused of aiding the rebels. Once again the old distrust of the Scots by the English proved too strong for cooperation.

Local defense was agreed to in the northern counties of England. Lord Rutherford, the ranking lord present in Fife, was unable to get money to defend that Scottish county. Lord Lonsdale was ordered to do, in Westmorland and Cumberland, exactly what Rutherford wanted to do, but

Lonsdale had fewer than 600 men, and they were almost unorganized.[26] It was a policy that showed an unrealistic view of the situation. Local defense was possible only where the nobles were willing to lead it, and in those places it should have been encouraged. Yorkshire was the one county that really made an effort at defense. The Earl of Malton and the Archbishop of York led the organization, and almost all elements of society joined. Viscount Irwin was given the right to grant commissions in the East Riding, and it is probable that Malton and the D'Arcys had similar rights in their Ridings. Stores, arms, and ammunition were ordered sent to the three Lords Lieutenant from Hull.[27] With this supply, plus military authority and attitude, Malton, Irwin, D'Arcy, and the Archbishop were able to establish a force that, though not strong, was capable of some defense. If others had done as much, the rebels might never have reached Derby.

Returning again to the time of Prestonpans, that battle caused another danger to the government. The news of the defeat caused stocks to fall, and a run on the Bank of England was started. One clergyman favorable to the government blamed the opponents of the cabinet for the run on the Bank. This seems quite unlikely, however, for just at that time Tweeddale and Granville began to stress unity of the nation. The merchants of London saved the situation by forming an association to receive and make payments in notes.[28] These powerful London interests prevented any serious damage to the prestige of the cabinet and helped Pelham remain in power. This was not to be the only time that Pelham's cultivation of the London merchants and monied groups paid political dividends. Their cooperation with him in 1746 has already been noted, and after the war there were to be similar instances.

The financial crisis, in spite of its brief nature, and the defeat of Prestonpans marked the end of a time of hope on the part of the cabinet and the beginning of a time of real disaster. The second phase of the rebellion began early in October. This was the critical period, for during the following sixty days the rebel army was at the height of its power and had almost free scope to exploit its advantage. It was also the period in which the extreme weakness of the Jacobite cause in England was proved completely. Even more than by the final military defeat of Prince Charles at Culloden Moor, the Jacobites were ruined by their own ineffectiveness, for at the high point of power they achieved nothing. That discouraged more prospective adherents than any military defeat.

During this period rumors played freely over Great Britain. Often minor participants in the rebellion were captured, and they reported all kinds of plans on the part of the rebel army. They also related that there were many active rebels among the English. These rumors upset any considered estimation of the military situation. Other reports circulated news of landings in the west of England and Catholic support of them. Still others announced that French ships were loose in the Channel and preparing to aid the rebels. And finally, there were many reports that additional clans, such as the Mackenzies, Fraziers, and Macintoshes, were joining the Stuart army. Above all else the great fear of a French invasion was widespread and created further anxiety. Many warnings of this nature reached Newcastle and the cabinet.[29] One particular word of an actual invasion at Hastings caused a cabinet meeting in the small hours of the morning. That the invasion turned out to be smugglers pursued by Admiral Vernon's men only proved how on edge the cabinet was.[30] The government did its own share in provoking these rumors, sending spies indiscriminately into Scotland, France, and parts of England and accepting their reports without attempt to learn whether they were true. In the face of the rumors, the cabinet delayed making any decisions other than those absolutely necessary in order to retain its position. Chesterfield continued to send reports, based on Irish intelligence, that there was no danger from the rebellion and that it could be easily met.[31] The government was slow in making decisions, but Chesterfield completely failed to grasp the situation when he reported no danger. He was, however, right in his over-all estimate that the rebellion did not have the strength to be successful. The rumors were only important because there was no accurate way to check them, and the cabinet was often afraid to act against them lest it make a mistake.

To take some action, while waiting for an army to collect, the government tried to promote local defense. For example, Sussex landowners and men of wealth pledged money to form a system of defense. The Dukes of Dorset and Richmond, as well as Newcastle and Henry Pelham, each contributed £500; Lords Gage and Abergavenny, the Bishops of Chichester and St. Davids, and the Dean and Chapter of Chichester each gave £200. Three others gave £100 each, and many contributed lesser sums.[32] The Treasury made money available to northern English officials, such as the Mayor of Newcastle-upon-Tyne, to pay for their defense.[33] But again, local defense was most well organized in Yorkshire. The rapid work of Malton, Irwin, D'Arcy, and the Archbishop paid returns in the form of an organization that could make use of supplies while most other areas merely wasted what was sent to them.

Arms were supplied, though far fewer than were requested. The central government, realizing that its supplies were not equal to the task, sent reasonable instructions to Yorkshire. The main order was to obstruct and distress the rebels if they entered Yorkshire and especially to make it difficult for them to get provisions—in other words, to avoid open battle but otherwise delay them as much as possible.[34] These were the best possible orders to be sent to such a local force, and showed that someone in London saw what could be expected and was working for time to assemble an English army. Lady Isabella Finch wrote to her brother, Lord Malton: "you've got imense Reputation, by supporting the Government at your own Expence" against possible rebel attack.[35]

The Yorkshire organization was worth fitting out with arms, but it was only a good example among bad copies. In no other county was there anywhere near as much work done and as many results achieved, and this probably had some weight in Jacobite councils when they decided to push into England in the west.

In October the Scots revived their plan to arm loyal companies. This time some of the most important nobles joined in the move. Marchmont applied again to Newcastle, who gave a favorable hearing to the plan. However, when Stair approached Harrington, the earl was rebuffed and was told that only Argyll would be allowed to arm in Scotland. Pelham had discussed the matter with Marchmont's brother and attempted to get an independent view of Scotland from him. When Stair proposed a specific plan to the Council, most members were surprised and delayed making a decision. In a few days it became clear that Pelham had decided against the plan, and it was finally rejected by the cabinet.[36] Instead Pelham favored the hiring of more Hessian troops. The cabinet named the Earl of Home as commander of Edinburgh with power to enlist men; the like power was given to the Earl of Glencairn as commander of Glasgow. It was obvious that the English cabinet was afraid to trust the great Scottish lords for political reasons, and therefore took a compromise position that could not work.

The rebels easily captured Edinburgh except for the castle. The flight southward of Archibald Stewart, the Provost of Edinburgh, reflected the turmoil of the borderlands and the army. Very unjustly he had been blamed by everyone for the fall of the capital, and he resented the reflections cast on him.[37] Other reports reaching London were even more exaggerated and suggested that the whole north of England was in a chaotic condition. The government, frightened, ordered Cope to be examined by a court-martial. He was relieved of his command, and Marshal Wade was sent north to replace him. Pelham had so far lost his calm at this time that he joined in the applause for Wade with hopes that the Marshal would succeed where Cope had failed.[38] The rebels in Edinburgh broke connections completely between the north and England. This meant that news and reports of the rebels' progress was even poorer than before. Now the government could not even receive accurate accounts of rebel moves in the Lowlands. The absolute lack of news is shown by the many different reports on the Jacobite army in Edinburgh and especially in its departure from the capital. It was small wonder that the swift fall of Carlisle to the rebels produced the utmost confusion, for no one had known what to expect. Even the unruffled Hardwicke showed signs of succumbing to terror at the arrival of the news.[39] Everything now waited on the arrival of the "white hope," the Duke of Cumberland.

When the rebel army moved south from Carlisle, no one in London knew what road it would take or what was the goal of the march. New-

castle reflected the general fear and excitement of the London inhabitants
in his series of letters to the Duke of Richmond during the invasion of
England by Charles Edward. Moreover, the nature of the rebel army
made it almost impossible to form a defense without overwhelming
numbers, for the rebel troops were largely irregulars who were accustomed to the hills and cross-country travel. Every move by a small
English defensive force was futile, because the rebels would simply
detour around it and then proceed south.[40] The English army had no
general or officers who understood this fluid type of battle line, and
consequently what troops there were in the west were useless. Nature
also helped the rebels, for the very severe weather prevented Marshal
Wade from crossing the mountains from the east. He finally retired to
Newcastle-upon-Tyne. Thus the only English army actually in the north
was prevented from making contact with the Jacobite army. Any future
success, as has been noted, depended on the Duke of Cumberland, who
was organizing his army, brought from Flanders, at Oxford.[41] By this
time Pelham's usual calm had returned, and he wrote,

> I find your neighbors are alarmed at the approach of the rebels. I don't won-
> der at it, but, by our intelligence, it does not look as if they meant to come
> your way to York. They are undoubtedly not so terrible as they have been
> lately represented, nor so insignificant as they were thought by some at first.
> Thank God, we have now an army in England.[42]

The farther the rebel army came south, the more sensible the government
became, because it soon was clear that the goal would have to be either
Chester or Derby. News from the invaded area came more quickly to
London, and it could be trusted to a much greater degree. It also became
plain that no English would be rising to join the Stuart cause, and this
removed one of the cabinet's fears.

Early in December another flurry of fear seized southern England
when it was learned that the French were embarking troops at Dunkirk.
The old scare of French invasion was loose, from London to the east
and south. The cabinet therefore had to provide for southern defenses
without weakening Cumberland. The only widespread fear regarding
the rebels at this time was that they might slip away from their pursuit of
Cumberland and join the French when they landed. Pelham asked the
Commons for money to pay 6,000 Hessians to defend southern England.[43]
An invasion by France was without doubt the major fear throughout the
rebellion. It explains—as fear of the rebels does not—the care taken to
keep some troops in the south, though they were needed in the north. It
explains why arms and supplies were kept in London instead of being sent
north. And it explains why the cabinet eyed the rebellion with a cautious
look, lest it have its back completely turned to the Channel. The French
fear vanished quickly, for when the rebels left Derby and turned back
northward, the government realized there was no coordinated attack

planned. After initial fears of the direction of the rebels from Derby, the leaders of the English army, local militia, and ministry settled down to await news of a speedy suppression of the rebellion.[44] Unfortunately the conquest of the rebel army did not occur as rapidly as most thought it would, for a major battle had to be fought. Rightly, however, the government considered the dangerous phase of the rebellion to be over at this point.

The early months of 1746 were disappointing to the English, for although the rebel army retreated steadily northward, there was no victory. In fact, most of the small engagements were won by the Scots. Duncan Forbes bombarded London with pleas for arms and money with which to organize an army in the north of Scotland. His relative, John Forbes, wrote that the pressure was removed from the cabinet and it was unlikely that the President's requests would be filled.[45] Lord Stair answered the pleas finally with small amounts of arms and money sent by sea, but recommended that Forbes continue to supply himself by contracts that could be settled later.[46] One major reason for the apparent indifference of the cabinet was the great amount of time consumed in preparing for the political crisis of February 10, 1746, which has already been discussed. One of the steps in the political attack on Granville was the complete removal of Tweeddale from his employments.[47] The marquis had mismanaged Scottish affairs in the early stages of the rebellion and deserved dismissal for that reason, but as a political friend of Granville he was even more vulnerable to attack by the Pelhams. They had to use the threat of the rebellion to be sure of victory over Granville, and until the political victory was won they were handicapped in directing the war. It was not surprising to find that they turned their attention to those matters once the immediate crisis was past.

The news of the defeat of Marshal Wade at Falkirk turned eyes momentarily northward. Cumberland, who was busy organizing southern defenses, was sent to Scotland again to restore confidence. London then returned to the more congenial pursuit of a political foe and left the duke to care for the military enemy. After February 14 and the complete triumph of the Pelham cabinet, attention again turned northward.

Cumberland pursued a policy of harsh treatment of the country through which his army moved. The cabinet had little to do with his decisions, which he made as the field commander. By no means was the cabinet in full accord with the policy, but since the leaders were not firmly agreed on what should be done, they passively accepted Cumberland's acts as necessary. Lord Chesterfield was the one cabinet member who urged extremely stern treatment of the Scots and in fact even advocated more severe penalties than Cumberland meted out.[48] Until the middle of April, Cumberland advanced cautiously; he wisely made sure of the rear areas before he advanced. The careful military methods paid dividends, for an increasing number of the rebel leaders fell into

English hands and were sent south. Finally, on April 14, while the English were camped on Culloden Moor, Prince Charles tried a surprise attack, which failed, and in the ensuing battle Jacobitism was destroyed as an effective force in Great Britain.[49]

The Battle of Culloden Moor resulted in the death or capture of many rebel leaders, though the prince escaped to become the wandering "Bonnie Prince Charlie" of legend until the following September, when he escaped to France.[50] The principal military task remaining was to clear the Highlands of the isolated armed bands that had escaped the battle. The government in London was finally relieved of the one situation which could have made possible a successful French invasion, and the ministers were jubilant at the success. Pelham himself was strangely quiet, and no letters of his remain to explain his views. However, his placid approach to almost every problem is perhaps sufficient reason why there is no note of rejoicing by him.

The ordinary functions of government could not be restored in Scotland until Cumberland's mopping-up operations were completed. Therefore in large measure the duke was dictator of the northern kingdom. Judges were ordered to discontinue their circuits for the time being. Prisoners were to be tried, and the three most important ones—the earls of Kilmarnock and Cromartie and Lord Balmerino—were sent to the Tower. Troops were reduced, and Pelham directed the return of some to England. Duncan Forbes tried to regulate the actions of some of the lesser rebellious nobles. Pelham was sent secret reports on Jacobite activities and names of men to be watched. And Cumberland started the machinery that would eventually rewrite many Scottish laws so that a similar rebellion would not occur again.[51] These moves were all useful, or at least attempted to be useful. Cumberland, however, did much to destroy any return of good will by his final military acts of brutality and repression. They were unnecessary in most cases, and his fears and hatred of the Scots were unreasonable.[52] A certain amount of the blame for his actions during the summer must be laid on the cabinet, especially the Secretaries of State, but in the last analysis Cumberland alone must be declared guilty. That a large yearly annuity was approved for Cumberland after Culloden Moor was not unusual, but flattery of the man was not necessary. Culloden Moor, however, remained the one great victory of the English in the War of the Austrian Succession, and that determined the favored position of the Duke of Cumberland.

CHAPTER XIV

Settlement of the Jacobite Question

❧ AS EARLY AS January 30, 1746, the cabinet was asked to make decisions on the treatment of prisoners captured and on a settlement in Scotland. At that time Cumberland advised a harsh policy.[1] As his armies pressed north, he became more outspoken in his opinions, and ten days before Culloden Moor he said:

> All in this country are almost to a man Jacobites; and the mild measures will not do. You will find, that the whole of the laws of this *ancient kingdom* must be new modelled. . . . Were I to enumerate the villains and villainies this country abounds in, I should never have done.[2]

As long as Cumberland was in Great Britain, he made his views important. At one point during the summer Pelham wrote that Cumberland would probably direct Scottish policy and expressed the belief and hope that the duke would act correctly.[3]

On the other hand, Duncan Forbes, Lord Stair, and the Earl of Crawford pressed for lenient treatment of the Highlanders and a policy of clemency.[4] These three men irritated Cumberland and caused him to insist on having his way. Pelham took a quiet hand in the quarrel and pursued a compromise policy. He proceeded severely against some leaders, but recognized that Cumberland's ideas were unsound and could achieve no lasting result but hatred.[5] As leader of the cabinet, Pelham had to keep Cumberland's favor because of the European war and because the prince was George's favorite. It was impossible to follow any other course of action.

From the summer of 1746 until his death, Pelham kept a careful watch on affairs in Scotland. He did not openly attempt to issue orders, for that was in the department of the Secretaries, but little hints occur at random which indicate that Pelham was at work. Sometimes he took part in government meetings dealing with Scotland. By 1749 Hardwicke made most of the decisions on Scottish matters because they were largely legal. Pelham saw and approved the Chancellor's acts before anything was done, and Newcastle was merely given a chance to approve without taking an active part. At other times Pelham dealt directly with Scots and tried to win their support by favors and flattery. But most important of all, he had his own secret sources of information in Scotland. The other cabinet officers did not know who his informants were, and they are unknown today. Some news must have come to Pelham from the Treasury officials in Scotland, and Robert Dundas was quite probably one of Pelham's main sources of information.[6] From the few remnants of this correspondence available today, the news sent was of all kinds and covered items from regular government matters to Jacobitism. Pelham was probably the best informed cabinet member on the subject of Scotland, and his sensible approach to the settlement was probably the result of his clearer picture of the northern kingdom.

The cabinet moved quickly to bring some leaders of the rebellion to trial, and on July 28, 1746, Hardwicke was created Lord High Steward of Great Britain to preside at a trial for high treason against Kilmarnock, Cromartie, and Balmerino.[7] These men were lodged in the Tower of London under the special guard of General Williamson, but they were allowed to write letters and receive visitors. Balmerino even wrote to Newcastle for favors, which were granted.[8] The men were tried in Westminster Hall by the House of Lords and found guilty. The usual sentence was passed, but the Earl of Cromartie was reprieved and finally pardoned as a sign of the king's mercy. The trial was carried off with dignity and legality, though there was never any question of the final verdict. In fact, all three admitted their guilt, and the public was only surprised at the few who were tried. Soon after the trial Simon Fraser, Lord Lovat, one of the principals of the rebellion, was captured and sent to Edinburgh Castle. The following March 9 Hardwicke was again created Lord High Steward, and Lovat, the wily old Scot, was brought to trial before the House of Lords. Lovat used all his tricks during the trial to keep from being found guilty, but to no avail. The Lords found him guilty by the unanimous vote of 117 to 0. No one found time to sympathize with the old man, who had earlier been pardoned for his part in the rebellion of 1715. In April the last action for these trials took place when Hardwicke received £1,000 to cover his expenses as Lord High Steward.[9] The Chancellor had done his job well and with dignity, and his fellow ministers and the king rewarded him generously.

While these four major trials were being held, the cabinet was preparing the legal case against the lesser captives. Lord George Murray, one of Prince Charles's principal advisers, was taken, but he gave full evidence to the government and was never tried. Murray testified in secret examinations before Hardwicke, Newcastle, Harrington, and Pelham. The evidence obtained was largely unused because the ministers were satisfied with the four examples already made and held the other prisoners at their mercy. By February 1747 Hardwicke insisted that some agreement must be reached on the disposition of the prisoners still in custody. After much discussion the cabinet leaders decided to issue an act of indemnity for all the lesser people involved, in order to reduce the murmuring of the citizens and because further investigations might prove embarrassing to themselves. Lord George Murray had let the names of a few people, like

Sir Watkin William Wynn, slip into his testimony, and the Tories joined the Whigs to prevent any further errors. Murray also mentioned a Sir John Dayles, who was a member of parliament, and Pelham was afraid that any such citations would seriously reflect on the administration. Many years later Philip Yorke noted on the bottom of one of the letters discussing the situation that there was a "remarkable shyness" on the part of both Pelhams in regard to involving any Englishman in the rebellion.[10] He even suggested that they may have had a personal reason not to proceed further. The personal implication must be regarded as false, since all other proof is against it, but some others of the administration might not have been so unassailable.

From 1746 until 1748 there were many pleas for mercy for prisoners not covered by the general pardon. The lords still in custody exerted all the influence they could through friends and relatives. By the end of 1748 almost all prisoners had been released or tried for a crime.[11] Jacobitism did not cease with the military defeat and the following trials, but it did become almost hopeless and lost many past or prospective adherents. On the treatment of individual rebels, therefore, Cumberland's harsh policy was supplanted by the more merciful one of the Pelhams. This fact alone goes far toward placing responsibility for the cruelties of the last weeks of the military campaign squarely on Cumberland. It was against the character of either Pelham or Newcastle to support brutality, and Pelham never reversed his policies so sharply in any other case.

There were several other problems arising out of the rebellion. Many requests were received asking payment for damage done to property. Several of the Scots lords demanded repayment of their money spent in defense. The Church of Scotland was granted money each year from 1749 to 1752 to pay itinerant preachers who were supposed to promote protestantism in the Highlands. And rewards for Jacobite information were paid out often. The sums of money involved were seldom great, but they did restrict other activities which the cabinet wanted to undertake at various times. It must have been expensive to meet these demands and still pay for government. To all of these must be added the political and administrative expenses in Scotland, which were large.[12]

The first important problem that arose in the administration of Scotland—one unconnected with the rebellion—was the death of Duncan Forbes, Lord President of the Sessions, in December 1747. The cabinet spent considerable time finding a successor to the efficient and trusted Forbes.[13] In the end Pelham chose Robert Dundas for the important post, but Forbes's experience and respect were sorely missed. Positions on the Board of Sessions were always considered very important, and the cabinet was careful in its nominations. In 1750 another vacancy occurred on the Board, and the correspondence on the replacement briefly summarizes the Pelhams' attitudes. Henry Pelham notified Newcastle of the vacancy and said:

He [President of the Sessions] recommended nobody, but wished we would well consider whom to recommend to the King. This last man, tho a good Lawyer did sadly. We both agree that no hasty engagement should be made. Ability and above all Loyalty is to be considered. and out of what shop to be sure of that I protest I don't know.[14]

Newcastle's reply expressed another aspect of the problem of any high office at the time. On the matter of the vacant judgeship, he wrote:

I entirely agree with you, That great Care should be taken, in filling it up; And That, above all Things, No one should be put in, That is not zealous for the Government. And being so in His Own Person, is not sufficient; For If His Friends, & Connections, are not zealous Friends also; He may do almost as bad, as If He was ill-intention'd Himself.[15]

There were three attributes desired by the Pelhams for any person appointed to office in Scotland: knowledge, efficiency, and political reliability. It is not without importance that such views were held by the leading members of the English cabinet. That contemporaries recognized the reasonableness of the Pelhams' demand is shown in the stressing of ability in all recommendations to fill vacant positions sent to Pelham. In this particular case, the Earl of Morton sent a list of well-qualified choices.[16] Clearly the Pelhams were interested in naming a capable official, perhaps even more than they were in the case of equally important English posts.

The same problem of reliable Scots always came up when an election drew near. Pelham was interested in the slate of sixteen Scottish peers, and carefully went over the list with Argyll and Newcastle before approving each choice. Political reliability was, of course, the primary requisite in these cases, but for Treasury positions and Scottish administrative places, knowledge and efficiency were the main considerations with Pelham. When Robert Dundas died in August, 1753, the same three qualifications were again stressed, and this was in the midst of an election year when all interest might reasonably be expected to center on politics.[17] No one could claim that the Pelhams were always successful in their selection of officials for Scotland, but the evidence supports the claim that, at least, Henry Pelham tried to name the best available men.

Another aspect of the settlement was legislative in nature. Following the rebellion, parliament enacted three main bills that dealt with the reorganization of Scotland's old laws to make new rebellions more difficult. The first bill was directed at disarming the Highlanders; the second attacked the heritable jurisdictions of the chiefs of the clans; and the third regulated the disposition of the estates forfeited by their owners because of Jacobite activity and participation in the rebellion. All three were necessary, and the last two did much, eventually, to consolidate the Union of 1707. While parts of the first bill, such as the banning of Highland dress, were foolish and made reconciliation more difficult, over the long period these were forgotten. On the whole the three bills represented a policy of moderation, in contrast to Cumberland's harsh military suppression, and the cabinet deserved credit for pushing them through parliament.

As soon as the news of Culloden Moor reached London, the cabinet set to work to enact the legislation necessary to prevent another rebellion. Hardwicke, as the highest legal authority in the cabinet, engaged in a series of consultations with Scottish lawyers on the terms of such a bill. When he had outlined an effective bill, he sent it to Pelham for approval. Pelham, after approving the suggested measure, forwarded it to the Attorney-General for preparation in final form and predicted that passage by the Commons would be swift.[18] The bill as finally drafted stated as its purpose:

> An Act for the more effective disarming the Highlands in Scotland; and for more effectual securing the Peace of the said Highlands; and for restraining the Use of the Highland Dress; and for indemnifying the Judges and other Officers of the Court of Judiciary in Scotland for not performing the Northern Circuit.[19]

It was therefore designed to meet immediate problems and reduce localism. In the first aim it was successful, but, as for the second, it had a negative effect for many years: It merely drove local loyalties underground. The bill became law in June in spite of the protests of faithful Scots like Lord Glenorchy, who pointed out in specific instances the flaws that would make it impossible to enforce and also the fact that it reduced the power of the loyal lords even more than that of the disloyal. As a result of such reasoned protests and its own doubts, the cabinet decided to move slowly in further legislation against the Scots. Newcastle sent for Forbes to come to London and advise on future laws so that the cabinet would be spared further criticism.[20]

It was almost a year before the next major bill on Scotland was passed. Hardwicke again worked long hours preparing a measure for the abolition of the heritable jurisdictions, those private systems of law courts that flourished among some of the clans. In February 1747 the cabinet met to make final decisions on the prospective bill. Pelham had insisted that action be taken so that the legislature could pass the bill during the current session. He expected trouble in the Commons over it, and the Speaker was dubious that it could be passed. Pelham and Onslow had been worried by the great number of letters, memorials, notes, and protests against the bill, and they wanted to present it before opposition could grow even greater.[21] The bill as presented proclaimed itself:

> An Act for taking away and abolishing the Heretable Jurisdictions in that Part of Great Britain called Scotland; and for making Satisfaction to the Proprietors thereof; and for restoring such Jurisdictions to the Crown; and for

making more effectual Provision for the Administration of Justice throughout that Part of the United Kingdom, by the King's Courts and Judges there; and for rendering the Union of the Two Kingdoms more complete.[22]

After long and heated debate the Commons passed the bill by 233 to 102, and a month later the Lords approved it by a 79 to 16 vote.[23] The opposition in the Commons was so large because the bill provided a convenient "screen" for all who disliked the Pelhams, and in both houses Tories made up almost the entire opposition. By the end of 1747 William Grant, Lord Advocate of Scotland, had listed the value of the jurisdictions as claimed by the lords. There were 157 claims set at a value of £582,990, and with this as a basis the measures of the bill were put into action.[24] In a peaceful fashion the Pelham administration had enacted one of the most salutory laws of the eighteenth century.

The other major bill was much longer in the process of passage. In December 1746 William Grant initiated the measure by proposing methods of dealing with the forfeited estates of the rebels. During 1747 steps were taken in Scotland by the Barons of the Exchequer for the administration of the estates. And this indeterminate status lasted until 1752 when parliament enacted:

A Act for annexing certain forfeited Estates in Scotland to the Crown unalienably; and for making Satisfaction to the lawful Creditors thereupon; and to establish a Method of managing the same; and applying the Rents and Profits thereof, for the better civilizing and improving the Highlands of Scotland; and preventing Disorders there for the future.[25]

The bill set up a commission of Scottish lords, officials, and prominent commoners to administer the forfeited estates. Because the commission was large and rather unwieldy, Pelham and Hardwicke made decisions and relied on the President of the Sessions and Lord Justice Clerk to carry them out.[26] In the final result the commission made the small decisions and the cabinet leaders made the major ones. It was a very practical division and held the possibility of improving conditions in the Highlands.

Various other bills were passed, but the three above were the keystones in the structure of a new Scotland. The Lord Provost of Edinburgh wrote, "There has been more real good done to this part of the united kingdom, During the currency of this present parliament, Than Ever has been done for it since it was a nation." [27] Historians have long recognized this contribution of the Pelham administration.

After the collapse of the rebellion in 1746 and Cumberland's tactics in the mopping-up campaign, Jacobitism hid its head. During the years in which the cabinet and parliament were considering the enactment of remedial legislation, the old Jacobite leaders fled abroad or quietly stayed at home to avoid notice. In reality Jacobitism died during these years from the succession of wounds it had received. However, as in the days of Walpole, it rose as a political issue. This time it became a weapon in the hands of the opposition. It is true that occasionally nonpolitical charges of Jacobitism were raised, but these were exceptions.[28]

In 1752 the first of two Jacobite charges was laid against the Pelham administration by its political enemies. Rumors were spread first about some of the minor political agents of the Pelhams, and the groundwork for the attack was laid. Then in March the Duke of Cumberland, the new leader of one faction of the opposition, gave the king a packet of papers that purported to be proof of widespread Jacobite activity by officials in Scotland. The most specific charge was that the Pelham administration had appointed and maintained known Jacobites in important and lucrative posts in Scotland. Pelham was angry, and announced that he considered the whole thing a direct attack on himself because he had refused to satisfy Cumberland's desire for power and especially military authority. He therefore undertook a careful examination of the charges with the approval of the king. From the beginning Pelham wanted a secret enquiry conducted by himself, while Newcastle wished to make it public and reap any political advantages possible. It was finally agreed that Holdernesse should conduct a public examination based on information from official sources while Hardwicke secretly collected information from private sources. The investigation progressed through the spring without revealing any startling reports. The leaders of the government were rather pleased than otherwise, for they felt the results would vindicate them.[29] The king was immensely pleased with Pelham for the examination and praised him highly.

Pelham used all kinds of people, from the Lord President of the Sessions to army officers and native Scots, as his sources of information. He ordered that all suspected persons should be immediately removed, and he happily reported to Newcastle that the number dismissed was much smaller than he had thought probable. In fact, only one important office was proved to be held by a Jacobite or Non-Juror: the Lord Justice Clerk.[30] When the results were made public, the opposition suffered for having made the charges, for no one would believe that Andrew Fletcher, the Lord Justice Clerk, and a few minor officeholders were serious threats. Pelham gained greatly by admitting that errors might have been made and by trying to correct them. The final result was that Pelham was more secure in power than before, with the support of both the king and the public.

In spite of the failure of the Jacobite charges in 1752, the same opposition group tried again the next year. As the general charges had failed, in their second attempt Cumberland, Bedford, and their friends backed specific charges against a few men. Early in February, Lord Ravensworth told Pelham that he had strong evidence of Jacobitism against Andrew Stone, William Murray, and the Bishop of Gloucester—the principal

members of the Prince of Wales' Household. On February 15, Lord
Ravensworth presented his accusations before the Privy Council, made
up of Canterbury, Hardwicke, Granville, Grafton, Devonshire, Argyll,
Newcastle, Hartington, Holdernesse, Anson, and Pelham.[31] Since Newcastle was particularly alarmed by the charges against Stone because they
came close to him personally, he was given every opportunity to defend
himself.[32] Ravensworth's evidence finally depended on the testimony of a
certain Mr. Fawcett, who, when examined by the Council, became involved in many contradictions and refused to make definite statements.
In the quarrel between Ravensworth and Fawcett on the nature of the
latter's testimony, the Dean of Durham supported Ravensworth's position. Stone was then called to present his defense. He denied the charges
completely and introduced the Bishops of St. Asaph and Gloucester and
Mr. Caley as witnesses to prove his innocence. The next day William
Murray, the Solicitor-General, was called at his own request, and he
likewise denied all charges. Murray took the view that the charges were
already disproved by the evidence. A few days later the Council unani-
mously agreed that the charges were "false, scandalous, & malicious." [33]
All three men were cleared.

The pleasure of the members of the government at the unanimity of
the decision was best expressed by Pitt when he said, "I . . . rejoice
sincerely in the unanimous and honourable justification of those Gentlemen, whose names had been so strangely attack'd." [34] It was not surprising to find the three cleared, since the cabinet dominated the Council, but unanimity was a great success for the government. The Bedford
Whigs were not willing, however, to let the matter drop, and they
brought the charges into the House of Lords. Pelham and Newcastle
considered this a direct attack on themselves, and they collected their
friends and allies to defeat the move.[35] They won success there, since
only political purposes motivated Bedford and the whole house knew it.
After this defeat the clamor died down, and Jacobitism in all its aspects
was finished for the remainder of Pelham's life.[36]

The entire history of Jacobitism during Pelham's administration further expanded his prestige and importance. He had been the leader in
dealing with the rebellion. If any member of the cabinet had retained
his presence of mind, it was Pelham, and he had made every effort to prepare the armed defense. He had favored a lenient program after the rebellion, and he had taken a large part in organizing the remedial legislation and getting its various bills passed by parliament over opposition.
And finally, he had met political attacks using Jacobitism as a cover and
had defeated them. He admitted that his administration was not perfect
and tried to correct its imperfections. Only a man secure in his knowledge of his ability could have done that. At the end Pelham was more
firmly entrenched in the king's favor and more strongly approved by the
public than before. He deserved his victory.

BOOK THREE

The Domination of Henry Pelham

CHAPTER XV

Foreign Policy, 1748–1754

🌱 FOLLOWING THE TREATY of Aix-la-Chapelle, peace returned to Europe, but it was an unstable peace. Beyond the geographic limits of Europe, England and France continued their rivalries in India, the West Indies, and continental America. Only a thin line separated these clashes from a full-scale war. Within Europe the peace was only a little more secure, for Austria was unreconciled to the terms of the treaty and Prussia was seeking further recognition. Other nations, such as Spain and Holland, were negotiating to recover their declining fortunes. In the face of these unsettled conditions, every European government attempted to establish alliances that would protect its own position.

In the English cabinet it was Newcastle who sought a means of consolidating the unstable peace of Europe. The most obvious prospect was to settle German affairs in such a way that both Austria and Prussia would be satisfied; then an overwhelming alliance could be formed against France. An opportunity presented itself in the old custom of electing a King of the Romans as heir to the Holy Roman Empire. Austria originated the question to insure the Hapsburg titular position in Germany, and George II and Newcastle grasped at the possibility of electing Archduke Joseph and thereby stabilizing relations in Germany. The plans and negotiations to achieve this election occupied almost three years and were the central aim of Newcastle's foreign policy.

By May 1750 Newcastle had enthusiastically proposed plans to gain the election with Prussian approval and thus oblige Austria. Pelham agreed that Newcastle should try to win the support of the electors but opposed using English subsidies to do it. He feared that without lavish subsidies Austria would not make the necessary concessions to please the other electors.[1] From the very beginning of the negotiations, therefore, he insisted that a minimum of money be spent. Hardwicke wrote to Newcastle and warned him that care must be taken if Pelham was to agree, for

> Your Grace knows very well the weight I lay upon the First of them, the Election of a King of the Romans, tho' I find it is not look'd upon by some others in the same degree. Your Brother yields to the face of it, but I find suspects that some Game may be play'd between the Court of Vienna, & those Electors, who alledge Grievances against them, to try to make up ye Differences by English money, instead of that Court's yielding to their Demands.[2]

171

Newcastle's plan was based on the fact that the electors were divided into three groups: those who supported a Hapsburg candidate (Bohemia, Mainz, Trier, and Hanover), those who opposed a Hapsburg (Brandenburg and the Palatinate), and those who were neutral (Bavaria, Cologne, and Saxony). Since a majority vote was required, at least one of the neutrals had to be won over to the support of the Austrians. During the war England had formed a subsidy treaty with Cologne for troops. Newcastle renegotiated this to include a secret understanding about the vote. However, he felt that Bavaria should be added to make the final result certain. His aim was, therefore, to negotiate a treaty with Bavaria similar to the one with Cologne, which ostensibly supplied troops to England when needed, in return for a subsidy, but secretly pledged the Bavarian vote to Austria. It was this use of subsidies to gain a non-English purpose to which Pelham objected. He was especially wary of doing anything that might revive the old charges of "Hanoverian minister."

While Newcastle was in Hanover during the summer he actively pursued the election scheme, always assuring Pelham that the Bavarian treaty was the only one he needed, though he might like a Saxon treaty also. Pelham, in return, accepted the Bavarian subsidy but insisted that payment be tied to the actual election. By the end of June Newcastle found the Bavarian negotiation was bogging down. He began to hint to Pelham that another treaty with Saxony would speed the entire affair and make it certain.[3] In reply Pelham said almost nothing except in regard to expenses:

> The Civil list, you know is much in debt. . . . I have endeavored to lessen the expences att home as much as possible, and have succeeded as far as relates to my own Office but a long series of uninterrupted extravagance to call it by no worse name, having got into all the great offices of the Kingdom, makes it very difficult, if not impracticable for the best intentioned to get the better of habit and custom.[4]

Nevertheless Newcastle continued to treat with Bavaria and to dream about Saxony.

Because of Austrian refusal to make concessions to Bavaria, it seemed during July that the prospective treaty had failed. Newcastle was quite discouraged. A few days later, however, the duke's patience was rewarded, for Bavaria gave in to the proposals and signed the treaty.[5] Pelham, Hardwicke, Pitt, and others were greatly pleased, but they were premature in their praise. No sooner had the Bavarian matter been settled than the Archbishop of Cologne made new demands.

Cologne's attitude made Newcastle furious, and he fired off letters of protest in all directions. He knew no reason for the renunciation of the treaty unless it was greed for money. But Newcastle had an alternative plan. He committed himself to the task of using the Cologne subsidy to pay either Saxony or the Palatinate and thereby replace the loss of Cologne's troops and vote.[6] At the same time the Elector Palatine indicated that he would negotiate if Austria would not refuse to make concessions.[7] The Palatinate was kept from negotiating because Austria refused to accept its terms and especially because France backed the decision. Throughout the rest of 1750 and 1751, the prospects for the election and the treaties swung back and forth from gloomy to bright.

At the beginning of May 1752, Pelham, Hardwicke, Holdernesse, and Granville approved Newcastle's renewed insistence on Austrian concessions but sounded a warning to Newcastle to beware of Austrian secret negotiations with other nations. By the end of the month it was painfully clear that Austria had no intention of ever negotiating. Again Newcastle was furious, and Pelham was disappointed, though he told his brother that he had always expected this.[8] Newcastle, however, soon regained his enthusiasm for the election even without Austrian help. He sounded out the other electors and came to the conclusion that if the Palatinate was paid a subsidy of £50,000 or £60,000, a unanimous vote could be achieved with French approval.[9] Since Newcastle was afraid that this new approach to the election would not gain Pelham's support, he used Hardwicke to present the proposition to the cabinet leaders. The Chancellor made the suggestion, believing that though Pelham was against it, he would eventually agree to save Newcastle embarrassment. In fact Pelham gave in surprisingly easily, with the stipulation that if the plan did not achieve the goal, then the whole election should be dropped. On this basis Newcastle continued to negotiate but with ever-decreasing hopes of success.[10]

In a letter dated August 5, Newcastle wrote Pelham of a new problem: the king's refusal to agree to a payment to the Count Palatine. George II had employed a tactic to which Newcastle had no answer when he asked, "What will your Brother say?"[11] George had shrewdly guessed that Pelham agreed to the negotiation only to keep political peace and that he would switch to the king's side if the monarch strongly objected. Newcastle, with the ground thus cut from under his feet bitterly condemned the courts of France, Prussia, and Austria for having caused so much delay that George changed his mind. In reply Pelham told his brother that he had agreed because if the plan should succeed the money would be well spent.[12] George knew his ministers well and correctly guessed that Pelham would slip out of the treaties if he could do so without irritating Newcastle. Yet this was not the full picture of George's sudden reversal of position. He confided to his Hanoverian ministers, Munchausen and Steinberg, who reported to Newcastle, that he had given up reliance on Austria and wanted the money as a subsidy for Russia.[13] The king was sure that he could "cajole and Manage Mr. Pelham," and his rejection of German alliances was a step in this "managing." George had made only one miscalculation: Pelham would not agree to the Russian subsidy once he had escaped from the German ones. The Prime Minister told George Dodington that he was "always against these subsidies" and had approved spending money for them only when it was to be paid for concrete acts, for then the expenditure could be defended in parliament.[14] The king's action was the final blow to Newcastle's favorite scheme. The Foreign Secretary was unable to overcome Austrian opposition to concessions, Prussian and French enmity, Pelham's unwilling support, and the king's about-face. The policy had the complete approval of Lord Granville and William Pitt, being the same as that pursued by Granville earlier and to be pursued by Pitt later. These two had varying degrees of success, but during the years of Newcastle's efforts almost all conditions were against it. Pelham's disapproval was much more nearly in line with the political facts of 1749–52 and, though he opposed the policy for what would now be called isolationist reasons, he deserves credit for realizing that it would not succeed.

Throughout the eighteenth century the payment of subsidies was the commonly accepted method of negotiating treaties between two states. England, France, Holland, and any other state that was financially able paid large sums of money to lesser states, usually for the promise of troops when needed. As the negotiations over the election of a King of the Romans showed, Pelham was against the normally accepted methods of conducting foreign policy. It was not merely a particular case to which Pelham objected but to subsidies in general, unless definite benefits would result.[15]

Pelham opposed subsidies, but he let Newcastle continue their use and agreed to pay the money involved when Newcastle found no alternative. Pelham's general attitude was that each subsidy was to be the last and no more would be negotiated.[16] He was forced into this untenable position because almost every other member of the British government believed in subsidies, and he could not fight both political friends and enemies.

Of all the subsidies suggested or actually negotiated by Newcastle, Pelham supported the Bavarian treaty most actively. He agreed to it rather easily, since the terms were moderate. Most important, he actively introduced, defended, and got parliament to approve it when it came before the Commons. Newcastle's proposal for a Saxon treaty was cautiously presented to Pelham after he had flatly rejected a loan for that country, and final agreement on the subsidy came at a secret meeting of Newcastle, Hardwicke, and Pelham. As has already been noted, Pelham needed little persuasion, largely because the funds had already been voted for Cologne and the Saxon treaty would mean only a shift of recipient. He really had not changed his opinion about the efficacy of such treaties, but he did present this one to the Commons in his best parliamentary style. Moreover, in spite of his general opposition to subsidies, once they had been negotiated and voted, he loyally supported them and always was able to produce the money when it had to be delivered.[17] Thus it may be said that even those most opposed to subsidies recognized them as one of the safest ways to regulate foreign affairs.

Because of Pelham's known opposition to subsidies, the Elector Palatine presented his demands for English gold in the form of unpaid debts from the War of the Spanish Succession. Pelham, furious at this attempt to extort money from England, flatly denied the justice of any Palatine claims and said that they had all been paid after 1713. As far as any claims for the 1743 campaign were concerned, he said he could produce the Count Palatine's receipt to prove payment. Pelham believed that Cologne, the Palatinate, and Bavaria were working together secretly to force large payments from England to their own advantage. He therefore rejected the Palatine's demands, and they consequently turned again to a subsidy. Pelham finally gave in to this—with qualifications—in order to further the existing foreign negotiations.[18] And once again a subsidy proved to be the easiest way to conduct foreign affairs.

England also tried, through her envoys, to break any subsidy treaties France had contracted, or was projecting, with small countries. One example was the series of instructions sent by Newcastle to Walter Titley, English envoy in Denmark, from May 1749 until December 1753.[19] Throughout the years the English feared that France would draw Denmark more firmly to the French side by means of subsidies. It is plain that the English government was so convinced of the usefulness of subsidies that it left other aspects of diplomacy unexplored. That had long been the cry against Granville by the Pelhams, and by 1752 it was Pelham's clear criticism of Newcastle's policy.

Newcastle's negotiations with the German electors on the election of a King of the Romans and on subsidies was the main diplomatic endeavor of England during the last half of Pelham administration. Yet it was not the most important, though its failure reduced the position of England on the continent to a dangerous state. However, while Newcastle was learning the truth of the Austrian state of mind, other diplomatic efforts were proving more advantageous. In August 1749 General Wall, the Spanish ambassador to England, approached Newcastle and Pelham with a proposal for negotiating a new treaty to replace the trade treaty of 1715. He even hinted that it might be possible to form an alliance of Spain, Holland, and England. After preliminary conferences, the scene was shifted to Madrid, and Sir Benjamin Keene was made the English participant. For the next ten months Keene labored to reach an agreement acceptable to his government, and by July 1750 Pelham agreed to accept the Spanish minister Carvajal's terms, even though he did not like them and felt the South Sea Company would have to be compensated. The interesting point about these negotiations was that Pelham was the cabinet member who directed Keene's moves. Neither Newcastle nor Bedford, in whose department they fell, was very active. Newcastle even wrote that he left the matter to Pelham, who, he hoped, could work out a plan to please every-one concerned.[20] It was the only time Newcastle ever uncomplainingly turned over any part of a foreign affair to another minister.

Under Pelham's leadership the Lords Justices and the cabinet agreed to Keene's negotiation, which reduced Spanish compensation to the South Sea Company to £100,000 if the Spanish agreed to restore the privileges of the treaties of 1667, 1713 (Utrecht), and 1715. Newcastle also agreed to the treaty, though he criticized some of the clauses that were drawn up by Keene and Carvajal. The treaty restored to the British the immunities and privileges of the time of Charles II and gave them the position of a "most favored nation." In return Britain renounced the Asiento Treaty and took £100,000 for compensation. In reality the treaty was very impor-tant, for it revived British trade with the Spanish homeland as well as with the New World and restored the trade the British had lost as a result of the wars from 1700 to 1750. It did what the War of the Austrian Suc-cession failed to do: reestablish trade on a peaceful basis.[21] Of all the treaties negotiated during the peacetime years of the Pelham administra-tion, this was the most successful, and it is the one treaty in which Henry Pelham took a personal part.

Pelham was quite pleased with the treaty in its final form. He told Pitt that it was the best news since Aix-la-Chapelle and a great stroke of luck that France had not interfered. He told both Newcastle and Stone of his pleasure with the treaty because it gave a definite basis for relations be-tween the two countries. He also told Newcastle that he would manage the South Sea Company through his friend John Bristow and thus the treaty would function smoothly. Newcastle returned his congratulations to Pelham, but with a few disparaging remarks about Keene's ability.[22] The duke could not resist the chance to slight a successful negotiator— perhaps because the duke was in the midst of his unrewarding piece of German diplomacy. The treaty succeeded because Pelham did not in-sist that Keene achieve impossible ends. His summary of the terms sent to Pitt showed a solid grasp of foreign affairs and a willingness to seek advice from others who lacked special knowledge of the details.[23] Keene was given general instructions and then left to work out the specific points. Pelham could delegate authority to others and support their decisions, and this ability was one of the secrets of his success in the domestic and political arena as well as in this one responsible experience in foreign affairs.

During the years following the Treaty of Aix-la-Chapelle there were many points at which Anglo-French interests clashed. In the first place, France worked behind the scenes to disrupt the election of the King of the Romans.[24] Obviously it was to French interest to keep Germany upset, for then no union could be formed and any country causing future trouble would find a ready ally in one of the German states. However, this meant that Newcastle had to give up hope that he could solve the German problem.

Second, the old problem of the West Indies remained unsettled. During the War of the Austrian Succession France had occupied certain of the West Indian islands and refused to evacuate them at the end of the war. The Treaty of Aix-la-Chapelle had left this thorny question to future negotiations, but the two countries made little progress in their talks. Both Bedford and Holdernesse protested to the French about their dilatory tactics after agreeing to withdraw, and both feared that the French were merely making excuses.[25] The English cabinet refused to take any action against the French forces, so the matter was left as it was, with the French making the final decision on when to withdraw.

Connected with the French position in the West Indies was the colonial situation in general. In 1749 the English colonists in North America complained of French aggressions. Nova Scotia was the scene of the most flagrant French attempts to push the English out of a border region, and the English cabinet officially complained of such actions throughout the period of peace.[26] Again the protests had little effect, for the French continued their slow advance into Nova Scotia. No final settlement of this dispute was reached by peaceful means. The same pressure was applied by France in other areas to take advantage of the strong position gained in the recent war. By the summer of 1752 Newcastle had ordered a strong squadron to patrol the coast of Africa, to maintain the English position against French interference. It was specifically stated that the squadron must be stronger than any force the French could collect there.[27] The competition in India continued almost as if the war were still in progress. Thus over the entire colonial world England and France stood opposed, and France held the initiative. Diplomacy failed to find a solution for any of the problems, and only after Pelham's death was war to decide the final victor.

Another important problem was that of the defenses of Dunkirk, which had produced quarrels from 1727 to 1730 and, by the terms of the Treaty of Aix-la-Chapelle, were supposed to be destroyed. The French refused to dismantle the sea defenses. The English protested, and negotiations were begun. These negotiations were largely conducted in secret by the French envoy, Mirepoix, and Pelham, who showed unusual interest in this particular question of foreign affairs. At the first recorded meeting, held in April 1750 and attended by Newcastle, a general discussion of foreign affairs was conducted. Pelham then continued the negotiations alone, and they dragged on until he was glad to see Mirepoix leave. Throughout 1751 and 1752 the negotiations stood still, partly because of deliberate French tactics and partly because of ministerial changes in France. Finally, in September 1753, the English government lost patience and agreed with the Dutch on a final draft to be sent to the French. This had very little effect.[28] The French were making the best of their position of control. Pelham had not been successful as a diplomat, and Dunkirk became another cause of friction between the two countries.

A last Anglo-French problem arose over the payment of English debts to some Prussians. In order to force payment Frederick II had banned English goods, and the English seized some Prussian ships in retaliation. France, as the ally of Prussia, offered to negotiate a settlement, but the English cabinet refused to recognize French interference. The negotiations over these issues carried on throughout 1753, and though Pelham agreed to raise £15,000 to pay the debts, Frederick refused to come to terms. Newcastle was firmly convinced that French diplomacy was the reason for Frederick's stubborn stand, and he was probably right. In any event Anglo-Prussian relations were still upset in February 1754, just before Pelham's death, and France was still making the most of the situation.[29] Here is another example of Pelham's habit of claiming no knowledge of, or influence in, foreign affairs. Yet he followed the negotiations carefully, knew exactly what was going on, and, more important, took part in the decisions. The whole of Anglo-French diplomacy from Aix-la-Chapelle until his death showed clearly Pelham's increasing influence in the planning and conduct of foreign affairs.

The English position in foreign negotiations was further weakened during the years from 1750 to 1752, for a quarrel with the Dutch over the Barrier forts kept the two countries from acting together. Dayrolles, the English envoy in the Hague, was presented with demands for money to support the Dutch occupation of the forts. Pelham insisted that a military man be sent to aid Dayrolles. Newcastle agreed to Pelham's directions and left control of the negotiations to the Prime Minister, with the advice of Sir John Ligonier. Pelham, Newcastle, Hardwicke, and Stone were the only men who knew the secrets of the negotiations as they progressed. As late as May 1752 the negotiations were still unfinished.[30] The Dutch were angry because the English sided with the Austrians and never gave up their demands for the Barrier forts, which the Treaty of Utrecht, as they interpreted its terms, accorded to them.

Other small problems arose during these years. One perennial problem, that of the Polish crown, was brought up by Sir Charles Hanbury Williams. Pelham was fearful that any tampering with the Polish election would restore the situation of 1733.[31] Newcastle agreed with Pelham's refusal to have anything to do with Hanbury Williams' scheme, so nothing was done; but the fear showed how narrow was the margin of peace in Europe. Another problem was caused by the Barbary pirates. The English took an active role, diplomatic and naval, in the Moorish world of North Africa.[32] As usual, when money was involved, Pelham had the last word in any decision. Thus when true English trade interests were involved, as they were in the Mediterranean and not in Poland, the cabinet moved to attain the particular ends.

From 1750 until Pelham's death, the foreign affairs of England were in a muddled, though not a particularly dangerous, state. German affairs were unsatisfactory in both Austrian and Prussian cases. France stirred up trouble wherever it could be done with little cost to the French. Spanish-English relations grew steadily brighter; in fact, they were an outstanding success. Dutch friendship was somewhat strained, and the positions of the lesser countries were sometimes advantageous and sometimes not. It was a period of general instability for all countries. Newcastle summarized the English position very well in July 1750 and informed Pelham of his estimate.[33] In 1752 Pelham could describe the international picture as in a state of change, but made the cheerful observation that "this country increases in wealth every year." He also warned that England must move cautiously because there was no justification for a new war and no allies to help finance and fight one.[34]

In general William Pitt agreed with Pelham and Newcastle in their assessment of the international scene in the last year of the Pelham administration.[35] In other words, though the cabinet was relatively unsuccessful in diplomacy, it saw and understood the English position rather accurately. The most striking feature of foreign affairs during these last years was Pelham's greatly increased share in their direction. There are many instances of Pelham's and Holdernesse's directing policy, and there is even stronger evidence that Pelham became Newcastle's only important confidant when the duke was in London.[36] Once again the conclusion is clear: the longer Pelham remained First Lord of the Treasury, the more nearly he assumed the power of a Prime Minister. And perhaps his greatest success was that, though he increased his power even at the expense of Newcastle, the duke did not object or become more jealous.

CHAPTER XVI

Domestic Policy and Legislation, 1748–1754

❧ THE RETURN OF PEACE had two effects on the distribution of patronage. First, the reduction in size of the army made fewer positions available for distribution and, second, there was less need of finding real military men. Political appointments became the rule again. However, there was a surprising absence of requests for military office; in fact, it was the beginning of 1750 before any real request reached Pelham.[1] In the fall of 1749 Hardwicke had asked that his third son, Joseph, be made an aide-de-camp to the king, but he was refused by Pelham, who recommended Colonel Boscawen. Hardwicke was extremely angry at Pelham and did not forgive him until November, when Joseph was named to another vacancy. All was smooth again by the following July, when Joseph was named envoy to the Hague.[2] Even when the highest ranking Whigs, therefore, sought patronage, which was not always granted, it was from Pelham that they sought it.

Hardwicke also used his influence to gain favors for his second son, Charles, and these Pelham arranged to secure. George Grenville obtained Pelham's support to gain a peerage for his mother, and Attorney-General Ryder attempted to get a peerage for himself. Anson used his friendship with Pelham to secure firm political advantages in Plymouth. And George Dodington worked through Pelham to regain his position at Court after the death of Frederick, Prince of Wales. Pelham spent a considerable time over these patronage requests and favors demanded by men who already were in office.[3]

If the high officials sought further advantages, the lesser people asked for almost every type of job. Pelham, as head of the Treasury, received a steady stream of requests for revenue and related offices at his disposal. Frequent requests were for Riding Officer posts, jobs in the Wine License Office, Stamp Office, Customs Offices, contracts to supply army and navy, and any number of sinecures.[4] The requests came from all parts of England, Scotland, Wales, and Ireland and from every class, from earls to local townsmen. Even when Pelham refused a favor, he continued to be asked for the desired thing—often through new channels.[5] On the other hand, Pelham continued to hold the government together by the use of patronage, as the case of Robert Nugent, in 1751, shows.[6] The real problem of patronage was expressed by Pelham himself in the following words:

> The vacancy of a searchers place att Whitehaven by the death of Mr. Tate, I have known for some time; Sr. James Lowther having been an earnest sollicitor for that employment, both before and after the poor mans death, Sr. Charles Howard, Lord Carlisles Brother has also put in his claim pretty strongly. But I was in hopes as it is a sinecure of no great value, a friend of my own, who is willing to resign a better employment in another Port, might have succeeded. He is of that country, and wishes to retire from business to his own home, upon this small income of about one hundred pounds a year. If your Lordship thinks this reasonable, I will make my excuse to the other Gentlemen, and direct the Patent, as I intended. But if your Lordship is of another opinion, no private acquaintance of mine shall stand in the way of your real service, and we must then endeavor to pacifie Sr. James as well as we can, who I know has this much att heart, and whose family as well as Lord Carlisles is growing very considerable in that part of England.[7]

A great variety of petitions came to Pelham for jobs other than places in the Treasury. Henry Fielding, the novelist and judge, recommended a friend as Keeper of New Prison. There were many requests for colonial posts, positions in the British Museum, sheriffs, or just pleas for the first suitable vacancy. Even more time-consuming were the requests for personal favors, such as letters of introduction to Englishmen abroad or pleas for pardons.[8] These had to be attended to or the local support at election time would be lost. In fact, Pelham and Newcastle were always short of available jobs and the means of granting favors were limited. The two men had great trouble restraining the king from filling vacancies until they had candidates. Therefore they often made George promise to hold certain offices open until they were ready to fill them.[9] This was not always easy, for many other men were trying to influence the king. However, they usually obtained his word by pressure or cajolery. In almost all these cases Pelham was the ultimate dispenser of patronage, as letters written to him during his illness in 1753 and to Newcastle after Pelham's death indicate.[10] The latter, especially, disclose that many times Pelham did not even consult the duke, who was almost swamped with work sorting out promises that Pelham was supposed to have made.

The ecclesiastical hierarchy provided another major area of patronage. Though Pelham insisted throughout his life that he had no share in the distribution of these positions, he was constantly requested to use his influence with the king to obtain church appointments and livings. Newcastle often consulted with Pelham on pleas directed to himself, and together the two men decided whether to recommend the applicant or not. Pelham took part in the promotion of most bishops, both in England and Ireland, and urged the king to make the final decisions in line with his and Newcastle's recommendations.[11] The lesser offices of prebendary and canon often came to Pelham's attention, and though he was less interested in these, he made recommendations to Newcastle and the king. Even in the case of small livings he made suggestions and sometimes demanded places to pay political debts. This political aspect of patronage was what interested Pelham, and he usually had an extremely important voice in the appointments, if not actually the deciding voice.[12] Thus his protestations of nonactivity may be disregarded. Especially when there were any political implications, a considerable influence may be assigned to him in the nominations of church dignitaries and clergymen.

From Scoland Pelham received three general types of requests. First, there were direct applications for patronage jobs. These were often transmitted through Scottish officials, such as the Lord Advocate or the Lord Chief Baron. Second, there was the nominating of the sixteen Scottish peers every seven years. This inevitably produced a problem, since only sixteen out of many could be selected and the Scots considered such a post one of the highest honors that could be bestowed. For instance, in 1749 Lord Marchmont applied to fill the vacancy caused by the death of Lord Crawford. When the Pelhams did not reply directly, he threatened to make trouble in the House of Commons through his brother. Pelham did not like the idea of choosing Marchmont, but he said they would have to agree if Argyll could be persuaded. And third, there were Scottish applications for parliamentary seats, which provided much difficulty because of local rivalries and the strong local power of the lords.[13]

Patronage had an extremely critical effect on parliamentary votes, for the granting of a job was the surest way to obtain the support of the members of both houses. In a few cases the refusal of a request led the disappointed man to join the opposition. Most important of all, the voters of any constituency were most easily persuaded to vote for the ministry's candidate if some patronage had been spread among their fellows. This was particularly true during the last years of the Pelham administration, when there was no real issue and the results of the approaching elections would depend on local influence. Sir Charles Bishop and Edward Walpole were two specific examples of the electoral power of patronage.[14] Pelham was deeply interested in both cases, for they would affect his control of the Commons. A similar example in the House of Lords was Sir Charles Wyndham, who inherited a title and moved into the upper house. At the time of the change he requested the right to select his successor in the Commons with the veiled threat that unless he received it he might not support the government.[15] Since Pelham quickly agreed, there was no problem, but the incident showed the wide ramifications of patronage.

Though the principal means of extending patronage was by posts in the government offices or by special favors and concessions, sometimes direct pensions were granted. Pelham had to deal with all requests for pensions because he controlled the purse strings. Requests came from all parts of England and even from America and the West Indies. Often they were merely attempts to gain a living at public expense, and Pelham, with political expediency always in mind, rejected many. However, he was not above providing for his own relatives, as witness the care he and Newcastle used in seeking the king's approval of a pension for their cousin James Pelham.[16] George II would not always agree to Pelham's suggestions, and then the minister would have to discover another way to provide for the applicant. In 1750, for instance, George refused to grant a pension to one of Richmond's protégés, even though this was the duke's dying wish.[17] In all these pension matters Pelham directed the cabinet's decisions, even though Newcastle usually presented the applications to the king and argued the case with the monarch.

These pensions are usually held up as the outstanding example of corruption in the eighteenth century, and no doubt many were merely payment of personal or political debts. However, there is another side to the problem which should never be forgotten—that many pensions were quite legitimate and in fact the only way to carry on an efficient government. In days when there were no retirement funds, old government workers had to be cared for in some way. Colonial governors and ambassadors were shuffled around, and some method had to be found to keep them in the public service while they were between posts and without salaries. Temporary pensions were the answer. There were also a surprising number of poor widows and widows of public servants on the pension list, and they too deserved consideration. A certain Elizabeth Hay was a good example of this type of pensioner.[18] Most of these payments were quite small, and the many types of recipients put the matter of pensions in some proper perspective in contrast to the common accusations of mere corruption.

The five years following the end of the war were years of little controversy. Pelham continued to push the same policy of moderation, economy, and compromise that he had begun to advocate during the war. The annual Mutiny Bill created a yearly battle between the government and the opposition. During these years Pelham strove persistently to reduce the size of the armed forces. In the parliamentary fights the efforts of the opposition were not nearly so important as the disagreement within the ministry. In 1749 those who advocated large forces were led by Fox in the Commons and Bedford and Sandwich in the Lords.[19] However, the votes were merely recorded as smaller majorities. The question of the size of the navy produced similar trouble, with Pelham and Pitt strongly against the plans of the Admiralty to keep the naval forces near wartime strength. The running battle within the ministry, begun in 1749, lasted until Bedford and Sandwich left the cabinet. In January 1751 a move was made in parliament to reduce the navy to 8,000 men. Pitt rebelled and asked for 10,000. Publicly Pelham stood between the two sides. Behind the scenes, however, he worked for the smaller figure, and Pitt was soundly defeated when the vote was taken. Economy and moderation were Pelham's guiding principles, and he could count on the majority of both houses to support him. Pelham allowed Pitt to pursue his own course, and defended the Paymaster and his friends because he knew his own side held the majority. He could afford to be generous.[20]

The same spirit influenced most of the other types of bills introduced during these years. For example, a turnpike bill had been introduced by Bedford and his friends. Pelham and Newcastle at first favored it, but when local people of the area to be affected started to riot and demonstrate against the turnpike, they backed off. Bedford was defeated on the vote, though to maintain peace Pelham and Newcastle both voted in favor of it. They had, however, assured the defeat by organizing their friends, under the Duke of Grafton, to vote against the measure.[21] The Pelhams thus showed their interest in the improvement of the road system by their early support and later face-saving device, but they also showed their acute sensitiveness to popular reaction.

On the other hand, the bill to reform the calendar, which raised loud popular protest, was consistently supported by Pelham and Hardwicke. Lord Macclesfield and Lord Chesterfield had introduced it, to bring the English calendar into agreement with the continental Gregorian one, and with the ministers' help it easily passed parliament.[22] Popular shouts to "return our eleven days" were ignored because of the obvious merit of the plan. Money was also granted to support the General Assembly of the Church of Scotland every year. Therefore the ministry and parliament continued to recognize the differences between the two sections of Great Britain and the provisions of the Act of Union. New regulations were issued to tighten up the laws of quarantine. Pelham proposed and managed the passage of new restrictions on the sale of gin and other spirits. A bill was introduced that attempted to unify all earlier legislation regarding the poor. It tried what the mid-eighteenth century thought was a practical approach, but it really accomplished little. There was also an attempt to legislate on the control of public places of entertainment and on the need to reduce the number of crimes punishable by hanging. None of these matters produced much real opposition, and Pelham had a relatively easy time with the proposed legislation. In fact, opposition was so weak that he delayed the usual November opening of parliament in 1752 until after Christmas. Not only were sessions shorter that year, but daily meetings seldom lasted long in the Commons.[23] Only two major bills produced real controversy during these peaceful years.

The first of the controversial bills had to do with the naturalization of Jews. The bill was passed in the winter session of 1752–53 with little difficulty. Pelham sponsored it and was warmly supported by Pitt for humanitarian reasons, since it would correct a long-held discrimination.[24] It was not in the least radical, for it gave citizenship only to Jews who had long been resident in Great Britain. There was little reaction until the new elections were called, and then the Bedford Whigs and other opposition groups used it as an issue to arouse the voters against the ministry. Thus by July, the cabinet began to waver, and Pelham told Newcastle the measure would probably have to be repealed. Newcastle was sure of the necessity for this, and by the end of the month the brothers agreed to support repeal during the next session unless the popular clamor died. During the fall the papers of the opposition loudly attacked the measure and the government, and some friends of the ministry wanted to reply in kind. Halifax was the one important official who opposed repeal, and he did so only because it set a "bad" example. In November Hardwicke drafted a repeal that was eventually passed by both houses.[25] Therefore, after a courageous effort, Pelham gave in to popular pressure and repealed one of the most honorable and worthwhile pieces of legislation of his entire administration.

The second of the controversial bills was Hardwicke's marriage bill, which he sponsored to correct the evils of the "Fleet Street clergy" elopements and the blackmail often resulting from them. In essence the bill made a license necessary for any marriage not preceded by the reading of the banns in the parish church. This would force unscrupulous and dishonorable clergymen, who lived in many cities but especially around Temple Bar, out of business. It was an honest effort to correct an evil, and Pelham joined with Hardwicke to get the bill passed. This would not have been difficult except that Henry Fox, who had himself been married in this fashion, led an attack against it and was supported by the Bedfordites. Pelham had some long and difficult debates before the bill was finally passed in the late spring of 1753 by a majority of more than two to one. Pelham was pleased with his success, for the opposition arguments had turned into a personal attack on the brothers and Hardwicke. George II had strongly supported the bill, and the three ministers were particularly in his favor for their stand. When Fox tried to get the king to oppose it, George told him that he got only what he deserved for opening the attack.[26] Thus the second great controversial piece of legislation ended with a resounding triumph for the ministry.

In spite of the varied legislation in many fields, the most important act passed by parliament in these years was financial and almost solely the work of Pelham. At the end of the war, Pelham began talking about his "great plan" to reduce and consolidate the national debt. In 1733 Walpole had begun the policy of raiding the sinking fund to make up yearly deficits, and from that time on there was little effort to manage or reduce the debt. It stood at £46,275,038 in 1738, and by 1749 it had grown to £77,125,617. Moreover, in 1738 the debt was fairly easy to manage because it was owed mostly to three companies: the South Sea Company, the East India Company, and the Bank of England. During the war, however, there was a definite policy of borrowing from the public without

the interposition of the companies. This created a large variety of creditors. In 1748 the debt was roughly divided as follows:

Bank of England	£11,686,000
East India Company	4,200,000
South Sea Company	27,302,203
Civil List Debts	1,000,000
Perpetual Annuities	25,000,000
Total	**£69,188,203**

This list indicates that more than £7,000,000 remained in miscellaneous
small debts.[27] Obviously the management of the debt had become much
more complex.

Pelham immediately after the war reduced the current expenses of the
government in order that he might have a balanced budget. In a short
time he had managed to reduce expenses about £5,000,000 annually.[28]
Then in the spring of 1749 he introduced his scheme to reduce interest on
the debt and to consolidate the many types of debt. The essential plan
was to offer bank annuities for sale at 3 per cent. In order to force the
creditors to accept these, the rate of interest of 4 per cent on outstanding
debts was to drop to 3½ per cent in December 1750 and then to 3 per
cent in December 1757. The bill passed on December 20, 1749, and in
1750 was further modified to advance the 3 per cent rate to 1755. The
plan was almost completely successful. Under the terms of the two bills,
and a lesser one of 1751, almost the whole debt was converted into 3 per
cent bank annuities or 3 per cent bank consolidated annuities.[29] These
two became the principal form of debt, representing a definite change
from company debt to outside debt, and the Bank of England became the
only real agency of public credit negotiation. From 1750 the South Sea
Company had no real importance in handling public debt functions, and
after 1755 the East India Company stopped doing so. Pelham rendered
his chief service to the nation by this operation, which completely reorganized national finance and created some sort of system. The incidental effect of the conversion was to remove the political importance of
the two companies until the East India Company rose again through its
political rule of India.

Because the reduction in expenses disturbed his foreign plans, Newcastle did not favor active operation of the plan. Hardwicke and Pelham
tried to convince him of its value, and he reluctantly agreed.[30] Even such
dubious political allies as Dodington approved and supported the plan.
The only real opposition in parliament was by the "hard core" of the
Prince of Wales' party.[31] The real opponents were the holders of the
debt in the various companies and the foreign creditors. The companies
were finally won over by various small concessions and Pelham's tact. By

May 1750 the conversions were going smoothly, and Pelham was highly pleased; by June only £3,268,871 remained outstanding.[32] Newcastle had become thoroughly convinced of the value of the plan, and he wrote to Pelham with enthusiasm:

> This is a most prodigious thing; and gives the King the most real Comfort, and satisfaction. I had Twenty Friends dine with me yesterday: And It was the greatest Pleasure to me, to hear how they all talk'd, upon this Subject. You cannot conceive how much Weight, Credit, & Solidity, It is universally thought, abroad, to give to the King; and His Government.[33]

A final effort in financial reorganization was an act of 1752 that slightly tightened the irregular practice of taking money from the sinking fund for yearly expenses. The whole problem of the debt had become simpler, and the idea of debt reduction from the sinking fund had been largely abandoned in favor of the new idea of debt management. Therefore the importance of the fund was considerably reduced and irregular borrowing was less of a problem. Pelham had achieved a financial reform considerably greater than anything achieved by Walpole or to be achieved in the future until the ministry of the younger Pitt.

In the last years of his administration Pelham faced many problems other than those of actual legislative procedure. In order to overcome obstacles in the easiest possible way, he insisted with increasing frequency that both foreign and domestic matters be kept calm. The desire for quiet was the principal reason why he agreed to Newcastle's subsidies to German states. It was also an important consideration in his support of the Spanish treaty and the work he did to gain the approval of the Bank and the South Sea Company.[34] By 1750 the much-desired calm was achieved, and during the summer Hardwicke was able to say that the most vexing problem was an application for a fishing charter. Almost all politicians, government and opposition, left London, and at one time in October Pelham and the Archbishop of Canterbury were the only officials in the capital legally able to sign orders.[35] The opposition was almost inactive, and during the autumn Lord Bute politely asked Pelham's leave to resign his pension so that he could become a member of the Bedchamber of the Prince of Wales.[36] Even more important, the calm extended to the general population of England. William Murray reported:

> The Exportation of Corn for almost 6 Months past has been immense above £140,000 Bounty paid during that Time! The Demands still continue to such a Degree that they are hard at work in the yards building new Corn ships, the shipping We had not being sufficient. & there is this year the Prospect of a plentifull Harvest, so that the Farmers own Themselves satisfied with the Crop & the Market. The Commissioners for Woolen & other Goods are greater than ever was known, whether it be owing to a Scarcity in the Spanish W. Indies

occasioned by the War, or that the French have not yet returned to their Manufactures, I don't know; but the Fact is certainly so.[37]

With merchants, shipbuilders, farmers, and everyone interested in wool living in prosperity, the whole economy of England would be on a high level. This helped account for the ease of financial conversion and gave the government popularity. The quiet of politics was thus easily explained, for the opposition could find little public discontent on which to build strength. The same situation was reflected throughout the period from 1749 until 1754, though such specific statements apply most fully to 1750.

In parliament the postwar years showed a wide variety of business. In 1749 Pelham extended his direction of parliamentary matters to the House of Lords, for at that time he organized the passage of money bills through the upper house.[38] This action definitely increased his relative strength within the cabinet. In 1750 court-martial and turnpike bills aroused sharp parliamentary debates, demonstrating the government's varied interests.[39] In the early session of 1751 the most controversial issue was a pamphlet that attacked the Duke of Cumberland as a prospective Richard III. Parliament took up this issue of libel against a member of the royal family. Pelham was determined that parliament should take a position against such attacks, and he spoke strongly in the Commons against the paper, *Constitutional Queries*. With the support of his friends, he got parliamentary approval of a condemnation, which speedily followed an Order in Council.[40] Records of two meetings held in March, 1751, show how the ministerial leaders collected their votes for an important issue. One was at Sir Thomas Robinson's home, where thirty-three leaders of the Commons met to decide on the policy to be pursued. The same day twenty-eight Lords met at Newcastle House to discuss parliamentary plans.[41] These meetings were not unusual but common occurrences when organized methods were to be decided. The Pelhams in this way assured their parliamentary success. Pelham also had to arrange for the publication of the Journals of the House of Commons and the date of the meeting of new parliamentary sessions.[42] These were all small matters, but they demonstrate the variety as well as the detail of the work. They also show the lack of important issues during these peaceful years.

Perhaps even more illuminating than the variety of parliamentary business was the great number of matters that came to Pelham's attention as First Lord of the Treasury. The Customs Books and Letter Books reveal many problems dealing with customs regulations, smuggling, customs officials, income, expense, and orders.[43] These demonstrate clearly the methods used to maintain a smooth, regular flow of work in the most important single department of the government.

Furthermore, Pelham took some part in the domestic affairs acted on by the Secretaries of State. For instance, in 1752 he advised the Earl of Holdernesse, the current Secretary, as to the steps necessary to prevent contraband trade and secret correspondence between Emden and Scotland. Again in 1753, Anthony Todd, who examined, opened, read, and copied all letters in and out of England by regular mail, wanted additional help for his office. He gained Newcastle's support, but Pelham had to approve this increase of the Post Office staff before any steps could be taken. And, as another example, in 1753 Pelham was presented with the question of paying the workmen who were constructing the new Horse Guards Palace or facing their refusal to continue. The money had not been provided, and Pelham had to provide it by any expedient he could conveniently find. Even local government problems, such as the appearance of some treasonable pamphlets in Leicester, were placed in the hands of Newcastle and Pelham. Local cases were often appealed to the Privy Council, and the appointment of sheriffs was always a problem. Thus Pelham and the rest of the cabinet were deeply involved in the local administration of justice and law enforcement.[44] These are ordinary functions of a government, but the important thing here is that the highest leaders of the cabinet attended to them.

On the other hand, the government processes often moved extremely slowly and often without approval by the proper authorities. When George Dodington resigned his office of Treasurer of the Navy, his accounts had to be approved by a special warrant instead of the usual audit because the records were incomplete.[45] The slowness of operation is best shown by the fact that in 1749, 1750, and 1751 Pelham still held funds from his term of office as Paymaster. During those years his final accounts were allowed and the balance was ordered turned over to Pitt.[46] The army funds were troublesome in another way, for often allowances were insufficient to cover the normal expenses in this peacetime period. In 1749 the Deputy-Paymaster ran short of funds and asked Pitt to appeal to Pelham to allow unusual methods of financing the army. Pelham must have made special arrangements, for the money was obtained. However, no long-term corrections were made. By March 1750 Pelham had arranged only one reform, which allowed the Paymaster to issue money on the warrant or order of the Captain General of the Forces or Commander in Chief of the Forces instead of the old cumbersome method in which the Secretary of State had to approve.[47] This was only a small improvement, which helped reduce the time necessary to audit accounts, but it did show that Pelham attempted to make the outdated government procedures more sensible.

One last domestic problem was the money spent for secret service purposes. The records for this expenditure are fragmentary for the peacetime years as well as the wartime ones. They were kept by Pelham and his personal secretary, John Roberts, and their loss or deliberate de-

struction makes it difficult to learn what occurred. However, one summary has survived; it shows government figures indicating to whom the
money was given for disbursement.[48]

Paid to	1751	1752	1753	1754
Newcastle	£ 3,000–0–0	£ 3,000–0–0	£ 3,000–0–0	£ 591–13–4
Bedford	1,356–3–3			
Holdernesse	1,564–7–8	3,000–0–0	3,000–0–0	3,000– 0–0
John Scrope	40,000–0–0	8,000–0–0		
James West		21,000–0–0	44,000–0–0	52,000– 0–0
Total	£45,920–10–11	£35,000–0–0	£50,000–0–0	£55,591–13–4

Two things are immediately clear: The secret service expenses went up
during the peacetime years and the Treasury (Scrope and West) received
the overwhelming share of the money. From this brief statement it is
perfectly plain that Pelham commanded most of the funds available for
secret service purposes. What happened to the money is unknown, except that many legitimate costs of foreign affairs were paid out of the
£6000 the Secretaries of State received, and many honest pensions were
paid to deserving people from the Treasury's share. Since only £25,000
more was spent in the election campaign of 1753 and 1754 than in the
two previous years, the government could not have spent such vast sums
as it has been accused of doing. Moreover, a share of that increase was
spent for necessary expenses involved in the changes in the government
following Pelham's death. Beyond that nothing can be said, for evidence
is lacking.

CHAPTER XVII

Postwar Government Problems

ESSENTIALLY conditions in parliament, the Privy council, the ministry, and the cabinet remained the same during the years after the war as they had been before, despite the change of personnel. It would therefore be unprofitable to cover the many details discussed previously, and much more useful to examine major changes in the ministry and the cabinet. However, one should always keep in mind the picture of Pelham in the House of Commons and Newcastle and Hardwicke in the House of Lords. Their methods and techniques were the same as earlier. They maintained an even more complete control of the legislature than during the war. On major issues the leaders were in full agreement, even though Horace Walpole was right when he wrote:

> At this time all was faction, and splitting into little factions. The Pelhams were ill with one another, and ill with the Bedfords. The latter Duke would have set up Fox against Mr. Pelham; and the former Duke was countenancing Pitt and his clan against the Duke of Cumberland, who was united with the Bedfords. The Prince's Court, composed of the refuse of every party, was divided into twenty small ones. Lord Egmont at the head of one, Nugent of another, consisting of himself and two more, Lady Middlesex and Doddington of a third, the chief ornament of which was the Earl of Bute, a Scotchman. . . . The Jacobites had quarrelled at Oxford on the choice of a member, and would not join with the Prince, who courted them. Lord Granville, Lord Chesterfield, and Lord Winchelsea, were each separately courted by the Duke of Newcastle, and Lord Oxford by Mr. Pelham, who at the same time was making new connections, trying to preserve the old ones, adopting his brother's jealousies, and yet threatening to resign on account of them.[1]

It was this very factionalization, which Walpole saw so clearly, that made the peaceful control of parliament possible. Every group supported the cabinet at one time or another because of fear of the rival opposition groups.

Nevertheless there was trouble within the ministry and cabinet, for that was where some men had enough power to try and get more. The most important test of strength was the struggle between Bedford and the Pelhams that lasted from the end of the war until June 1751. The rivalry had two roots: Newcastle's anger at Sandwich during the peace negotiations and Bedford's incapacity for, and indifference to, his duties.

191

Because Bedford heartily espoused Sandwich's cause, the resentment of the Pelhams was concentrated on him, and his position became the symbol of the brothers' control of the government. Moreover, coals were heaped on the fire when Cumberland, angry at Pelham's refusal to concede him complete control of the army, joined Bedford and thus gave him added prestige.

In 1747 the differences between Bedford and the rest of the cabinet came out in the open. Early in the year Chesterfield reported that Bedford was trying to establish a party composed of himself, Sandwich, Cumberland, Lord Gower, and their followers.[2] Bedford hoped to gain Gower through Lord Trentham, who was Gower's son and Bedford's brother-in-law and strongly opposed to the Pelhams. By December Bedford had actively opposed Pelham by working for Trentham's election to the Commons in a special vote at Westminister. He failed, and made Gower angry by bringing his family to defeat.[3] Newcastle used this violation of Pelham's directions to prepare the way for his plan to get rid of the troublesome "little" duke.

During the meeting of parliament in the spring of 1750, the Pelhams and Bedford called a truce in their quarreling. Once parliament was over, however, and the king and Newcastle had gone to Hanover, the arguments and dissatisfactions began again. This time Pelham was extremely irritated at Bedford's neglect of duty, and he expressed his feelings to Newcastle off and on throughout the summer. Newcastle, for his part, complained loudly of Bedford's incompetence and especially of his lack of cooperation with himself as senior Secretary.[4] It was the old story of Newcastle's jealousy of any possible rival, but this time Pelham agreed that the culprit was impossible to deal with. In July Newcastle began his active campaign to get rid of Bedford. He wrote Pelham that he knew the difficulties of forcing Bedford out and that therefore he would himself resign and become President or Privy Seal. This was of course a ridiculous proposal, for it would destroy the cabinet. Newcastle knew this, but it was his method of pressuring Pelham to oust Bedford. Pelham and Hardwicke discussed Newcastle's letter and sent answers urging that nothing be done for the present. Pelham added that it would be better that he himself resign than that Newcastle act alone. These letters, and many others, had the desired effect. Newcastle agreed to wait until his return to England before taking any definite steps against Bedford.[5]

Pelham thought the affair was settled for the time being, but Newcastle merely shifted to another attack. About the middle of August the duke began to report that the king was out of patience with Bedford and wanted to remove him from office. He blandly said that he had done nothing to encourage the king but rather had held back the royal resentment. While Newcastle was writing these assurances to London, he was working to gain Lady Yarmouth's aid for his plan to oust Bedford. These two concocted a scheme for Bedford to succeed either Dorset as President or Richmond as Master of the Horse. Newcastle later told Pelham of the plan but presented it as initiated by the king and Lady Yarmouth.[6]

Pelham and Hardwicke saw through the subterfuge and recognized that Newcastle's earlier praise of the Earl of Holdernesse indicated that he was the desired replacement. Pelham accepted the scheme to shift offices, if Bedford agreed, but he objected to Holdernesse as Secretary of State and suggested the Earl of Halifax. Hardwicke agreed with Pelham, thus irritating Newcastle.[7] However, Pelham clearly indicated that he preferred to leave things as they were. Newcastle, angry, wrote that George personally picked Holdernesse as the future Secretary.[8] Then at the end of September a new obstacle rose in Newcastle's path: The king began to hedge on the removal of Bedford. Moreover, Bedford changed his mind about shifting offices unless he could name his own successor, which was an obviously unreasonable request and unacceptable to Pelham. Therefore Pelham again urged that Bedford be retained in office. Newcastle's anger broke out anew, and he denounced Pelham. The quarrel thus begun continued through the rest of the year. No decision was reached, even though Lady Yarmouth finally told Newcastle that the king would approve the change if Pelham asked it. When Newcastle returned to England he still needed Pelham's approval of the removal.[9] Matters remained at this impasse until the session of parliament was over.

Pelham's great fear was that removing Bedford would provoke a series of cabinet problems that would bring down the ministry. Therefore he tried desperately to find a compromise. By March 1751, however, he decided that Bedford had to go because of his connivance with Cumberland in the opposition. Pelham's only stipulation was that he be permitted to pick the time, after careful thought and discussion with Hardwicke and Murray. During the spring he prepared the king for the coming change.[10] The death of the Prince of Wales had destroyed the opposition, so that the time was ripe for Pelham to act. Bedford tried to prevent the ax from falling but to no avail. On June 13 Sandwich was removed from the Admiralty according to Pelham's plan, and Bedford immediately resigned.[11] Newcastle had his way, but Pelham had prepared the actual resignation so that Bedford would carry only minimum strength to the opposition.

While the Bedford-Newcastle quarrel was dragging to completion, other serious cabinet problems developed. Most pressing was the number of vacancies in cabinet-rank posts caused by death. The Duke of Montagu died in 1749, the Earl of Pembroke in early 1750, and the Duke of Richmond in the summer of 1750. The two latter vacancies caused great competition among many lords.[12] In order to strengthen the cabinet, and because of the plan to remove Bedford, the Pelhams moved very slowly in filling the vacancies. In fact, it took a year to make the final decisions. Moreover, the summer of 1751 was the time agreed upon for the end of Harrington's administration of Ireland, and the Duke of Dorset and the king insisted that he resign. Dorset thereupon became Lord Lieutenant of Ireland and left another major cabinet vacancy in the office of Lord President. Thus in 1751 there were four openings, and when Bedford and Sandwich were removed two more were added.

Pelham, Newcastle, and Hardwicke spent many hours planning the changes. The aim of all three was to prevent any disturbance of the parliamentary political balance by the new appointments.[13] Newcastle and Pelham disagreed over the men to be added. Newcastle urged that the Duke of Leeds be named and strongly opposed Halifax, who was Pelham's choice. Pelham flatly rejected Sir Thomas Robinson and disapproved Holdernesse, who were Newcastle's nominees. But most controversial of all was Newcastle's suggestion that Granville be brought back into office. Pelham wanted Chesterfield returned and violently objected to Granville. Newcastle judged Granville more correctly than did Pelham, and when he wrote, "My Ld. Granville is no more the terrible man," he was exactly right.[14] Pelham's personal hatred of Granville clouded his usually excellent estimation of men, and he never was reconciled to Granville's return to office. The brothers did, however, agree on one thing: that either the Duke of Devonshire should be brought back into office or else a powerful member of the Devonshire faction should be brought in. This was only sensible, for Devonshire was the most powerful single member of the Whig aristocracy. In the end, Newcastle agreed that he would not insist on any particular person but would give in to Pelham's judgment.[15]

In June 1751, on the forced resignation of Bedford, the compromise between Pelham and Newcastle was announced. Newcastle had his way. Holdernesse became Secretary of State for the Southern Department and Granville became Lord President. Pelham's nominee, Admiral Anson, lately created Viscount Anson, became First Lord of the Admiralty; Viscount Hartington, the son of Devonshire, became Master of the Horse; the Duke of Marlborough remained as Lord Steward; and Halifax was to have increased power. George II personally picked the Earl of Albemarle to be the new Groom of the Stole. These changes recast the entire aspect of the cabinet, except that Pelham and Newcastle were more firmly in control than ever before.[16] At first the removal of Bedford seemed a blunder, but Newcastle's countermove of bringing in Granville more than compensated for the change. The king was extremely pleased; Granville was an excellent debater in the House of Lords, and he loyally supported the Pelhams' policies. Bedford merely joined Cumberland's opposition, where he took on some of the duke's unpopularity.[17] On the whole, both externally and internally, the cabinet was strengthened, and it was the last shift of the administration.

It did not solve all problems, for Lord Gower was in very poor health and there was strong and important competition for his place. Marlborough, Leeds, and the Duke of Rutland were dissatisfied, and they constantly demanded offices or changes.[18] These were not men who could be ignored, but Pelham successfully delayed any action on their demands for the rest of his life.

Newcastle began to promote the idea of restoring Granville to the cabinet in 1749, both to counteract Bedford and Cumberland and because Granville had strongly supported his foreign policy in the Lords. At that time Newcastle persuaded Pelham to allow Granville to become a Knight of the Garter. Publicly, therefore, the *rapprochement* was announced. During the struggle to reform the cabinet Newcastle worked to get Pelham's agreement, which was only reluctantly given. Pelham's real objection was that he feared Newcastle and Granville would join against him and push foreign affairs beyond the point to which he wished to go. He even said he could not long remain in office with Granville. Pelham was wrong, for Granville brought back Sir John Barnard's support and gained Robert Nugent from the opposition.[19] He fulfilled Andrew Stone's belief that he would cooperate, and he followed Newcastle's advice on how to overcome Pelham's objections. Once Granville was in office, Pelham had no reason to object to his policies, for he followed the leaders' wishes. Again Granville offered an example of his complete lack of understanding of politics and showed his essential unfitness to direct a ministry. He had no firm convictions except on an active foreign policy in Europe, though it did not especially matter to him what the policy was. However, he showed he had learned that he could not compete with Pelham.

Nevertheless 1752 was not a happy year for Pelham in regard to Granville. It was a well-known fact that Granville drank heavily during his later life. He came to official meetings several times under the influence of too much wine. Often this made him merely pleasant and witty, but sometimes it made him incapable of doing business. In August 1752 Pelham was extremely depressed over the death of his grandson. At one cabinet meeting at this time Granville imbibed too heavily. This was more than Pelham could tolerate. He lost his temper, and the cabinet was momentarily shaken. It took Stone a month to soothe Pelham's anger, and even then Pelham promised to continue with Granville only if they need not meet except on formal occasions.[20] Thus the cabinet went on, but Pelham was always uncomfortable with Granville.

There were other problems of personnel. Newcastle had quarrels with Pelham, Grafton, and Richard Arundel. Halifax clamored for promotion and threatened to resign. Gower's health, though improved in 1752, was always a problem. Fox, Pitt, and the Cobhamites became restless. These problems were not important, but they indicated one major point: the younger men were becoming eager for offices of the top rank. In other words, the men of Pelham's generation were beginning to lose their monopoly of power. Already Newcastle had adopted Holdernesse, one of the young men, as his colleague, though Holdernesse had no power in his own right.[21] He was unambitious and was the only partner who ever satisfied Newcastle, but others were not so content. This could easily have become a major threat if Pelham had not been such an excellent negotiator and peacemaker.

In 1751 Granville Gower, the son of the Lord Privy Seal, resigned from the Admiralty Board, and his method of resignation indicated Pelham's continued superiority in the cabinet. The eventual decline of dispute after the reshuffle of the cabinet showed that Pelham, Newcastle, Hardwicke, Granville, and Holdernesse were the "inner cabinet" which made ultimate decisions.[22] And among these men Pelham directed major decisions. At times during these later years Pelham actually made decisions, since the others left him in London alone. He seldom objected, for then there would be no disputes.

> Every one of the lords whom the king trusts with his private correspondence are in the country, except lord Holdernesse, You have my thoughts, therefore, naked, and without reserve. Lord Holdernesse is very good; but I cannot say I am much edified by conferences with him.[23]

It is clear from this and other examples that Pelham had accepted Holdernesse and found him, as Newcastle did, a willing helper but not a person to formulate policy. He was therefore a good person to fill the post of the second Secretary of State. With help from a man of this caliber Pelham was perfectly content to direct the government alone.

On the other hand, Pelham had uniformly good relations with the Cobhamite section of the Whigs during the peacetime years. Lyttelton specifically stated his pleasant relations with Pelham and would do nothing to irritate him. Pelham expressed his thanks to George Grenville for his services and was particularly solicitous at the time of Lord Cobham's death. But most important of all, Pitt remained perfectly contented with Pelham. Indeed, he was happy in his relationship with the entire ministry.[24] The petty squabbles of individual members of the ministry fall into their proper perspective when the essential agreement of the main groups is remembered.

The second major problem of the cabinet after the war was the argument between Dorset and Harrington over the Lord Lieutenancy of Ireland. Before 1750 Pelham and Newcastle had promised Dorset that he would succeed to the Irish post in that year. Because the king refused to appoint Harrington to any other position, the brothers wanted to leave him in Ireland. Dorset was insistent on being given the post, and the most Pelham was able to do was to get his agreement to wait until the next year. The Pelhams were forced to find an equivalent position for Harrington during the interval, and this was particularly difficult because Harrington's health was failing. In their minds this made a pension almost the only expedient.[25]

Late in August 1750 Harrington went to Pelham and begged to know his future disposition. Pelham was forced to tell him that the king was unalterably opposed to his holding any office because of the old grudge caused by the mass resignations of 1746. Harrington then demanded that the Pelhams support him as he had supported them at that earlier time, and Pelham promised to find some post.[26] Then Pelham proposed a plan to Newcastle:

> I have been thinking, tho I never mentioned it to him whether the old story of General of the Marines might not do, his friends, I have reason to believe will be satisfied with that, tho I dare say he himself will not be pleased. I should not according to my principles recommend a further expense on that head of service; but when I consider he won't last long, and that the opposition would probably be stop'd from attaching him, I had rather venture that reproach, than the other of suffering a man to drop for an offence which we drew him into, and in which we were as much concern'd as he. . . . I doubt we do not see this administration in its true light. Death or retreat has taken away all our old friends and fellow servants. The D. of Grafton Lord Chancellor and yourself excepted, in a little while there will not be one man in the Cabinet Councill, with whom we began the world, or have carried on business with, 'till within this very few years. I own this reflection often strikes me, and makes me greatly fear new experiments.[27]

Obviously Pelham felt very personally the impending fall of Harrington. Later he wrote letters to Newcastle telling him to demand something for Harrington and saying that he would take entire responsibility for the move in the House of Commons.

Hardwicke announced complete agreement with Pelham, and Newcastle promised to push George II to agree, in spite of the old man's hatred of Harrington.[28] In line with his promise Newcastle suggested that Harrington be made General of the Marines. The king flew into a rage and, according to Newcastle, said,

> The General of Marines was to be the Reward for every Body, that flew in His Face; that that was the Case of that old Rascal, Stair; that my Lord Harrington should have His Ears cut off. . . . That, as to the General of Marines, He should not have it, if *He* could hinder it; and, at last, said, "He deserves to be *hanged;* and I am ready to tell him so." [29]

In the end Newcastle obtained the king's permission to delay the entire affair until they returned to England, and he thought that then George would agree to Harrington's being given the sinecure. Dorset was informed and accepted the situation, so the difficult problem was solved in the summer of 1751.[30] Dorset remained a good friend of the Pelhams; therefore no loss resulted. The episode reflected two points: first, Pelham was able to enforce his wishes on ministry matters, and, second, the king wielded great power in the make-up of the government. Only by skillful management could Pelham or any other minister get his way—even in the composition of the cabinet—if the king objected strongly. It also demonstrated clearly the loyalty of Pelham to his colleagues and his very real concern for his friends. His possession of these traits, neither of which was very strong in most other mid-eighteenth-century politicians, shows the supposedly "cold" Henry Pelham in a more human light.

When one shifts from the sphere of the cabinet to the larger sphere of the Privy Council, one finds the same activities as in the earlier period. There were the same six types of sessions: full Council with or without the king, the general committee meetings, the Committee for Plantation Appeals, the Committee for Plantation Affairs, the Committee for Irish Bills, and the Committee for Jersey and Guernsey Affairs. The most interesting differences are that all met more frequently and that the number of meetings to deal with the Channel Isles increased considerably. It is also interesting that George II attended almost half (92 out of 188) of the full Council sessions, thus reflecting the rather active part that the monarch still played. The same offices were represented at the various meetings. The Lord President, both Dorset and Granville, attended with regularity. Pelham, Newcastle, Hardwicke, and Holdernesse attended important sessions. One of the legal members was normally present, especially when appeals were heard. And finally, the group of Privy Councilors outside the cabinet attended to give wider authority. By this time Cholmondeley, Hyndford, Lord Delawar, Edgcumbe, Finch, Legge, D'Arcy, Lord Cornwallis, Lord Berkeley of Stratton, and Sir George Lee were the most active participants. These men and less important members usually formed the majority in any vote. Thus the cabinet still used outsiders to legalize policies and decisions.

In the years from 1749 to 1754 the Lords Justices were established twice, in 1750 and 1752. In both cases they were all cabinet members. There was only one exception in 1752, when Pitt, though not a member, was ordered to be present at their meetings.[31] Again two of the Undersecretaries of State were made Secretaries of the Lords Justices. Therefore Pelham exercised an even more complete control over that body than during the war, for then outsiders were made actual members.

On another level of the government the foreign representatives of Britain in the European capitals gave a picture of the caliber of men attracted to what had almost become a career service. During the 1750's every ambassador, envoy, or minister, except Albemarle at Paris and Hanbury Williams at Berlin, was a man who made foreign service his main occupation. Each one, except Albemarle and the Earl of Rochford at Turin, was a member of the middle class. Sir Benjamin Keene, Robert Keith, and Solomon Dayrolles were excellent diplomats, who served Britain well in Madrid, Vienna, and Brussels. Others, like Joseph Yorke, Arthur Villettes, James Grey, and Horace Mann, were merely adequate. None was a complete failure except Hanbury Williams, who was highly incompetent both at Dresden and Berlin. The consuls and agents, who were maintained in thirty-two cities from St. Petersburg to Tunis and the Canary Islands, had little to do, but when ordered to act they normally dispatched their business well.[32] British interests were therefore well attended to in the years of peace.

Pelham's particular interest in the envoys was financial. He seldom issued orders to them except when money was involved, and even his letters were usually supplementary to those of the Secretaries. Pelham and the Treasury issued only one general order during the period: that no allowances be made for an ambassador's, envoy's, or minister's travel expenses unless the trip was specifically ordered by the king. This was a needed reform, for it eliminated one of the biggest chances of waste in the foreign service. However, Pelham's main connection with the envoys was through his approval or disapproval of their requests for extraordinary allowances. These ranged from expenses incurred in the ordinary performance of duties to Albemarle's expenses for special parties at the birth of the Duke of Burgundy. Most of the requests were carefully examined and passed only on merit.[33] Again it is plain that Pelham's demand for economy was enforced.

These examples give some idea of the functioning of the ministry during the peacetime years of the Pelham administration. They disclose four primary facts. First, Pelham was in complete control of his government. Second, his economy measures were put into effect as far as possible. Third, no startling innovations were introduced. And fourth, the petty quarrels among ministers were the main disturbances during the time. The two exceptions were in colonial and Irish matters, and it is now necessary to examine these briefly.

Colonial and Irish Affairs, 1748–1754

℞ T H E Y E A R 1 7 4 8 , which marked the split of the Pelham administration into two parts, even more definitely marked a change in attitude toward the colonies. Reform of structure had been given up earlier, but reform through personnel was begun by the appointment of the Earl of Halifax to the office of First Lord of Trade (or President of the Board of Trade). The more vigorous leadership was plain from the beginning, for the number of Privy Council meetings held to deal with colonial matters increased. In the eight war years under Monson's tenure of office 83 meetings had been held, but in the five years and two months of Halifax's tenure under Pelham there were 108.[1] This was true in spite of the military importance of the colonies during the war. Slightly over two thirds of the meetings dealt with appeals, and the rest with general colonial matters. As a result meetings on colonial matters were more frequent than on any other single problem of government. Moreover, the meetings were more regular than during the earlier period, with at least one session every month except in the usual vacation time of August, September, and October. Certainly an effort was made to regularize control of colonial affairs.

A definite effort was also made to increase efficiency of administration. When Halifax was appointed in 1748, the Pelhams had discussed and rejected a plan to make the First Lord of Trade a position of cabinet rank. Halifax was disappointed, and by 1750 he had begun to exert pressure to increase his power.[2] By the next summer he had made three specific recommendations for reform. First, the Commissioners of Trade were to have frequent access to the king on Plantation matters. Second, the Commissioners of Trade were to have power to nominate men for governors, deputy-governors, and secretaries in the colonies. Third, the First Lord of Trade was to be called to the cabinet with an increased salary.[3] These steps would effectively give the Board of Trade control over the colonies and colonial patronage.

Bedford, when he resigned, aimed a parting barb at the Pelhams over these proposed changes. He told the king, that H. M. would find that as soon as He was out of the Secretary's office, one considerable part of it, America, was to be lopped off & thrown into the hands of the first Commissioner of Trade, Lord Halifax. That this was an affair settled without H. M.'s privity. That it was true He (the D. of B.) & Lord Halifax were now not Friends; but that was not his Reason for mentioning it, for Lord Halifax might probably execute it as well as another. That his only reason for mentioning it was to shew the King that, not only Persons were to be ill-treated & removed out of the way, but the chief offices of the State were to be mangled, altered, & lowered at *their* pleasure, in order to promote the Scheme of engrossing all power to *Them* & their Creatures.[4]

The king remembered this interview, and though he admitted most of the reforms, he refused to allow the First Lord of Trade to become a member of the cabinet.[5]

In order to give some form of impartiality to the desired changes Pelham in 1749 appointed a committee to study all aspects of colonial affairs and make recommendations. It was a large committee made up of two distinct groups: (1) those named to give influence and whose attendance was not required (Hardwicke, Dorset, Gower, Pelham, Sandwich, Newcastle, Bedford, the Bishop of London, and Horatio Walpole) and (2) those named to do the actual work (Halifax, Robert Herbert, John Pitt, James Grenville, Lord Dupplin, Francis Fane, Sir Thomas Robinson, and Charles Townshend).[6] Just a glance at these lists reveals that the cabinet would dominate any decisions, for all members were holders of some office or other. Halifax pressed Newcastle throughout the autumn of 1751 to institute the recommended changes, and Newcastle at last gave in and agreed. In November Pelham gave his approval. During 1752 the various changes were introduced except that Halifax was never made a cabinet councilor.[7] The reforms were useful and without a complete reorganization of the government were as much as could be done. Pelham had actively urged the changes, and his administration contributed this distinct improvement to the better functioning of the government. It failed to achieve the desired results because the personnel during the succeeding decades was incapable and, even more important, because the entire government structure was unable to meet the demands made on it by eighteenth-century conditions in many areas. The failure in no way detracts from the sensible attempt to concentrate colonial authority in a single office whose major duty it would become.

The principal problem of the colonies during the peacetime years was the French encroachment on Nova Scotia. This problem consumed time, paper, and money. In 1750 the French advance into Nova Scotia became critical, and the cabinet tried to strengthen the British position by men, money, arms, and diplomacy.[8] Pelham, Newcastle, and Halifax took the lead and eventually sent enough material to Lord Cornwallis to make an actual defense possible. Pelham pushed the Commons and obtained the following sums:[9]

1751	£34,242–16s–11d
1752	46,738– 8 – 4
1753	47,448– 5 –10
1754	47,054–15 – 3

This was a large amount of money to be spent on any one colony, and it showed the importance Pelham attached to the English position there. Pitt strongly supported Pelham's views.[10] Again one can see that Pitt's supposedly new concepts were not new but were rooted in the policies of the preceding fifteen years, when Pelham and Newcastle controlled the government.

Closely connected with the Nova Scotia problems were the difficulties in the West Indies. These have already been referred to in Chapter X on the negotiations with France. However, besides the problem of the disputed islands there were other questions. Pelham in 1750 told Newcastle that England would have to solve these questions alone, for no other country would help. The Privy Council met to discuss them during the years, and approved as strong a policy as feasible. The French seizure of Turk Island in the Bahamas in 1753 was a final blow, and military and naval supplies were ordered shipped to Virginia in preparation for a fight. The Spanish moves against the Mosquito Coast brought a similar response to meet force with force.[11]

By 1753 the same determined opposition to French encroachments was the order for the North American continent. Money was spent to gain the Indians' support. In August word arrived that French forces were moving into the Ohio River Valley. Governor Dinwiddie demanded power to stop them.[12] Conditions were ripe for a future war, and the government in London supported a strong stand against French moves in any of the colonial areas. Therefore before Pelham's death the government was determined to defend its position even if war resulted.

Within the colonies the same general problems arose as during the earlier war period. Georgia was granted funds to improve its defense and increase settlement. Quarrels between colonial legislatures and governors had to be decided. One critical example was the fight in New York between the assembly and Governor Clinton over money. Additional time was spent on patronage applications for positions.[13] In all these matters Pelham was consulted, and in the case of expenditures he held the primary position.

During 1750 another effort at reform occurred. A move was afoot to create a bishopric for America and the West Indies. The Bishop of London, in whose jurisdiction the colonies were, strongly advocated a new bishop to improve the administration of the church in America. Newcastle agreed to the need for a thorough investigation, but he insisted that Pelham must be present. Pelham became deeply involved in this ecclesiastical affair and stood firmly against any new bishopric. His argument was simply that the Bishop of London was trying to dictate policy to the government.[14] The plan came to nothing because the civil government backed Pelham's stubborn stand.

A final area of interest was economic. The North American colonies were stoutly protected from foreign encroachment, and local colonial control was resisted because the London cabinet knew the value of the colonies as markets for British goods. There exists a summary of British exports to the colonies for the Pelham ministry period that shows the increasing value of this export trade:[15]

1740	£ 595,792– 6s– 0d
1741	647,968–16 –10
1742	583,252– 9 –11
1743	604,144–18 – 2
1744	448,129–17 – 8
1745	365,075–15 –11
1746	587,911–13 – 5
1747	612,166– 3 – 8
1748	622,300– 4 – 2
1749	994,568–15 – 1
1750	998,561–11 – 2
1751	943,882– 5 – 0
1752	869,180– 4 – 1
1753	1,118,378–15 –11
1754	921,465– 7 –11

Obviously an export trade of about £1 million a year during the peace years was worth fighting to preserve, especially in 1753 when it was well over that sum. Pelham was friendly enough with the merchants to know what the figures meant to them, and this goes far to explain his stand against French encroachments and a diminution of British control, even in the religious sphere.

The colonial picture would be incomplete without reference to India. By 1750 the London cabinet was aware that no peaceful solution to Anglo-French rivalry was possible. Admiral Boscawen kept the government informed of the state of Indian affairs, and the government backed the strong measures taken by the East India Company.[16] Again Pelham was involved in the decisions that eventually led to the Seven Years War. The circumstances were beyond the control of any man, even an advocate of complete economy. The English cabinet did only what was inevitable.

In sharp contrast to the attention paid to colonial matters, the Privy

Council devoted very little time to Ireland. According to the Privy Council Register, only fourteen (possibly fifteen) meetings of the Committee for Irish Bills were held in the five years.[17] In 1749 and again in 1751 there was only one meeting. This, in spite of the Irish parliament and the Lord Lieutenant, was not nearly enough attention to assure control. It was enough when the Lord Lieutenant was tactful and managed the Irish parliament, but otherwise trouble was bound to arise. Harrington had the necessary tact to keep peace while enforcing the English cabinet's views. The completeness of his control was shown particularly by the surplus he was able to build up in the treasury and his disbursement of those funds.[18] Pelham worked closely with Harrington on financial matters and often at other times. Thus there was a definite loss in efficiency of administration when Harrington was forced to resign.

In the summer of 1751 the Duke of Dorset started out well in Dublin. He and his son, Lord George Sackville, the Irish Secretary, at first kept in close touch with Pelham. However, by the time the Irish parliament met, Dorset felt that he was well enough settled to advance his own policies without London's support. The session of the commons was peaceful at first, but then the problem of how to dispose of the surplus funds was raised. Dorset wished to apply them to the English debt by issuing an order based on his own authority as regent for the king. Sackville wrote to discover if the king's direct order was needed to do this. Pelham responded that it would be better if Dorset arranged it as a voluntary offering from the Irish parliament but that he should move slowly. Things seemed to be going peacefully, and Pelham congratulated Dorset on a successful administration.[19] The English cabinet expected a continuation of the calm, but it was to be disappointed.

Behind the scenes in Ireland Lord George Sackville had formed a political alliance with George Stone, Archbishop of Armagh, and the two proceeded to organize an opposition to Henry Boyle, speaker of the Irish House of Commons. In May 1752 Dorset's administration of Ireland began to arouse open opposition, led by Boyle, and questions were even raised in England.[20] Newcastle voiced the view that Dorset might have to repair the quarrel with Boyle or be removed.[21] The basis of the trouble was, first, Dorset's support of his son and the Archbishop in their attempt to break the power of Boyle and, second, the charges of corruption laid against Sackville. Archbishop Stone, who was the brother of Andrew Stone and on particularly good terms with the Pelhams, denied the charges, but they continued. By the end of Dorset's first year in office the Primate reported that the Irish government was good but unpopular. In spite of these assurances Pelham and Newcastle were not satisfied. They discussed Ireland privately with Dorset, Andrew Stone, and Hardwicke; officially they discussed the problem with Hardwicke, Grafton, Devonshire, Hartington, Holdernesse, and Anson.[22]

Boyle had wisely attached his cause to the issue of how to spend the surplus funds in the Irish treasury. By doing this he gained great favor and support in the Irish parliament and built up solid opposition to the Sackville-Stone alliance. Affairs remained at an impasse throughout 1752 and 1753, and popular discontent appeared in Dublin. Dorset and Sackville made no effort to solve the problem; rather, they stubbornly insisted on prerogative and relied on support from London.[23]

In June 1753, backed by overwhelming parliamentary support, Boyle petitioned the king to demand the restoration of the Irish parliament's right to dispose of its surplus money as it wished. The English cabinet, the Privy Council, and the king were forced to reject the petition and support Dorset or face a loss of power in Ireland. The Irish Commons replied by rejecting Dorset's money bill, 122 to 117. The king and the English cabinet were angry and ordered Dorset to discipline the opposition by dismissing some of its members from their offices and pensions.[24] During these meetings in late 1753, Pelham was ill and therefore only indirectly involved. At the very end of the year the Earl of Kildare arrived in London to present the Irish Commons' views. Pelham, on his recovery, took an active part in the discussions and in preparing to meet Kildare. It was his specific order that established the cabinet policy of rejecting completely the Boyle-Kildare demands.[25] Kildare returned to Dublin unsatisfied, and Pelham sent Dorset the king's authority to proceed without the Irish Commons' vote of money.[26] These forceful moves were contrary to Pelham's usual careful balancing of forces, but if his advice to move slowly had been followed by Dorset they would have been unnecessary. Nevertheless, once the crisis had developed, Pelham felt he could do nothing but enforce authority.

The whole affair was an example of English contempt for the Irish. It also was the first of many attempts of the Irish to govern themselves. The uproar started by Sackville and Dorset was never really settled until after Pelham's death when Henry Boyle's support of the Lord Lieutenant was bought by a title. Pelham's health broke during the summer of 1753, and he was absent from the cabinet meetings much of the summer and occasionally during the fall and winter. Though he was kept informed, he lost his personal touch, and his careful attention to detail was sorely missed. Dorset must bear the major share of the blame, because his stubborn and stiff nature would permit no compromise and his support of Lord George Sackville led him into an indefensible position that nevertheless had to be defended. Dorset was without question the poorest Lord Lieutenant of Ireland named by Pelham. And unfortunately at the very time that the death of Pelham made a strong government essential, Dorset weakened it. The entire affair showed the importance of Pelham and his tact to the administration.

CHAPTER XIX

Postwar Opposition and Politics

℘ THE POLITICAL CALM of the peacetime years of Pelham's administration has been referred to many times. Certainly in parliament it was the most strikingly quiet period of the mid-eighteenth century. Much of the credit was due to Pelham's careful balancing of groups within the cabinet and to his thoroughness in preparing for new measures by tactful compromise before launching them. However, no cabinet or First Lord could kill opposition completely, for there were bound to be malcontents. Part of the reason for the political calm could, therefore, be found in the opposition itself.

After the war it would have been natural to expect a growing opposition, but such was not the case. The end of the war merely removed the one possible source of united opposition available to those out of power. An immediate scramble occurred, during which some opponents joined the government and the others broke into even smaller groups than before. In 1749, when the Mutiny Bill was presented to the House of Lords, the opposition was almost nonexistent. Granville, Winchelsea, and their few friends did not even attend the debates. The opposition tactics consisted of delay by violent attacks and divisions on each clause. In 1751, the vote on the address was carried by 203 to 74, and the land tax, an unpopular issue, was carried by an even greater majority, 229 to 28.[1] These were typical votes, showing no organization among the opposition members.

Part of the explanation was that the Prince of Wales and the Duke of Cumberland, who opposed the Pelhams after 1750, would have nothing to do with each other. Moreover, as Pelham clearly saw, Frederick was not respected or trusted by the public and Cumberland was feared by the vast majority of citizens.[2] The royal brothers were particularly ill suited to lead any concerted action either together or separately. Granville followed the cabinet's lead and rejoined it in 1751. Bath resumed his friendship with Newcastle. And last, Lord Bolingbroke's death in 1751 removed the one man capable of organizing the opposition.[3] A short examination of the two main groups will make even more clear the failure of any real opposition to develop.

Early in 1749 Horace Walpole described the party of the Prince of Wales, who, Walpole said, stayed till the Pelhams had bought off every man of parts in his train, and then began to form his own party. . . . You wil wonder what new resources the Prince has discovered—why, he has found them all in Lord Egmont. . . . All the old corps hate him, on my father's and Mr. Pelham's account; the new part of the ministry on their own. The Tories have not quite forgiven his having left them in the last Parliament: besides that, they are now governed by one Prowse, a cold plausible fellow, and a great well-wisher to Mr. Pelham.[4]

Moreover, Lord Strange and Robert Nugent were the other leaders, and they disliked Egmont. However, out of this combination Frederick tried to form an opposition. His one great strength was the age of the king, for the prince would be sure to have his way once he ascended the throne. In spite of these conditions there were only two important defections from the ministry: Dodington, the perpetual turncoat, and Lord Bute.[5]

In late 1749 Frederick and his followers laid plans for their assumption of power. A long list of corrections of evils was to be their order of business, and they distributed the cabinet offices among themselves. This was a classic study in impotence, especially when a few days later they agreed not to oppose the ministry's bills unless these were completely unacceptable.[6] Only Egmont refused to agree, and he opposed merely to oppose. In November 1750 the Prince of Wales was gleeful over the cabinet fight between Newcastle and Bedford because he was sure the cabinet would collapse. He even hinted that Newcastle had approached him to form a new ministry with Granville.[7] However, Pelham's temporary compromise destroyed any of Frederick's hopes that had been based on Egmont's wishes.

On March 21, 1751, the Prince of Wales' party was destroyed, for Frederick died early that morning. Everything was in chaos among his followers, and the leaders decided on a vague support for Pelham.[8] In reality it was every man for himself, and Lords Limerick, Westmoreland, Shaftesbury, Oxford, and Talbot and Francis Dashwood, Richard Glover, and George Dodington made the best possible settlement for themselves during the following spring.

The result of the destruction of Frederick's party was the Regency Bill, which would make the Princess of Wales regent if the necessity arose. The Pelhams proposed this to keep power from Cumberland, who was then their principal political enemy. Pelham sponsored it in the Commons, Newcastle and Devonshire in the Lords. There was a long and noisy debate by Cumberland's friends and the Bedford Whigs. But by the end of May 1751 it was safely passed, and the Pelhams were in complete control again.[9] The rest of the session was very quiet, for the friends of the late heir, except Egmont, were busy cultivating the triumphant ministers. Some of them were successful, but the case of Dodington showed that Pelham was in no hurry to provide for them. It was the spring of 1753 before that case was entirely settled.[10]

The total destruction of the Prince of Wales' party gave Pelham the opportunity he needed to satisfy Newcastle and dispose of Bedford. He waited until the end of the session of parliament and until the leaders of Frederick's party had committed themselves to him. Then he allowed Bedford to be ousted. He knew this would increase Cumberland's power, but since the Bedfordite-Cumberland coalition would be the only sizable group, the cabinet could afford the luxury of removing Bedford. Newcastle's recall of Granville left the opposition groups without any well-established leader. Pelham had taken advantage of the accident of Frederick's death and made political capital of it.

The Cumberland opposition grew from two sources: his own ambition and Bedford's dislike of Newcastle. Cumberland had been disappointed at the end of the war because the Pelhams had cut his military position to almost nothing and refused him other power. He and his sister Amelia were George's favorite children, and this was the great danger to the cabinet. They used their influence with the king to build a small group opposed to the government and especially to Newcastle. It did not really become important until 1750, when Bedford and his friends began to negotiate for support. Bedford's dislike of Newcastle was partly personal and partly inspired by Sandwich. The two dukes were at open war during 1750, and each stayed in office only because Pelham soothed and pressed them.[11] When Bedford was finally removed, he immediately formed an alliance with Cumberland, and that alliance was the basis of the only effective parliamentary opposition during the remaining years of the administration.

In 1752 Bedford tried to provoke a large opposition to the Saxon treaty but he failed by 249 to 54. He and Cumberland tried again in 1753, but they lost every time. The last two parliamentary sessions of Pelham's life were really the most quiet of any during his administration, for his only serious trouble came from the popular clamor over the Naturalization of Jews Bill. Even Egmont admitted the futility of any opposition. Pelham was satisfied with the situation, and he advised Newcastle to ignore any parliamentary or public attacks.[12] Pelham clearly was not worried, and he was right. The opposition was out of power until the cabinet let it in by compromise or accumulated mistakes. The whole history of the opposition during this period is one of futility and incompetence.

The last major task undertaken by Pelham before his death was the organization of the election campaign of 1754. A few examples will show that electioneering was not a separate occurrence every seven years but continuous process with high points of activity for about a year previous to each statutory election. In the first place, vacancies occurred from time to time because of the death or resignation of a member of the House of Commons, and these caused special elections. In 1750 there were three such vacancies, one each at Dorchester, East Grinsted, and Weymouth. In each case Pelham was called upon to make the final choice of government candidate after conference with all interested parties. In the Dorchester case, Pelham expressed his sole responsibility better than anyone else when he said,

> You know the only difficulty, I have assured him [John Pitt] I will do my best, when the King comes over, had I left it to be managed att Hanover [i.e., by Newcastle] I am moraly sure, it would not have ended well. But I hope when I can speak myself it will do.[13]

Obviously Pelham regarded himself as responsible for the elections and thought he could arrange matters better than anyone else. In 1751 William Cayley appealed to Newcastle, not to arrange his election but to persuade Pelham to arrange it. Later in that year the local politicians in Gloucester asked that Newcastle and Pelham suggest a candidate for a vacancy.[14] These events are sufficient to demonstrate the fact that the ministry, and especially Pelham, had a constant problem in the actual elections.

Second only to these interim elections was the problem of negotiating political authority. One example may perhaps suffice—George Dodington's negotiations. Early in 1752 Dodington approached Pelham with a request to regain some office, since the Prince of Wales' death had left him without a party, group, or job. Pelham wanted the parliamentary support of the two votes at Weymouth that Dodington controlled. Thus a compromise was effected, and each man got what he wanted.[15] Moreover, Dodington had an important voice in the choice of candidates at Bridgewater, along with Lord Paulet, Egremont, and Egmont. Dodington, Paulet, and Egremont agreed on a candidate and offered support to Pelham against an opposition set up by Egmont. This was a further extension of Pelham's deal with Dodington, combined with friendship for Egremont and Paulet.[16] This type of political activity had to be constantly carried on, or election time would find too many discontented people controlling local elections. Pelham's tact and compromise were great advantages in these affairs.

In fact, 1752 became a year of build-up for the next regular election. The opposition, mindful of the shrewd trick of 1747 when Pelham caught them unprepared by calling the election a year early, had no intention of being caught asleep again. Pelham, therefore, countered by beginning to electioneer early for the government. In general he found the country well disposed toward the cabinet. Sussex Pelham knew to be well in hand, and on a trip northward he found matters well enough except in Staffordshire, Huntingdonshire, and the northwest.[17] His one caution was expressed as follows:

> I am doing as much as I can privately, in many borroughs, and shall continue to act with as much caution as I can, for if burgessing begins so early; ill humour will arise in Parliament, and great expence both to the Publick and

individuals. Nothing however must be neglected, for I am of opinion the
quiet and ease of His Majestys future Government, and the prosperity of this
Nation in General, depends upon the choice of the next Parliament.[18]

Thus the careful economist appeared in the election procedure. Pelham
wanted to win a definite victory at the polls, but he wanted to win it as
cheaply as possible. And careful attention to detail and personal direction
were his methods of winning.

Newcastle and Pelham had been particularly attentive to Sussex electoral affairs. As early as 1749 they were preparing the way for continuation of their control. They named a cousin, Thomas Pelham, at a
special election that year, and in 1750 they reprimanded him for not
catering enough to his electorate. They arranged to take and manage
the Chichester interests of the Duke of Richmond after his death. And
Pelham frequently went to Sussex during 1752 and 1753 to attend personally to electoral matters.[19] His illness during the summer of 1753 made
him unavailable at times, but Newcastle arranged that Chief Justice Lee
hold his Lewes Assizes (a common electioneering chance) at a time
convenient for Pelham's presence. The brothers collected all their political
supporters from the Lords and Commons on August 29, 1753, at Lewes,
and there they nominated Pelham and John Butler to represent the
county of Sussex. The meeting proceeded in perfect agreement, and
Pelham was able to write a few days later that everything was under control. He was right, for even though he died before the election all the
brothers' nominees were returned.[20] It had been a completely successful
campaign.

However, Sussex was only part of Pelham's election campaign. In
Oxfordshire the Duke of Marlborough decided to upset the peaceful
balance between government Whigs, opposition Whigs, and Tories, and
Pelham supported his move as a chance to increase the parliamentary
majority.[21] Pelham entered into the campaign by issuing ordinances,
writing letters of recommendation, revoking licenses of publicans who
opposed Marlborough's men, and buying off James Ralph, the opposition
journalist who was active in the area.[22] Pelham used his vacation at
Scarborough, forced by poor health, to help solve Yorkshire election
quarrels among the Whig leaders, and he kept in touch with the young
Marquis of Rockingham as to affairs in the city of York.[23] Pelham and
Newcastle, compelled to take a direct hand in the Nottingham election,
exerted great pressure on most local leaders to make them accept Lord
Howe's candidate.[24] The Nottingham officials finally gave in, but only
after almost two months of persuasion. Through his earlier deal with
Dodington, Pelham practically directed the elections of Dorchester and
Bridgewater, and he did so with a minimum of trouble.[25] Besides these,
and in other places where Pelham was actively engaged in the elections
to some degree, he and Newcastle received reports from, and sent sug-

gestions to, Whigs all over England. They were assured of success from such widely separate spots as North Wales, Bristol, Staffordshire, Shropshire, Norfolk, Old Sarum, and Scotland.[26] The opposition was unable to break the complete system Pelham had established, for the Bedfordites and Tories would not unite. They were the only two sizable groups; all other opposition was local and unconnected with national issues. The result was a smashing victory for the government. Pelham had prepared so well that even his death did not upset the result.

One historian has estimated that the government spent only £30,000 on the whole general election. That seems a rather good guess, for the individual amounts listed by West for Newcastle to examine after Pelham's death total only about £12,000.[27] That exceedingly small amount shows that Pelham had been successful in his demands for economy.

Newcastle's ignorance of the men selected by Pelham to be candidates further bears out the idea that Pelham directed almost all aspects of the election alone. After Pelham's death, Lord Dupplin and John Roberts, Pelham's two personal aides, held a meeting with Newcastle at which they produced Pelham's list and showed the duke what decisions had been made. Contemporary historians have also noted the fact that Pelham alone ran the election.[28] Nothing could make plainer the fact that Pelham was indeed the Prime Minister. Newcastle would have given up his cherished election control under no other circumstances. Therefore until the very day of his death Pelham actively controlled his government and determined its course of action—and he did it alone whenever he desired.

CHAPTER XX

Henry Pelham

႘ IN DECEMBER 1753 Pelham became seriously ill, and for almost three weeks, from December 17 to January 4, he was isolated from the cabinet. Dr. Wilmot, Lord Dupplin, or John Roberts sent regular daily reports to Newcastle or the Earl of Lincoln, Pelham's son-in-law, on the progress of his recovery.[1] Wilmot, after opening a swelling that had formed, was unable to do anything for Pelham except bleed him. Nevertheless on January 7, 1754, he felt sufficiently well to attend to government business.[2] His apparent recovery was received happily by the entire ministry. Yet in spite of the fact that he attended to affairs of the government during the rest of January and February, he had not recovered. On February 2 another swelling developed, and doctors were called to open it.[3] This should have been a warning that all was not well, but instead the cabinet acted as if his return to work had marked a complete recovery. Pelham also acted as if he had regained his health. He attended a Privy Council meeting on March 1, and then he was forced to his bed. This time all Whigs were alarmed seriously at the possibility of his death.[4]

Their worst fears were justified, for Pelham died on March 6, 1754, early in the morning. Newcastle, overwhelmed by the news, shut himself up for two days without seeing anyone and left Hardwicke to hold the reins of government.[5] Condolences poured in to Newcastle from all parts of England. Almost every member of the ministry and every office-holder expressed sympathy for Newcastle and respect for Pelham's conduct of the government.[6] It is the evident honesty of expression in most of these letters that best testifies to the leadership Pelham had exerted for twelve years.

Not everyone felt saddened by the loss. Horace Walpole, dipping his pen in venom, dashed off several masterpieces of satire on the death of the minister:

> Mr. Pelham is dead! All that calm, that supineness, of which I have lately talked to you so much is at an end! there is no heir to such luck as his. The whole people of England can never agree a second time upon the same person for the residence of infallibility.[7]

Richard Glover left no doubt of his hatred of Pelham, whom he described as a gamester—narrow, false, ungrateful, and corrupt.[8] But

Walpole had made a slip in his comment. He paid Pelham a tribute when he admitted that "the whole people of England" were agreed in support of him. There are very few persons in history about whom an enemy could say that the whole nation followed them.

Not only were the governing groups upset by the loss of Pelham, but they immediately began the chaotic scramble for office and power that was characteristic of the next three years under Newcastle. Fox did not even have the common decency to wait until after Pelham's funeral. On the very day of the death he sought out Newcastle to request promotion. The old king was right when he said, "Now I shall have no more peace." The month of March was absolutely hectic.[9] In many ways Pelham had become indispensable, for he had kept the fine balance between strong rivalries and many groups. The new cabinet was decided on by Granville, Marlborough, Grafton, Devonshire, Argyll, Hartington, Holdernesse, Anson, and Hardwicke.[10] Newcastle and the king then approved the outline and tried to put it into effect; however, Newcastle was too obstinate to please Fox. Therefore Fox refused to become Secretary of State, and Newcastle changed the plans. The duke sorely missed the careful negotiation by which Pelham had solved equally great, or even greater, political crises. His only certainty was that he had succeeded Pelham in the Treasury post and was at last the most important minister in England.[11]

Pelham rendered one last service to the cabinet after his death. He had left specific orders to his secretary, John Roberts, to collect all his papers and lock them up until ordered to separate them and pass the proper ones on to a successor.[12] Thus Pelham left the one man who knew all about his private and public affairs at the disposal of a future government, in order to make a change of government easy. He also ensured thereby the secrecy of important matters. This was especially true of the secret service papers that were to be kept until the king's personal will was expressed.[13] Pelham's old friend Arundel was the only other person to help in securing the papers. However, Hardwicke gave Roberts the necessary legal and political advice.[14] These measures of secrecy were extremely important in the eighteenth century, and especially so in the period following Pelham, for the factions would have used any available information in the bitter fights to upset the succeeding government.

What was the man really like? The preceding pages have attempted to survey Henry Pelham's part as First Lord of the Treasury in a cabinet that lasted from August 1743 until March 1754. The major problems confronting that cabinet have been reviewed, and Pelham's role in their solution has been estimated. His relationships with other ministers and departments outside the Treasury have been examined. The extra-statutory aspects of his career, such as leadership in the Commons, election participation, and activity in the rough-and-tumble of eighteenth-century politics, have been especially commented on. But still the question of what the man was really like remains. That question can best be answered by a review of what his contemporaries and succeeding historians thought of him.

For many years in the nineteenth century the primary source of all information on the period was Horace Walpole. Historians accepted his word as final proof in any argument. However, as they sharpened the weapons of their craft, they found that though Walpole's facts might have been right, his conclusions were prejudiced and twisted to suit his personal feelings. Lord Holland, as early as 1846, noted Walpole's major prejudices when he edited the *Memoirs of George II*. Walpole, he said, always spoke of Pelham with dislike, of Hardwicke with hatred, and of Newcastle with contempt and aversion.[15] Therefore when Walpole said, "Sir Robert loved power so much, that he would not endure anything; Mr. Pelham loved it so well, that he would endure anything," [16] the statement cannot be accepted at its face value. In spite of this general attitude on the part of Walpole, he had the justice to say, "Let it be remembered . . . that, though he first taught or experienced universal servility in Englishmen, yet he lived without abusing his power, and died poor." [17] From an eighteenth-century mind accustomed to political corruption and especially to political opponents, this was a considerable compliment. Unfortunately the nineteenth-century historians forgot that when they found their sources in Walpole's words they also found Walpole's prejudices. These, therefore, color almost all nineteenth-century remarks.

Lord Chesterfield contrasted his views of various personages of his time with those of his contemporaries. In particular, he quoted the two authors of the *Continuation of Rapin* on Pelham. Nicholas Tindal, a strong Tory, wrote:

> Great Britain perhaps never enjoyed such a state of political tranquillity, as it did while Mr. Pelham was considered in the capacity of first minister; and, perhaps, he is the only instance upon record of a minister who made great virtues serve in place of great abilities. . . . His understanding was rather clear than bright, so that he seldom was deceived by the false glare of the medium through which he perceived objects. . . .
>
> Few private gentlemen were ever known to unite so much dignity and ease in their behaviour as he did; and he retained a complacency of manners towards those with whom he differed . . . that he seldom failed to win them over. His long experience in business undoubtedly contributed greatly to his success. . . . His disinterestedness was seen in the state of his private affairs, which . . . were but very indifferent at the time of his death.[18]

Tobias Smollett, who continued the work of Tindal wrote:

> Mr. Pelham was generally esteemed as a man of honesty and candour, actuated by a sincere love for his country. . . . His death . . . was . . . regretted by the nation in general, to whose affection he had powerfully recommended himself by the candor and humanity of his conduct and character,

even while he pursued measures which they did not entirely approve.[19]

Chesterfield, who was a much more friendly witness, agreed in general with his two sources:

> Mr. Pelham had good sense, without either shining parts or any degree of Literature. He had by no means an elevated or enterprizing genius, but had a more manly and steady resolution than his brother the Duke of Newcastle. He had gentleman-like frankness in his behaviour, and as great point of honour as a minister can have, especially a minister at the head of the Treasury, where numberless sturdy and insatiable beggars of condition apply, who cannot all be gratified, nor all with safety refused.
>
> He was a very inelegant Speaker in Parliament, but spoke with a certain candour and openness that made him well heard, and generally believed.
>
> He wished well to the Public, and managed the Finances with great care and personal purity. He . . . had many domestic Virtues and no Vices. If his place, and the power that accompanies it, made him some public enemies, his behaviour in both secured him from personal and rancorous ones. Those who wished him worst, only wished themselves in his place.[20]

These are three estimates from very different points of view, but the picture presented is strikingly the same.

William Pitt wrote that, political considerations aside, he was "sensibly touched with his loss, as a man, upon the whole, of a most amiable composition." [21] The Earl of Holdernesse, not an otherwise perspicacious person, reported, "The high & just Opinion the Nation in general had conceived of His Ability, & disinterested Integrity, has render'd Him, at once, an usefull Minister to the King, and a Favorite to the Nation." [22] And James Ralph, one of Pelham's most consistent foes, described his conversation as "genteel and elegant . . . beyond most others.[23] In fact, most of the estimates are well summed up by the Earl of Waldegrave, who said:

> Mr. Pelham died in March, 1754; and our tranquility, both at home and abroad, expired with him.
>
> He had acquired the reputation of an able and honest minister. had a plain, solid understanding, improved by experience in business, as well as by a thorough knowledge of the world; and without being an orator, or having the finest parts, no man in the House of Commons argued with more weight, or was heard with greater attention.
>
> He was a frugal steward to the public, averse to continental extravagance and useless subsidies; preferring a tolerable peace to the most successful war; jealous to maintain his personal credit and authority; but nowise inattentive to the true interest of his country.[24]

Thus contemporaries thought well of him, and political persuasion had little effect on their reasoned views once he was gone from the political scene. He was almost universally applauded for his public and private virtues, and his faults were usually ignored or described as minor traits.

His speaking ability in the Commons was agreed by all to be plain but forceful and honest. This honesty was the characteristic held up by all as his strongest claim to high distinction.

Though pamphlet warfare was strong during Pelham's life, and he was charged with almost every crime from stupidity to corruption and subversion of the English constitution, such charges do not appear in the opinions of contemporaries who attempted to be impartial. Laudatory pamphlets about him were almost as numerous as condemnatory ones. Both must be considered as what they were—politics, of the most violent sort, in action. But again, nineteenth-century historians chose to believe only those that fitted their preconceived ideas of eighteenth-century corruption and wickedness.[25]

The nineteenth-century historians largely ignored the first sixty years of the eighteenth century, or else they passed over that period—with which they felt so little in common—with generalities about corruption and the growth of the cabinet. Even Lecky, at the end of the century, largely ignored the political aspects of the eighteenth century and concentrated on its social aspects. A few individuals like William Pitt, because of his upright moral life, and Prince Charles Edward Stuart, because of his romantic escape from Scotland, appealed to the nineteenth century and were popular with the historians. But men of as widely divergent personalities as Bolingbroke, Robert Walpole, the Duke of Newcastle, Lord North, and William Pitt the younger were unpopular. Not all of these could be omitted, but they were treated as briefly as possible. Of course there were exceptions, as, for example, the great number of memoirs and letters that were published. In a true sense, however, they were not histories but only the raw materials of history. We may be most grateful today for these materials, but we sadly miss a tradition of history for the eighteenth century.

Early in the nineteenth century Archdeacon William Coxe produced his many memoir-like histories. For almost a century his was the only biographical work on Robert Walpole, and his work on Henry Pelham is still the only biography of that minister. He was old enough to remember contemporaries of Pelham, so that his works form a bridge between Pelham and later historians. However, he was prejudiced in favor of the "good old days," and his work must be judged on this basis. Nevertheless, as the only historian who ever saw the now lost Pelham papers, his estimation must carry weight. He summarized Pelham's career as follows:

> Towards him, even political rivalry seems scarcely to have engendered either prejudice or animosity; and in the estimate of the principles, by which he was guided, the ends which he pursued, and the means which he employed, both his opponents and friends, with little exception, cordially agree.
>
> His knowledge was rather useful than extensive; his understanding more solid than brilliant. His abilities did not burst forth with that splendor which has distinguished the opening career of many statesmen, but were gradually

developed by experience and practice, and seemed to grow equal to the occasions, by which they were called into action. He was slow and cautious in
deciding, yet firm and persevering, when his resolution was once formed;
though he knew the proper time and occasion, to bend to popular prejudice,
or public opinion. Instead of declining under the weight of years, his energies
continued to increase; and, at no period did he better assume the spirit and
authority of a great minister, than in that which immediately preceded his
dissolution.[26]

Later nineteenth-century historians occasionally mentioned Pelham
in general histories or biographies of other men. John Earle, in his volume on English premiers, devoted a short section to Pelham. His summary comment was that Pelham's great merit was that he was a "safe"
man. However, Earle failed to define what he meant by "safe." [27] Archibald Ballantyne, in his biography of Granville, took the side of his subject and denounced Pelham with violence.[28] These two were typical late
nineteenth-century comments—the slurring over or the attack. It can be
plainly stated that Earle was unjustified in his small allotment of time
and space. Pelham was First Lord of the Treasury for more than ten
years and George Grenville, Lord Grafton, and others for considerably
shorter periods, yet the author devoted space to them in an inverse relationship. Moreover, it cannot be argued that the late 1760's were more
vital than the 1740's, and certainly Grenville, Grafton, and Rockingham never did anything of importance equal to the financial reforms of
Pelham. Ballantyne's arguments simply are not supported by facts; he
believed his own prejudices.

By the time of World War I, the prejudices of nineteenth-century
morality were dying. Wartime power politics and the resurgence of economic nationalism made the milieu of England in this period more akin
to that of the mid-eighteenth century. Moreover, the opening of many
private collections of documents made new sources of information available. Historians began to reexamine the eighteenth century. Philip
Yorke, in his biography of Lord Hardwicke, described Pelham in much
more balanced terms than the earlier generations had done. In fact, his
over-all estimation was more accurate than any other, since he recognized
the essentially good characteristics of the minister:

Henry Pelham possessed great natural abilities and performed great services
to the nation. Though unlike Sir Robert Walpole in character, being timid
and pliant when opposed, reserved and fretful and wanting in optimism and
good humour, he inherited and carried on Walpole's great national policy—
the peaceful development of the country. He was a sound and successful
financial minister, an excellent and industrious man of business, a good
manager of Parliament and leader of the House of Commons. Actuated by an
honest and genuine love of his country, he upheld the government and
guided the state through times of dangerous crisis, during a great war, a great
rebellion and a hostile invasion, and his long tenure of power was marked by
the carrying through of many useful and important reforms.[29]

Basil Williams, in his general history of the first half of the eighteenth century, devoted most of his attention to the Duke of Newcastle and largely ignored Pelham except to note his financial reforms. He credited Pelham with being a "moderate" man and one able to conciliate opposition.[30] Lloyd Sanders, in his biography of Dodington, examined only the political aspects of the period, and on this basis he found Pelham far superior to the average politician.[31] But his picture is strictly limited, not that of a well-rounded man. Clive Bigham attempted a multiple biography of British prime ministers, which was by nature merely a series of brief sketches. His sketch of Pelham is exceedingly brief, but he recognized the fact that most historians have concentrated on Walpole and Pitt to the exclusion of everyone else during the first seventy years of the eighteenth century. His estimate of Pelham was that of a solid man and a minister of great merit.[32] A few years later F. J. C. Hearnshaw wrote the same kind of book on the eighteenth century alone. He allotted to Pelham only a few pages and found nothing to say about him except that he was a good politician who followed the lead of others.[33] A. S. Turberville's fine study of the House of Lords, without trying to examine Pelham, describes well how the oligarchic Whigs controlled the government—the ultimate result of the Pelham cabinet. Turberville thus implied that there was an excellent coordinating person behind the scene. He did not ascribe this coordination to Pelham, but he indicated that Pelham played the major part in the system.[34] Within the limited scope of his work he presented another aspect of Pelham's personal position and showed how the oligarchy began to lose control after Pelham's death.

In 1930 Sir Lewis Namier brought the revision of the historical interpretation of the eighteenth century to its climax by basing his study on private papers of the people involved. Namier's brilliant *Structure of Politics* changed the attitudes of historians and made eighteenth-century conservatism better understood. F. S. Oliver, in a popular book, represented these changed attitudes, for he depicted his historical figures as men without the Whig-Liberal bias of the nineteenth and early twentieth centuries. He presented Pelham as a capable administrator, a peacemaker, and a man of complete honesty.[35] Thus the wheel has turned a full cycle, and William Coxe's assessment has been heard again, but without partiality.

A recent general history of the time of Pitt and Walpole is the little survey of the eighteenth century by John Plumb. His summary of Pelham represents an advance from the popularization attempts of Oliver, for his work is based on a solid knowledge of eighteenth-century history and personalities. He wrote:

> Henry Pelham was not a great statesman, but his qualities have been underestimated because his early career was overshadowed by Sir Robert Walpole and his maturity by Pitt. His views on domestic affair were sound, liberal,

well in advance of his time; about foreign policy he thought very much as Pitt thought, but he was infinitely more circumspect. He learned all that could be learned from Walpole of the art of handling men, and for ten years he had held together a most heterogeneous collection of politicians in a common purpose. Opposition had ceased almost to exist. But by his death many men saw an opportunity to make a bid for power.[36]

This is the picture of a successful Prime Minister and a gifted politician.

The latest, and in some ways the most important, examination of Pelham is John Owen's *The Rise of the Pelhams*. It is mainly an examination in detail of the two years from 1742 to 1744, with special reference to parliamentary activity. Written under the influence of Sir Lewis Namier, it is extremely detailed and covers the composition of the House of Commons in a thorough manner. However, it does not really examine the administration or the House of Lords. More important as an assessment of Pelham, it devotes only one chapter to the period from 1744 to 1747 and nothing to the rest of Pelham's life. Nevertheless Owen summarized his attitude toward the First Lord as follows:

> Henry Pelham fully deserved his new title, for he was by 1747 a true "Minister for the King in the House of Commons" and "Minister for the House of Commons in the Closet." Drawing his strength from the two chief sources of political power, he rose above his titled colleagues in the Cabinet and, because he had to defend the *whole* of the Administration's policy in the Commons, he could not be confined merely to the business of the Treasury—he had become England's second Prime Minister.[37]

This, then, is a clear statement of full recognition of Pelham as the chief minister and maker of policy. The little that has been written about Pelham has varied from hatred and detestation to respect and even admiration. The more complete the data, the greater the attitude of respect.

As a man, particularly a young man, Pelham was a gay and pleasant companion, but as the years advanced and his responsibilities became greater, he lost much of his zest for life. He became rather cold and aloof and preferred to spend his time alone. Nevertheless his old spirit flashed occasionally in his fondness for his grandchildren and in his friendship for Lord Dupplin, Thomas Arundel, and a few younger men. It does not detract from his character that he was as fond of his brother at his death, in spite of Newcastle's quarrelsome nature and all the trouble it had caused, as he had been when both were youths. Historians, however, usually find it difficult to present a quiet and reserved man in a true manner. The answer is best found in the respect that almost all Englishmen felt for him in 1754. Walpole spread hatred everywhere he went. Pitt bred anger and resentment throughout his life. Newcastle usually was well liked but not respected. Granville was always distrusted. Henry Fox was feared and held in contempt. And Chesterfield, while usually liked, was considered too self-seeking. It was a true mark of Pelham's ability that he alone, among first-ranking contemporary politicians, was almost universally respected as a man and as a minister.

Pelham's administration of the Treasury was extremely successful in both war and peace. His reform of finances not only obtained value for money expended and saved the Treasury from considerable waste but also stressed the true use of money—not as valuable itself but only valuable for what it represented. Debt management and systematic control were his standards, and he overthrew outmoded ideas of the intrinsic evils of a debt. By doing this, Pelham arrived at the sensible idea of a government economy that could be expanded and contracted with the needs of the times. This was one of his two major contributions to England.

The other contribution was equally practical—his belief that party politics must not be carried to such lengths that the king's service (England's national policy) should suffer. This lesson he learned during the bitter fights of Walpole's administration, and when his opportunity came, he avoided the continuation of political warfare as far as possible. This was particularly important during the middle of the eighteenth century because political parties did not exist as such, and the many splinter groups were especially bitter in attacking one another. No one person or group could enforce peace, but Pelham negotiated it. The sixteen years following his death proved what chaos could result from lack of power or negotiating ability. George II recognized Pelham's service by putting almost complete power into his hands in the last years of the ministry. George had not liked Pelham at first, and it took seven years for Pelham to gain favor, but by 1750 George trusted his advice as thoroughly as he had once trusted Walpole. George II was not a brilliant man, but he knew from long experience the difficulty of government, and he wanted to avoid trouble. To that end he accepted both Walpole and Pelham, though disliking them at first.

Pelham took a sensible attitude toward the Jacobite rebellion. He refused to get alarmed by its military success and instead worked quietly to provide the military means to defeat it. In this he was aided by the excitable Newcastle, and the two eventually succeeded. He helped Cumberland's concentration of troops to meet the rebels between Derby and London. Once the rebels retreated to the north, Pelham agreed to a division of troops to prepare to meet the expected French invasion. When the rebellion was over he strongly supported reform of the laws of Scotland but was so opposed to Cumberland's violence in enforcing peace that he wished to deny military power to Cumberland after the war. On the whole his policy was one of reconciliation, even though he was unable to enforce it completely.

The same reform spirit that Pelham showed in regard to finance and Scottish laws was apparent in his general domestic policy. The calendar reform, bills for quarantine, tolerance for Jews, increasing efficiency in government departments especially in colonial administration and army payment—these demonstrated the ideas of Pelham in many fields. In foreign affairs he was also prepared to make constructive changes. He advocated an alliance with Prussia, even at the expense of the old alliance with Austria, thus preceding Pitt in recognition of the decline of the Hapsburgs and the rise of the Hohenzollerns. Under his prodding, the government's evaluation of the European balance underwent a gradual change, completed by Newcastle two years after Pelham's death. Only some of the reforms of the period originated with Pelham, but he saw the virtues of the others, accepted them, and promoted them. Until the time of the American Revolution no First Lord showed so strong a desire to reform the evils and inefficiencies of government. His guiding principle was to make the government work effectively and as cheaply as possible. To this end no established rule or law was sacrosanct; he was willing to change anything.

In the constitutional struggle between the king and parliament, Pelham always acted as the spokesman of parliamentary will, not the king's, even though he continually spoke of himself as the king's servant. This was one step further than Walpole had gone, for Sir Robert always acted as a minister responsible to the king. In particular, Pelham forced the constitutional issue of the cabinet's ultimate control in 1744 and 1746 when he compelled George II to oust Granville. His whole correspondence with Newcastle repeated his view that the monarch had to submit to his ministers' policies as the best policies. The policy worked under Pelham when the ministers controlled parliament and regarded themselves as the king's friends, but it failed later when parliamentary leaders were opposed to the king's friends. George III did only what his grandfather had done, but he did not have friends who belonged to the groups that controlled parliament until Lord North became First Lord. It was Pelham's conciliatory ability that enabled the government to function without difficulty from 1742 to 1754.

Pelham's various coalition ministries at one time or another contained almost all the competent political leaders. Granville, Chesterfield, and Newcastle were Secretaries of State who understood the nature of foreign policy and made concrete efforts to regulate Britain's affairs. Harrington and Holdernesse were capable functionaries who could carry out policies decided on by others. Admiral Anson was one of the best First Lords of the Admiralty of the eighteenth century, though Lord Sandwich was one of the less competent. Lord Hardwicke is usually considered one of the two outstanding legal officials of eighteenth-century England. The other was William Murray, who was Solicitor-General during Pelham's entire ministry and a close friend of Pelham. Devonshire, Chesterfield, and Harrington were good administrators of Ireland. Harrington, Dorset, and Granville performed the duties of Lord President with regularity and competence. Thus it can be said that Pelham organized a cabinet in which the major executive positions were normally held by men of above average ability for the eighteenth century. The point can be quickly proved by comparing them with the men who held the same offices under Walpole.

Among the lesser ministers of great ability were William Pitt, Henry Fox, Henry Bilson Legge, and Duncan Forbes, all of whom would rank high in any administration. Other members of the ministry, like George Grenville, George Lyttelton, and the Earl of Halifax, were assets to several governments. In fact, Pelham's government was made up of such a variety of groups that men who received their first office in it reappeared as leaders of the government for the next thirty years. Pelham selected the best from many groups and put them together. This explains some of the intracabinet quarreling, for men of such varied talents seldom get along well together.

The bad choices of ministers have already been noted—Monson, Bedford, and Dorset being the outstanding failures—and there were far too many of them to be disregarded. However, not all of them were free choices of the Pelhams, for some were leaders of factions who demanded office as the price of cooperation. This was the reason for Bedford's promotion and in part for Dorset's. On the whole Pelham managed to keep these incapable men out of major administrative offices. They were usually placed in secondary posts or honorary ones. Thus an effort was made to achieve efficiency within the existing system.

The Undersecretaries, who did much of the work, were often excellent selections. John Scrope and James West of the Treasury; Andrew Stone, Edward Weston, Thomas Ramsden, Hugh Valence Jones, and Claudius Amyand of the State Office; Thomas Corbet and John Cleveland of the Admiralty; Hutton Perkins in the Chancery were all men of extremely high administrative ability in their respective offices. The men named to high army command were less fortunate choices. The Earl of Stair had been a good commander, but he was too old by 1743. Sir John Cope and Field Marshal Wade were poor commanders. The Duke of Cumberland, the best new commander, was an unsuccessful one. Sir John Ligonier, who rose to prominence, was a moderately able man. There were some good men in the lower ranks, but the army system was so full of purchased commands that it bred poor commanders. The navy, on the other hand, produced several men who were truly capable: Admirals Anson, Ogle, Warren, Byng, Hawke, Knowles, Boscawen, Haddock, and Vernon. These were the men who made England's navy great during the wars of the period. Any administration that relied on such outstanding civil and naval commanders was bound to achieve some success. Conversely one that relied on such mediocre military figures was likely to fail. Yet on balance, the civil and naval professionals outweighed the military commanders.

In closing, Pelham's own position should be reviewed. He started his major cabinet activity as Paymaster-General and leader of the House of Commons in 1742. In 1743 he advanced to First Lord of the Treasury and Chancellor of the Exchequer. In 1744 he managed the removal of his strongest opponent, Granville, and established a new ministry that recognized him as leader. From 1745 until 1748 he consolidated his position in the realm of domestic and political affairs, demanding and obtaining the king's recognition of this position in 1746. During 1745 and 1746 he gained the king's faith by directing the defeat of the rebellion. From 1748 until 1754 he expanded his control over foreign affairs by taking an active part in them and by giving Newcastle instructions. By 1752 he was in almost complete control of the election machinery. After 1749 he met no serious opposition in the House of Commons, which he directed completely for the government. He was the principal distributor of patronage—civil and military and even, in part, ecclesiastical. By 1750 he was the minister most trusted and respected by George II, even though the king personally liked Granville and Newcastle better. By 1754 Henry Pelham was in as complete control of the government as Robert Walpole had been. The fact that he was liked by most people made him more secure.

Compared with the other ministers from Robert Walpole to Lord North, Pelham stands out as a true First Minister. He certainly deserves recognition as a Prime Minister, at least as much as Walpole or North. His talent for achieving his aims surpassed that of either of those men, and his power was still growing when he died. Whether the Seven Years War would have been too much for him cannot be answered. He always agreed with Pitt's foreign policy and desires for cooperation, and Pitt worked well with him. If Pitt and Newcastle made one of England's greatest ministries, one can only surmise what Pitt and Pelham might have done. Pelham had the happy faculty of gaining agreement among rivals, a faculty neither Pitt nor Newcastle had. On the other hand, he may have been fortunate in death as well as life, for the rising young men of the 1750's might have resented his power and position.

The least that can be said is that Pelham provided a stable government for England for twelve years. The most that can be said is that he provided a good government, which fulfilled the needs of England without regard to long-established rules and outmoded regulations. The truth lies somewhere between. Personally he was liberal in his views (except for those on Ireland), honest in his conduct, efficient in his methods, and willing to compromise. His one great defect was that he did not grasp the fact that the entire structure of the administrative branch of the government needed reorganization. He was perhaps the only man who could have negotiated this before 1783 without creating serious trouble. However, his whole background, his oligarchic friends, and his incessant demand that things be made to work within the existing framework prevented him from seeing that major need.

If the question of his lack of original ideas arises, the only answer is that this is a quality of one particular kind of genius. Pelham's genius was to make men get along and work together. In this he was successful the majority of the time. It was the practical application of ideas that interested him. Can one type of man get along without the other? Pelham was not a great intellect, not the equal of Granville, Chesterfield, or Pitt. But Granville never succeeded in politics, Chesterfield soon tired of politics, and Pitt almost expended himself in four brilliant years. Pelham never showed the spectacular greatness that Pitt did during the Seven Years War, but he steadily served the interests of England. In spite of all flaws, unfounded accusations, and preconceived principles of judgment, considering the office of Prime Minister only, Pelham was extremely successful. Marlborough and the two Pitts achieved greatness as war ministers, but Pelham was more successful as leader of an administration. Pelham's true importance is seen in the chaos of the years following his death. It was almost solely Pelham's work that prevented such chaos from developing in 1742. He made the obviously outdated English system of administration work and work well. He made the political Englishman, even the Duke of Newcastle, like it.

Henry Pelham, when all aspects of his career are examined, remains the most successful First Minister between Robert Walpole and William Pitt the younger. He directed no single brilliant victory in war, nor did he achieve any dramatic reform in domestic government. Instead he provided twelve years of responsible government that furthered reform within the oligarchic political structure of eighteenth-century England. He led in moderation and effectiveness. No other politician of his time was so successful in pursuing this middle road as Henry Pelham.

Notes

Notes

CHAPTER I

1. William Coxe, *Memoirs of the Administration of the Right Honourable Henry Pelham* . . . (London: Longman, Rees, Orme, Brown, and Green, 1829), I, 1–6.

2. To avoid confusion, Thomas Pelham will be referred to henceforth by his more familiar title, Duke of Newcastle, even though he did not receive the actual title until 1715. Stebelton H. Nulle, *Thomas Pelham-Holles, Duke of Newcastle, His Early Political Career, 1693–1724* (Philadelphia: University of Pennsylvania Press, 1931), p. 16.

3. British Museum, Additional MSS., 32686, ff. 251–58.

4. Nulle, *Newcastle*, p. 153.

5. B.M., Add. MSS., 33064, f. 439.

6. *Ibid.*, 32687, ff. 113–14.

7. *Ibid.*, 32686, f. 147.

8. Coxe, *Henry Pelham*, I, 7.

9. *Ibid.*, I, 18.

10. William M. Torrens, *History of Cabinets from the Union with Scotland to the Acquisition of Canada and Bengal* (London: W. H. Allen and Company, Limited, 1894), I, 273.

11. B.M., Add. MSS., 32678, ff. 113–14; *Ibid.*, 32691, f. 495.

12. Coxe, *Henry Pelham*, I, 21.

13. B.M., Add. MSS., 32686, ff. 163–64, 227, 230, 425. It should be remembered that Sunderland and Townshend were both brothers-in-law of Newcastle.

14. "Chronological Diary," p. 12, *The Historical Register*, VI (1721).

15. Though no one has discovered documentary proof, it is a reasonable conclusion that a position on the Treasury Board was considered the highest of secondary government positions in the eighteenth century. For a full discussion of the system of promotions see Richard Pares, *King George III and the Politicians* (Oxford: The Clarendon Press, 1953), pp. 1–65.

16. Charles Brechdolt Realey, *The Early Opposition to Sir Robert Walpole, 1720–1727* (Lawrence, Kansas: University of Kansas Press, 1931), p. 30.

17. Torrens, *Cabinets*, I, 284.

18. William Thomas Laprade, *Public Opinion and Politics in Eighteenth Century England* (London: The Macmillan Company, 1936), p. 245.

19. Nulle, *Newcastle*, pp. 134–35. *Cf.*, Donald G. Barnes, "Henry Pelham and the Duke of Newcastle," *The Journal of British Studies*, No. 2 (May 1962).

20. George Henry Rose (ed.), *A Selection from the Papers of the Earls of Marchmont* (London: John Murray, 1831), II, 3.

21. B.M., Add. MSS., 27732, f. 188.

22. David Harrison Stevens, *Party Politics and English Journalism, 1702–1742* (Chicago: University of Chicago Press, 1916), p. 88. This election brought the future Lord Wilmington into electoral alliance with the Pelhams and strengthened the friendship of the future Lord Hardwicke.

23. Nulle, *Newcastle,* pp. 151–52.

24. William Coxe, *Memoirs of the Life and Administration of Sir Robert Walpole* . . . (London: T. Cadell, Jun. and W. Davies, 1798), II, 255.

25. *Ibid.,* II, 257–58.

26. B.M., Add. MSS., 32686, f. 145. Even this early, Pelham learned of the secret desire of Townshend and Walpole to dominate or remove Carteret. It happened that Pelham made the wrong guess, for he thought Carteret would give in, once Sunderland and Stanhope were broken. He never suffered from that illusion again.

27. Coxe, *Robert Walpole,* II, 285.

28. Nulle, *Newcastle,* p. 154.

29. Coxe, *Robert Walpole,* II, 278.

30. B.M., Add. MSS., 32685, ff. 31–32, 33–34: Richard Steele to Pelham, May 27, 1720, and May 28, 1720. These demonstrate Pelham's good relations with the Sunderland-Stanhope group, which Walpole ignored because of Pelham's loyalty to him by 1723.

31. Basil Williams, *Carteret and Newcastle, A Contrast in Contemporaries* (Cambridge: The University Press, 1943), pp. 70–71.

32. "Chronological Register," p. 20, *The Historical Register,* IX (1924).

33. B.M., Add. MSS., 32687, f. 101. In discussion of a diplomatic appointment in Italy, Newcastle said, "If you should think it proper to make this Change, your Lop. will most certainly oblige me, but what I know will have more weight with you, will overjoy *old Harry.*"

34. Williams, *Carteret and Newcastle,* pp. 70–71.

35. Coxe, *Robert Walpole,* II, 300–1.

36. *Ibid.,* II, 301.

37. B.M., Add. MSS., 36134, ff. 276, 285; *ibid.,* 36135, f. 292; *ibid.,* 36136, f. 261; *ibid.,* 36137, ff. 16, 188.

38. William Cobbett, *The Parliamentary History of England from the Earliest Period to the Year 1803* (London: Longman, Hurst, Rees, Orme, and Brown, 1812), VIII, 455.

39. *Ibid. The Political State of Great Britain* (London: F. Baker, 1711–1741), XXIX, 362.

40. *The Historical Register,* X, 26.

41. B.M., Add. MSS., 32686, f. 130; *ibid.,* 35423, f. 1.

42. *Ibid.,* 33064, ff. 191–92.

43. *Ibid.,* 32686, ff. 209–10; *ibid.,* 32687, f. 17. In 1725 another Pelham cousin who had actively supported the brothers in Sussex and parliament died, and the usual maneuvering gives an example of the problems of eighteenth-century political life: *Ibid.,* 32687, ff. 79, 81.

44. Realey, *Early Opposition,* p. 185.

45. Jean Dumont, *Corps universel diplomatique du des gens* . . . (Amsterdam: Chez P. Brunel, 1731), VIII, Part II, 158.

46. Earl of Ilchester (ed.), *Lord Hervey and His Friends, 1726–38* (London: John Murray, 1950), p. 43.

47. *Ibid.,* p. 46.
48. Philip Dormer Stanhope, *The Letters of Philip Dormer Stanhope, Fourth Earl of Chesterfield,* edited by Bonamy Dobree (London: Eyre and Spottiswoode Publishers Ltd., 1932), II, 107; James F. Chance (ed.), *British Diplomatic Instructions, 1689–1789,* edited for the Royal Historical Society, Vol. I (London: Offices of the Society, 1922), p. 239; Coxe, *Robert Walpole,* II, 623, 627–28, 631, 521, 535, 637; Historical Manuscripts Commission, *Eleventh Report,* Appendix, Part IV, The Manuscripts of the Marquess Townshend (London: Her Majesty's Stationery Office, 1887), p. 121.
49. Williams, *Carteret and Newcastle,* pp. 68–69.
50. Lord John Hervey, *Some Materials Towards Memoirs of the Reign of King George II,* edited by Romney Sedgwick (London: [King's Printers], 1931), I, 120.
51. It is interesting to note that Pelham made no personal profit from the army money, though, unlike Pitt, he never made a show of his virtue and it has been largely passed without comment.
52. Hervey, *George II,* I, 120. Lord Hervey explains the appointment in a simple sentence, "Mr. Pelham . . . was strongly attached to Sir Robert, and more personally beloved by him than any other man in England."
53. B.M., Add. MSS., 27733, f. 11: Pelham to Essex, January 18, 1734. In this letter Pelham says, "There is little news stirring worth your notice, publick affairs in the House of Commons go as our friends would wish. . . . The Lords are many of them discontented, and from that enter into Clubs and Cabals of an ugly nature, but when any proposition comes before 'em, the King's friends have still a great majority."
54. Realey, *Early Opposition,* p. 236; Laprade, *Public Opinion,* p. 347.
55. Hervey, *George II,* I, 249.
56. E. L. Hargreaves, *The National Debt* (London: Edward Arnold and Company, 1930), pp. 31–52. This discusses the many schemes put forward for handling the debt by Archibald, Sir Humphrey Mackworth, and Sir John Barnard and Walpole's expedient to handle the problem by raiding the sinking fund, which solved nothing.
57. Hervey, *George II,* III, 731–32.
58. Hargreaves, *National Debt,* pp. 47–52.
59. Laprade, *Public Opinion,* p. 321. The admonition was voted on March 4, 1732.
60. *Ibid.,* p. 340.
61. B.M., Add. MSS., 27733, f. 11.
62. *Ibid.,* f. 35.
63. *Ibid.,* 32688, f. 345.
64. *Ibid.,* f. 339.
65. Laprade, *Public Opinion,* p. 342.
66. *Ibid.,* p. 345.
67. *Ibid.*
68. Ilchester, *Hervey,* p. 237; B.M., Add. MSS., 27732, f. 188. Pelham's attitude toward Walpole is shown when he says, "Sr. Robert is gone to Norfolk, and I can assure you was much your servant when he went, His thoughts and mine in relation to publick affairs are more correspondant, I began the world under him, and have never seen in all the actions of his life since my acquaintance with him the least reason to doubt of his friendship or integrity." Or two years later, B.M.,

Add. MSS., 27734, f. 2: "As you know he [Walpole] has ever been my oracle, I don't think it worth while to talk Politicks much with any one else, and when I know his opinion of things, which he is so good generaly to tell me sincerely, I can give a pretty good guess as to what will happen here."

69. B.M., Add. MSS., 32688, ff. 283–84, 305–6, 619–20, 337–38, 347–50, 421–23, 307–9; *ibid.*, 32689, ff. 9 and 100; *ibid.*, 27733, f. 63.

70. *Ibid.*, 27733, f. 84.

71. The eighteenth-century custom was to use the terms *government, ministry,* and *cabinet* in a loose fashion. The first two remain more or less general terms, but cabinet has taken on a specific meaning for the twentieth century. In the following pages I shall use "cabinet" as it was used in the eighteenth century, to mean those leaders of the government who were called to meetings of the cabinet council with regularity. An additional problem has been created by the use of terms *inner cabinet* and *formal cabinet* meetings. I shall refer to the former as special meetings and usually indicate who was present. The term *cabinet* will be used to indicate regular meetings of the larger group. This, in general, seems to me the usage most consistent with the period under discussion.

CHAPTER II

1. Laprade, *Public Opinion,* p. 381.

2. B.M., Add. MSS., 9198, ff. 40–41.

3. Hervey, *George II,* III, 708; Bodleian Library, North MSS., a. 4, f. 152.

4. Hervey, *George II,* III, 716.

5. *Ibid.,* III, 733.

6. *Ibid.,* III, 735–38.

7. B.M., Add. MSS., 32690, ff. 425–27.

8. Stanhope, *Letters,* II, 311.

9. Coxe, *Robert Walpole,* III, 507: Bolingbroke to William Wyndham, February 3, 1738.

10. B.M., Add. MSS., 32691, f. 83.

11. Hervey, *George II,* III, 829.

12. Historical Manuscripts Commission, *Manuscripts of the Earl of Egmont— Diary of the First Earl of Egmont* (London: His Majesty's Stationery Office, 1923), II, 486.

13. Coxe, *Henry Pelham,* I, 11–13. In August, Newcastle also had a quarrel with Horatio Walpole, which Pelham had to smooth over: B.M., Add. MSS., 32691, ff. 293–94.

14. Coxe, *Robert Walpole,* III, 111; Coxe, *Henry Pelham,* I, 12; Laprade, *Public Opinion,* p. 400. Pelham during this time had cultivated good relations with many of the lesser members of the ministry: B.M., Add. MSS., 32691, f. 345.

15. *Ibid.,* 32799, f. 211; *ibid.,* 32691, ff. 468–69.

16. *Ibid.,* 32691, ff. 317–21.

17. *Ibid.,* 32692, ff. 377–84; *ibid.,* 35406, f. 164; Philip C. Yorke, *The Life and Correspondence of Philip Yorke . . . Lord High Chancellor of Great Britain* (Cambridge: The University Press, 1913), I, 229, 232.

18. B.M., Add. MSS., 32692, f. 370.

19. Laprade, *Public Opinion,* p. 416.

20. B.M., Add. MSS., 32692, f. 435.

21. *Ibid.,* 35423, f. 5; Coxe, *Henry Pelham,* I, 14; Yorke, *Hardwicke,* I, 240.

22. H.M.C., *Egmont Diary,* III, 141; Stanhope, *Letters,* II, 404.

23. Vera L. Brown, "South Sea Company and Contraband Trade," *American Historical Review,* XXXI (1926), 662–78.

24. Laprade, *Public Opinion,* p. 406.

25. B.M., Add. MSS., 28132, f. 13: Norris' Journal, June 6, 1739.

26. Yorke, *Hardwicke,* I, 223.

27. H.M.C., *Egmont Diary,* III, 141. Egmont noted that "Lord Harrington is so indolent he joins himself to none." The second group was the balance of power within the ministry.

28. B.M., Add. MSS., 32992, f. 302.

29. *Ibid.,* 28132, ff. 13, 40–41, 63.

30. Bodleian Library, North MSS., d. 5, f. 67.

31. Cambridge University Library, Cholmondeley-Houghton MSS., 3306: Pelham to Walpole; B.M., Add. MSS., 32691, ff. 403 and 438; *ibid.,* 32692, ff. 374 and 377.

32. Public Record Office, State Papers, Domestic, George II, No. 50, not folioed. This includes both the Order in Council creating the Lords Justices, and their instructions. The men named for this office were the Archbishop of Canterbury, Hardwicke, Wilmington, Hervey, Dorset, Grafton, Richmond, Bolton, Devonshire, Montagu, Newcastle, Pembroke, Ilay, Harrington, Walpole, and Wager. The creation of the Lords Justices was based on the precedent of the usual method of ruling Ireland and the regency created at the time of Richard II.

33. P.R.O., S.P., Dom., Geo. II, No. 50, *passim.*

34. B.M., Add. MSS., 32693, f. 190, 250, 304; *ibid.,* 32698, ff. 233–34, 306–7; *ibid.,* 32697, f. 355.

35. *Ibid.,* 33441, ff. 6–7.

36. *Ibid.,* 32693, f. 485; *ibid.,* 32696, ff. 5–6, 11, 19–20, 340, 393, 440, 442.

37. *Ibid.,* 33073, f. 178. It was at this point that Newcastle was able to elect his friend and secretary, Andrew Stone, to Commons from Hastings; B.M., Add. MSS., 32696, ff. 375, 381, 383–84.

38. *Ibid.,* 32697, ff. 13, 45, 164, 194; *ibid.,* 32699, f. 10; B.M., Stowe MSS., 155, f. 116.

39. B.M., Add. MSS., 40828, f. 74.

40. *Ibid.,* 32697, f. 501; *ibid.,* 32698, ff. 34 and 243.

41. L. G. Wickham Legg (ed.), *British Diplomatic Instructions, 1689–1789,* Vol. VI, edited for the Royal Historical Society (London: Offices of the Society, 1930), pp. 231–39; James F. Chance (ed.), *ibid.,* Vol. III, edited for the R.H.S. (London: Offices of the Society, 1926), pp. 124–29; B.M., Add. MSS., 9132, ff. 68–70.

42. *Ibid.,* 32693, f. 334; *ibid.,* 35407, f. 17.

43. *Ibid.,* 32697, f. 194.

44. *Ibid.,* 35407, f. 59; *ibid.,* 32697, ff. 432–33.

45. *Ibid.,* 32698, f. 36.

46. *Ibid.,* ff. 16–22, 55; William Coxe, *Memoirs of Horatio, Lord Walpole Selected from His Correspondence and Papers and Connected with the History of the Times, from 1678 to 1757* (London: T. Cadell, Jun. and W. Davies, 1802), p. 237.

47. Coxe, *Henry Pelham,* I, 20–23.

48. B.M., Add. MSS., 32698, ff. 114–17.

49. H.M.C., *Egmont Diary,* III, 140.

50. B.M., Add. MSS., 9176, f. 55.

51. *Ibid.*, 32697, ff. 215 and 310.

52. *Ibid.*, 32698, ff. 11, 73, 317, 346.

53. *Ibid.*, 32693, f. 51; *ibid.*, 33034, f. 33.

54. Tobias Smollett, *The History of England, Written Originally in French by Rapin de Thoyras . . . With the Reign of George III* (London: John Harrison, 1789) , V, 537.

55. B.M., Add. MSS., 33034, ff. 21–23. Among others in the Lords were the following, who later made peace with Pelham: Bedford, Argyle, Berkshire, Winchelsea, Chesterfield, Sandwich, Rockingham, Halifax, Cobham, Clinton, North, Carteret, Gower, Middleton, and Bathurst.

56. H.M.C., *Egmont Diary*, III, 116.

57. Laprade, *Public Opinion*, p. 428.

58. Stanhope, *Letters*, II, 433.

59. B.M., Add. MSS., 23805, f. 307, indicates that in the summer Newcastle was cultivating Carteret.

60. P.R.O., Chatham MSS., 83, not folioed.

61. *Ibid.*, 33, not folioed: Richard Glover to Lyttelton.

62. John Murray Graham, *Annals and Correspondence of the Viscount and the First and Second Earls of Stair* (Edinburgh: William Blackwood and Sons, 1875) , II, 268–69: Chesterfield to Stair, March 6, 1741.

63. Stanhope, *Letters*, II, 462. John B. Owen, *The Rise of the Pelhams* (London: Methuen & Co., 1957) , pp. 1–40, shows the ministry lost only twelve seats from their usual majority.

64. Stanhope, *Letters*, II, 467; Coxe, *Robert Walpole*, III, 579.

65. B.M., Add. MSS., 22628, f. 79.

66. *Ibid.*, 47137, not folioed.

67. Mrs. Paget Toynbee (ed.) , *The Letters of Horace Walpole, Fourth Earl of Orford, Chronologically Arranged and Edited with Notes and Indices* (Oxford: The Clarendon Press, 1903) , I, 140–41.

68. B.M., Add. MSS., 32698, ff. 409 and 413.

69. Laprade, *Public Opinion*, p. 426.

70. H.M.C., *Egmont Diary*, III, 244.

71. Coxe, *Robert Walpole*, III, 587.

72. It was significant that Carteret confined his attack to Walpole and did not bring Newcastle into question.

73. Laprade, *Public Opinion*, p. 429.

74. Toynbee, *Walpole's Letters*, I, 162.

75. *Ibid.*, I, 164–68.

76. Coxe, *Robert Walpole*, III, 592, 594; H.M.C., *Egmont Diary*, III, 244, 251, 252–53.

77. Richard Glover, *Memoirs by a Celebrated Literary and Political Character from . . . 1742 to . . . 1757 . . .* (London: John Murray, 1814) , pp. 3–4.

78. *Ibid.*, pp. 5–6.

79. H.M.C., *Egmont Diary*, III, 251.

80. *Ibid., Fourteenth Report*, Appendix, Part IX. The Manuscripts of The Earl of Buckingham, The Earl of Linsey, The Earl of Onslow, Lord Emly, Theodore J. Hare, Esq., and James Round, Esq., M.P. (London: Her Majesty's Stationery Office, 1895) , p. 81.

81. B.M., Add. MSS., 9200, f. 80.

82. [Glover], *Memoirs,* pp. 7–12. Glover had a particularly low opinion of Argyle, which was probably due to this restoration.

83. B.M., Add. MSS., 47092, p. 118.

84. Toynbee, *Walpole's Letters,* I, 180.

85. P.R.O., S.P., Dom., Geo. II, No. 58; *ibid.,* King's Warrant Book, XXXIV, pp. 491–92.

86. *Ibid.,* Treasury Minute Book, XXIX, p. 7.

87. James Oswald, *Memorials of the Public Life and Character of the Right Hon. James Oswald, of Dunniker* (Edinburgh: Archibald Constable and Co., 1825), p. 33.

88. Emily J. Climenson, *Elizabeth Montagu: The Queen of the Blue-Stockings, Her Correspondence from 1720 to 1761* (London: John Murray, 1906), I, 102.

89. B.M., Add. MSS., 32699, f. 78.

90. *Ibid.,* 47137, not folioed.

91. H.M.C., *Egmont Diary,* III, 253–55.

92. *Ibid.,* III, 258.

93. Horace Walpole, *Memoirs of the Reign of King George the Second,* edited by Lord Holland (London: Henry Colburn, 1846), I, xv; [John Almon], *Anecdotes of the Life of the Right Honourable William Pitt, Earl of Chatham . . . from the Year 1736 to the Year 1778* (London: L. B. Seeley, 1796), I, 82–112; Basil Williams, *The Life of William Pitt, Earl of Chatham* (London: Longmans, Green, and Co., 1915), I, 89.

94. H.M.C., *Egmont Diary,* III, 262. Other men were suspicious of Carteret and not of Pulteney: B.M., Add. MSS., 32699, ff. 111–12.

95. *Ibid.,* 35360, f. 75.

96. H.M.C., *Report on the Manuscripts of Mrs. Stopford-Sackville of Drayton House, Northamptonshire* (London: His Majesty's Stationery Office, 1904), I, 37: Orford to Dorset, March 20, 1742.

97. B.M., Add. MSS., 33052, ff. 210–59: Report of the Committee of Secrecy, June 30, 1742.

98. H.M.C., *Fourteenth Report,* Appendix, Part IX, p. 84.

CHAPTER III

1. Toynbee, *Walpole's Letters,* I, 171–72.

2. B.M., Add. MSS., 32699, f. 390.

3. Toynbee, *Walpole's Letters,* I, 352 and 355.

4. B.M., Add. MSS., 32700, ff. 205–6.

5. Toynbee, *Walpole's Letters,* I, 361. The actual cabinet crisis will be discussed later.

6. Coxe, *Henry Pelham,* I, 83.

7. B.M., Add. MSS., 32701, f. 23.

8. Coxe, *Henry Pelham,* I, 91–93. A similar letter of October has been recorded, *ibid.,* I, 103–6, which indicates that Walpole was anxious that Pelham have full use of his long experience.

9. B.M., Add. MSS., 32701, ff. 117–20.

10. Coxe, *Henry Pelham,* I, 100–2.

11. *Ibid.,* I, 94.

12. B.M., Add. MSS., 32701, ff. 148–49. It is possible that Walpole's improved relations with William Pitt were responsible for his softened attitude toward the Cobhamites: Williams, *William Pitt,* I, 92.

13. B.M., Add. MSS., 32701, f. 243.

14. *Ibid.,* 35351, f. 44. Just what part Walpole played will be made clear in the discussion of the crisis to follow.

15. P.R.O., Privy Council Register, Nos. 8 and 9, George II, *passim.* Chief Justice Willes was the principal participant during 1742 and 1743.

16. *Ibid.*

17. *Ibid.*

18. For this reason I shall concentrate on the position occupied by Pelham and indicate other domestic events only when they seem to warrant it.

19. B.M., Add. MSS., 35453, ff. 160–61.

20. P.R.O., Treasury Minute Book, XXIX, p. 69: July 1, 1742. Pelham argues the soldiers' position before the Treasury Board, made up of Wilmington, Sandys, Compton, Rushout, and Gybbon.

21. *Ibid.,* Customs Book, XV, 213–14; *ibid.,* King's Warrant Book, XXXV, 174–75; *ibid.,* XXXIV, 490; B.M., Add. MSS., 45733, not folioed: April 24, 1742, and June 3, 1742.

22. Duncan Warrand (ed.), *More Culloden Papers* (Inverness: Robert Carruthers & Sons, 1927), III, 193; P.R.O., S.P., Dom., Geo. II, No. 58, *passim;* B.M., Add. MSS., 8870, ff. 65–66; *ibid.,* 34736, f. 27.

23. H.M.C., *Tenth Report,* Reports on the Manuscripts of the Earl of Eglinton, Sir J. Stirling Maxwell, Bart., C. S. H. Drummond Moray, Esq., C. T. Weston Underwood, Esq., and G. Wingfield Digby, Esq. (London: Her Majesty's Stationery Office, 1885), p. 277.

24. *Historical Memoirs of His Late Royal Highness William Augustus, Duke of Cumberland* . . . (London: T. Waller, 1767), p. 34 and Appendix II; B.M., Add. MSS., 22536, f. 17. This was the first time that Pelham was added to the board of the Lords Justices, and it shows his importance, though he was only Paymaster.

25. *Ibid.,* 33052, ff. 268–77: attacks from Henley's Oratory by a Tory clergyman and spokesman.

26. *Ibid.,* 35423, ff. 13–14.

27. *Ibid.,* 32700, f. 149.

28. P.R.O., Chatham MSS., 83, not folioed.

29. B.M., Add. MSS., 22528, f. 79.

30. *Ibid.,* 38455, f. 41.

31. *Ibid.,* 32699, f. 471.

32. Toynbee, *Walpole's Letters,* I, 307.

33. B.M., Add. MSS., 35407, f. 299.

34. *Ibid.,* 35454, ff. 304–5.

35. *Ibid.,* 35454, ff. 331–32.

36. *Ibid.,* 32699, ff. 234, 549; *ibid.,* 32993, ff. 223 and 227; P.R.O., S.P., Dom., Geo. II, No. 62, not folioed; H.M.C., *Tenth Report,* Weston-Underwood MSS., p. 278.

37. P.R.O., Customs Book, XV, p. 384.

38. B.M., Add. MSS., 32700, f. 146.

39. *Ibid.*, 8870, f. 57.

40. *Ibid.*, 32699, ff. 280–81.

41. *Ibid.*, 32699, f. 29; Yorke, *Hardwicke*, I, 310; Toynbee, *Walpole's Letters*, I, 226–27.

42. H.M.C., *Report on the Manuscripts of the Duke of Buccleuch and Queensberry* . . . (London: Her Majesty's Stationery Office, 1899), I, 399–400: Earl of Winchelsea to Duke of Montagu. Montagu was troublesome to the European war also, but Carteret and Newcastle forced him to act in this case, which they considered more vital, or else issued the orders on their own authority. It would be hard to find a more inefficient minister than Montagu at any time.

43. B.M., Add. MSS., 22542, ff. 4–15.

44. *Ibid.*, 32701, f. 25.

45. *Ibid.*, 22539, f. 11.

46. *Ibid.*, 6911, ff. 17–20.

47. P.R.O., Granville MSS., box 1, not folioed: Pelham to Gower, September 30, 1742.

48. *Ibid.*, King's Warrant Book, XXXV, pp. 208–9.

49. B.M., Add. MSS., 35870, f. 85.

50. *Ibid.*, 22542, ff. 104–17.

51. P.R.O., Treasury Minute Book, XXIX, p. 243.

52. B.M., Add. MSS., 23815, f. 351.

53. *Ibid.*, 22545, ff. 59–63.

54. *Ibid.*, 22531, f. 27. The treaty gave about two years' relief from Prussian attacks.

55. James F. Chance (ed.), *British Diplomatic Instructions, 1689–1789,* Vol. V, edited for the Royal Historical Society (London: Offices of the Society, 1928), pp. 89–114; *ibid.*, III, 129–37; B.M., Add. MSS., 35407, Andrew Stone, May 28, 1743.

56. *Ibid.*, 22545, ff. 144–72; *ibid.*, 22526, f. 43.

57. *Ibid.*, 35870, ff. 60–63.

58. *Ibid.*, 33004, ff. 57–58.

59. *Ibid.*, 22536, ff. 131–36; *ibid.*, 35407, f. 235. It is interesting to note that earlier in the year Wilmington and Bath had agreed with the Pelhamites' objections to the various schemes of Carteret while he was in Europe.

60. Yorke, *Hardwicke*, I, 317; B.M., Add. MSS., 35423, f. 15; Graham, *Stair Correspondence,* II, 450–51.

61. H.M.C., *Fourteenth Report,* Appendix, Part IX, 90.

62. *Ibid.*, *Buccleuch MSS.*, I, 407; Graham, *Stair Correspondence,* II, 454–56; B.M., Add. MSS., 22537, ff. 419–22.

63. One of the most brilliant and sustained attacks was the result of a pamphlet entitled "The Case of the Hanover Troops," which laid the blame for all English troubles since 1714 on Hanoverian schemes. In answer there followed rapidly "The Interest of Great Britain Steadily Pursued," "The Interest of Hanover Steadily Pursued," "A Farther Vindication of the Case of the Hanover Troops," and "A Vindication of a Late Pamphlet, Intitled, The Case of the Hanover Troops." These papers were on a fairly high level and appealed to the intelligent on both sides, but pamphlets like "The Whigs and the Nurse," "Beef and Butt Beer, against Mum and Pumpernickle," "The Yellow Sash," and

"Serious Considerations on the Present State of Affairs, Both at Home and Abroad" were undoubtedly designed to appeal to the mob of London, for they were outright scurrilous.

64. B.M., Add. MSS., 22545, f. 95: Minute of the Cabinet, July 29, 1742; *ibid.,* 33004, f. 55: Minute of the Privy Council, July 30, 1742.

65. *Ibid.,* 38330, f. 264; *ibid.,* 33046, f. 136.

66. *Ibid.,* 33034, f. 97.

CHAPTER IV

1. H.M.C., *Egmont Diary,* III, 263.

2. B.M., Add. MSS., 32699, f. 265.

3. Graham, *Stair Correspondence,* II, 286; B.M., Add. MSS., 35407, f. 243; P.R.O., Granville MSS., box 1: Chesterfield to Gower, July 15, 1742.

4. B.M., Add. MSS., 23811, f. 332.

5. Lord John Russell (ed.), *Correspondence of John, Fourth Duke of Bedford Selected from the Originals at Woburn Abbey* (London: Longman, Brown, Green, and Longmans, 1842), I, 10–11.

6. Toynbee, *Walpole's Letters,* I, 250.

7. P.R.O., Granville MSS., box 1: Chesterfield to Gower, July 22, 1742.

8. B.M., Add. MSS., 32699, f. 347; *ibid.,* 35407, ff. 137–38.

9. *Ibid.,* 35407, ff. 141–42; *ibid.,* 32699, ff. 400–1.

10. P.R.O., Granville MSS., box 1: Pelham to Gower, September 30, 1742, to October 20, 1751.

11. B.M., Add. MSS., 32699, f. 401; *ibid.,* 35407, f. 244.

12. *Ibid.,* 35455, ff. 74–77, 120–21, 173, 187–88, 211–12, 248–49, indicate that in several ways Pelham was involved in almost all directions of the war.

13. *Ibid.,* 35423, ff. 9–10; also f. 7 shows that Pelham had access to the king beyond what was ordinary for a Paymaster-General.

14. Toynbee, *Walpole's Letters,* I, 322.

15. *Ibid.,* I, 338.

16. H.M.C., *Fourteenth Report,* Appendix, Part IX, 87.

17. B.M., Add. MSS., 43441, not folioed: Keene to de Castres, May 10, 1743.

18. *Memoirs of Cumberland,* p. 133 n.

19. Coxe, *Henry Pelham,* I, 74; B.M., Add. MSS., 22529, f. 272.

20. *Ibid.,* 22536, f. 77.

21. *Ibid.,* 32701, ff. 117–20; *ibid.,* 35455, ff. 265–66, 267; *ibid.,* 22537, ff. 419–22, 423, 425.

22. *Ibid.,* 32700, ff. 183–84. Richmond was an old friend and political ally of Newcastle and Pelham in Sussex and in national affairs. He seems to have acted as their secret source of information about Carteret and the king while all three were on the continent.

23. *Ibid.,* 32700, f. 278.

24. *Ibid.,* f. 298.

25. Toynbee, *Walpole's Letters,* I, 365.

26. Coxe, *Henry Pelham,* I, 469; H.M.C., *Buccleuch MSS.,* I, 406.

27. B.M., Add. MSS., 32700, ff. 314–15: Newcastle to Orford, July 22, 1743.

28. *Ibid.,* ff. 335–36.

29. *Ibid.,* 32701, f. 5.

30. *Ibid.*, 32701, ff. 13–14.

31. *Ibid.*, 35455, ff. 262–63: August 12, 1743.

32. *Ibid.*, 32701, f. 23.

33. *Ibid.*, ff. 29–30.

34. Williams, *Carteret and Newcastle.* Basil Williams sees mainly the brilliant and flashy side of Carteret and seldom the foolish, incapable side. He is right to contrast the two men but often wrong in his distinctions.

35. B.M., Add. MSS., 32701, f. 27.

36. *Ibid.*, ff. 29–30.

37. *Ibid.*, 35407, f. 251; *ibid.*, 32701, f. 55.

38. *Ibid.*, 34731, f. 7; *ibid.*, 35351, f. 40; H.M.C., *Buccleuch MSS.*, I, 407.

39. Rose, *Marchmont Papers*, II, 309–10: Bolingbroke to Marchmont, August 25, 1743. Bolingbroke was unable to understand why there should be any possible contender with Pelham for the Treasury.

40. Coxe, *Henry Pelham*, I, 91–93.

41. *Ibid.*, I, 87–88.

42. H.M.C., *Egmont Diary*, III, 273. If this entry is correct, as seems probable, the argument of J. C. Earle that Carteret and the king gave Pelham the Treasury post to hide their foreign negotiations from parliament does not hold; for there would be no reason not to award the Garter to Bath. *Cf.* John Charles Earle, *English Premiers from Sir Robert Walpole to Sir Robert Peel* (London: Chapman and Hall, 1871), I, 86.

43. B.M., Add. MSS., 43441, not folioed: Keene to de Castres, September 16, 1743.

44. P.R.O., Granville MSS., box 1: Pelham to Gower, August 30, 1743; B.M., Add. MSS., 32701, ff. 74–76; *ibid.*, 35407, f. 255.

45. P.R.O., Treasury Minute Book, XXIX: September 2, 1743.

46. B.M., Add. MSS., 32701, f. 85: Stone to Newcastle, September 3, 1743. Stone reported his news at second hand from John Scrope, Secretary of the Treasury, who had held office since 1724.

47. Coxe, *Henry Pelham*, I, 96–98: Hardwicke to Newcastle, September 8, 1743.

CHAPTER V

1. Coxe, *Henry Pelham*, I, 77.

2. B.M., Add. MSS., 32701, f. 184.

3. *Ibid.*, ff. 238–39.

4. *Ibid.*, f. 243.

5. *Ibid.*, 35407, ff. 265–66; *ibid.*, 32701, f. 150.

6. H.M.C., *Egmont Diary*, III, 276–77.

7. B.M., Add. MSS., 35337, ff. 1–5: Philip Yorke's Journal.

8. *Ibid.*, 35423, f. 17.

9. Toynbee, *Walpole's Letters*, I, 388.

10. Coxe, *Henry Pelham*, I, 94; B.M., Add. MSS., 32701, ff. 148–49.

11. *Ibid.*, f. 150.

12. *Ibid.*, 35407, f. 275: Newcastle to Hardwicke, October 1, 1743.

13. P.R.O., Granville MSS., box 1, not folioed: Chesterfield to Gower, October 2, 1743.

14. B.M., Add. MSS., 32701, f. 170: Trevor to Newcastle, October 20, 1743; H.M.C., *Fourteenth Report*, Appendix, Part IX, 91: Newcastle to Trevor, October 28, 1743; Warrand, *More Culloden Papers*, III, 161–62: Ilay to Duncan Forbes, November 29, 1743.

15. Toynbee, *Walpole's Letters*, I, 393. Horace Walpole estimated 300 votes for the Court and 205 for the opposition, if all went well. B.M., Add. MSS., 22540, f. 292.

16. *Ibid.*, 35337, f. 19. He was easily elected and took his place again on December 19.

17. [Almon], *Pitt*, I, 183–95.

18. P.R.O., Treasury Minute Book, XXIX, 365. They were sworn in on December 29.

19. H.M.C., *Egmont Diary*, III, 278: December 9, 1743. The Earl of Bath also wanted the job for himself or Lord Carlisle, and Carteret's move drove a wedge between the two men.

20. B.M., Add. MSS., 32701, f. 310.

21. Coxe, *Horatio Walpole*, pp. 253–54.

22. H.M.C., *Report on the Manuscripts in Various Collections*, Vol. VI, The Manuscripts of Miss M. Eyre Matcham; Captain H. V. Knox; Cornwallis Wykeham-Martin, Esq; etc. (Dublin: His Majesty's Stationery Office, 1909), pp. 16–18; William James Smith (ed.), *The Grenville Papers: Being the Correspondence of Richard Grenville Earl Temple, K.G., and the Right Hon. George Grenville, Their Friends and Contemporaries* (London: John Murray, 1852), I, 19; Stanhope, *Letters,* II, 528–29.

23. B.M., Add. MSS., 22540, ff. 89–90.

24. [Almon], *Pitt,* pp. 134–42; Smollett, *Continuation of Rapin,* V, 251.

25. B.M., Add. MSS., 43441, not folioed: May 10, 1743.

26. Rose, *Marchmont Papers,* II, 302: July 26, 1743.

27. H.M.C., *Various Collections,* Vol. VI, Matcham MSS., p. 18.

28. *Ibid., Tenth Report,* Weston-Underwood MSS., p. 278; Russell, *Bedford Correspondence,* I, 16; [Almon], *Pitt,* I, 143–82; B.M., Add. MSS., 35876, f. 221; *ibid.,* 35337, ff. 6, 9–19.

29. [Glover], *Memoirs,* p. 21.

30. P.R.O., Granville MSS., box 1, not folioed: Chesterfield to Gower, October 2, 1743.

31. B.M., Add. MSS., 35587, ff. 186, 188, 194.

32. Russell, *Bedford Correspondence,* I, 14–15.

33. Rose Mary Davis, *The Good Lord Lyttelton, A Study in Eighteenth Century Politics and Culture* (Bethlehem, Penna.: Times Publishing Company, 1939), p. 125.

34. H.M.C., *Egmont Diary,* III, 281: January 5, 1744.

35. *Ibid.,* III, 281: January 6, 1744.

36. B.M., Add. MSS., 35337, ff. 22–25: January 11, 1744. The vote was 277 to 165 for the Flanders campaign.

37. [Almon], *Pitt,* I, 183–95.

38. Davis, *Lyttelton,* p. 186.

39. [Glover], *Memoirs,* pp. 23–25.

40. B.M., Add. MSS., 35337, ff. 36, 41–42.

41. Toynbee, *Walpole's Letters,* II, 2.

42. H.M.C., *Fourteenth Report,* Appendix, Part IX, 93.

43. Coxe, *Horatio Walpole,* pp. 267–68 n.

44. *Ibid.,* p. 261.

45. B.M., Egerton MSS., 1721, ff. 59–60.

46. B.M., Add. MSS., 35423, f. 19: March 15, 1744.

47. *Ibid.,* 35337, f. 65; Coxe, *Horatio Walpole,* p. 264.

48. *Ibid.,* p. 263; H.M.C., *Egmont Diary,* III, 296; B.M., Add. MSS., 35337, ff. 69–71.

49. Rose, *Marchmont Papers,* II, 329–30.

50. B.M., Add. MSS., 9146, f. 115.

51. *Ibid.,* 35354, f. 42: Hardwicke to Joseph Yorke, April 27.

52. *Ibid.,* 35408, f. 9.

53. Coxe, *Henry Pelham,* I, 155–57.

54. B.M., Add. MSS., 35408, ff. 21–22: June 6, 1744.

55. *Ibid.,* 32703, ff. 108–10: Newcastle to Pelham, June 10, 1744. Newcastle asked that this letter be absolutely secret from all but Hardwicke and Andrew Stone.

56. *Ibid.,* 32703, ff. 156–57: Hardwicke to Newcastle, June 24, 1744.

57. Rose, *Marchmont Papers,* I, 9–10: August 7, 1744.

58. *Ibid.,* I, 10–11: August 7, 1744.

59. *Ibid.,* I, 16: August 11, 1744.

60. *Ibid.,* I, 15: August 11, 1744.

61. *Ibid.,* I, 19–20.

62. B.M., Add. MSS., 35408, f. 34: Newcastle to Hardwicke, August 8, 1744.

63. *Ibid.,* 32703, ff. 281–82. Newcastle again repeated his resolution to resign before the meeting of parliament unless his friends forced a solution by removing Lord Carteret.

64. *Ibid.,* f. 283.

65. Coxe, *Henry Pelham,* I, 169–71.

66. Rose, *Marchmont Papers,* I, 44–45.

67. *Ibid.,* I, 39: September 2, 1744. It is clear that some Tories and opposition Whigs did not know the extent of the political deals afoot, for some were still planning to attack the whole cabinet. Bolingbroke therefore wanted an issue that could bring all elements of the opposition together behind Pelham. H.M.C., *Various Collections,* Vol. VI, Matcham MSS., p. 18.

68. Rose, *Marchmont Papers,* I, 44–45.

69. B.M., Add. MSS., 35408, f. 53: Newcastle to Hardwicke, September 14, 1744.

70. Coxe, *Horatio Walpole,* p. 272.

71. Rose, *Marchmont Papers,* I, 48.

72. H.M.C., *Various Collections,* Vol. VI, Matcham MSS., p. 19: Letter by Waller, October 7, 1744; Rose, *Marchmont Papers,* I, 67–68: October 22, 1744; *ibid.,* I, 73–88: November 6–24, 1744.

73. *Ibid.,* I, 56; B.M., Add. MSS., 35587, ff. 314 and 317.

74. Rose, *Marchmont Papers,* I, 72–73.

75. B.M., Add. MSS., 35337, f. 82; *ibid.,* 32703, ff. 315 and 329.

76. There is some discrepancy in the exact date of the delivery of the paper to the king. William Murray gives October 28 (Rose, *Marchmont Papers,* I, 69), while Philip Yorke gives October 31 (B.M., Add. MSS., 35337, f. 82). The latter seems the more likely date.

77. *Ibid.,* 33066, ff. 16–19; *ibid.,* 32703, ff. 363–64.

78. *Ibid.*, 32703, ff. 365–66; *ibid.*, 35408, ff. 74–75; *ibid.*, 32703, f. 367; *ibid.*, 35408, f. 76.

79. On October 18, 1744, Carteret's mother, the Countess of Granville, died, and he inherited the title. From this point on he will be referred to as Earl Granville.

80. B.M., Add. MSS., 35870, f. 63.

81. *Ibid.*, 35408, f. 86.

82. Rose, *Marchmont Papers,* I, 73.

83. Coxe, *Robert Walpole,* III, 603–4: Horatio Walpole to Orford, November 8, 1744. This letter gives further proof that Pelham was accepted by the old Whigs as the leader of their faction.

84. *Ibid.*, III, 601–2: Cholmondeley to Orford, November 5.

85. Rose, *Marchmont Papers,* I, 81–82.

86. *Ibid.*, I, 70–71, 75, 77; B.M., Add. MSS., 35337, f. 84.

87. *Ibid.*, 35408, f. 88.

88. *Ibid.*

89. Rose, *Marchmont Papers,* I, 77 and 80.

90. *Ibid.*, I, 83–84: November 15, 1744.

91. *Ibid.*, I, 88–89: November 24, 1744. Granville also tried to make separate deals with Pelham and Harrington, which would split the ranks of the old Whigs. These moves merely show how little he understood the facts of political life. *Cf.* B.M., Add. MSS., 32703, ff. 407–9: Stone to Newcastle, November 4, 1744; *ibid.*, 35408, f. 90.

92. *Ibid.*, 35408, f. 90.

93. Cambridge University Library, Cholmondeley-Houghton MSS., 90/29: December 12, 1744.

94. B.M., Add. MSS., 32703, f. 429: Hardwicke to Newcastle, November 19, 1744.

95. *Ibid.*, 35337, f. 85; H.M.C., *Egmont Diary,* III, 303; Toynbee, *Walpole's Letters,* II, 59.

96. Rose, *Marchmont Papers,* I, 91.

97. B.M., Add. MSS., 35337, ff. 85–86.

98. Coxe, *Horatio Walpole,* pp. 278–79; Toynbee, *Walpole's Letters,* II, 63–64.

99. B.M., Add. MSS., 32703, ff. 427–28; *ibid.*, 35408, ff. 80–85.

100. Williams, *Pitt,* I, 129; Lord Fitzmaurice, *Life of William Earl of Shelburne afterwards First Marquess of Lansdowne with Extracts from his papers and Correspondence* (London: Macmillan and Co., Limited, 1912), I, 39–40, 41; Tobias Smollett, *A Complete History of England from the Descent of Julius Caesar, to the Treaty of Aix la Chapelle, 1748* (London: Richard Baldwin, 1760), XI, 195–96; Keith Grahame Feiling, *The Second Tory Party, 1714–1832* (London: Macmillan and Co., Limited, 1938), pp. 43, 44, 47.

101. Stanhope, *Letters,* II, 541: Chesterfield to Newcastle, December 1, 1744.

102. Sir Richard Lodge (ed.), *Private Correspondence of Chesterfield and Newcastle, 1744–46,* edited for the Royal Historical Society, Camden Series, Vol. XLIV (1930), p. 3; B.M., Add. MSS., 32703, f. 454.

103. [Glover], *Memoirs,* pp. 30–31, 34–35.

104. [Almon], *Pitt,* I, 201–2; John H. Plumb, *Chatham* (London: Collins Clear-Type Press, 1953), pp. 29–31; Toynbee, *Walpole's Letters,* II, 65–66.

105. *Ibid.*, II, 59: November 26, 1744.

106. Coxe, *Robert Walpole,* III, 605–6.

107. B.M., Add. MSS., 35408, f. 99: Stone to Hardwicke, December 6, 1744; B.M., Stowe MSS., 254, ff. 1–2: Minute of a Cabinet Paper by Lord Chancellor Hardwicke. This Minute summarizes the position of the Pelhamites as follows: "The principal point of the public service, is to continue the war till a reasonable peace can be obtained. . . . The present Ministers are sincerely for it; so are the Whigs attached to them; Earl of G[ranvill]e has to preserve the K[ing]s favour given him strong assurances on this Head. The body of the Tories, & the present Opposition are so well satisfied with his removal, so as to profess themselves ready to concur heartily in supporting the War; but their concurrence cannot be expected, without advantages & favours from the Government. Coalition is attainable, without letting any of them into Posts of great power, tho' some places of Profit & Honour, must be necessarily bestowed amongst them. By such a scheme all divisions of men will be united, and the carrying on the War, become a national measure."

108. Edward R. Turner, *The Cabinet Council of England in the Seventeenth and Eighteenth Centuries, 1622–1784* (Baltimore: Johns Hopkins Press, 1930–1932), II, 7–8; Toynbee, *Walpole's Letters*, II, 64–65; Coxe, *Henry Pelham*, I, 197–98; *Memoirs of Cumberland*, pp. 176–77.

109. *Ibid.* Sheffield City Library, Wentworth-Woodhouse MSS., M4, f. 1.

110. Toynbee, *Walpole's Letters*, II, 65.

111. Coxe, *Horatio Walpole*, pp. 279–80.

112. B.M., Add. MSS., 23819, f. 24: Pelham to Robinson, December 5, 1744; H.M.C., *Fourteenth Report*, Appendix, Part IX, 108–9: Pelham to Trevor, November 27, 1744.

113. Coxe, *Henry Pelham*, I, 198–99; H.M.C., *Fifteenth Report*, Appendix, Part VII, The Manuscripts of the Duke of Somerset, the Marquis of Ailesbury, and the Rev. Sir T.H.G. Puleston, Bart. (London: Her Majesty's Stationery Office, 1898), p. 331: Lord Barrymore to Francis Price, January 4, 1745; Coxe, *Henry Pelham*, I, 199–203, 204; B.M., Add. MSS., 35870, ff. 87–91; *ibid.*, 32704, ff. 72–74; H. R. Duff (ed.), *Culloden Papers: comprising an extensive and interesting correspondence from the year 1625 to 1748* (London: T. Cadell and W. Davies, 1815), p. 197.

114. B.M., Add. MSS., 32704, ff. 24–25: Newcastle to Chesterfield, January 22, 1745; *ibid.*, 35408, f. 114: Newcastle to Hardwicke, January 5, 1745; P.R.O., Chatham MSS., 61: Richard Grenville to Pitt, January 12, 1745; H.M.C., *Fourteenth Report*, Appendix, Part IX, 110: Stephen Poyntz to Trevor, January 9, 1745; Duff, *Culloden Papers*, p. 198: Andrew Mitchell to Duncan Forbes, January 29, 1745; Toynbee, *Walpole's Letters*, II, 68 and 73.

115. B.M., Add. MSS., 35588, f. 7: Bolingbroke to Hardwicke, January 14, 1745; *ibid.*, 32704, f. 145: Pelham to Newcastle, April 4, 1745.

116. *Ibid.*, 35337, ff. 86–87; Lord Mahon, *History of England from the Peace of Utrecht to the Peace of Versailles*, (London: John Murray, 1851–54), III, Appendix, p. lviii.

117. Toynbee, *Walpole's Letters*, II, 70.

118. *Ibid.*, II, 87; *cf.*: B.M., Add. MSS., 35588, f. 23: Bolingbroke to Hardwicke, February 20, 1745; Stanhope, *Letters*, II, 572: Chesterfield to Newcastle, March 1, 1745; Lodge, *Chesterfield and Newcastle*, pp. 35–36: Chesterfield to Newcastle, March 19, 1745; Coxe, *Horatio Walpole*, p. 374: Horatio Walpole to Philip Yorke, May 25, 1745; Toynbee, *Walpole's Letters*, II, 76, 80–81.

119. Stanhope, *Letters*, II, 569: Chesterfield to Newcastle, March 9, 1745.

CHAPTER VI

1. Henry Finch was a member of the family of the Earl of Nottingham and an important member of the Whig oligarchy in the House of Commons.

2. Sheffield City Library, Wentworth-Woodhouse MSS., M3, f. 122: November 18, 1742.

3. *Ibid.,* f. 123.

4. P.R.O., S.P., Dom., Regencies, 34, not folioed: Newcastle to Carteret, May 24, 1743. This is a clear example, for Pelham was described as taking care to secure the borough held by Sir Charles Wager, who was dying, from its patron, Governor Edward Trelawny.

5. B.M., Add. MSS., 32706, f. 279.

6. Rose, *Marchmont Papers,* I, 218–19: Marchmont Diary, October 21, 1747.

7. B.M., Add. MSS., 32713, f. 414.

8. *Ibid.,* 32715, ff. 32–33.

9. H.M.C., *Report on the Manuscripts of Lady du Cane* (London: His Majesty's Stationery Office, 1905), p. 54: James Henshaw to Vice-Admiral Medley, April 30, 1745.

10. Smith, *Grenville Papers,* I, 35–39: George Grenville to Thomas Grenville, May 13, 1745, which gives the vote as 258 to 73.

11. H.M.C., *Lady du Cane MSS.,* p. 54.

12. Toynbee, *Walpole's Letters,* II, 3.

13. Russell, *Bedford Correspondence,* I, 86–89; *ibid.,* I, 76; H.M.C., *Report on the Manuscripts of the Marquess of Lothian Preserved at Blicking Hall, Norfolk* (London: His Majesty's Stationery Office, 1905), p. 160; Toynbee, *Walpole's Letters,* II, 147.

14. B.M., Add. MSS., 32707, ff. 149–50, 155–56.

15. H.M.C., *Lothian MSS.,* p. 160.

16. Also interesting is the fact that three other Prime Ministers (Duke of Grafton, Marquis of Rockingham, and Lord North) were sons of very close political allies of the Pelhams.

17. B.M., Add. MSS., 46974, not folioed: John Cust to Lord Perceval, June 6, 1747.

18. H.M.C., *Report of Manuscripts in Various Collections, Vol. VIII, The Manuscripts of the Hon. Frederick Lindley Wood; M. L. S. Clements, Esq.; S. Philip Unwin, Esq.* (London: His Majesty's Stationery Office, 1913), p. 171: June 11, 1747.

19. B.M., Add. MSS., 35360, f. 167: June 16, 1747.

20. *Ibid.,* 32711, f. 233: June 7, 1747. Smollett remarked in his *History of England* (V, 271) that "the elections for the new parliament in England had been conducted so as fully to answer the purposes of the duke of Newcastle, and his brother Mr. Pelham."

21. *Ibid.,* 32711, f. 233. I have deliberately used Henry Pelham's name alone, since Newcastle himself referred to his brother as "premier," which suggests that Pelham was definitely deciding issues on the election. Otherwise Newcastle would never have used the term.

22. *Ibid.,* 32711, ff. 353–54.

23. *Ibid.,* 32710, f. 5.

24. *Ibid.,* f. 135.

25. *Ibid.,* 32711, ff. 197 and 254.

26. *Ibid.,* f. 429: Newcastle to the Mayor, Jurass, & Freemen of Hastings, June 20, 1747.

27. *Ibid.,* f. 442: Newcastle to Seaford Corporation, June 20, 1747; *ibid.,* f. 552.

28. *Ibid.,* ff. 526, 540, 542.

29. *Ibid.,* 32710, f. 9.

30. *Ibid.,* 32711, ff. 418–19.

31. *Ibid.,* ff. 433–35, 436–37.

32. *Ibid.,* f. 479.

33. Robert J. Phillimore (ed.), *Memoirs and Correspondence of George, Lord Lyttelton, from 1734–1773* (London: James Ridgway, 1845), I, 256–58.

34. B.M., Add. MSS., 15946, f. 44.

35. *Ibid.,* 34734, f. 31.

36. *Ibid.,* 32711, f. 513: William Cayley to Newcastle, June 24, 1747.

37. Russell, *Bedford Correspondence,* I, 210–11: Lord Fane to Bedford, May 7, 1747.

38. Phillimore, *Lyttelton,* I, 256–58: Pelham to Lyttelton, July 11, 1747.

39. B.M., Add. MSS., 32714, f. 44: Tankerville to Newcastle, January 11, 1747.

40. *Ibid.,* 35351, ff. 109–10: Philip Yorke to Hardwicke, June 21, 1747.

41. *Ibid.,* ff. 124–25: Philip Yorke to Hardwicke, August 4, 1747.

42. *Ibid.,* ff. 126–27: Hardwicke to Philip Yorke, August 6, 1747.

43. Warrand, *More Culloden Papers,* V, 181–82: Andrew Mitchell to Duncan Forbes, May 21, 1747.

44. P.R.O., Chatham MSS., 31, not folioed: Hew Dalrymple to Pitt, June 21, 1747.

45. *Ibid.*

46. Smith, *Grenville Papers,* I, 63–64: Colonel Speed to Richard Grenville, June 29, 1747.

47. B.M., Add. MSS., 46977, not folioed: Cary to Viscount Perceval, n.d.; *ibid.,* 32711, f. 617: Newcastle to Borough Bridge and Alborough.

48. *Ibid.,* 46974, not folioed: Henry Fox to Lord Perceval, October 12, 1747.

49. P.R.O., Chatham MSS., 83, not folioed.

50. Oswald, *Memorials,* p. 61: January 29, 1748.

51. Phillimore, *Lyttelton,* I, 256–58: Pelham to Lyttelton, July 11, 1747.

52. Coxe, *Horatio Walpole,* p. 329: Pelham to Horatio Walpole.

53. B.M., Add. MSS., 35363, ff. 178–79: Philip Yorke to Joseph Yorke, July 24, 1747; *ibid.,* 35354, ff. 314–16: Hardwicke to Joseph Yorke, August 21, 1747.

54. Coxe, *Horatio Walpole,* pp. 338–39: Horatio Walpole to Cumberland, August 26, 1747.

55. Appendix III.

56. B.M., Add. MSS., 32704, ff. 17–18: Newcastle to Pelham, January 19, 1745.

57. If the papers of Henry Pelham could be found, some further light might be thrown on these meetings. These papers have been traced only until the 1820's, when they were in the hands of John Roberts, the son of Pelham's private secretary. They were seen at that time by Archdeacon Coxe and used for his biography of Pelham.

58. Stanhope, *Letters,* III, 665: Chesterfield to Newcastle, September 12, 1745.

59. B.M., Add. MSS., 32709, f. 16: Chesterfield to Stone, October 6, 1746.

60. *Ibid.*, 32708, f. 330: Hardwicke to Newcastle, September 19, 1746.

61. *Ibid.*, 32714, ff. 367–68: Newcastle to Cumberland, March 22, 1748.

62. *Ibid.*, 32709, ff. 9–12: Pelham to Hardwicke, October 4, 1746; *ibid.*, 32714, f. 6: Pelham to Stone, January 3, 1748; Coxe, *Horatio Walpole,* p. 329: Pelham to Horatio Walpole, n.d.

63. B.M., Add. MSS., 35633, f. 94: Horatio Walpole to Charles Yorke, May 24, 1748.

64. Rose, *Marchmont Papers,* I, 222–23: Marchmont Diary, October 27, 1748.

65. B.M., Add. MSS., 32709, ff. 65–66: Pelham to Newcastle, October 18, 1746.

66. *Ibid.*, 32711, f. 328: Pelham to Newcastle, June 13, 1747. This is only one example of the deep affection that existed between the brothers and that ultimately prevailed in all disagreements.

67. P.R.O., S.P., Dom., Geo. II, No. 68: Newcastle to Devonshire, September 21, 1745; B.M., Add. MSS., 35409, f. 100: Newcastle to Hardwicke, September 5, 1747; *ibid.*, 32714, f. 535: Newcastle to Cumberland, April 26, 1748.

68. *Ibid.*, 32713, f. 32: Hardwicke to Newcastle, September 6, 1747; *ibid.*, 32715, f. 475: Hardwicke to Newcastle, July 29, 1748.

69. *Ibid.*, 32711, f. 334: Earl of March to Newcastle, June 13, 1747.

70. *Ibid.*, 32703, f. 34: Lord Somerville to Newcastle, May 12, 1744. The request seems to have been to become a Scottish peer, but it is not quite clear from Somerville's letter.

71. *Ibid.*, 32710, f. 319: John Roberts to Stone, March 6, 1747.

72. Sheffield City Library, Wentworth-Woodhouse MSS., M5, f. 45: Rockingham to Pelham, July 5, 1746. Rockingham also sought the support of Newcastle; *ibid.*, M5, f. 44.

CHAPTER VII

1. B.M., Add. MSS., 35337, f. 112: Chesterfield to Philip and Charles Yorke, February 14, 1748.

2. Sheffield City Library, Wentworth-Woodhouse MSS., M3, f. 169: Isabella Finch to Malton, October 2, 1744.

3. Plumb, *Chatham,* pp. 28–31: "Pelham was subtle and dexterous. . . . Pelham had fixed Pitt. There can be no doubt that [Pitt] had been completely outmanoeuvered in 1746."

4. B.M., Add. MSS., 32707, f. 300: Sandwich to Newcastle, June 11, 1746.

5. Coxe, *Henry Pelham,* I, 341–42: Pelham to Trevor, October 29, 1746.

6. *Ibid.*

7. *Ibid.*, I, 343–44.

8. Rose, *Marchmont Papers,* I, 218–19: Marchmont Diary, October 21, 1747; Earl of Chesterfield, *An Apology for a Late Resignation in a Letter from an English Gentleman to His Friend at the Hague* (London: John Freeman, [1748]), pp. 16–17; B.M., Add. MSS., 35337, f. 112: Chesterfield to Philip and Charles Yorke, February 14, 1748.

9. *Ibid.*, 35423, f. 23: Pelham to Hardwicke, July 18, 1746; Russell, *Bedford Correspondence,* I, 423: Pelham to Bedford, 1748; B.M., Add. MSS., 32716, f. 217: Pelham to Newcastle, September 13, 1748.

10. *Ibid.*, 32704, f. 280: Richmond to Newcastle, May 18, 1745. Pelham's

military experiences were mostly confined to being Secretary at War from 1724 to 1730.

11. *Ibid.,* f. 307: Newcastle to Harrington, May 21, 1745; P.R.O., S.P., Dom., Regencies, 35, not folioed: Harrington to Pelham, June 2, 1745; *ibid.:* Harrington to Newcastle, June 2, 1745.

12. *Ibid.,* Harrington to Cumberland, May 29, 1745.

13. B.M., Add. MSS., 34523, f. 34: Henry Legge to Bedford, March 6, 1746.

14. P.R.O., Privy Council Register, No. 11, George II, p. 168.

15. Russell, *Bedford Correspondence,* I, 216: Pelham to Bedford, May 15, 1747.

16. *Ibid.,* I, 217: Pelham to Bedford, May 16, 1747. Perhaps a partial explanation for Pelham's activity with regard to the navy was that very often the navy clashed with the customs. Nevertheless Pelham was also active in non-Treasury affairs. *Cf.,* B.M., Add. MSS., 32713, f. 174: Bedford to Newcastle, September 30, 1747; Russell, *Bedford Correspondence,* I, 275: Bedford to Sandwich, October 19, 1747.

17. B.M., Add. MSS., 32717, f. 264: Pelham to Newcastle, November 4, 1748.

18. *Ibid.,* 32716, f. 397; *ibid.,* 35410, ff. 23–24.

19. *Ibid.,* 38331, f. 125.

20. P.R.O., Treasury Board Papers, Treasury Minute Book, XXX–XXXII, *passim;* August 1743–March 1754.

21. The positions were not completely sinecures, as they later became. The Board was required to pass on customs and other financial matters, but the junior members merely followed the lead of the First Lord.

22. B.M., Add. MSS., 32717, ff. 264 and 314; Coxe, *Henry Pelham,* II, 333.

23. P.R.O., S.P., Dom., Regencies, 41, not folioed: Bedford to Newcastle, August 26, 1748, and August 30, 1748.

24. B.M., Add. MSS., 32716, f. 134: August 28, 1748.

25. *Ibid.,* 15955, f. 236: August 30, 1748.

26. It must be remembered that in 1760 Lord Bute moved into the office of Groom of the Stole. He was obviously very important to the cabinet, for he represented the new king. These offices were not mere "rubber stamps," but they were rapidly losing their effective political power to the other ministers.

27. B.M., Add. MSS., 32716, ff. 65–66: August 16, 1748.

28. B.M., Stowe MSS., 308, ff. 15–16: Chesterfield's Character of Newcastle.

29. This is hardly a contemporary criticism, since Pitt was one of the first Englishmen to grasp this source of power. Newcastle certainly did better than Carteret in gaining the ruling class to his side.

30. B.M., Add. MSS., 32715, ff. 246–63, 277–93, 378–400; *ibid.,* 32716, ff. 26–27; *ibid.,* 32717, ff. 12–13, 52–69, 222, 227–28; *ibid.,* 35410, ff. 70–71, 80–81, 74–75, 101; Coxe, *Henry Pelham,* II, 322–23. These letters cover the period from June 29 to November 19.

31. B.M., Add. MSS., 32716, ff. 154–58; *ibid.,* 35410, ff. 3, 53–55, 78–79, 93–94. These letters cover the period from September 2 to November 8.

32. *Ibid.,* 32717, ff. 80–84, 161–62; *ibid.,* 35410, ff. 72–73.

33. Coxe, *Henry Pelham,* II, 326–28: Pelham to Newcastle, October 11, 1748.

34. B.M., Add. MSS., 25423, f. 65: Pelham to Hardwicke, September 25, 1748.

35. *Ibid.,* f. 75: Pelham to Hardwicke, October 22, 1748.

36. *Ibid.,* f. 78: Pelham to Hardwicke, November 7, 1748.

37. *Ibid.,* ff. 79–81: Pelham to Hardwicke, November 14, 1748.

38. Coxe, *Henry Pelham,* II, 30: Pelham to Newcastle, September 2, 1748. This is a definite expression of defeatism and wish to withdraw into England. Since Pelham was primarily interested in domestic matters, it is not surprising.

39. *Ibid.,* I, 425: June 10, 1748. This is representative of many letters.

40. *Ibid.,* I, 341–42: Pelham to Trevor, October 29, 1746.

41. B.M., Add. MSS., 35408, f. 280: Newcastle to Hardwicke, October 28, 1746.

42. Coxe, *Henry Pelham,* I, 342–43; Russell, *Bedford Correspondence,* I, 169–70.

43. *Ibid.,* I, 170, 171–73.

44. Stanhope, *Letters,* III, 818: November 28, 1746.

45. B.M., Add. MSS., 35589, f. 222: Chesterfield to Hardwicke, April 22, 1747.

46. Stanhope, *Letters,* III, 966–67: July 17, 1747.

47. Lodge, *Correspondence of Newcastle and Chesterfield,* p. xliv.

48. Coxe, *Henry Pelham,* I, 456: Pelham to Newcastle, July 22, 1748; B.M., Add. MSS., 35423, f. 48: Pelham to Hardwicke, July 25, 1748; *ibid.,* 32715, f. 459: Pelham to Newcastle, July 26, 1748; *ibid.,* 32716, ff. 28–31: Pelham to Newcastle, August 9, 1748.

49. Coxe, *Henry Pelham,* I, 460.

50. P.R.O., S.P., Dom., Various, 308, not folioed; *ibid.,* Regencies, 311, not folioed.

51. Warrand, *More Culloden Papers,* III, 198–99: Robert Craigie [Lord Advocate] to Duncan Forbes, January 10, 1744.

52. Coxe, *Horatio Walpole,* pp. 284–85: Fox to Hanbury-Williams, September 19, 1745.

53. Yorke, *Hardwicke, passim,* gives a full discussion of the legal aspects of Hardwicke's career.

54. B.M., Add. MSS., 35587, f. 243: Carteret to Hardwicke, April 1, 1744; "He [Bath] approv'd extremely ye Speech, & Motion; but desir'd to be excus'd from drawing ye Address. I therefore joyn wth the Duke of Newcastle in desiring Yr Lp to draw ye Address, wch no one can do so well." *Ibid.,* 32711, f. 176: Hardwicke to Newcastle, May 29, 1746.

55. *Ibid.,* 32708, f. 328.

56. *Ibid.,* 9200, ff. 109–10.

57. Russell, *Bedford Correspondence,* I, 108–9.

58. *Ibid.,* I, 191–94: Sandwich to Bedford, November 24, 1746.

59. Sir John Barrow, *The Life of George Lord Anson* . . . (London: John Murray, 1839), p. 153. Barrow gives Sandwich's duties as peace negotiator at Aix and Bedford's predilections for Woburn Abbey as the reasons for Anson's power, but neither Bedford nor Sandwich was interested in the daily problems of the department. They would likely have left these affairs to Anson even if they had been in London regularly.

60. *Ibid.,* pp. 201–3: Anson to Sandwich, February 15, 1748, and Sandwich to Anson, March 5, 1748.

61. Rose, *Marchmont Papers,* I, 213: September 16, 1747.

62. *Ibid.,* I, 91.

63. W. E. H. Lecky, *A History of England in the Eighteenth Century* (New York: D. Appleton and Company, 1878–90), chapters on Ireland. W. Ernst, *Memoirs of the Life of Philip Dormer, Fourth Earl of Chesterfield* . . . (London: Swan Sonnenschein & Co., 1893), *passim.* Claud Nugent, *Memoir of Robert, Earl Nugent* . . . (London: William Heinemann, 1898), *passim.*

64. Paget Toynbee (ed.), *Supplement to the Letters of Horace Walpole . . .* (Oxford: The Clarendon Press, 1925), III, 19: Horace Walpole to Lady Louisa Lennox, October 14, 1773. He probably exaggerated the extent of the quarrel.

65. Coxe, *Henry Pelham,* I, 343–44, 345.

66. Russell, *Bedford Correspondence,* I, 179; Coxe, *Henry Pelham,* I, 344.

67. *Ibid.* Russell, *Bedford Correspondence,* I, 178.

68. P.R.O., S.P., Dom., Geo. II, No. 64: Montagu to Newcastle, October 28, 1744. He wanted specific orders from both Newcastle and Pelham.

69. B.M., Add. MSS., 35423, f. 44: July 24, 1748.

70. *Ibid.,* 32705, f. 201: September 21, 1748.

71. P.R.O., Privy Council Register, George II, No. 8–12. Since these records are not always complete, Dorset may have missed other meetings, but they were not recorded as Council meetings. The record does, however, give an idea of his regularity, for he missed only 31 out of 274 meetings of all kinds, and six were definitely excused in advance.

72. B.M., Add. MSS., 35423, f. 44.

73. H.M.C., *Egmont Diary,* III, 141; Yorke, *Hardwicke,* I, 229–32.

74. During the eighteenth century, appointment to the office of Groom of the Stole seems to have been left to the king. Pembroke was George's choice and Albemarle certainly was chosen by George. Bute was plainly chosen by George III as one of his first acts.

75. B.M., Add. MSS., 32716, ff. 65–66: Pelham to Newcastle, August 16, 1748; *ibid.,* 35409, f. 189: Newcastle to Hardwicke, July 17, 1748; *ibid.,* 32703, f. 55: Richmond to Newcastle, May 20, 1744.

76. *Ibid.,* 32714, ff. 200–1: Richmond to Newcastle, February 9, 1748.

77. *Ibid.,* f. 235: Richmond to Newcastle, February 17, 1748.

78. The disappearance of the papers of the Duke of Argyll (Campbell Papers) is a most serious loss to a complete understanding of eighteenth-century political life during the time of Walpole and Pelham.

CHAPTER VIII

1. B.M., Add. MSS., 43771, not folioed: John Calcraft to Pitt, May 9, 1746.

2. *Ibid.,* 15955, f. 123: Lord Vere Beauclerk to Anson, April 9, 1747.

3. Barrow, *Anson,* p. 197: Anson to Sandwich, February 1748.

4. *Ibid.,* p. 198: Sandwich to Anson, February 1748.

5. Lloyd Sanders, *Patron and Place-hunters: A Study of George Bubb Dodington, Lord Melcombe* (London: John Lane, 1919), *passim.*

6. B.M., Add. MSS., 40817, f. 158: Vernon to Dodington, December 26, 1744.

7. *Ibid.,* 32715, f. 457: July 25, 1748: "I think I cou'd be of Some use in that Station; at least I'll promise you the letters from the Colonies shou'd not lye unopen'd." Here is one explanation for the future rift between the American colonies and England.

8. *Ibid.,* ff. 438–39: Pelham to Newcastle, July 22, 1748.

9. *Ibid.,* 32716, ff. 28–31, 38–39, 96–97, 99–100, 313.

10. *Ibid.,* ff. 293: September 17, 1748.

11. *Ibid.,* 32707, f. 142: Chesterfield to Newcastle, May 1, 1746.

12. P.R.O., Chatham MSS., 26: Nath. Clements to Pitt, March 8, 1745.

13. B.M., Add. MSS., 32716, ff. 28–31: Pelham to Newcastle, August 9, 1748.

14. The part of Finch in the crisis of February 1746 will be discussed later.

15. P.R.O., Privy Council Register, George II, No. 8–12. A list of the Privy Councillors for each year appears at the opening of each volume.

16. John Holliday, *The Life of William Late Earl of Mansfield* (London: P. Elmsly and D. Bremner, 1797), *passim*.

17. B.M., Add. MSS., 34734, f. 25: Thos. Sheppard to West, June 9, 1747; *ibid.*, f. 50: Grimston to West, February 14, 1748.

18. P.R.O., King's Warrant Book, XXXVII, 76 and 115.

19. *Ibid.*, pp. 8, 152, 169, 395, 65.

20. B.M., Lansdowne MSS., 660, ff. 78–102. The orders by Scrope give an example of the work of the Treasury in the case of Thomas Lawther's accounts. The auditing lasted from August 29, 1744, until November 26, 1744, and Scrope kept close watch on the proceedings.

21. B.M., Add. MSS., 34734, f. 25.

22. P.R.O., King's Warrant Book, XXXVII, *passim*, pp. 46–393.

23. B.M., Add. MSS., 32717, ff. 290–93: Pelham to Stone, November 8, 1748. This is an almost perfect example of these letters, for in it Pelham discusses foreign policies, personal questions, and the Duke of Newcastle. Stone is obviously considered as a friend.

24. *Ibid.*, 32703, ff. 415–16: John Burnaby to Stone, November 8, 1744. There are many other letters of a similar nature in the Newcastle papers.

25. *Ibid.*, 32715, ff. 306–8: July 17, 1748.

26. P.R.O., S.P., Dom., Various, 308, not folioed: Edward Weston and Andrew Stone named Secretaries, April 25, 1743; *ibid.*, 311, not folioed: Andrew Stone and Thomas Ramsden named Secretaries, May 1, 1745; *ibid.*, Various, Regencies, 315, not folioed: Richard Aldworth and John Potter named, May 12, 1748.

27. It is interesting to note that Hutton Perkins seems to have been related to the Pelhams in some fashion, for he was involved in the settlement of the Newcastle estates in 1741 along with the lesser Pelhams, the Earl of Godolphin, Mr. Godolphin, Lord Monson, Mr. Monson, and Viscount Vane, who were definitely relatives with valid claims against the estates: B.M., Add. MSS., 33138, ff. 60–62, 50–59.

28. P.R.O., Treasury Board Papers, CCCXXII, not folioed: April 5, 1746.

29. *Ibid.*, CCCXXI, not folioed: June 3, 1746. Henry Finch, Thomas Ripby, William Kent, and Westby Gill were the members.

30. Rose, *Marchmont Papers*, II, 368: July 21, 1747.

31. B.M., Add. MSS., 33054, f. 268; Toynbee, *Walpole's Letters*, II, 355: December 26, 1748.

32. H.M.C., *Fourteenth Report*, Appendix, Part IX, pp. 145, 149–51.

33. B.M., Add. MSS., 35410, ff. 17–18; *ibid.*, 32717, f. 383.

34. P.R.O., Privy Council Register, George II, No. 8, pp. 157, 240, 311, 386.

35. *Ibid.*, Nos. 8–12, *passim*. Lord Cholmondeley should be added as a very active Privy Councillor, but his position was somewhat different from that of these men. He had been a cabinet member who retained his Council importance after Gower succeeded him as Lord Privy Seal; he also was a Lord Lieutenant of several shires.

36. Robert Walpole was sworn into office on January 5, 1749; Henry Fane was a relative of the Pelhams. William Sharpe and Philip Sharpe were probably relatives of the Treasury Solicitor, John Sharpe. William Blair was a friend of the Pelhams.

37. The Earl of Ilay was a member of the regency, but technically not of the cabinet, though for all practical purposes he was also a cabinet member. He later became one officially.

38. P.R.O., S.P., Dom., Various, Regencies, 311, not folioed; *ibid.*, Various, 308, not folioed.

39. *Ibid.*, Various, Regencies, 315, not folioed.

40. *Ibid.*, 308, *passim; ibid.*, 311, *passim; ibid.*, 315, *passim; ibid.*, 110, *passim; ibid.*, Part I, 128, *passim.*

CHAPTER IX

1. B.M., Add. MSS., 32699, f. 301: Pulteney to Newcastle, June 27, 1742.

2. Pelham replaced Wilmington in August 1743, and reorganized the Treasury Board in December 1743 and again in December 1744. *Cf.* P.R.O., S.P., Regencies, 33, unfolioed: Carteret to Newcastle, August 16, 1743; P.R.O., Treasury Minute Book, XXX, p. 106: January 1, 1745.

3. H.M.C., *Fourteenth Report,* Appendix, Part IX, p. 133: Pelham to Trevor, November 8, 1745.

4. B.M., Add. MSS., 35423, f. 11: Pelham to Stair, May 13, 1743.

5. H.M.C., *Fourteenth Report,* Appendix, Part IX, pp. 97–98: Pelham to Trevor: May 29, 1744.

6. *Ibid.*, p. 114; *ibid.*, Lothian MSS., p. 151.

7. Russell, *Bedford Correspondence,* I, 190: George Grenville to Bedford, November 19, 1746.

8. Coxe, *Henry Pelham,* I, 373–75: Pelham to Cumberland, September 8, 1747.

9. B.M., Add. MSS., 32714, f. 326: Newcastle to Cumberland, March 11, 1747.

10. *Ibid.*, 32717, f. 264: November 4, 1748.

11. *Ibid.*, 35337, f. 60: Yorke's Journal, March 19–20, 1744.

12. Toynbee, *Walpole's Letters,* II, 169: January 17, 1746.

13. P.R.O., Chatham MSS., 74, f. 130: Notes & Memoranda.

14. *Ibid.*

15. *Ibid.*, Treasury Board Papers, CCCXVIII, No. 38.

16. *Ibid.*, No. 39.

17. B.M., Add. MSS., 35337, f. 45: Yorke's Journal, February 6, 1744.

18. *Ibid.*, ff. 45–46: February 13, 1744.

19. *Ibid.* Yorke said Pelham won the vote by only twenty-three votes. "Nor was the smallness of it Matter of Surprise to Those Who considered how Many were either by Themselves or their Friends, deeply concerned in one part or other of the Sugar Trade."

20. Williams, *Pitt,* I, 120.

21. B.M., Add. MSS., 35337, ff. 50–51: Yorke's Journal, February 20, 1744.

22. *Ibid.*, f. 51: February 22, 1744.

23. *Ibid.*, f. 68: April 5, 1744; Williams, *Pitt,* I, 120.

24. B.M., Add. MSS., 38331, ff. 51–53: Exchequer Reports, January 5, 1746.

25. P.R.O., Treasury Board Papers, CCCXXIX: February 28, 1746.

26. H.M.C., *Egmont Diary,* III, 315: March 10, 1746.

27. B.M., Add. MSS., 43441, unfolioed: Keene to de Castres, March 18, 1746.

28. *Ibid.*, 35363, ff. 143–44: Philip Yorke to Joseph Yorke, December 23, 1746.

29. P.R.O., Treasury Board Papers, CCCXXIII: Lotteries of 1719 and 1746 compared.

30. Under Newcastle, after Pelham's death in 1754, this plan did not work; therefore Pelham's ability must have been a primary factor.

31. B.M., Add. MSS., 33046, f. 230.

32. There was a similar office at Gibraltar.

33. P.R.O., Treasury Board Papers, CCCX, No. 6, unfolioed: Pelham's Report on Methods of Paying the Army, January 11, 1743.

34. *Ibid.,* Treasury Minute Book, XXIX, 257: May 18, 1743.

35. *Ibid.,* XXX, 11: April 12, 1744; B.M., Add. MSS., 38330, f. 284: April 19, 1744.

36. P.R.O., King's Warrant Book, XXXVI, 34–38: King to William Benson and William Aislabie, November 22, 1744.

37. *Ibid.,* Chatham MSS., 32, unfolioed: Furze to Pitt, August 25, 1746.

38. *Ibid.,* North Britain Book, XIV, 195: Henry Fane to Allen Whiteford, August 13, 1745.

39. B.M., Add. MSS., 32993, ff. 415: Pelham's Memoranda on Economy in Military Part of the Government, June 5, 1748; Coxe, *Henry Pelham,* I, 433: Pelham to Newcastle, July 5, 1748.

40. B.M., Add. MSS., 32716, f. 139: Cumberland to Newcastle, September 2, 1748.

41. *Ibid.,* 33046, ff. 236–39: Account of Naval Money.

42. Russell, *Bedford Correspondence,* I, 197–98: Legge to Bedford, November 28, 1746.

43. *Ibid.,* I, 200: George Grenville to Bedford, December 1, 1746.

44. Several plans of naval campaigns had to be curtailed or eliminated at least in part because of a shortage of money toward the end of the war.

45. P.R.O., King's Warrant Book, XXXV, 209–10; B.M., Add. MSS., 38330, f. 266.

46. *Ibid.,* S.P., Dom., Regencies, 31, unfolioed: Carteret to Newcastle, May 18, 1743.

47. There is strong reason to believe that on Pelham's death John Roberts, his private secretary, destroyed the secret service records—if Pelham's letters to Newcastle mean what they seem to imply.

48. B.M., Add. MSS., 33038, ff. 231–34.

49. P.R.O., S.P., Dom., Regencies, 32, unfolioed: Carteret to Newcastle, July 5, 1743.

50. *Ibid.,* Various, 4, last paper: Council Minute, November 24, 1743.

51. *Ibid.,* King's Warrant Book, XXXV, 444–45, 445–46; B.M., Add. MSS., 22533, f. 217; Chance, *British Diplomatic Instructions,* V, 115–19.

52. B.M., Add. MSS., 35337, ff. 90–94: Yorke's Journal, February 1, 6, 18, 1745; H.M.C., *Fourteenth Report,* Appendix, Part IX, 118: Chesterfield to Weston, July 6, 1745.

53. *Ibid.,* Pelham to Weston, July 9, 1745.

54. P.R.O., Treasury Board Papers, CCCXX, unfolioed: Pelham to Fox, and Arundel to Montagu, March 15, 1746; B.M., Add. MSS., 32707, ff. 67–68: Newcastle to Cumberland, April 17, 1746. Pitt strongly supported Pelham in the Commons debates.

55. Coxe, *Henry Pelham,* I, 330–31: Pelham to Robinson, July 18, 1746.

56. B.M., Add. MSS., 32714, f. 326; *ibid.,* 35423, ff. 38–39, 40, 42; ibid., 32714,

f. 67; Coxe, *Henry Pelham,* I, 397–99. Pelham also rejected the idea of paying damages to various German princes through whose lands the British armies had passed: *ibid.,* II, 32.

57. B.M., Add. MSS., 15870, f. 229: Pelham to Dayrolles, August 5, 1748.

58. *Ibid.,* 32715, f. 10; *ibid.,* 32717, f. 193; *ibid.,* 35423, f. 54; Russell, *Bedford Correspondence,* I, 377; *ibid.,* I, 547–48; Coxe, *Henry Pelham,* I, 433–35.

59. B.M., Add. MSS., 32715, f. 239: Andrew Stone to Newcastle, June 27, 1748. "The King took Notice of what your Grace mentions relating to the Payment of the Austrian Subsidy; upon which, His Majesty continues to think, there may be a great Difficulty; and indeed He has always treated this Point, as a Thing, that would not easily be got over. He said, He knew, Your Grace would be glad to find an Expedient to make it practicable: But what would Mr. Pelham say? I told him, I was persuaded, in the present Circumstances, Mr Pelham would be equally glad to do it: and that Mr. Wasner told me, that Mr Pelham assured him, when He left London, that if they could find a way to make it legal, He should be very glad to pay the money. To which His M[ajes]ty answer'd: that that was because Mr Pelham knew, that no such way could be found."

60. P.R.O., S.P., Dom., Regencies, 35, unfolioed: Harrington to Newcastle, June 23, 1745; Stanhope, *Letters,* III, 1014: Chesterfield to S. Dayrolles, September 22, 1747.

61. B.M., Add. MSS., 32715, f. 184: Pelham to Newcastle, June 10, 1748.

62. P.R.O., Treasury Board Papers, CCCXXIII, unfolioed: R. Spence (secretary of the Royal Africa company) to Treasury, August 14, 1746.

63. B.M., Add. MSS., 32716, ff. 1–3: Pelham to Newcastle, August 2, 1748; Russell, *Bedford Correspondence,* I, 582–85: Sandwich to Bedford, December 1, 1748.

64. B.M., Add. MSS., 32717, f. 314: Newcastle to Hardwicke, November 14, 1748; Coxe, *Henry Pelham,* II, 333: Newcastle to Pelham, November 15, 1748.

CHAPTER X

1. P.R.O., S.P., Dom., Regencies, 31, unfolioed: Carteret to Newcastle, June 16, 1743.

2. *Ibid.,* 33, unfolioed: Memorial of the Earl of Stair.

3. *Ibid.,* 32, unfolioed: Carteret to Newcastle, July 5, 1743.

4. *Ibid.,* 34, unfolioed: Newcastle to Carteret, July 15, 1743. Hardwicke, Pelham, Harrington, Wilmington, and Bath all agreed.

5. *Ibid.,* 33, unfolioed: Carteret to Newcastle, September 2, 1743.

6. B.M., Add. MSS., 35337, f. 30: Yorke's Journal, January 18, 1744.

7. H.M.C., Various, VIII, Wood MSS., p. 104: Pelham to Irwin, January 23, 1744.

8. Sheffield City Library, Wentworth-Woodhouse MSS., M6, f. 55: Malton to Dr. Griffith, February 4, 1744; B.M., Add. MSS., 35337, f. 46: Yorke's Journal, April 1744; *ibid.,* 32702, ff. 195–219; Coxe, *Horatio Walpole,* pp. 260–61: Horatio Walpole to Mr. Milling.

9. B.M., Add. MSS., 35337, f. 46: Yorke's Journal, [February] 1744.

10. *Ibid.,* 28157, ff. 130–31: Newcastle to Norris, February 9, 1744.

11. *Ibid.,* 22541, f. 130: Extract from an anonymous letter from Paris, February 21, 1744, that gives the destination as Ireland or, if that failed, Scotland.

12. Graham, *op. cit.,* II, 307: King's Warrant, February 24, 1744.

13. Coxe, *Horatio Walpole,* p. 259: Horatio Walpole to Trevor, March 3, 1744.

14. B.M., Add. MSS., 35337, ff. 53–54: Yorke's Journal, February 24, 1744; *ibid.,* f. 47. The address of loyalty was opposed by Waller, Dodington, Vernon, Dashwood, Strange, Pitt, Lyttelton, and Lord Hillsborough, though all but Vernon and J. Philips eventually agreed.

15. *Ibid.,* 32702, f. 215: Mr. Pybus to ?, February 26, 1744; *ibid.,* 35337, ff. 44–45: Yorke's Journal, spring of 1744, where he noted that the fear had subsided because the government realized that an invasion of Ireland or Scotland could be put down only with ruin to the invading forces.

16. *Ibid.,* 32702, f. 260: Admiralty to Newcastle, March 24, 1744; *ibid.,* 35337, f. 65: Yorke's Journal, n.d. The English declaration was drawn up by Andrew Stone.

17. P.R.O., Customs Book, XV, 407: Scrope to ?, March 22, 1744.

18. H.M.C., *Fourteenth Report,* Appendix, Part IX, 95: Pelham to Trevor, April 19, 1744; *ibid.,* pp. 95–96: Trevor to Pelham, May 15, 1744 N.S.

19. *Ibid.,* pp. 96–97: Trevor to Pelham, May 26, 1744 N.S.; *ibid.,* p. 98: Pelham to Trevor, June 12, 1744; *ibid.,* pp. 103–8: Trevor to Pelham, November 30, 1744 N.S.

20. *Ibid., Tenth Report,* Weston Underwood MSS., p. 281: Pelham to Weston, August 19, 1744.

21. Rose, *Marchmont Papers,* I, 3: Marchmont Diary, August 1, 1744.

22. B.M., Add. MSS., 23819, f. 24: Pelham to Robinson, December 25, 1744.

23. *Ibid.,* 32703, f. 270: Hardwicke to Newcastle, August 16, 1744; *ibid.,* 35587, f. 275: Carteret to Hardwicke, August 15, 1744.

24. Coxe, *Henry Pelham,* I, 163–64.

25. B.M., Add. MSS., 4325, ff. 129–30: Bolingbroke to Hardwicke, August 17, 1744.

26. *Ibid.,* 35337, f. 87: Yorke's Journal, January 28, 1745.

27. Coxe, *Henry Pelham,* I, 237–38: Cumberland to Newcastle, May 22, 1745; *ibid.,* I, 239: Cumberland to ?, June 13, 1745; *ibid.,* I, 255–58: Newcastle to Argyle, August 14, 1745; *ibid.,* I, 259–60: Newcastle to Argyle, August 21, 1745; Coxe, *Horatio Walpole,* pp. 285–87: Horatio Walpole to Mr. Yorke, June 1, 1745; B.M., Add. MSS., 35354, ff. 135–36: Hardwicke to Joseph Yorke, August 23, 1745; *ibid.,* 32705, f. 113: Cumberland to Newcastle, September 6, 1745 N.S.

28. *Ibid.,* 32705, f. 379: Chesterfield to Newcastle, November 25, 1745.

29. *Ibid.,* 35408, ff. 126–27: Stone to Hardwicke, February 9, 1745; *ibid.;* H.M.C., *Fourteenth Report,* Appendix, Part IX, p. 115: Pelham to Weston, June 11, 1745.

30. Russell, *Bedford Correspondence,* I, 22–25; Coxe, *Henry Pelham,* I, 255–58; Russell, *Bedford Correspondence,* I, 22–25, 35.

31. B.M., Add. MSS., 35354, ff. 135–36; *ibid.,* 32705, f. 113; Russell, *Bedford Correspondence,* I, 25–27, 36.

32. P.R.O., S.P., Dom., Regencies, 36, unfolioed: Harrington to Trevor, July 15, 1745; B.M., Add. MSS., 32705, f. 2: Philip Journeaulx to Newcastle, August 2, 1745; *ibid.,* f. 92: Newcastle to Cumberland, August 10, 1745; *ibid.,* f. 100: Newcastle to Harrington, August 22, 1745; Russell, *Bedford Correspondence,* I, 28–30: Vernon to Bedford, August 28, 1745. The Jacobite rebellion will be discussed as a separate problem in a later chapter.

33. *Ibid.,* I, 28–30: Bedford to Harrington, July 26, 1745.

34. Barrow, *Anson,* pp. 128–29.

35. Lodge, *Correspondence of Chesterfield and Newcastle,* pp. 6–10, 12–17, 33, 50; Stanhope, *Letters,* II, 563.

36. B.M., Add., MSS., 32704, f. 337: June 14, 1745; H.M.C., *Fourteenth Report,* Appendix, Part IX, pp. 121–24, 126–27, 128, 135; Coxe, *Henry Pelham,* I, 282–83.

37. D. B. Horn, *Sir Charles Hanbury Williams and European Diplomacy 1747–58* (London: George G. Harrop & Company, Ltd., 1930), p. 21; Lodge, *Correspondence of Chesterfield and Newcastle,* xxv. Both books indicate that the Pelham administration moved toward such an alliance, and Lodge named Pelham as a leader of the action.

38. Coxe, *Horatio Walpole,* pp. 288–90: May 29, 1745; B.M., Add., MSS., 35408, ff. 179–80: August 11, 1745.

39. Lodge, *Correspondence of Chesterfield and Newcastle,* pp. 63–65: Newcastle to Chesterfield, September 5, 1745. Newcastle indicated that Granville recovered much of his importance with the king because of this treaty.

40. Sheffield City Library, Wentworth-Woodhouse MSS., M1, unfolioed: Fitzwilliam to Malton, November 30, 1745.

41. H.M.C., *Fourteenth Report,* Appendix, Part IX, p. 129: Pelham to Trevor, August 9, 1745; Lodge, *Correspondence of Chesterfield and Newcastle,* pp. 53–55.

42. P.R.O., S.P., Dom., Regencies, 37, unfolioed: Newcastle to Harrington, May 17, 1745; Stanhope, *Letters,* III, 654: Chesterfield to Trevor, August 13, 1745.

43. B.M., Add., MSS., 38197, ff. 39–40; P.R.O., S.P., Dom., Geo. II, No. 81, unfolioed: Minute of Council, February 3, 1746; *ibid.:* Newcastle to Sir George Oxenden, February 20, 1746.

44. H.M.C., *Fourteenth Report,* Appendix, Part IX, pp. 142–43: Trevor to Pelham, February 25, 1746; Russell, *Bedford Correspondence,* I, 106: Anson to Bedford, May 20, 1746; Coxe, *Henry Pelham,* I, 329: Pelham to Horatio Walpole, June 12, 1746.

45. B.M., Add., MSS., 33046, f. 172: Council Minute, April 4, 1746.

46. P.R.O., Chatham MSS., I, f. 8: Furze to Pitt, July 31, 1746 N.S.

47. Russell, *Bedford Correspondence,* I, 143–44, 146–47.

48. H.M.C., *Tenth Report,* Weston Underwood MSS., p. 295: Poyntz to Weston, December 4, 1746; Russell, *Bedford Correspondence,* I, 138, 153–54.

49. B.M., Add. MSS., 9185, f. 37: Robinson to Granville, March 9, 1746; *ibid.,* ff. 38–39: other letters of Robinson that confirm the confusion.

50. Chance, *British Diplomatic Instructions,* III, 138–44.

51. P.R.O., Chatham MSS., 32, unfolioed: Peregrine Furze to Pitt, July 15, 1746; B.M., Add. MSS., 9146: Horatio Walpole to Pelham, before August 15, 1746.

52. Stanhope, *Letters,* III, 804: Chesterfield to Hyndford, November 4, 1746; Chance, *British Diplomatic Instructions,* V, 119–29: Chesterfield to Guy-Dickens, November 7, 1746, to February 5, 1748.

53. Coxe, *Horatio Walpole,* pp. 307–8: Pelham to Horatio Walpole, August 23, 1746; *ibid.,* pp. 309–14: Horatio Walpole to Yorke, October 6, 1746.

54. Russell, *Bedford Correspondence,* I, 203–5: Newcastle to Bedford, January 7, 1747.

55. *Ibid.,* I, 206: Newcastle to Bedford, January 14, 1747.

56. B.M., Egerton MSS., 929, ff. 168–72: Warren to Newcastle, January 17, 1747; B.M., Add. MSS., 35409, f. 5: Stone to Hardwicke, March 7, 1747.

57. *Ibid.,* 35409, f. 9; W. S. Taylor and J. H. Pringle (eds.), *Correspondence of William Pitt, Earl of Chatham* (London: John Murray, 1838), I, 19: Thomas Orby Hunter, deputy paymaster in Flanders, to Pitt, May 9, 1747; P.R.O., Chatham MSS., I, f. 20: Hunter to Pitt, April 21, 1747 N.S.

58. Smith, *Grenville Papers,* I, 63–64; Russell, *Bedford Correspondence,* I, 229–30, 232–33; Phillimore, *Lyttelton,* I, 258–59; Coxe, *Henry Pelham,* I, 375–76; B.M., Add., MSS., 32712, f. 21; *ibid.,* 32713, f. 16.

59. H.M.C., *Tenth Report,* Weston Underwood MSS., p. 297: Bishop Trevor to Weston, July 16, 1747.

60. B.M., Add. MSS., 32809, f. 78: Cumberland to Chesterfield, July 31, 1747.

61. *Ibid.,* 32710, ff. 467–68, 471; Stanhope, *Letters,* III, 914; B.M., Add., MSS., 32711, ff. 233–34; *ibid.,* 32712, ff. 2–3; *ibid.,* 32713, ff. 51–64; *ibid.,* 15869, f. 183; Russell, *Bedford Correspondence,* I, 222–26; Stanhope, *Letters,* III, 985; Coxe, *Henry Pelham,* I, 370–73; Coxe, *Horatio Walpole,* p. 353.

62. B.M., Add. MSS., 15955, f. 147: Bedford to Anson, August 23, 1747.

63. *Ibid.,* 32713, f. 95: Newcastle to Hardwicke, September 21, 1747; *ibid.,* 35409, f. 132: Newcastle to Hardwicke, September 30, 1747.

64. *Ibid.,* 32713, f. 232.

65. Chesterfield, *An Apology,* pp. 16–17; Coxe, *Henry Pelham,* I, 403: February 27, 1748; *ibid.,* I, 426: June 14, 1748.

66. Phillimore, *Lyttelton,* I, 390; Coxe, *Henry Pelham,* I, 405–6. Cumberland himself gave orders that the English should retreat if the French advanced; B.M., Add. MSS., 142, f. 115: Cumberland to Albemarle, April 5, 1748 N.S.

67. Coxe, *Henry Pelham,* I, 406: Newcastle to Cumberland, April 1, 1748.

68. B.M., Add. MSS., 32715, f. 44: Cumberland to Newcastle, May 9, 1748.

69. *Ibid.,* 32714, f. 14; *ibid.,* 32716, ff. 11–14; Coxe, *Henry Pelham,* I, 445; Russell, *Bedford Correspondence,* I, 307, 316, 508–10.

70. B.M., Add. MSS., 35423, f. 52; *ibid.,* 32715, f. 412; *ibid.,* 35423, f. 70; Russell, *Bedford Correspondence,* I, 519–21.

71. B.M., Add., MSS., 32717, ff. 175–77: Newcastle to Pelham, October 23, 1748. Newcastle's plan was to build a supreme navy, reach an understanding with the Prince of Orange, retain Austria, gain Russia, and avoid provoking Prussia; *ibid.,* 35410, ff. 86–91: November 6, 1748: Coxe, *Henry Pelham,* II, 332.

72. H.M.C., *First Report of the Royal Commission on Historical Manuscripts* (London: George Edward Eyre and William Spottiswoode, 1870), Appendix, p. 415: Stone to Richmond, May 1746; Stanhope, *Letters,* III, 763: May 20, 1746.

73. B.M., Add. MSS., 32707, ff. 234–35, 289, 390; Coxe, *Horatio Walpole,* p. 322.

74. B.M., Add. MSS., 32708, f. 52: Pelham to Newcastle, August 10, 1746; Coxe, *Henry Pelham,* I, 331–33: Pelham to Horatio Walpole, July 29, 1746.

75. B.M., Add. MSS., 32708, ff. 182, 389; *ibid.,* 32709, f. 33; *ibid.,* 5797, ff. 1–142; Russell, *Bedford Correspondence,* I, 138–40; Coxe, *Henry Pelham,* I, 336–37; Coxe, *Horatio Walpole,* p. 314.

76. *Ibid.,* p. 317–20; Coxe, *Henry Pelham,* I, 368 and 492; B.M., Add. MSS., 35423, f. 28.

77. *Ibid.,* 35354, ff. 314–16; Coxe, *Horatio Walpole,* p. 329.

78. B.M., Add. MSS., 32713, ff. 22, 178–79; *ibid.,* 35423, f. 67; *Russell Correspondence,* I, 246. Pelham in particular felt that Cape Breton had to be restored to France in order to regain French conquests in the Netherlands: B.M., Add. MSS., 35337, f. 110. Some Englishmen, like Sandwich and Bedford, were

even willing to cede Gibraltar to Spain in return for trade concessions from that nation: Russell, *Bedford Correspondence,* I, 287–88.

79. Taylor and Pringle, *Correspondence of Pitt,* I, 26–28: Newcastle to Pitt, January 19, 1748; B.M., Add. MSS., 25561, ff. 103–4: Memorial of the South Sea Co. Directors to Newcastle, February 16, 1748; Coxe, *Henry Pelham,* I, 496: Newcastle to Cumberland, March 22, 1748; B.M., Add. MSS., 32714, ff. 387–88: Newcastle to Cumberland, March 25, 1748.

80. Coxe, *Henry Pelham,* I, 400; B.M., Stowe MSS., 262, ff. 1–2: Cumberland to Sandwich, March 22, 1748.

81. Russell, *Bedford Correspondence,* I, 346–48: Note of the French, April 7, 1748. Newcastle, Pelham, Hardwicke, Bedford, Gower, Dorset, and the king were the men who agreed to the note.

82. B.M., Add. MSS., 32714, ff. 452–53: Pelham to Newcastle, April 8, 1748.

83. Coxe, *Henry Pelham,* I, 418–19 and 420–21: April 12 and 25, 1748.

84. Smith, *Grenville Papers,* I, 74: Pelham to George Grenville, April 30, 1748; Coxe, *Horatio Walpole,* p. 359.

85. Coxe, *Henry Pelham,* I, 496–500: May 1/April 20, 1748; B.M., Add. MSS., 9187, ff. 176–80: May 5, 1748.

86. *Ibid.,* 32715, f. 204; Coxe, *Henry Pelham,* I, 426.

87. Russell, *Bedford Correspondence,* I, 381: Bedford to Sandwich, June 23, 1748.

88. B.M., Add. MSS., 32715, ff. 299–300; *ibid.,* 32716, ff. 38–39; Coxe, *Henry Pelham,* I, 453.

89. P.R.O., S.P., Dom., Regencies, 40, unfolioed: Bedford to Newcastle, July 29, 1748; B.M., Add. MSS., 32715, ff. 478–81; *ibid.,* 23829, f. 279.

90. There is a vast correspondence back and forth among Newcastle, Pelham, Hardwicke, Bedford, Sandwich, and Robinson on the subject of a peace without Austria and the quarrels over this issue. It is unnecessary and impossible to list specific letters, but the following references include the most important sources: *ibid.,* 35409, ff. 197–226; *ibid.,* 32716, ff. 5–70, 242–66; Coxe, *Henry Pelham,* I, 464–65; *ibid.,* II, 4–21, 314–26; Russell, *Bedford Correspondence,* I, 405–52, 516–18, 540–52.

91. *Ibid.,* I, 27–272; Coxe, *Henry Pelham,* II, 330–31.

92. Hostages were to be held until Britain restored its conquests.

93. B.M., Add. MSS., 32716, f. 341; *ibid.,* 32717, ff. 214–15; *ibid.,* 23830, ff. 158–59: Minutes of the Lords Justices, November 8, 1748; *ibid.,* 32815, ff. 33–34; P.R.O., S.P., Dom., Regencies, 39, unfolioed: Bedford to Newcastle, July 22, 1748; *ibid.,* 42, unfolioed: Bedford to Newcastle, October 11, 1748; *ibid.,* 43, unfolioed: Newcastle to Bedford, October 19, 1748; Russell, *Bedford Correspondence,* I, 529–38; Nugent, *Memoir of Nugent,* p. 252.

94. B.M., Add. MSS., 32716, ff. 78, 147–50, 345–48; *ibid.,* 32717, ff. 126–27; P.R.O., S.P., Dom., Regencies, 42, unfolioed: Newcastle to Bedford, September 4, 1748; Coxe, *Henry Pelham,* II, 323–24.

95. *Ibid.,* I, 466; B.M., Add. MSS., 32716, ff. 21–24.

96. *Ibid.,* f. 45: August 11, 1748.

97. *Ibid.,* ff. 180–81, 196–97; *ibid.,* 35363, f. 221.

98. *Ibid.,* 32716, ff. 345–48; *ibid.,* 35423, ff. 61, 72–73; *ibid.,* 32717, f. 35.

99. *Ibid.,* ff. 8–9; Russell, *Bedford Correspondence,* I, 270–72: October 18–28, 1748.

CHAPTER XI

1. P.R.O., S.P., Dom., Regencies, 34, unfolioed: Stone and Weston to Carteret, June 17, 1743; *ibid.*, 32, unfolioed: Carteret to Newcastle, June 24, 1743; *ibid.*, Various, 132, p. 259: Secretary's Letter Book, 1740–45, Newcastle to Attorney-General and Solicitor-General, November 14, 1743.

2. *Ibid.*, Regencies, 31, unfolioed: Carteret to Newcastle, May 22, 1743.

3. Cambridge University Library, Cholmondeley-Houghton MSS., 3165: Charles Gibson to Orford, July 16, 1743; *ibid.*, 3167: Gibson to Orford, August 13, 1743.

4. P.R.O., Treasury Minute Book, XXIX, 381: January 30, 1744; *ibid.*, S.P., Dom., Geo. II, No. 64, unfolioed: Carteret to Thos. Lane and Earl of Arran, September 26, 1744.

5. *Ibid.*, King's Warrant Book, XXXV, 444: June 13, 1744; Toynbee, *Letters*, II, 28–29.

6. Sheffield City Library, Wentworth-Woodhouse MSS., M6, f. 70; Duff, *Culloden Papers*, p. 195; Cambridge University Library, Cholmondeley-Houghton MSS., 3177.

7. B.M., Add. MSS., 35337, ff. 95–109: Yorke's Journal, February 20 to April 10, 1745; Sheffield City Library, Wentworth-Woodhouse MSS., M1, unfolioed: Fitzwilliam to Malton, December 10, 1745; Toynbee, *Letters*, II, 87.

8. B.M., Add. MSS., 32709, f. 78: Pelham to Stone, October 22, 1746.

9. *Ibid.*, 32713, f. 205: Richmond to Newcastle, October 2, 1747.

10. Sheffield City Library, Wentworth-Woodhouse MSS., M6, ff. 111–12; *ibid.*, M5, f. 91; B.M., Add. MSS., 32711, ff. 144 and 574; *ibid.*, 32712, f. 299; *ibid.*, 32713, f. 393.

11. *Ibid.*, 32710, ff. 436–37: April 15, 1747; *ibid.*, 35957, f. 30: November 14, 1747 N.S.

12. *Ibid.*, 33034, f. 115: List sent to the Lords Justice Clerk, June 18, 1747.

13. *Ibid.*, 32711, ff. 493–95: Newcastle to Lothian, June 23, 1747.

14. *Ibid.*, 32716, ff. 229, 233, 273–78, 255–56.

15. *Ibid.*, f. 231: Pelham to Newcastle, September 16, 1748.

16. *Ibid.*, 32714, ff. 86 and 264; *ibid.*, 32994, f. 16; *ibid.*, 32716, ff. 122–23, 273–78; *ibid.*, 32717, f. 572.

17. Toynbee, *Letters*, V, 306–7: Horace Walpole to Mann, March 11, 1748.

18. P.R.O., Chatham MSS., 55, unfolioed; B.M., Add. MSS., 32717, f. 237; Stanhope, *Letters*, III, 1119; Phillimore, *Lyttelton*, I, 266–68.

19. B.M., Add. MSS., 32715, f. 457: Earl of Morton to Newcastle, July 25, 1748.

20. P.R.O., Privy Council Register, Vol. VIII–XII, *passim*.

21. Cambridge University Library, Cholmondeley-Houghton MSS., 3196.

22. B.M., Add. MSS., 32714, f. 107: January 26, 1748.

23. *Ibid.*, 32717, ff. 218–19; P.R.O., Treasury Board Papers, CCCXX, unfolioed; *ibid.*, Chatham MSS., 34, unfolioed. Governor Shirley seems to have been a particular friend of Pelham's, for there are many letters in this period dealing with the financial problems of the former and seeking the latter's aid: Huntington Library, Huntington MSS., 9699, 9700, 9701, 9703, 9704, 9706, 9707, 9709, 9717, 9718, 9719, 9723.

24. B.M., Add. MSS., 32706, f. 235.

25. *Ibid.,* 32705, ff. 41, 43, 45.

26. P.R.O., Treasury Board Papers, CCCXXI, *passim;* see especially letter from Thos. Corbet to John Scrope, March 15, 1746.

27. *Ibid.,* Egremont MSS., No. 17, *passim;* especially Memorandum with regard to Acts of Gov't relating to the Mosquito shore.

28. *Ibid.,* S.P., Dom., Regencies, 39, unfolioed; B.M., Add. MSS., 23830, ff. 223–24.

29. Russell, *Bedford Correspondence,* I, 64: March 28, 1746.

30. *Ibid.,* 65–69: March 30, 1746.

31. B.M., Add. MSS., 32707, f. 25: April 6, 1746.

32. *Ibid.*

33. Russell, *Bedford Correspondence,* I, 129: July 17, 1746.

34. *Ibid.,* 132: July 19, 1746.

35. B.M., Add. MSS., 32708, f. 118: August 21, 1746.

36. *Ibid.,* ff. 138–39; *ibid.,* f. 150.

37. *Ibid.,* f. 162: August 27, 1746.

38. Sheffield City Library, Wentworth-Woodhouse MSS., M5, f. 55: October 18, 1746.

39. Smith, *Grenville Papers,* I, 56–57.

40. B.M., Add. MSS., 32715, f. 457; *ibid.,* 32716, f. 63.

41. Russell, *Bedford Correspondence,* I, 441–42: August 11, 1748.

42. *Ibid.,* 497–98: September 3, 1748.

43. *Ibid.,* 505–6: September 7, 1748.

44. B.M., Add. MSS., 46973, unfolioed: Will. Cooley to Lord Perceval, July 6, 1744.

45. *Ibid.,* 32711, ff. 114–15: George Stone to Newcastle, May 22, 1747.

46. *Ibid.,* 32704, f. 34: Stanhope, *Letters,* III, 742–43.

47. P.R.O., Privy Council Register, Nos. 8–11, George II, *passim.*

CHAPTER XII

1. Plumb, *Chatham,* pp. 27–28; [Glover], *Memoirs,* pp. 38–42.

2. [Almon], *Pitt,* I, 205–10.

3. B.M., Add. MSS., 32705, f. 174: Chesterfield to Newcastle, September 12, 1745.

4. *Ibid.,* 35351, f. 80; Coxe, *Henry Pelham,* I, 265.

5. B.M., Add. MSS., 35396, f. 321: Thomas Birch to Philip Yorke, September 14, 1745.

6. *Ibid.,* 32705, ff. 233–34: Chesterfield to [Stone], September 30, 1745.

7. *Ibid.,* f. 285: Chesterfield to Newcastle, October 24, 1745.

8. *Ibid.,* 35408, f. 188: Newcastle to Hardwicke, September 15, 1745.

9. H.M.C., *First Report,* Appendix, p. 415.

10. B.M., Add. MSS., 32705, ff. 318–37: Newcastle to Chesterfield, November 20, 1745.

11. *Ibid.,* 35588, f. 166.

12. Lodge, *Correspondence of Chesterfield and Newcastle,* p. 90.

13. P.R.O., Granville Papers, Box 1, unfolioed: December 3, 1745.

14. B.M., Add. MSS., 32706, ff. 17–29; Stanhope, *Letters,* III, 718–19.

15. B.M., Add. MSS., 32706, f. 36.

16. *Ibid.,* 32707, f. 336: Newcastle to Cotton, January 19, 1746.

17. *Ibid.*, 35351, f. 98.

18. Coxe, *Henry Pelham*, I, 290–92; Rose, *Marchmont Papers*, I, 171.

19. B.M., Add. MSS., ff. 187–88: Hardwicke to Joseph Yorke, February 11, 1746.

20. There is a great correspondence on the subject of the resignation, among which the following are important: B.M., Add. MSS., 32706, ff. 136 and 140; Rose, *Marchmont Papers*, I, 171; Coxe, *Henry Pelham*, I, 289; Coxe, *Horatio Walpole*, p. 295; Russell, *Bedford Correspondence*, I, 61–62; Stanhope, *Letters*, III, 729–31; H.M.C., *Egmont Diary*, III, 314.

21. B.M., Add. MSS., 43441, ff. 6–7.

22. Sheffield City Library, Wentworth-Woodhouse MSS., M6, extra folio between 88 and 89.

23. B.M., Add. MSS., 32706, ff. 151–59.

24. Coxe, *Henry Pelham*, I, 290–92.

25. H.M.C., *Lothian MSS.*, p. 158.

26. Rose, *Marchmont Papers*, I, 173.

27. B.M., Add. MSS., f. 100: Hardwicke to Philip Yorke, February 12, 1746.

28. H.M.C., *Fourteenth Report*, Appendix, Part IX, 141–42; Toynbee, *Letters*, II, 175–78; Coxe, *Henry Pelham*, I, 292.

29. Smith, *Grenville Papers*, I, 50.

30. B.M., Add. MSS., 35360, ff. 153–54.

31. H.M.C., *Egmont Diary*, III, 315.

32. B.M., Add. MSS., 35385, f. 50: Charles Yorke to Joseph Yorke, February 15, 1746; *ibid.*, 43441, f. 8.

33. *Ibid.*, 35870, f. 117: Notes of meeting, in Hardwicke's handwriting.

34. P.R.O., S.P., Dom., Various, 133, p. 70; B.M., Add. MSS., 32706, ff. 164–65.

35. Plumb, *Chatham*, p. 36. This seems a more nearly correct conclusion than that reached by O. A. Sherrard in his recent biography of Chatham and in other works.

36. Coxe, *Henry Pelham*, I, 482–83; Stanhope, *Letters*, III, 733.

37. B.M., Add. MSS., 32706, ff. 221–24.

38. H.M.C., *Egmont Diary*, III, 315.

39. Coxe, *Horatio Walpole*, p. 307.

40. Coxe, *Henry Pelham*, I, 376.

41. B.M., Add. MSS., 35363, f. 187.

42. H.M.C., *Tenth Report*, Weston-Underwood MSS., p. 299.

43. Toynbee, *Letters*, II, 300–1.

44. Russell, *Bedford Correspondence*, I, 320–23.

45. B.M., Add. MSS., 47090, unfolioed: Speeches of Egmont; *ibid.*, 47092, unfolioed: original pagination 1–5 and 32–58.

46. Phillimore, *Lyttelton*, I, 295.

47. Glover, *Memoirs*, p. 45.

48. Russell, *Bedford Correspondence*, I, 206–7: January 14, 1747; Stanhope, *Letters*, III, 1043: October 23, 1747; *ibid.*, 1088: January 26, 1748; Rose, *Marchmont Papers*, I, 262–63: December 24, 1747; Coxe, *Henry Pelham*, I, 389–92: February 17, 1748.

49. B.M., Add. MSS., 32713, ff. 26–27: September 5, 1747.

50. *Ibid.*, 32714, f. 187: Newcastle to Andrew Stone, February 6, 1748.

51. Russell, *Bedford Correspondence*, I, 323–24.

52. [Chesterfield], *Apology, passim.*

53. Stanhope, *Letters,* III, 1096.
54. *Ibid.,* 1132.
55. B.M., Add. MSS., 32710, ff. 189, 269–70, 273.
56. Rose, *Marchmont Papers,* I, 177–88, 189.
57. Russell, *Bedford Correspondence,* I, 282–83; Rose, *Marchmont Papers,* I, 264; Barrow, *Anson,* p. 198; B.M., Add. MSS., 35410, ff. 19–21; *ibid.,* 32717, f. 205.
58. Oswald, *Memorials,* pp. 402–3; Horn, *Hanbury Williams,* p. 46.
59. Russell, *Bedford Correspondence,* I, 262.
60. Rose, *Marchmont Papers,* I, 222–23: October 27, 1747.
61. B.M., Add. MSS., 32717, ff. 23–26: Pelham to Newcastle, October 4, 1748; *ibid.,* ff. 184–91: Pelham to Newcastle, October 25, 1748.
62. *Ibid.,* 35410, ff. 95–96: Newcastle to Hardwicke, November 14, 1748.

CHAPTER XIII

1. B.M., Add. MSS., 32700, ff. 9–10, 17–18, 30–31.
2. *Ibid.,* 22533, ff. 10–11, 13–15, 17–18, 19, 25–29, 31–32.
3. *Ibid.,* 22544, f. 53; Warrand, *More Culloden Papers,* IV, 1–3. One report even accused the Methodists of giving aid to the Pretender: *ibid.,* 32702, f. 81.
4. *Ibid.,* f. 88; *ibid.,* 32703, f. 50; *ibid.,* 35337, ff. 56–57; H.M.C., *Egmont Diary,* III, 289.
5. B.M., Add. MSS., 35337, f. 76: Yorke's Journal, April 27, 1744, and May 3, 1744; Coxe, *Henry Pelham,* I, 252.
6. B.M., Add. MSS., 32704, f. 125: March 6, 1745.
7. *Ibid.,* ff. 160, 162–63, 244, 442, 455–57; H.M.C., *Tenth Report,* Weston-Underwood MSS., pp. 286–87.
8. B.M., Add. MSS., 35870, f. 99; Coxe, *Henry Pelham,* I, 252–55.
9. [Glover], *Memoirs,* pp. 38–42.
10. B.M., Add. MSS., 37176, unfolioed: August 1, 1745.
11. Lord Mahon, *History of England from the Peace of Utrecht to the Peace of Aix-la-Chapelle* (London: John Murray, 1839), III, Appendix, xxii: Charles Edward to James III, August 4, 1745; P.R.O., S.P., Dom., Geo. II, No. 67, unfolioed: August 22, 1745; *Ibid.,* Treasury Board Papers, CCCXXI, *passim.*
12. Duff, *Culloden Papers,* p. 203, 204–5; Graham, *Memoirs of Stair,* II, 318: Loudoun to Stair.
13. B.M., Add. MSS., 32705, f. 18; *ibid.,* 35450, f. 32: August 15, 1745.
14. Rose, *Marchmont Papers,* I, 105–8: Marchmont Diary, September 27, 1745. Marchmont also failed to get any decision from Tweeddale when he used the Duke of Queensberry as his agent: *ibid.,* I, 110–13.
15. B.M., Add. MSS., 35396, f. 302; P.R.O., S.P., Dom., Regencies, 36, unfolioed: Harrington to Newcastle, August 2, 1745.
16. Coxe, *Henry Pelham,* I, 258–59; B.M., Add. MSS., 32705, f. 100: Newcastle to Harrington, August 22, 1745.
17. Coxe, *Henry Pelham,* I, 264: September 5, 1745.
18. H.M.C., *Fourteenth Report,* Appendix, Part IX, p. 131.
19. *Ibid., First Report,* Appendix, p. 415: Newcastle to Richmond, September 21, 1745; Coxe, *Henry Pelham,* I, 264–65: Fox to Hanbury Williams, September 19, 1745.
20. *Ibid.,* I, 244: Newcastle to Cumberland, September 4, 1745; *ibid.,* I, 255–58: August 14, 1745; P.R.O., S.P., Dom., Geo. II, No. 67, unfolioed: Tankerville to

Newcastle, August 16, 1745; *ibid.:* William Stodart to Newcastle, August 27, 1745; Sheffield City Library, Wentworth-Woodhouse MSS., M4, f. 28: letter to Lord Malton, September 5, 1745.

21. *Ibid.,* M4, f. 48; B.M., Add. MSS., 32705, ff. 113, 144; H.M.C., *Lothian MSS.,* p. 148; Coxe, *Henry Pelham,* I, 244–45; Graham, *Memoirs of Stair,* II, 320–21.

22. Coxe, *Henry Pelham,* I, 268–69: September 25, 1745.

23. *Ibid.,* I, 259–60; Sheffield City Library, Wentworth-Woodhouse MSS., M4, f. 29.

24. Duff, *Culloden Papers,* pp. 208–9, 219, 399; P.R.O., North Britain Book, XIV, 195: John Scrope to the Barons of the Exchequer, September 10, 1745; *ibid.,* Treasury Board Papers, CCCXVIII, No. 10, 10a.

25. Duff, *Culloden Papers,* pp. 395–96: September 6, 1745; Rose, *Marchmont Papers,* I, 98–100: September 20, 1745; Warrand, *More Culloden Papers,* IV, 71: September 12, 1745; *ibid.,* I, 101: September 21, 1745.

26. B.M., Add. MSS., 32705, f. 102: August 22, 1745; P.R.O., S.P., Dom., George II, No. 67: September 9, 1745.

27. Sheffield City Library, Wentworth-Woodhouse MSS., M4, ff. 27, 32; *ibid.,* M11, unfolioed: list of those present at the General Meeting, September 23, 1745; H.M.C., *Various MSS.,* VIII, Wood MSS., p. 106: September 10, 1745; P.R.O., S.P., Dom., Various, No., 132, 414–15: Secretary's Letter Book, Newcastle to Montagu, September 21, 1745.

28. Climenson, *Elizabeth Montagu,* I, 207; B.M., Add. MSS., 35396, f. 328: Rev. Thos. Birch to Philip Yorke, September 28, 1745; Duff, *Culloden Papers,* pp. 226–27: Andrew Mitchell to Forbes, October 2, 1745.

29. Sheffield City Library, Wentworth-Woodhouse MSS., M1, unfolioed: Correspondence Book I, October 1, 1745; Smith, *Grenville Papers,* I, 41–42: George Grenville to Richard Grenville, October 5, 1745; Russell, *Bedford Correspondence,* I, 52: Admiral Anson to Bedford, October 17, 1745; Rose, *Marchmont Papers,* I, 141: October 15, 1745; B.M., Add. MSS., 35870, ff. 102–13, 115–17: nine such reports between November 30 and December 31, 1745.

30. Sheffield City Library, Wentworth-Woodhouse MSS., M4, extra folio between 148 and 149.

31. B.M., Add. MSS., 32705, f. 251: Newcastle to Chesterfield, October 9, 1745; *ibid.,* ff. 242, 285, 417: Chesterfield to Newcastle, October 5 and 24, 1745, December 6, 1745; *ibid.,* Stowe MSS., 158, f. 203: Newcastle to Cumberland, December 1, 1745.

32. B.M., Add. MSS., 33058, f. 462: October 11, 1745.

33. P.R.O., Treasury Minute Book, XXX, 192: October 15, 1745.

34. H.M.C., Various MSS., VIII, Wood MSS., p. 110: Newcastle to Irwin, October 7, 1745; *ibid.,* p. 114: Newcastle to Irwin, October 23, 1745; *ibid.,* p. 125: Newcastle to Irwin, November 15, 1745; Sheffield City Library, Wentworth-Woodhouse MSS., M4, f. 110: Newcastle to Malton, October 17, 1745.

35. *Ibid.,* M1, unfolioed: correspondence Book I, November 5, 1745.

36. Rose, *Marchmont Papers,* I, 124, 129, 146–47, 150, 153, 154, 158–59: entries from October 7 to November 28, 1745.

37. Oswald, *Memorials,* pp. 128–29: Stewart to Oswald, November 15, 1745.

38. Coxe, *Horatio Walpole,* pp. 290–91; Smith, *Grenville Papers,* I, 42–44: George Grenville to Thomas Grenville, n.d.; H.M.C., *Various MSS.,* VIII, Wood MSS., pp. 115–16: Pelham to [Irwin], October 24, 1745.

39. Russell, *Bedford Correspondence,* I, 51: Stair to Bedford, October 11, 1745; Sheffield City Library, Wentworth-Woodhouse MSS., M1, unfolioed: Letter Book I, James Gilchrist to Malton, October 20, 1745; Graham, *Memoirs of Stair,* II, 323; Stair to Forbes, November 18, 1745; Duff, *Culloden Papers,* p. 255: Mitchell to Forbes, November 19, 1745; B.M., Add. MSS., 32705, f. 316: Hardwicke to Newcastle, November 17, 1745.

40. P.R.O., S.P., Dom., Geo. II, Nos. 67–83, *passim.*

41. B.M., Add. MSS., 34731, f. 26: Sarah West to Thomas Steavens, November 26, 1745.

42. H.M.C., *Various,* VIII, Wood MSS., p. 135: Pelham to Irwin, November 30, 1745.

43. B.M., Add. MSS., 35363, f. 109: Philip Yorke to Joseph Yorke, December 10, 1745; *ibid.,* 35354, ff. 154–55: Hardwicke to Joseph Yorke, December 12, 1745; Sheffield City Library, Wentworth-Woodhouse MSS., M4, f. 155: Henry Finch to Malton, December 19, 1745.

44. Barrow, *Anson,* pp. 118–19: Thomas Anson to George Anson, December 7, 1745; Sheffield City Library, Wentworth-Woodhouse MSS., M4, f. 147: Countess of Malton to Malton, December 10, 1745; B.M., Add. MSS., 35354, ff. 170–72: Hardwicke to Joseph Yorke, December 28, 1745.

45. Duff, *Culloden Papers,* p. 468: January 9, 1746.

46. Warrand, *More Culloden Papers,* IV, 184–85: Stair to Forbes, January 9, 1746, and Stair to Loudoun, January 9, 1746.

47. *Ibid.,* IV, 184–85; Duff, *Culloden Papers,* p. 264: Newcastle to Forbes, January 11, 1746.

48. Stanhope, *Letters,* III, 745–48, 750, 753–55.

49. H.M.C., *Tenth Report,* Weston-Underwood MSS., p. 445. On one day, April 15, twelve nobles and officers were captured.

50. *Ibid.,* pp. 442–45: Cumberland to Newcastle, April 18, 1746; *cf. ibid.,* letter of Fawkener, April 19, 1746.

51. P.R.O., S.P., Dom., Various, IX, 25: Newcastle to Lord Justice Clerk, April 17, 1746; B.M., Add. MSS., 32707, f. 253: May 27, 1746; *ibid.,* 32992, f. 213, 124–26; H.M.C., Buccleuch MSS., I, 408–9: Forbes to Montagu, June 6, 1746; Coxe, *Henry Pelham,* I, 301–2: Cumberland to Newcastle, April 23, 1746.

52. *Ibid.,* I, 303: Cumberland to Newcastle, July 17, 1746.

CHAPTER XIV

1. P.R.O., S.P., Dom., Geo. II, no. 81, unfolioed: Minute, February 3, 1746.

2. Coxe, *Henry Pelham,* I, 299–300; Cumberland to Newcastle, April 4, 1746.

3. *Ibid.,* I, 331–33: Pelham to Newcastle, July 29, 1746.

4. Warrand, *More Culloden Papers,* V, 71–72: Cumberland to Newcastle, April 30, 1746.

5. Coxe, *Henry Pelham,* I, 333–36: Pelham to Horatio Walpole, August 23, 1746.

6. Warrand, *More Culloden Papers,* V, 136–37: Pelham's letter of September 29, 1746; B.M., Add. MSS., 34523, f. 43: Pelham to Bedford, May 1747; *ibid.,* Stowe MSS., 158, ff. 203–10: Examination of Dr. Arch. Cameron, April 17, 1753; *ibid.,* Add. MSS., 35447; f. 21; David Bruce to Hardwicke, August 10, 1749; *ibid.,* f. 81: June 6, 1750; *ibid.,* ff. 132–33: November 8, 1750; *ibid.,* 34523, f. 43:

Pelham to Bedford, May 1747; *ibid.*, 35447, f. 305: December 2, 1752; *ibid.*, 33050, f. 431: Pelham's Notes.

7. *Ibid.*, 36271E: Warrant for creation of Hardwicke as Lord High Steward.

8. B.M., Stowe MSS., 158, f. 224: July 30, 1746.

9. P.R.O., S.P., Dom., Geo. II, no. 87, unfolioed: Council Minute, September 18, 1746; B.M., Add. MSS., 36271F: Warrant for the creation of Hardwicke; H.M.C., *Egmont Diary*, III, 318: March 18, 1747; Stanhope, *Letters*, III, 887: Chesterfield to Cumberland, March 20, 1747; P.R.O., King's Warrant Book, XXXVII, 38, unfolioed: April 14, 1747.

10. B.M., Stowe MSS., 254, ff. 3–7; *ibid.*, Add. MSS., 32710, f. 207: February 6, 1747; *ibid.*, f. 343: Hardwicke to Newcastle, March 14, 1747; *ibid.*, 32711, f. 233: Newcastle to Cumberland, June 7, 1747; *ibid.*, f. 301: Hardwicke to Newcastle, June 11, 1747; *ibid.*, 35409, f. 7: Newcastle to Hardwicke, March 16, 1747.

11. *Ibid.*, 35446, *passim; ibid.*, 23830, ff. 98–99: John Potter to Robinson, October 24, 1748.

12. P.R.O., Treasury Board Papers, CCCXXI, *passim;* B.M., Add. MSS., 32714, f. 48; P.R.O., North Britain Book, XV, ff. 59, 247–48; *ibid.*, ff. 1–4: Civil List in Scotland, June 24, 1748 to September 29, 1748, gives the total for three months as £9,691–9–5½.

13. Rose, *Marchmont Papers*, I, 260–62: December 24, 1747.

14. B.M., Add. MSS., 32722, ff. 210–11.

15. *Ibid.*, ff. 328–30.

16. *Ibid.*, 32723, f. 322: November 30, 1750.

17. *Ibid.*, ff. 348–49: Pelham to Newcastle, July 24, 1753; *ibid.*, 32727, ff. 125–26: Pelham to Newcastle, May 8, 1752; *ibid.*, 32732, f. 410: Newcastle to Argyll, August 4, 1753; *ibid.*, f. 541: Robert Dundas to Newcastle, August 26, 1753; Coxe, *Henry Pelham*, II, 413: Pelham to Newcastle, April 17, 1752.

18. B.M., Add. MSS., 35363, f. 126: Philip Yorke to Joseph Yorke, May 17, 1746; *ibid.*, 35423, f. 23: Pelham to Hardwicke, May 22, 1746.

19. *Ibid.*, 35876, ff. 238–43: printed copy of bill, May 1746.

20. *Ibid.*, 35451, f. 40: Glenorchy to Philip Yorke, June 26, 1746; Warrand, *More Culloden Papers*, V, 112–13: Alexander Brodie (Lord Lyon) to Forbes, July 1, 1746.

21. B.M., Add. MSS., 32710, f. 207: Hardwicke to Stone, February 16, 1747; *ibid.*, f. 209: Hardwicke to Newcastle, February 16, 1747; *ibid.*, 35446, ff. 151–200.

22. *Ibid.*, 35876, ff. 256–65: printed copy of the bill.

23. *Ibid.*, 35363, f. 157: Philip Yorke to Joseph Yorke, April 20, 1747; *ibid.*, f. 164: Philip Yorke to Joseph Yorke, May 29, 1747; *ibid.*, 33034, f. 113: May 21, 1747.

24. *Ibid.*, 35446, f. 218: Grant to Newcastle, November 19, 1747.

25. *Ibid.*, 35890, unfolioed: Grant to Lords of the Treasury, December 2, 1746; *ibid.*, 32713, f. 405: November 17, 1747; *ibid.*, 35877, ff. 78–85: printed copy of the bill.

26. *Ibid.*, 35890, f. 248: July 14, 1752; *ibid.*, 32728, f. 372: Hardwicke to Newcastle, July 24, 1752.

27. *Ibid.*, 35447, f. 275: Drummond to Hardwicke, August 22, 1752.

28. *Ibid.*, 32710, f. 258: excerpt included in Robert Smith to Newcastle, March 1, 1747.

29. *Ibid.*, 6871, f. 50: Mitchell to Newcastle, February 26, 1752; *ibid.*, 32726,

ff. 314–15, 497; *ibid.*, 32727, ff. 27–28, 47, 192; Coxe, *Henry Pelham*, II, 414–15, 420.

30. *Ibid.*, II, 435, 440–41, 416–18; B.M., Add. MSS., 32730, f. 38.

31. Horace Walpole, *Memoirs of the Reign of King George the Second,* edited by Lord Holland (London: Henry Colburn, 1846), I, 303; B.M., Add. MSS., 33050, ff. 200–9: February 15, 1753.

32. *Ibid.*, 32731, f. 211: Stone to Newcastle, n.d.; *Cf.* ff. 212, 214, 216.

33. *Ibid.*, 33050, ff. 213–22, 231–32, 234–39, 240–51, 260–63, 264, 266, 271–94, 331–42, 256–58; *ibid.*, 35870, ff. 2226–29. *Cf.* Romney Sedgwick's discussion of the subject in the introduction to his *Letters from George III to Lord Bute.*

34. B.M., Add. MSS., 32731, f. 244: Pitt to Newcastle, March 10, 1753.

35. *Ibid.*, f. 264: Newcastle to Pelham, March 12, 1753; *ibid.*, f. 265: Newcastle to Lord Abergavenny, March 17, 1753.

36. Stanhope, *Letters*, V, 2014: Chesterfield to Solomon Dayrolles, April 6, 1753.

CHAPTER XV

1. Coxe, *Henry Pelham*, II, 338–41; B.M., Add. MSS., 32720, f. 387: May 23, 1750; *ibid.*, 32721, ff. 9–10: June 1, 1750.

2. *Ibid.*, f. 47: June 6, 1750.

3. *Ibid.*, ff. 80, 143–44, 156, 307–12. The last is an excellent review of the entire negotiation.

4. *Ibid.*, f. 355: July 13, 1750. *Cf. ibid.*, ff. 254–55, 337.

5. *Ibid.*, 32722, ff. 16–19, 76–77, 122–28, 185–87, 379–81, 406–9: correspondence of August and September 1750; *ibid.*, 35411, f. 1: August 1, 1750; Coxe, *Henry Pelham*, II, 362–65, 373–77; P.R.O., Chatham MSS., I, f. 41: August 24, 1750; Taylor & Pringle, *Pitt's Correspondence*, I, 43–44; Horn, *Williams*, pp. 48–50.

6. B.M., Add. MSS., 32723, ff. 136–37: October 10, 1750 (it seemed at that time that even Prussia would support the treaty) ; *ibid.*, 32824, ff. 25, 100; Coxe, *Henry Pelham*, II, 373–77; Yorke, *Hardwicke*, II, 26.

7. B.M., Add. MSS., 32824, ff. 144–45: October 5, 1750.

8. *Ibid.*, 32727, ff. 39: May 1, 1752, and 230–34: May 21, 1752; Coxe, *Henry Pelham*, II, 421–22: May 20, 1752.

9. B.M., Add. MSS., 32728, ff. 27–35: June 18, 1752.

10. *Ibid.*, ff. 120, 139–46, 196; 282; *ibid.*, 32729, f. 201; P.R.O., S.P., Dom., Regencies, 48, unfolioed: H. V. Jones to Claudius Amyand, July 17, 1752; Coxe, *Henry Pelham*, II, 441–45.

11. B.M., Add. MSS., 32729, ff. 25–26: August 5, 1752.

12. *Ibid.*, ff. 400–1: September 29, 1752; Coxe, *Henry Pelham*, II, 447–49: Newcastle to Pelham, September 19, 1752.

13. *Ibid.*, II, 455: October 3, 1752.

14. George Bubb Dodington, *Diary of George Bubb Dodington* (Salisbury, 1784), p. 103: October 4, 1752.

15. B.M., Add. MSS., 32722, f. 283: August 31, 1750.

16. *Ibid.*, 32719, f. 188: September 26, 1749.

17. Coxe, *Henry Pelham*, II, 76: Pelham to Hanbury Williams, February 28, 1749; *ibid.*, II, 349: July 2, 1750; Coxe, *Horatio Walpole*, p. 398; Walpole,

George II, I, 48: February 22, 1751; *ibid.,* I, 243: January 23, 1752; B.M., Add. MSS., 32724, ff. 129–34: February 22, 1750; *ibid.,* 32723, f. 65: Newcastle to Pelham, September 30, 1750. *Cf. ibid.,* 32725, ff. 134–36, 220.

18. P.R.O., S.P., Dom., Regencies, 47, unfolioed: September 30, 1750, and October 9, 1750; B.M., Add. MSS., 32824, ff. 170–71: Pelham to Holdernesse, October 9, 1750; *ibid.,* 32728, ff. 139–46: Pelham to Newcastle, July 1, 1752. *Cf. ibid.,* 32826, f. 286: October 9, 1750.

19. Chance, *British Diplomatic Instructions,* V, 144–53.

20. B.M., Add. MSS., 32719, f. 92: Newcastle to Bedford, September 1, 1749; *ibid.,* 32721, f. 267: Hardwicke to Newcastle, July 5, 1750; Pelham's scheme for the South Sea Company compensation was to turn the £3,500,000 unsubscribed annuities into their stock on favorable terms; *ibid.,* ff. 386–93: Newcastle to Pelham, July 18, 1750.

21. P.R.O., S.P., Dom., Regencies, 45, unfolioed: August 16, 1750, and August 29, 1750; B.M., Add. MSS., 32722, ff. 223–33: August 23, 1750; William Coxe, *Memoirs of the Kings of Spain of the House of Bourbon from the Accession of Philip the Fifth to the Death of Charles the Third* (London: Longman, Hurst, Rees, Orme, and Brown, 1813), III, 99: Commercial Treaty of Madrid; *cf.* B.M., Add. MSS., 32824, f. 76: Keene to Newcastle, October 9, 1750 (Keene's report on the negotiations); Jean O. McLachlan, *Trade and Peace with Old Spain, 1667–1750* (Cambridge: University Press, 1940), *passim,* but especially the foreword by Harold Temperley for a summary of the importance of the treaty of 1750, pp. ix–xi. The book contains a complete examination of the commercial problem.

22. P.R.O., Chatham MSS., I, ff. 47–48: Pelham to Pitt, October 12, 1750; B.M., Add. MSS., 32723, ff. 142–44, 152–53: Pelham's letters of October 1750.

23. Taylor & Pringle, *Pitt's Correspondence,* I, 52–53: October 20, 1750.

24. L. G. Wickham Legg (ed.), *British Diplomatic Instructions, 1689–1789,* Vol. VII, edited for the Royal Historical Society (London: Offices of the Society, 1934), pp. 13, 16–18, 20–23, 33–34, 40–41.

25. *Ibid.,* pp. 5–7: Private instructions to Albemarle, June 12, 1749; *ibid.,* pp. 16, 34, 39, 40.

26. *Ibid.,* pp. 7–10, 18–19.

27. P.R.O., S.P., Dom., Regencies, 48, unfolioed: July 15, 1752.

28. B.M., Add. MSS., 32720, ff. 233–34: Newcastle to Stone, April 20, 1750; *ibid.,* ff. 245–49: Pelham to Newcastle, April 25, 1750; *ibid.,* 32725, f. 122: Pelham to Stone [?], September 5, 1751; *ibid.,* 35870, f. 230: September 18, 1753; *ibid.,* 32732, ff. 696–702: September 21, 1753; *ibid.,* f. 489: Pelham to Newcastle, August 18, 1753. Pelham urged that a very firm position be taken and insisted upon.

29. Legg, *British Diplomatic Instructions,* VII, 36–38: February 15, 1753; *ibid.,* VII, 45: February 7, 1754; B.M., Add. MSS., 32844, f. 94: April 14, 1753; *ibid.,* 32732, ff. 373–76: Pelham to Newcastle, July 28, 1753; *ibid.,* Newcastle to Pelham, July 27, 1753.

30. *Ibid.,* 32721, ff. 440–41: Pelham to Newcastle, July 24, 1750; *ibid.,* 32722, ff. 20–21: Newcastle to Pelham, August 1, 1750; *ibid.,* 32726, f. 116: Newcastle to H. V. Jones, February 9, 1750; *ibid.,* 32727, f. 39: Pelham to Newcastle, May 1, 1752.

31. *Ibid.,* 32728, f. 55: Stone to Newcastle, June 9, 1752; *ibid.,* 32722, f. 358: Newcastle to Pelham, September 7, 1750.

32. P.R.O., S.P., Dom., Various, CXXXVI, 5: Secretary's Letter Book, 1749–1760, Aldworth to West, September 27, 1749.

33. B.M., Add. MSS., 32731, ff. 226–30: July 4, 1750; *ibid.*, ff. 420–23: July 20, 1750.

34. Coxe, *Henry Pelham*, II, 464: October 19, 1752; B.M., Add. MSS., 32732, ff. 225–26: July 13, 1753.

35. *Ibid.*, ff. 32726, ff. 460–61: Pitt to Newcastle, August 14, 1753.

36. *Ibid.*, 32726, f. 140; *ibid.*, 32727, f. 73; *ibid.*, 32729, f. 283; *ibid.*, 32732, ff. 559, 630–31.

CHAPTER XVI

1. B.M., Add. MSS., 32720, f. 1: Lauderdale to Newcastle, January 1, 1750.

2. *Ibid.*, 32719, f. 165; *ibid.*, ff. 126–28, 272.

3. *Ibid.*, 35423, f. 121; *ibid.*, 32719, ff. 314–15: Hardwicke to Newcastle, December 17, 1749; *ibid.*, 32725, f. 196: Anson to Newcastle, September 21, 1750; Smith, *Grenville Papers*, I, 89–90: George Grenville to Richard Grenville, October 3, 1749; Dodington, *Diary*, pp. 86–87.

4. B.M., Add. MSS., 32719, ff. 201 and 350; *ibid.*, 32724, f. 49; *ibid.*, 32725, ff. 413–14, 466; *ibid.*, 32726, f. 193; P.R.O., Customs Book, XVII, 9; Sheffield City Library, Wentworth-Woodhouse MSS., M.5, ff. 160–61; Bodleian Library, North MSS., d.6, f. 201; Toynbee, *Letters*, III, 132–33.

5. B.M., Add. MSS., 33087, f. 272: E. Prole to Lord Abergavenny, April 17, 1753; *ibid.*, Stowe MSS., 155, f. 127: January 26, 1753.

6. Nugent, *Memoir*, pp. 254–56: Pelham to Nugent, September 21, 1751, and September 27, 1751.

7. P.R.O., Egremont MSS., 28, unfolioed: Pelham to Egremont, August 21, 1753.

8. B.M., Add. MSS., 32685, f. 59: January 15, 1750; *ibid.*, 32730, f. 275; *ibid.*, 32731, ff. 440–41; *ibid.*, 32732, ff. 61, 86, 147, 270–71, 601; *ibid.*, 36269, ff. 1–19; Oswald, *Memorial*, pp. 289–91.

9. B.M., Add. MSS., 32722, f. 44: Newcastle to Pelham, August 3, 1750.

10. *Ibid.*, 32992, f. 219: William Gage to Newcastle, summer 1753; *ibid.*, 32734, ff. 242–402.

11. *Ibid.*, 32721, f. 203: Newcastle to Pelham, June 29, 1750; f. 362: Pelham to Newcastle, July 13, 1750; ff. 500–2: Pelham to Newcastle, July 31, 1750; H.M.C., *Stopford-Sackville MSS.*, I, 181: Newcastle to Dorset, January 31, 1752.

12. B.M., Add. MSS., 32725, ff. 229–57, 368; *ibid.*, 32731, f. 422: Pelham to Newcastle, May 3, 1753.

13. *Ibid.*, 35447, f. 1: William Grant to Hardwicke, January 3, 1749; *ibid.*, 35423, ff. 85–86: Pelham to Hardwicke, May 2, 1749; *ibid.*, 32719, f. 330: Alexander Hume Campbell to Newcastle, December 24, 1749; f. 337: Pelham to Newcastle, December 25, 1749; Oswald, *Memorial*, pp. 343–44.

14. B.M., Add. MSS., 32723, f. 105: Pelham to Newcastle, October 5, 1750; f. 184: Newcastle to Pelham, October 23, 1750; *ibid.*, 32726, f. 58: Edward Walpole to Newcastle, January 18, 1751.

15. *Ibid.*, 32720, f. 90: Wyndham to Newcastle, February 9, 1750.

16. *Ibid.*, 32718, f. 100: T. Robinson, Governor of Barbados, to Newcastle, February 22, 1749; *ibid.*, 32721, f. 383: Newcastle to Pelham, July 18, 1750.

17. *Ibid.*, 32722, ff. 149, 297–98.

18. *Ibid.*, 32720, ff. 199–200: William Shirley to Newcastle, April 10, 1750; *ibid.*, 33054, f. 426: George II to Commissioners of the Treasury, May 25, 1750; *ibid.*, 32725, f. 69: August 19, 1751.

19. *Ibid.*, 35355, ff. 38–39: Hardwicke to Joseph Yorke, April 2, 1749.

20. Toynbee, *Letters*, II, 365–66; *ibid.*, III, 32; Walpole, *George II*, I, 12–13, 17–18; Davis, *Lyttelton*, p. 204. The size of the vote has been variously reported as 167 to 107 or 189 to 106; the only absolutely certain aspect is that a very large majority followed the Pelhams: B.M., Add. MSS., 32724, f. 105: Newcastle to James Pelham, January 30, 1751.

21. Toynbee, *Letters*, II, 427: February 25, 1750. The same problem of popular opposition arose strongly again in 1753, when the local citizens of Yorkshire damaged several turnpikes under construction. In this case troops were used to restore order: B.M., Add. MSS., 32732, ff. 88, 111–12, 182–83; P.R.O., S.P., Dom., Geo. II, 126, unfolioed: Mr. Francis, March 6, 1754. Pelham insisted on force, but also that measures be taken to convince the people of the usefulness of turnpikes.

22. Walpole, *George II*, I, 50–51: February 25, 1751.

23. P.R.O., North Britain Book, XV, 58: May 1, 1749, April 9, 1750, April 24, 1751, March 26, 1752, and May 10, 1753; *ibid.*, Customs Book, XVII, 356–61: March 1, 1754; *ibid.*, Letter Book, XXI, 9: May 3, 1751; Walpole, *George II*, I, 106: April 23, 1751; B.M., Add. MSS., 35879, ff. 8–27; *ibid.*, 34524, f. 67: Pelham to Hardwicke, October 10, 1752; *ibid.*, 32730, f. 63: Pelham to Newcastle, October 9, 1752; H.M.C., *Various MSS.*, VIII, Wood MSS., p. 175: February 5, 1752.

24. Williams, *Pitt*, I, 174–75.

25. Coxe, *Henry Pelham*, II, 467: July 13, 1753; *cf.* R. J. Robson, *The Oxfordshire Election of 1754* (London; Geoffrey Cumberlege, 1949) ; B.M., Add. MSS., 32732, ff. 297–300, 323; *ibid.*, 35398, ff. 145 and 168; *ibid.*, 32733, ff. 236–39: Halifax to Newcastle, November 12, 1752; f. 213: Hardwicke to Newcastle, November 8, 1753; Dodington, *Diary*, p. 170: November 15, 1753.

26. Toynbee, *Letters*, III, 161: May 24, 1753; Walpole, *George II*, I, 342; B.M., Add. MSS., 32732, ff. 3–4: Amyand to Newcastle, June 1, 1753; ff. 22–23: Amyand to Newcastle, June 4, 1753 (the vote was 125 to 56) ; *ibid.*, 35423, f. 160; *ibid.*, 35398, f. 116; Stanhope, *Letters*, V, 2030–31; Bodleian Library, North MSS., d.6, f. 195: Legge to Guilford, June 2, 1753.

27. Hargreaves, *National Debt*, pp. 52–53.

28. Williams, *Pitt*, I, 168.

29. Hargreaves, *National Debt*, p. 54.

30. B.M., Add. MSS., 32719, f. 84: Hardwicke to Newcastle, August 30, 1749.

31. Dodington, *Diary*, p. 17: November 28, 1749.

32. B.M., Add. MSS., 35468, f. 223: Pelham to Robert Keith, April 11, 1750; *ibid.*, 32720, f. 266: Pelham to Newcastle, April 30, 1750; f. 412: Murray to Newcastle, May 25, 1750; *ibid.*, 32721, ff. 10–11: Pelham to Newcastle, June 1, 1750.

33. *Ibid.*, f. 15: Newcastle to Pelham, June 1, 1750.

34. Rose, *Marchmont Papers*, II, 387–89: Pelham to Marchmont, September 1, 1750; B.M., Add. MSS., 32722, ff. 275–78: Pelham to Newcastle, August 31, 1750; *ibid.*, 32723, f. 176: Pelham to Newcastle, October 19, 1750; P.R.O., Chatham MSS., I, ff. 47–48: Pelham to Pitt, October 12, 1750.

35. B.M., Add. MSS., 32722, f. 173: August 17, 1750; *ibid.*, ff. 322–23: September 4, 1750; *ibid.*, 32723, ff. 116–17: October 9, 1750.

36. *Ibid.*, f. 176: October 19, 1750.
37. *Ibid.*, 32721, f. 263: Murray to Newcastle, July 5, 1750.
38. *Ibid.*, 32718, f. 211: Hardwicke to Newcastle, May 24, 1749; *ibid.*, f. 215: Pelham Note, May 26, 1749.
39. Dodington, *Diary*, p. 20: January 23–29, 1750.
40. B.M., Add. MSS., 32724, ff. 83–84: Hardwicke to Newcastle, January 20, 1751; *ibid.*, 35606, f. 15: Pelham to Philip Yorke; P.R.O., S.P., Dom., Geo. II, no. 116, unfolioed: Order in Council, February 5, 1751; Walpole, *George II*, I, 11: January 22, 1751.
41. B.M., Add. MSS., 32994, f. 271: March 20, 1751; f. 272: March 20, 1751.
42. P.R.O., King's Warrant Book, XXXIX, 36: March 7, 1752; B.M., Add. MSS., 32729, ff. 278–79: Pelham to Newcastle, September 15, 1752.
43. P.R.O., Customs Book, XVI, p. 24; *ibid.*, Letter Book, XX, *passim; ibid.*, Reference Book, XI, pp. 240–44: April 1743 to March 1754.
44. *Ibid.*, S.P., Dom., Regencies, 128, Part II, unfolioed: Holdernesse to Newcastle, May 29, 1752; *ibid.*, Chatham MSS., 83, unfolioed: Todd to Newcastle, January 2, 1753; *ibid.*, Works Office Letter Book, Set I, No. 3, 1744–61: James Ware to Thomas Ripley, October 23, 1753; B.M., Add. MSS., 32732, f. 28: Todd to H. V. Jones, June 4, 1753; *ibid.*, 32992, ff. 84–87: Newcastle to Rutland and Mayor of Leicester; *ibid.*, 32719, f. 44: Newcastle to Sir Charles Eversfield, August 11, 1749; *ibid.*, 35603, f. 242: Pelham to Hardwicke, July 31, 1750.
45. P.R.O., King's Warrant Book, XXXIII, p. 515: King (Pelham, Lyttelton, Campbell) to Clerk of the Signet, January 18, 1749.
46. *Ibid.*, XXXVII, 550: King (Lyttelton, Campbell, Grenville) to Pelham, March 21, 1749; *ibid.*, XXXVIII, 14: King (Grenville, Lyttelton, Vane) to William Benson, July 12, 1749; *ibid.*, pp. 282–83: King (Campbell, Lyttelton, Vane) to Pelham, January 22, 1751.
47. P.R.O., Chatham MSS., 55, unfolioed: A. Sawyer to Pitt, November 14, 1749; *ibid.*, A. Sawyer to Pitt, December 6, 1749; B.M., Add. MSS., 38331, ff. 139 and 141.
48. *Ibid.*, 29465, ff. 19–20.

CHAPTER XVII

1. Walpole, *George II*, I, 47: 1751.
2. Stanhope, *Letters*, IV, 1322: Chesterfield to Solomon Dayrolles, March 31, 1749.
3. H.M.C., *Lady duCane MSS.*, pp. 203–4: December 5, 1749.
4. B.M., Add. MSS., 32721, ff. 39–40, 258, 453; *ibid.*, 32722, ff. 30–35, 112; *ibid.*, 35411, f. 7; Coxe, *Henry Pelham*, II, 340–42, 351–52.
5. B.M., Add. MSS., 32721, f. 240: July 4, 1750; ff. 359–60: Pelham to Newcastle, July 13, 1750; ff. 467–68; *ibid.*, 32722, ff. 48, 16–19; *ibid.*, 35410, ff. 275–78: Hardwicke to Newcastle, July 13, 1750.
6. *Ibid.*, 32722, ff. 114–21: August 12, 1750; ff. 195–96, 200.
7. *Ibid.*, 32722, ff. 251–55: Pelham to Stone, August 24, 1750; f. 284: Hardwicke to Newcastle, August 31, 1750.
8. *Ibid.*, 32722, ff. 300–17: Newcastle to Pelham, September 2, 1750; *ibid.*, 35411, ff. 49–56: Newcastle to Hardwicke, September 8, 1750.
9. *Ibid.*, 32723, ff. 54–57: Newcastle to Pelham, September 29, 1750; f. 103: Pelham to Newcastle, October 5, 1750; ff. 124–27: Newcastle to Hardwicke,

October 10, 1750; f. 155: Newcastle to Hardwicke, October 14, 1750; P.R.O., Chatham MSS., I, ff. 45–46: Pitt to Newcastle, October 1750 (Pitt believed that he had been the major peacemaker between Pelham and Newcastle, but the brothers had merely agreed in principle, not in detail) ; ff. 199–200: Newcastle to Pelham, October 30, 1750; Toynbee, *Letters*, III, 23: November 19, 1750.

10. B.M., Add. MSS., 32724, ff. 175–78: Stone to Newcastle, March 10, 1750; ff. 190–91: Pelham to Newcastle, March 16, 1751; Walpole, *George II*, I, 3.

11. B.M., Add. MSS., 32724, f. 358: Newcastle to Sandwich, June 13, 1751; f. 360: Richard Aldworth to Albemarle, June 14, 1751; Walpole, *George II*, I, 193.

12. B.M., Add. MSS., 32720, f. 80; *ibid.*, 32722, ff. 71–72, 90–92, 110, 214–16; *ibid.*, 35411, ff. 32–41.

13. *Ibid.*, 32722, ff. 143–46, 175–76, 214–16; *ibid.*, 35411, ff. 11–12, 32–41.

14. *Ibid.*, 32722, ff. 214–16, 300–17; *ibid.*, 35411, ff. 117–23; *ibid.*, 35423, ff. 105–8.

15. *Ibid.*, 35411, ff. 49–56; Coxe, *Henry Pelham*, II, 396–98: September 29, 1750.

16. B.M., Add. MSS., 32724, f. 356: Devonshire to Newcastle, June 13, 1751; Toynbee, *Letters*, III, 57; Walpole, *George II*, I, 193; Dodington, *Diary*, p. 80.

17. A. S. Turberville, *The House of Lords in the Eighteenth Century* (Oxford: The Clarendon Press, 1927) , p. 270.

18. B.M., Add. MSS., 32728, f. 328; *ibid.*, 32730, f. 405; *ibid.*, 28051, f. 356.

19. Stanhope, *Letters*, IV, 1362: Chesterfield to Solomon Dayrolles, June 23, 1749; Walpole, *George II*, I, 46; B.M., Add. MSS., 32722, ff. 343–50: Pelham to Newcastle, August 7, 1750.

20. *Ibid.*, 32724, ff. 362–63: Stone to Newcastle, June 15, 1751; *ibid.*, 32729, ff. 210–11, 232, 238–39, 402: Pelham to Newcastle, September 29, 1752; *ibid.*, 35411, ff. 257–60: Newcastle to Hardwicke, June 15, 1751; *ibid.*, 35423, f. 126.

21. *Ibid.*, 32721, f. 268; *ibid.*, 32722, f. 110; *ibid.*, 33087, f. 133; B.M., Egerton MSS., 1733, f. 121; Coxe, *Henry Pelham*, II, 441; Phillimore, *Lyttelton Memoirs*, II, 435.

22. P.R.O., Granville MSS., box 1, unfolioed: Granville Gower to Pelham, 1751; B.M., Add. MSS., 32728, f. 119: Hardwicke to Newcastle, June 26, 1752.

23. Coxe, *Henry Pelham*, II, 457: Pelham to Newcastle, October 5, 1752.

24. B.M., Add. MSS., 4254, f. 1: Lyttleton to Bolingbroke, April 14, 1749; *ibid.*, 9190, f. 201; *ibid.*, 32722, ff. 30–35, 258–59; Smith, *Grenville Papers*, I, 79–80: September 11, 1749; P.R.O., Chatham MSS., 52, unfolioed: Pelham to Pitt, n.d.

25. B.M., Add. MSS., 32720, ff. 245–49; *ibid.*, 32722, ff. 23–24; Coxe, *Henry Pelham*, II, 333–35, 337–38.

26. B.M., Add. MSS., 32722, ff. 243–48: Pelham to Newcastle, August 24, 1750.

27. *Ibid.*, ff. 246–48.

28. *Ibid.*, 32722, ff. 331–32, 353–54, 416–17: September 14, 1750; *ibid.*, 35411, ff. 90–91, 112–13, 115–16; Coxe, *Henry Pelham*, II, 382–83: Hardwicke to Newcastle, August 31, 1750.

29. B.M., Add. MSS., 32723, ff. 134–35: Newcastle to Pelham, October 10, 1750.

30. *Ibid.*, 32723, ff. 130–31: Newcastle to Dorset, October 10, 1750.

31. P.R.O., Chatham MSS., 17, unfolioed: Amyand to Pitt, April 14, 1752.

32. *Ibid.,* 84, unfolioed: Lists of Ministers and Consuls in the Southern and Northern Departments.

33. Coxe, *Henry Pelham,* II, 76: Pelham to Hanbury Williams, February 28, 1749; B.M., Add. MSS., 32718, ff. 195, 205; *ibid.,* 32721, 89, 143–44, 194–96: Pelham to Newcastle, June 28, 1750; *ibid.,* 32722, ff. 26–29, 36–37; *ibid.,* 32726, f. 254; *ibid.,* 32733, f. 6; *ibid.,* 32994, f. 83: November 16, 1749.

CHAPTER XVIII

1. P.R.O., Privy Council Register, George II, nos. 12–15, *passim; ibid.,* Privy Council Minutes, 1670–1776: Minute Books of Walter Cary and Gilbert West.

2. B.M., Add. MSS., 32723, f. 312: Halifax to Newcastle, November 28, 1750.

3. *Ibid.,* 32725, f. 17: August 6, 1751. Later in the month Halifax added the recommendation that all colonial dispatches be handled through the Board of Trade. Matters such as Indian problems would be shifted from the Secretary of State; *ibid.,* ff. 81–91: August 25, 1751, with enclosed paper of June 23, 1749.

4. *Ibid.,* f. 60: Hardwicke to Newcastle, August 13, 1751.

5. *Ibid.,* f. 378: Newcastle to Halifax, November 7, 1751.

6. *Ibid.,* ff. 81–89: June 23, 1749.

7. *Ibid.,* ff. 154, 160, 295, 398, 455: Pelham to Newcastle, November 29, 1751; *ibid.,* 32994, ff. 286–87: Halifax's Paper of December 17, 1751, at the bottom of which Newcastle noted Pelham's general approval; *ibid.,* 32726, f. 20; *ibid.,* 12428, ff. 31–69; *ibid.,* 32729, f. 404; *ibid.,* 32732, f. 90.

8. *Ibid.,* 32721, ff. 42–43, 81, 87–88, 156, 185, 256; *ibid.,* 32722, ff. 1–3; *ibid.,* 32723, f. 243; *ibid.,* 32724, ff. 131–33, 165; *ibid.,* 32727, ff. 73–174; *ibid.,* 32728, f. 71; *ibid.,* 32836, ff. 300–31; *ibid.,* 32994, f. 300; *ibid.,* 35870, ff. 160–61; Coxe, *Henry Pelham,* II, 346–47; Huntington Library MSS., Loudoun Papers, 323: Contract between Lords of Treasury and William Baker of London, March 29, 1751; *ibid.,* 441: Peregrine Furze to Thomas Saul, April 25, 1753.

9. P.R.O., King's Warrant Book, XXXVIII, 210, 330, 347, 472, 491; *ibid.,* XXXIX, 74, 116, 134, 194, 382.

10. B.M., Add. MSS., 32721, ff. 129–30: Pitt to Newcastle, June 19, 1750.

11. *Ibid.,* 32721, f. 114: June 15, 1750; *ibid.,* 35870, ff. 188–90a, 195–96, 205–6; *ibid.,* 32732, ff. 556–57: Holdernesse to Newcastle, August 27, 1753; *ibid.,* ff. 546–47: H. V. Jones to Newcastle, August 27, 1753; P.R.O., Egremont MSS., 17, unfolioed: March 26, 1753.

12. *Ibid.,* 32732, ff. 450, 452–53: August 12, 1753; Huntington Library MSS., Loudoun Papers, 443a: August 10, 1753; *ibid.,* 447a: Holdernesse to Dinwiddie, August 28, 1753.

13. P.R.O., S.P., Dom., Various, 136, ff. 5, 7; *ibid.,* King's Warrant Book, XXXVIII, p. 34, f. 206; B.M., Add. MSS., 35870, f. 210: October 18, 1750; *ibid.,* 32722, ff. 212–13: September 1, 1750; *ibid.,* 35909, f. 148: August 31, 1751; Huntington Library MSS., 9918: Lords Justices to William Pitt, April 28, 1752.

14. B.M., Add. MSS., 32720, f. 156: Bishop of London to Newcastle, March 23, 1750; *ibid.,* f. 160: Newcastle to Bishop of London, March 23, 1750; *ibid.,* 35423, f. 94: Pelham to Hardwicke, May 21, 1750; *ibid.,* 35909, ff. 137–38: May 18, 1750.

15. P.R.O., Treasury Papers Supplementary, unfolioed: Exports to America. *Cf.* Huntington Library MSS., Abercromby Papers, AB976: May 1752, Summary of Trade of American Colonies by General James Abercromby.

16. B.M., Add. MSS., 32721, ff. 206–7: Boscawen to Newcastle, June 1750; *ibid.*, 33031, f. 6: Petition of English Merchants, July 18, 1750; *ibid.*, 35870, f. 186: Council Meeting, August 9, 1750.

17. P.R.O., Privy Council Register, George II, nos. 12–15, *passim;* B.M., Add. MSS., 35870, ff. 166–69: June 28, 1750.

18. *Ibid.*, 35423, ff. 115–16: Pelham to Hardwicke, October 22, 1750; H.M.C., *Tenth Report,* Weston-Underwood MSS., p. 304: Pelham to Harrington, November 7, 1749.

19. H.M.C., *Stopford-Sackville MSS.*, I, 175: Pelham to George Sackville, July 8, 1751; *ibid.*, 176–78: Sackville to Pelham, October 8, 1751, Pelham to Sackville, October 11, 1751, Pelham to Sackville, October 21, 1751; *ibid.*, I, 178–79: Pelham to Sackville, January 19, 1752; *ibid.*, I, 182: Pelham to Sackville, March 16, 1752.

20. B.M., Add. MSS., 32727, ff. 230–34: Pelham to Newcastle, May 21, 1752.

21. Coxe, *Henry Pelham,* II, 425: Newcastle to Hardwicke, May 31, 1752; *ibid.*, II, 425–26: Newcastle to Pelham, May 31, 1752.

22. *Ibid.*, II, 429–30: Newcastle to Pelham, June 12, 1752; H.M.C., *Stopford-Sackville MSS.*, I, 184–86: Primate to Pelham, July 25, 1752; B.M., Add. MSS., 32995, f. 38: December 26, 1753.

23. H.M.C., *Stopford-Sackville MSS.*, I, 189: Primate to Sackville, February 10, 1753.

24. B.M., Add. MSS., 32732, ff. 118–23; *ibid.*, ff. 116–17; *ibid.*, 32733, f. 515: December 1753; *ibid.*, 503–10: Dorset to Newcastle, December 21, 1753; *ibid.*, ff. 578: Holdernesse to Dorset, December 28, 1753; *ibid.*, 35870, ff. 235–36: Holdernesse to the Lord Chancellor of Ireland, June 29, 1753, Privy Council to Dorset, November 28, 1753.

25. *Ibid.*, 32733, ff. 604–5; *ibid.*, 32734, ff. 21–24; Stanhope, *Letters,* V, 2070–71.

26. H.M.C., *Stopford-Sackville MSS.*, I, 204–5: Sackville to Pelham, January 14, 1754; *ibid.*, I, 208: Pelham to Dorset, February 28, 1754.

CHAPTER XIX

1. B.M., Add. MSS., 35355, ff. 38–39: Hardwicke to Joseph Yorke, April 2, 1749; *ibid.*, 35355, f. 61: Cumberland to Joseph Yorke, April 10, 1749; Dodington, *Diary,* p. 57; Walpole, *George II,* I, 32–33.

2. B.M., Add. MSS., 32721, ff. 10–11: Pelham to Newcastle, June 1, 1750.

3. *Ibid.*, 32720, ff. 175, 207–8; Dodington, *Diary,* p. 84: December 12, 1751.

4. Toynbee, *Letters,* II, 360: Walpole to Mann, March 4, 1749.

5. Stanhope, *Letters,* IV, 1333: April 25, 1749; Dodington, *Diary,* pp. 2–5, 7 (Pelham parted from him without anger and Dodington soon regretted his hasty action) ; H.M.C., *Various MSS.*, VI, Matcham MSS., p. 20; B.M., Add. MSS., 32723, f. 176.

6. Dodington, *Diary,* p. 10: October 13, 1749; *ibid.*, pp. 10, 61; H.M.C., *Tenth Report,* Weston-Underwood MSS., pp. 304–5.

7. B.M., Add. MSS., 47073, unfolioed: Memoranda of Egmont, November 24, 1750.

8. Dodington, *Diary,* pp. 62, 64–68, 70–71, 73, 75; Coxe, *Henry Pelham,* II, 165; B.M., Add. MSS., 46975, unfolioed: R. Cenley to Egmont, March 27, 1751.

9. Walpole, *George II,* I, 114–15; Dodington, *Diary,* p. 77.

10. Coxe, *Henry Pelham,* II, 206–7; Stanhope, *Letters,* V, 1798, 1978; H.M.C.,

Tenth Report, Weston-Underwood MSS., pp. 306–7; Dodington, *Diary,* pp. 86, 88–95, 116–17, 123, 149–50.

11. Coxe, *Henry Pelham,* II, 336; Walpole, *George II,* I, 99, 103–5.
12. B.M., Add. MSS., 32721, f. 3: Hardwicke to Newcastle, June 1, 1750; *ibid.,* 32723, f. 304: Hardwicke to Newcastle, November 27, 1750; *ibid.,* 32726, ff. 82–84: Newcastle to Dorset, January 25, 1752; *ibid.,* 35432, f. 90; *ibid.,* 47092, *passim; ibid.,* 32732, f. 323: July 20, 1753; H.M.C., *Tenth Report,* Weston-Underwood MSS., p. 307: Bishop Thomas to Weston, January 30, 1752; *ibid., Various MSS.,* VIII, Wood MSS., p. 175; Dodington, *Diary,* pp. 56, 158–62; P.R.O., Chatham MSS., I, ff. 49–50: Pelham to Pitt, October 20, 1750.
13. *Ibid.,* Chatham MSS., I, ff. 49–50.
14. B.M., Add. MSS., 2725, ff. 213–14: September 26, 1751; *ibid.,* f. 387: Henry Gally to Newcastle, November 9, 1751.
15. Dodington, *Diary,* p. 85: February 2, 1752; Sanders, *Dodington,* p. 182.
16. P.R.O., Egremont MSS., 28, unfolioed: Pelham to Egremont, September 19, 1752; Dodington, *Diary,* p. 105: October 11, 1752, and October 13, 1752.
17. B.M., Add. MSS., 32728, f. 65; *ibid.,* 32729, ff. 9, 336; *ibid.,* 32730, f. 47; Coxe, *Henry Pelham,* II, 464.
18. B.M., Add. MSS., 32728, ff. 319–20: Pelham to Newcastle, July 20, 1752.
19. *Ibid.,* 32718, f. 242; *ibid.,* 32723, f. 143: Pelham to Newcastle, October 12, 1750; *ibid.,* 32725, f. 117; *ibid.,* 32728, f. 239; *ibid.,* 32732, ff. 67–69.
20. *Ibid.,* 32732, ff. 99, 105, 473–74, 568–69; P.R.O., Egremont MSS., 28, unfolioed: Newcastle to Egremont, August 11, 1753; B.M., Add. MSS., 41354, f. 14: Pelham to Martin, September 1, 1753; *ibid.,* 32735, f. 94: April 15, 1754. *Cf. ibid.,* 32732, f. 613; *ibid.,* 32992, ff. 99–102.
21. Robson, *Oxfordshire Elections,* p. 15.
22. *Ibid.,* pp. 29, 53, 87; B.M., Add. MSS., 32731, ff. 238 and 282; *ibid.,* 34734, f. 66.
23. *Ibid.,* 32732, ff. 225–26, 297–304; Sheffield City Library, Wentworth-Woodhouse MSS., R 1 (a) , f. 33; *ibid.,* F 35a, unfolioed: J. Fountayne to Fitzwilliam, November 25, 1753.
24. B.M., Add. MSS., 32732, ff. 223, 347–49, 429, 437, 456, 493–94.
25. Dodington, *Diary,* pp. 163–66, 168–71.
26. B.M., Add. MSS., 9232, ff. 8–9; *ibid.,* 32732, ff. 72, 233, 361, 659; *ibid.,* 32735, ff. 34 and 36; *ibid.,* 35606, f. 83. Pelham and Newcastle discussed some of the reports and tried to evaluate them: *ibid.,* 32733, ff. 138–39.
27. Robson, *Oxfordshire Elections,* p. 161; B.M., Add. MSS., 32734, ff. 239–40.
28. *Ibid.,* 32995, ff. 63–67: March 15, 1754; f. 94; Smollett, *Continuation of Rapin,* V, 302.

CHAPTER XX

1. B.M., Add. MSS., 32733, ff. 464, 466, 468, 472, 474, 479, 491, 525, 531, 539, 559, 561, 594; *ibid.,* 32734, ff. 7, 11, 15.
2. *Ibid.,* ff. 21–22.
3. *Ibid.,* f. 100.
4. *Ibid.,* f. 173.
5. Coxe, *Henry Pelham,* II, 307; P.R.O., Chatham MSS., I, f. 55.
6. B.M., Add. MSS., 32734, ff. 175, 180, 208, 214–15, 216, 220, 222, 224, 231, 233, 259; *ibid.,* 32735, f. 6; *ibid.,* 35448, f. 76; *ibid.,* 35364, f. 5; *ibid.,* 35388, f. 10;

ibid., 43443, unfolioed: Keene to Castres, March 29, 1754; *ibid.*, 9201, f. 103; P.R.O., S.P., Dom., Geo. II, no. 126, unfolioed: Ereskine (Lord Justice Clerk) to Newcastle, March 14, 1754; Stanhope, *Letters*, V, 2096; Phillimore, *Lyttelton*, II, 450; Smith, *Grenville Papers*, I, 105–6; Dodington, *Diary*, pp. 175–78, 181–91; Lord Rosebery, *Lord Chatham: His Life and Connections* (New York: Harper & Brothers Publishers, 1910) , p. 89.

7. Toynbee, *Letters*, III, 216: Walpole to Mann, March 7, 1754; *cf. ibid.*, pp. 212–15, 218, 223.

8. [Glover], *Memoirs*, pp. 48–49.

9. B.M., Add. MSS., 34723, f. 48; *ibid.*, 35356, f. 230; *ibid.*, 43443, unfolioed: Keene to Castres, April 6, 1754; H.M.C., *Various MSS.*, VIII, Wood MSS., p. 177; Smith, *Grenville Papers*, I, 110–22; Taylor and Pringle, *Pitt's Correspondence*, I, 85–87.

10. B.M., Add. MSS., 35870, ff. 245–46: March 12, 1754.

11. P.R.O., Treasury Minute Book, XXXII, 180: Treasury Board Meeting, March 20, 1754.

12. B.M., Add. MSS., 35423, f. 167: Roberts to Hardwicke, March 6, 1754.

13. *Ibid.*, f. 168: Roberts to Hardwicke, March 7, 1754.

14. *Ibid.*, f. 170: Roberts to Hardwicke, March 7, 1754. The advice was so well followed that today there is no knowledge of what was in the private papers or even what became of them after they passed into the hands of Roberts' son—if indeed all of them were passed to him.

15. Walpole, *George II*, I, xxvi.

16. *Ibid.*, I, 231.

17. *Ibid.*, I, 371.

18. [Philip Dormer Stanhope], *Characters by Lord Chesterfield Contrasted with Characters of the Same Great Personages by Other Respectable Writers* (London: Edward and Charles Dilly, 1778) , pp. 39–40.

19. *Ibid.*, p. 40.

20. *Ibid.*, p. 39; B.M., Stowe MSS., 308, f. 17. A very similar characterization is to be found in the Sheffield City Library, Wentworth-Woodhouse MSS., R.93, unfolioed, where it is ascribed to William Burke. My surmise is that if Burke wrote it, he copied Chesterfield.

21. Smith, *Grenville Papers*, I, 106: Pitt to Lyttleton and the Grenville brothers, March 7, 1754.

22. B.M., Add. MSS., 9193, ff. 87–88: Holdernesse to Robert Keith, April 26, 1754.

23. James Ralph, *A Critical History of the Administration of Sir Robert Walpole* . . . (London: J. Hinton, 1743) , p. 521.

24. James, Earl of Waldegrave, *Memoirs from 1754 to 1758* (London: John Murray, 1821) , p. 18.

25. Some of the more prominent pamphlets of the sort are *An Examination of the Principles* . . . *of the Two B[rothe]rs, A Second Series of Facts and Arguments, The Ordinary of Newgate's Account of the Behaviour* . . . *of Several Malefactors* . . . *To Which Is Annexed, Mr. P[elha]m's Speech Immediately Before His Execution,* and *A Tale of Two Tubs.* On the other side there were *An Ode on the Death of Mr. Pelham, A Letter to the Author of an Examination of the Principles* . . . *of the Two B[rothe]rs, The Conduct of the Two B[rothe]rs Vindicated, The Discovery,* and *A Modest and Impartial Reply* . . . *to A Second Series of Facts and Arguments.*

26. Coxe, *Henry Pelham,* II, 301; *cf.* Coxe, *Horatio Walpole,* pp. 408–9.

27. John Charles Earle, *English Premiers from Sir Robert Walpole to Sir Robert Peel* (London: Chapman and Hall, 1871) , I, 90.

28. Archibald Ballantyne, *Lord Carteret: A Political Biography, 1690–1763* (London: Richard Bentley & Son, 1887) , *passim.*

29. Yorke, *Hardwicke,* I, 284.

30. Williams, *Pitt,* I, 109.

31. Sanders, *Dodington,* p. 184.

32. Clive Bigham, *The Prime Ministers of Britain, 1721–1921* (London: John Murray, 1922) , p. 41.

33. F. J. C. Hearnshaw, *British Prime Ministers of the Eighteenth Century* (London: Ernest Benn Limited, 1928) , Chapter III.

34. Turberville, *House of Lords,* pp. 278–79.

35. F. S. Oliver, *The Endless Adventure* (London: Macmillan and Co., Limited, 1930–35) , III, 49.

36. Plumb, *Chatham,* pp. 42–43.

37. John B. Owen, *The Rise of the Pelhams* (London: Methuen & Co., Ltd., 1957) , p. 319.

Bibliography

Bibliography

BIBLIOGRAPHIES AND REFERENCE WORKS

Cheney, C. R. *Handbook of Dates for Students of English History*. London: Offices of the Royal Historical Society, 1948.

Dunkin, E. H. W. *A Calendar of the Deeds and Other Documents in the Possession of the Sussex Archaeological Society*.

Grose, Clyde L. *A Select Bibliography of British History, 1660–1760*. Chicago: University of Chicago Press, 1939.

Haydn, Joseph. *The Book of Dignities*. Edited by Horace Ockerby. Third Edition. London: W. H. Allen & Co., Limited, 1894.

Pargellis, Stanley, and Medley, D. J. *Bibliography of British History: The Eighteenth Century, 1714–1789*. Oxford: The Clarendon Press, 1951.

MANUSCRIPTS

Bodleian Library
  North Manuscripts
British Museum
  Additional Manuscripts
    15955–15957: Anson Papers
    34412: Auckland Papers
    4223, 4254, 4324A, 4325: Birch Collection
    22526–22545: Carteret Papers
    43771: Chatham Papers
    9131–9132, 9146–9147, 9176–9201, 9231–9232: Coxe Papers
    15869–15875, 15887: Dayrolle Papers
    46972–46977, 47072–47073, 47090–47092, 47137: Egmont Papers
    27732–27735: Essex Papers
    35337, 35351–35388, 35406–35472, 35584–35592, 35602–35609, 35633, 35679, 35692, 35853, 35869–35890, 36119, 36125, 36134–36137, 36248, 36269, 36271.E, 36271.F, 38161: Hardwicke Papers
    38854: Hodgkin Papers
    43441–43443: Keene Papers
    28051: Leeds Papers
    38197, 38330–38331, 38373, 38455, 38476: Liverpool Papers
    34523–34525: Mackintosh Collections
    41254–41355: Martin Papers
    6911, 11394, 30170: Miscellaneous Papers
    6807, 6871: Mitchell Papers
    5737: Musgrave Papers

32679, 32684–32737, 32799–32876, 32894, 32934, 32992–32995, 33004, 33008–
    33009, 33018, 33028–33075, 33198, 33201, 33344: Newcastle Papers
28148, 28151–28152, 28156–28157: Norris Papers
33087, 33136, 33138–33141, 33162–33163, 33167, 33441: Pelham Papers
23805–23830: Robinson Papers
25560–25561: South Sea Company Papers
22628: Suffolk Papers
41654–41656: Townshend Papers
23630–23634, 23642: Tyrawly Papers
40815–40817, 40827–40828, 40846–40847: Vernon Papers
21555: Walpole Papers
34287, 34731–34736: West Papers
45733: Wilmington Papers
Egerton Manuscripts
    1721–1722, 1733: Bentinck Papers
    1955: Miscellaneous Papers
    2528–2529: Haddock Papers
    929: Halifax Papers
    2687–2689, 2691: Titley Papers
Lansdowne Manuscripts
    660
Sloane Manuscripts
    4225
Stowe Manuscripts
    142, 155, 158, 251–252, 254–256, 262, 308
Cambridge University Library
Cholmondeley-Houghton Manuscripts
Huntington Library
Loudoun Papers:
    323, 441, 443a, 447a
Huntington Library Manuscripts:
    9918
Abercromby Papers:
    AB976
Nottingham University Library
Pelham Papers
Public Record Office
Chatham Papers:
    1–6, 17, 19, 25–26, 31–35, 38–40, 48–49, 51–52, 54–55, 61, 70–71, 74, 83–84,
    95, 98–100
Egremont Papers:
    17, 28
Granville Papers:
    1–3, 384A
Miscellaneous Papers of the P.R.O.: Papers on the Exchange of the Prisoners,
    1744
Privy Council: Minutes of the Clerks of the Council. Miscellaneous, 1670–1776
Privy Council Papers: 30
Privy Council Register: 8–15
State Papers, Domestic, Entry Books: 82–85

State Papers, Domestic, George II: 50–126
State Papers, Domestic, King's Letters: 162
State Papers, Domestic, Regencies: 303–322
State Papers, Domestic, Secretary's Letter Books: 129–136
State Papers, Domestic, Undersecretary's Letter Books: 148
State Papers, Domestic, Various: 3–5, 8–9, 15, 19, 21, 27–28
State Papers, Military: 14–19
State Papers, Naval: 139
State Papers, Regencies: 31–50, 100–123, 126–128
Treasury Papers: Affairs of Taxes: 4–5
Treasury Papers: Crown Lease Book: 6–8
Treasury Papers: Customs Book: 15–17
Treasury Papers: Irish Book: 9
Treasury Papers: King's Warrant Book: 34–39
Treasury Papers: Letter Book: 19–21
Treasury Papers: Lord Chamberlain's Warrant Book: 2
Treasury Papers: Miscellaneous—Various—Canada, 1744–1776
Treasury Papers: Money Book: 40–42
Treasury Papers: North Britain Book: 13–16
Treasury Papers: Order Book: 17–18
Treasury Papers: Reference Book: 11
Treasury Papers: Treasury Board Papers: 308–355
Treasury Papers: Treasury Fee Book: 9–10
Treasury Papers: Treasury Minute Book: 29–32
Treasury Papers: Warrants Not Relating to Money: 27
Treasury Papers: Supplementary (c. 1731–1800)
Works Papers: Letter Book Set I, No. 2–3
Sheffield City Libraries:
Wentworth-Woodhouse Muniments: M1–M20, R1, R93, R145, R166, F35

PRINTED PRIMARY SOURCES: BOOKS

[Almon, John.] *Anecdotes of the Life of the Right Honourable William Pitt, Earl of Chatham; and of the Principal Events of His Times: with His Speeches in Parliament, from the Year 1736 to the Year 1778.* London: L. B. Seeley, 1796.

Anson, Sir William R. (ed.). *Autobiography and Political Correspondence of Augustus Henry, Third Duke of Grafton, K.G. from Hitherto Unpublished Documents in the Possession of His Family.* London: John Murray, 1898.

Bell, Robert Fitzroy (ed.). *Memorials of John Murray of Broughton Sometime Secretary to Prince Charles Edward, 1740–1747.* Edited for the Scottish History Society. First Series. Vol. XXVII. Edinburgh: University Press, 1898.

Blailie, Walter Biggar (ed.). *Origins of the 'Forty-Five and Other Papers Relating to That Rising.* Edited for the Scottish History Society. Second Series. Vol. II. Edinburgh: University Press, 1916.

Chance, James Frederick (ed.). *British Diplomatic Instructions, 1689–1789.* Vol. III. Denmark. Edited for the Royal Historical Society. London: Offices of the Society, 1926.

———. *British Diplomatic Instructions, 1689–1789.* Vol. V. Sweden. Edited for the Royal Historical Society. London: Offices of the Society, 1928.

Chesterfield, Earl of. *An Apology for a Late Resignation in a Letter from an English Gentleman to His Friend at the Hague.* London: John Freeman, 1748.

Climenson, Emily J. *Elizabeth Montagu: The Queen of the Blue-Stockings, Her Correspondence from 1720 to 1761.* London: John Murray, 1906.

Cobbett, William. *The Parliamentary History of England from the Earliest Period to the Year 1803.* Vol. XII–XIV. London: Longman, Hurst, Rees, Orme, & Brown, 1812.

Coxe, William. *Memoirs of the Administration of the Right Honourable Henry Pelham, Collected from the Family Papers, and Other Authentic Documents.* London: Longman, Rees, Orme, Brown, and Green, 1829.

————. *Memoirs of the Life and Administration of Sir Robert Walpole, Earl of Orford with Original Correspondence and Authentic Papers, Never Before Published.* London: T. Cadell, Jun. and W. Davies, 1798.

————. *Memoirs of Horatio, Lord Walpole Selected from his Correspondence and Papers, and Connected with the History of the Times, from 1678 to 1757.* London: T. Cadell, Jun. and W. Davies, 1802.

Duff, H. R. (ed.). *Culloden Papers: Comprising an Extensive and Interesting Correspondence from the Year 1625 to 1748* . . . London: T. Cadell and W. Davies, 1815.

Dumont, Jean. *Corps universel diplomatique du droit des gens; contenant un recueil des traitez d'alliance, de Paix, de treve, de neutralité, de commerce, de échange.* Amsterdam: Chez P. Brunel, R. et G. Wetstein, et G. Smith, Henri Waesberge, et Z. Chatelain, 1731.

Ellis, Sir Henry (ed.). *Original Letters of Eminent Literary Men of the Sixteenth, Seventeenth, and Eighteenth Centuries.* Edited for the Camden Society. Old Series. Vol. XXIII. London: Camden Society, 1843.

Fitzmaurice, Lord. *Life of William Earl of Shelburne afterwards First Marquess of Lansdowne with Extracts from his Papers and Correspondence.* London: Macmillan and Co., Limited, 1912.

Fox, John Charles (ed.). *The Official Diary of Lieutenant-General Adam Williamson, Deputy-Lieutenant of the Tower of London, 1722–1747.* Edited for the Camden Society. Series III. Vol. XXII. London: Offices of the Society, 1912.

[Glover, Richard.] *Memoirs by a Celebrated Literary and Political Character from the Resignation of Sir Robert Walpole, in 1742, to the Establishment of Lord Chatham's Second Administration, in 1757; Containing Strictures on Some of the Most Distinguished Men of That Time.* London: John Murray, 1814.

Graham, John Murray. *Annals and Correspondence of the Viscount and the First and Second Earls of Stair.* Edinburgh: William Blackwood and Sons, 1875.

Grant, W. L., and Munro, James (eds.). *Acts of the Privy Council of England.* Colonial Series. Vol. III. Hereford: His Majesty's Stationery Office, 1910.

Harris, James Howard, Third Earl of Malmesbury (ed.). *A Series of Letters of the First Earl of Malmesbury His Family and Friends from 1745–1820.* London: Richard Bentley, 1870.

Hervey, Lord John. *Some Material Towards Memoirs of the Reign of King George II.* Edited by Romney Sedgwick. London: King's Printers, 1931.

Historical Manuscripts Commission. *First Report of the Royal Commission on Historical Manuscripts.* London: George Edward Eyre and William Spottiswoode, 1870.

Historical Manuscripts Commission. *Third Report of the Royal Commission on Historical Manuscripts*. London: George Edward Eyre and William Spottiswoode, 1872.

————. *Tenth Report*. Reports on the Manuscripts of the Earl of Eglinton, Sir J. Stirling Maxwell, Bart., C. S. H. Drummond Moray, Esq., C. T. Weston Underwood, Esq., and G. Wingfield Digby, Esq. London: Her Majesty's Stationery Office, 1885.

————. *Eleventh Report*. Appendix, Part IV. The Manuscripts of the Marquess Townshend. London: Her Majesty's Stationery Office, 1887.

————. *Twelfth Report*. Appendix, Part V. The Manuscripts of His Grace the Duke of Rutland, K. G., Preserved at Belvoir Castle. Vol. II. London: Her Majesty's Stationery Office, 1889.

————. *Thirteenth Report*. Appendix, Part VII. The Manuscripts of the Earl of Lonsdale. London: Her Majesty's Stationery Office, 1893.

————. *Fourteenth Report*. Appendix, Part III. The Manuscripts of the Earl of Marchmont. Her Majesty's Stationery Office, 1894.

————. *Fourteenth Report*. Appendix, Part IX. The Manuscripts of the Earl of Buckinghamshire, the Earl of Lindsey, the Earl of Onslow, Lord Emly, Theodore J. Hare, Esq., and James Round, Esq., M. P. London: Her Majesty's Stationery Office, 1895.

————. *Fifteenth Report*. Appendix, Part VII. The Manuscripts of the Duke of Somerset, The Marquis of Ailesbury, and the Rev. Sir T. H. G. Puleston, Bart. London: Her Majesty's Stationery Office, 1898.

————. *Report on the Manuscripts of the Duke of Buccleuch and Queensberry, K. G., K. T., Preserved at Montagu House, Whitehall*. Vol. I. London: Her Majesty's Stationery Office, 1899.

————. *Report on the Manuscripts of the Earl of Denbigh Preserved at Newnham Paddox, Warwickshire* (Part V). London: His Majesty's Stationery Office, 1911.

————. *Manuscripts of the Earl of Egmont. Diary of the First Earl of Egmont (Viscount Percival)*. Vol. III. London: His Majesty's Stationery Office, 1923.

————. *Report on the Manuscripts of Mrs. Frankland-Russell-Astley, of Chequers Court, Bucks*. London: Her Majesty's Stationery Office, 1900.

————. *Report on the Manuscripts of Mrs. Stopford-Sackville of Drayton House, Northamptonshire*. Vol. I. London: His Majesty's Stationery Office, 1904.

————. *Report on the Manuscripts of Lady duCane*. London: His Majesty's Stationery Office, 1905.

————. *Report of the Manuscripts of the Marquess of Lothian Preserved at Blickling Hall, Norfolk*. London: His Majesty's Stationery Office, 1905.

————. *Calendar of the Manuscripts of the Marquis of Bath Preserved at Longleat, Wiltshire*. Vol. I. London: His Majesty's Stationery Office, 1904.

————. *Report on Manuscripts in Various Collections*. Vol. VI. The Manuscripts of Miss M. Eyre Matcham; Captain H. V. Knox; Cornwallis Wykeham-Martin, Esq.; etc. Dublin: His Majesty's Stationery Office, 1909.

————. *Report on Manuscripts in Various Collections*. Vol. VIII. The Manuscripts of the Hon. Frederick Lindley Wood; M. L. S. Clements, Esq; S. Philip Unwin, Esq. London: His Majesty's Stationery Office, 1913.

Historical Memoirs of His Late Royal Highness William-Augustus, Duke of Cumberland. Including the Military and Political History of Great Britain, during that Period. London: T. Waller, 1767.

Journals of the House of Commons. Vol. XXIII–XXVI.

Journals of the House of Lords. Vol. XXV–XXVIII.

Legg, L. G. Wickham (ed.). *British Diplomatic Instructions, 1689–1789.* Vol. VI. France, 1727–1744. Edited for the Royal Historical Society. London: Offices of the Society, 1930.

––––––. *British Diplomatic Instructions, 1689–1789.* Vol. VII. France, 1745–1789. Edited for the Royal Historical Society. London: Offices of the Society, 1934.

Lodge, Sir Richard (ed.). *Private Correspondence of Chesterfield and Newcastle, 1744–46.* Edited for the Royal Historical Society. Camden Series. Vol. XLIV. London: Offices of the Society, 1930.

Mackay, William (ed.). *The Letter-Book of Bailie John Stewart of Inverness 1715–1752.* Edited for the Scottish History Society. Second Series. Vol. IX. Edinburgh: University Press, 1915.

Mahon, Lord (Philip Henry Stanhope). *History of England from the Peace of Utrecht to the Peace of Versailles, 1713–1783.* Vol. I, Appendix, The Stuart Papers. London: John Murray, 1831.

Millar, A. H. (ed.). *A Selection of Scottish Forfeited Estates Papers 1715; 1745.* Edited for the Scottish History Society. First Series. Vol. LVII. Edinburgh: University Press, 1909.

Munro, James (ed.). *Acts of the Privy Council of England.* Colonial Series. Vol. IV. London: His Majesty's Stationery Office, 1911.

Nugent, Claud. *Memoir of Robert, Earl of Nugent with Letters, Poems, and Appendices.* London: William Heinemann, 1898.

Oswald, James. *Memorials of the Public Life and Character of the Right Hon. James Oswald, of Dunnikier.* Edinburgh: Archibald Constable and Co., 1825.

Phillimore, Robert (ed.). *Memoirs and Correspondence of George, Lord Lyttelton from 1734–1773.* London: James Ridgway, 1845.

[Ralph, James.] *A Critical History of the Administration of Sir Robert Walpole, Now Earl of Orford. Collected Chiefly from the Debates in Parliament, and the Political Writings on Both Sides.* London: J. Hinton, 1743.

Rose, George Henry (ed.). *A Selection from the Papers of the Earls of Marchmont.* London: John Murray, 1831.

Russell, Lord John. *Correspondence of John, Fourth Duke of Bedford Selected from the Originals at Woburn Abbey.* London: Longman, Brown, Green, and Longmans, 1842.

Sichel, Walter. *Bolingbroke and His Times.* Vol. I. Selected Correspondence. London: James Nisbet & Co., Limited, 1901.

Smith, William James (ed.). *The Grenville Papers: Being the Correspondence of Richard Grenville Earl Temple, K. G., and the Right Hon. George Grenville, Their Friends and Contemporaries.* London: John Murray, 1852.

[Stanhope, Philip Dormer.] *Characters by Lord Chesterfield Contrasted with Characters of the Same Great Personages by Other Respectable Writers.* London: Edward and Charles Dilly, 1778.

––––––. *The Letters of Philip Dormer Stanhope, Fourth Earl of Chesterfield.* Edited by Bonamy Dobree. London: Eyre and Spottiswoode (Publishers), Limited, 1932.

Taylor, W. S., and Pringle, J. H. (ed.). *Correspondence of William Pitt, Earl of Chatham.* London: John Murray, 1838.

Toynbee, Mrs. Paget (ed.). *The Letters of Horace Walpole Fourth Earl of*

Orford, Chronologically Arranged and Edited with Notes and Indices. Oxford: The Clarendon Press, 1903.

Toynbee, Paget (ed.). *Supplement to the Letters of Horace Walpole Fourth Earl of Orford*. Oxford: The Clarendon Press, 1925.

Waldegrave, James, Earl of. *Memoirs from 1754 to 1758*. London: John Murray, 1821.

Walpole, Horace. *Memoirs of the Reign of King George the Second*. Edited by Lord Holland. London: Henry Colburn, 1846.

Warner, Rebecca (ed.). *Original Letters, from Richard Baxter, Matthew Prior, Lord Bolingbroke, Alexander Pope, Dr. Cheyne, Dr. Hartley, Dr. Samuel Johnson, Mrs. Montague, Rev. William Gilpin, Rev. John Newton, George Lord Lyttelton, Rev. Dr. Claudius Buchanan, etc. with Biographical Illustrations*. Bath: Richard Cruttwell, 1817.

Warrand, Duncan (ed.). *More Culloden Papers*. Inverness: Robert Carruthers & Sons, 1927.

Wyndham, Henry Penruddocke (ed.). *The Diary of the Late George Bubb Dodington, Baron of Melcombe Regis: from March 8, 1748–49, to February 6, 1761*. Dublin: William Porter, 1784.

Yorke, Philip C. *The Life and Correspondence· of Philip Yorke, Earl of Hardwicke, Lord High Chancellor of Great Britain*. Cambridge: University Press, 1913.

PRINTED PRIMARY SOURCES: NEWSPAPERS

Gentleman's Magazine and Historical Chronicle. Vol. XII–XXIV (1724–1754). London: Edward Cave, Jr., 1724–1754.

Historical Register. Vol. IX (1724). London: C. Meere, 1724.

Political State of Great Britain. London: F. Baker, 1711–1741.

PRINTED PRIMARY SOURCES: PAMPHLETS

A Letter from a By-stander to a Member of Parliament . . . London: J. Roberts, 1741.

Miscellaneous Thoughts on Present Posture Both of Our Foreign and Domestic Affairs. [1741.]

A Proper Answer to the By-Stander . . . London: T. Cooper, 1742.

A Full Answer to the Letter from a By-Stander . . .

The New-comers: or, the Characters of John the Carter, Sandy Long-bib, Daniel Raven, and Old Will with the Spencer Wig. To Which Is Added, The Character and History of Will Trimmer . . . London: J. Mechell, 1742.

An Epistle to the Right Honourable William Pulteney, Esq; Upon His Late Conduct in Public Affairs. London: B. Dod, 1742.

The False Patriot: A Satyrical Epistle to W[illiam] P[ultene]y, Esq; On His Being Created E[ar]l of B[a]th. London: T. Johnson, 1742.

A Vindication of the Conduct of a Certain Eminent Patriot . . . London: S. Lyne, 1742.

The S[ta]te M[iniste]rs Are Come; or a New Doctor for a Crazy Constitution. 1742.

A New C[our]t Ballad. Dublin: James Stone, 1742.

A Congratulatory Letter To a Certain Right Honourable Person, Upon His Late Disappointment. London: J. Mechell, 1743.

A Proper Reply to a Late Infamous and Scurrilous Libel, Intitled, A Congratulatory Letter to a Certain Right Honourable Person Upon His Late Disappointment. London: J. Robinson, 1743.

The Patriot and the Minister Review'd . . . London: S. Dial, 1743.

Faction Detected, by the Evidence of Facts. Dublin: G. Faulkner, 1743.

The Detecter Detected . . . London: M. Cooper, 1743.

A Review of the Whole Political Conduct of a Late Eminent Patriot, and His Friends for Twenty Years Last Past . . . London: M. Cooper, 1743.

An Enquiry into the Independency of a Dependent L[or]d . . . London: W. Webb, 1743.

A Letter to the Reverend Dr. Zachary Pearce . . . *In Which the Secret History and Real Tendency of* . . . *Faction Detected by the Evidence of Facts, Are Clear'd Up* . . . London: M. Cooper, 1743.

Public Discontent Accounted for from the Conduct of Our Ministers in the Cabinet, and of Our Generals in the Field . . . London: M. Cooper, 1743.

The Desertion Discussed: Or, the Last and Present Opposition Places in Their True Light . . . London: M. Cooper, 1743.

The Case of the Hanover Forces in the Pay of Great Britain . . . London: T. Cooper, 1743.

The Interest of Great Britain Steadily Pursued . . . London: J. Roberts, 1743.

The Interest of Hanover Steadily Pursued since the A[ccessio]n . . . London: M. Cooper, 1743.

A Farther Vindication of the Case of the Hanover Troops . . . London: M. Cooper, 1743.

A Vindication of a Late Pamphlet, Intitled, The Case of the Hanover Troops Considered . . . London: T. Cooper, 1743.

The Wife and the Nurse: A New Ballad. London: W. Webb, 1743.

Beef and Butt Beer, Against Mum and Pumpernickle. H[a]n[ove]r Scrubs, or a Bumper to Old England, — Huzza. A Drinking Song. London: B. C., 1743.

The Yellow Sash . . . London: 1743.

Serious Considerations on the Present State of Affairs, Both at Home and Abroad . . . London: C. Cobbett, 1744.

A Defence of the People: or, Full Confutation of the Pretended Facts, Advanc'd In a Late Huge, Angry Pamphlet; Call'd Faction Detected . . . London: J. Robinson, 1744.

The New Opposition Compared with the Old in Point of Principles and Practices . . . London: W. Bickerton, 1744.

An Apology for the Conduct of the Present Administration . . . London: M. Cooper, 1744.

The Conduct of the Allies and the Management of the War Impartially Examined . . . London: M. Cooper, 1744.

Of the Use and Abuse of Parliaments . . . London: 1744.

An Ode, Imitated from Ode XI. Book 2d. of Horace . . . London: W. Webb, 1745.

Place-Book for the Year Seventeen-Hundred, Forty-Five. New Ballad. London: W. Webb, 1745.

King George's Title Asserted . . . London: Bickerton, 1745.

285

The New Court Secret; A Melancholy Truth . . . London: 1746.
An Essay Towards Deciding the Important Question, Whether It Be a National Advantage to Britain to Insure the Ships of Her Enemies? . . . London: J. Robinson, 1747.
The State of the Nation for the Year 1747, and Respecting 1748 . . . London: M. Cooper, 1747.
The Ordinary of Newgate's Account of the Behaviour, Dying Words, and Confession. . . . To Which Is Annexed, Mr. P[elha]m's Speech Immediately Before His Execution. London: W. Webb, 1747.
An Apology for the Conduct of a Late Celebrated Second-rate Minister, from the Year 1729, at Which Time He Commenc'd Courtier, till within a Few Weeks of His Death, in 1746 . . . London: W. Webb, 1747.
A Proper Answer to a Late Scurrilous Libel Entitled, An Apology for the Conduct of a Late Celebrated Second-rate Minister . . . London: M. Cooper, 1747.
A Free Comment on the Late Mr. W[innin]g[to]n's Apology for His Conduct . . . London: W. Webb, 1748.
A Modest Apology for My Own Conduct. London: M. Cooper, 1748.
The Finesse of Rantum Scantum, A New Diverting Dialogue Betwixt Tom and Harry, Fratres Fraterrimi. London: A. Hill, 1748.
The Puppet Shew: A Poem Humbly Inscribed to H[enry] P[elham]. London: M. Cooper, 1748.
The Resignation Discussed. In Which Many of the False Facts Are Detected . . . London: J. Roberts, 1748.
The Conduct of the Government With Respect to Peace and War, Stated. London: J. Owen, 1748.
An Examination of the Principles, and Enquiry into the Conduct of the Two B[rothe]rs . . . London: A. Price, 1749.
A Letter to the Author of An Examination of the Principles; and an Enquiry into the Conduct of the Two Brothers . . . Dublin: James Esdall, 1749.
The Conduct of the Two B[rothe]rs Vindicated . . . London: M. Cooper, 1749.
A Second Series of Facts and Arguments; Tending to Prove that the Abilities of the Two B[rothe]rs, are not More Extraordinary Than Their Virtues . . . London: A. Price, 1749.
A Modest and Impartial Reply to a Pamphlet Lately Published, Entitled A Second Series of Facts and Arguments . . . London: James Roberts, 1749.
A Ballad. To the Tune of Chevy Chase. London: H. Carpenter, 1749.
A Dialogue Betweeen Thomas Jones, A Life-guard-man, and John Smith, Late Serjeant in the First Regiment of Foot-Guards, Just Returned from Flanders. London: J. Raymond, 1749.
A Tale of Two Tubs: or, the B[rothe]rs on Querpo. London: A. Price, 1749.
Titus Antigallicus, An Ode for the Thanksgiving Day. 1749.
An Occasional Letter from a Gentleman in the Country to His Friend in Town . . . London: 1749.
A Plain Account of the Old and New Stiles . . . *and the Difficulties attending a Perpetual Reformation of the Calendar, are Shortly Resolved* . . . London: A. Miller, 1751.
National Expectations on the Late Change in the Ministry . . . London: M. Cooper, 1751.
The Discovery, and Ode to Mr. P[elha]m. London: Paul Vaillant, 1752.
An Edict to His Grace the D. D[orset]. L[ieutenant] G[eneral] and G[overnor]

G[eneral] of Ireland. and to His M[ajest]y's P[riv]y C[ounci]l of the said
Kingdom. London: Robert Swan, 1753.

An Ode on the Death of Mr. Pelham. London: M. Cooper, 1754.

A Letter to the Author of the Ode on Mr. Pelham's Death . . . London: W.
Reeve, 1754.

An Epistle from John More Apothecary of Abchurch-Lane, to L[ord] C[arteret]
Upon His Treatiee of Worms. London: W. Webb, n. d.

The Courtier and Patriot. An Epistle to His Grace the Duke of Newcastle.
London: G. Woodfall, n. d.

An Occasional Letter to the Right Honourable H[enry] P[elham], Esq. London: H. Carpenter, n. d.

A Letter from a Person of Distinction to the Rt. Hon. J[ohn] E[arl] of
Eg[mon]t . . . London: J. Cobham, n. d.

SECONDARY WORKS: BOOKS

Ballantyne, Archibald. Lord Carteret: A Political Biography, 1690–1763. London: Richard Bentley & Son, 1887.

Barrow, Sir John. The Life of George Lord Anson, Admiral of the Fleet; Vice-
Admiral of Great Britain; and First Commissioner of the Admiralty, Previous
to, and during the Seven Years' War. London: John Murray, 1839.

Bigham, Clive. The Prime Ministers of Britain 1721–1921. London: John
Murray, 1922.

Chance, James Frederick. Notes on the Diplomatic Relations of England and
Germany. List of Diplomatic Representatives and Agents, England and North
Germany, 1689–1727. Edited by Charles Harding Firth. Oxford: B. H. Black-
well, 1907.

————. Notes on the Diplomatic Relations of England with the North of Europe.
List of English Diplomatic Representatives and Agents in Denmark, Sweden
and Russia, and of those Countries in England, 1689–1762. Edited by Charles
Harding Firth. Oxford: B. H. Blackwell, 1913.

Clark, Dora Mae. The Rise of the British Treasury: Colonial Administration in
the Eighteenth Century. New Haven: Yale University Press, 1960.

Conn, Stephen. Gibraltar in British Diplomacy in the Eighteenth Century. New
Haven: Yale University Press, 1942.

Cooper, William Durant. The Parliamentary History of the County of Sussex;
and of the Several Boroughs and Cinque Ports Therein. Lewes: Sussex Press,
1834.

Coxe, William. History of the House of Austria from the Foundations of the
Monarchy by Rudolph of Hapsburgh to the Death of Leopold the Second:
1218 to 1792. London: T. Cadell and W. Davies, 1807.

————. Memoirs of the Kings of the House of Bourbon from the Accession of
Philip the Fifth to the Death of Charles the Third: 1700 to 1788 Drawn from
Original and Unpublished Documents. London: Longman, Hurst, Rees, Orme,
and Brown, 1813.

Davis, Rose Mary. The Good Lord Lyttelton, A Study in Eighteenth Century
Politics and Culture. Bethlehem, Penn.: Times Publishing Company, 1939.

Earle, John Charles. English Premiers from Sir Robert Walpole to Sir Robert
Peel. London: Chapman and Hall, 1871.

Ellis, Kenneth. *The Post Office in the Eighteenth Century.* London: Oxford University Press, 1958.

Ernst, W. *Memoirs of the Life of Philip Dormer Fourth Earl of Chesterfield with Numerous Letters now First Published from the Newcastle Papers.* London: Swan Sonnenschein & Co., 1893.

Eyck, Erich. *Pitt Versus Fox: Father and Son, 1735–1806.* London: G. Bell and Sons, Ltd., 1950.

Feiling, Keith Grahame. *The Second Tory Party, 1714–1832.* London: Macmillan and Co., Limited, 1938.

Grego, Joseph. *A History of Parliamentary Elections and Electioneering from the Stuarts to Queen Victoria.* London: Chatto & Windus, 1892.

Hargreaves, E. L. *The National Debt.* London: Edward Arnold & Co., 1930.

Hearnshaw, F. J. C. *British Prime Ministers of the Eighteenth Century.* London: Ernest Benn, Limited, 1928.

Henderson, Alfred James. *London and the National Government, 1721–1742.* Durham, N. C.: Duke University Press, 1945.

Holliday, John. *The Life of William Late Earl of Mansfield.* London: P. Elmsly and D. Bremner, 1797.

Horn, D. B. (ed.). *British Diplomatic Representatives 1689–1789.* Edited for the Royal Historical Society. Camden Series. Vol. XLVI. London: Offices of the Society, 1932.

————. *Sir Charles Hanbury Williams and European Diplomacy (1747–50).* London: George G. Harrop & Company Ltd., 1930.

Laprade, William Thomas. *Public Opinion and Politics in Eighteenth Century England.* London: The Macmillan Company, 1936.

Leadam, Isaac S. *The History of England from the Accession of Anne to the Death of George II (1702–1760).* London: Longmans, Green, and Co., 1912.

Lecky, W. E. H. *A History of England in the Eighteenth Century.* New York: D. Appleton and Company, 1878–1890.

Legge, F. G. Wickham. *Notes on the Diplomatic Relations of England and France. List of Diplomatic Representatives and Agents, England and France, 1689–1763.* Oxford: B. H. Blackwell, 1909.

Lewis, Wilmarth Sheldon. *Three Tours Through London in the Years 1748–1776–1797.* New Haven: Yale University Press, 1941.

Lodge, Richard. *Great Britain and Prussia in the Eighteenth Century.* Oxford: The Clarendon Press, 1923.

McLachlan, Jean O. *Trade and Peace with Old Spain, 1667–1750.* Cambridge: University Press, 1940.

Namier, Lewis Bernstein. *The Structure of Politics at the Accession of George III.* London: Macmillan and Co., Limited, 1929.

Nulle, Stebelton H. *Thomas Pelham-Holles, Duke of Newcastle, His Early Political Career, 1693–1724.* Philadelphia: University of Pennsylvania Press, 1931.

Oliver, F. S. *The Endless Adventure.* London: Macmillan and Co., Limited, 1930–35.

Owen, John B. *The Rise of the Pelhams.* London: Methuen & Co., Ltd., 1957.

Pares, Richard. *King George III and the Politicians.* Oxford: The Clarendon Press, 1953.

————. *War and Trade in the West Indies, 1739–1763.* Oxford: The Clarendon Press, 1936.

Pemberton, W. Baring. *Carteret: The Brilliant Failure of the Eighteenth Century*. London: Longmans, Green and Co., 1936.

Plumb, John H. *Chatham*. London: Collins Clear-Type Press, 1953.

————. *Sir Robert Walpole*. London: The Cresset Press, 1956, 1960.

Realey, Charles B. *The Early Opposition to Robert Walpole, 1720–1727*. Lawrence, Kansas: University of Kansas Press, 1931.

Riker, Thad Weed. *Henry Fox, First Lord Holland: A Study of the Career of an Eighteenth Century Politician*. Oxford: The Clarendon Press, 1911.

Robertson, Sir Charles Grant. *England Under the Hanoverians*. London: Methuen & Co., Ltd., 1911.

Robson, Robert. *The Attorney in Eighteenth Century England*. Cambridge: University Press, 1959.

————. *The Oxfordshire Election of 1754, A Study in the Interplay of City, County and University Politics*. London: Geoffrey Cumberlege, 1949.

Rosebery, Lord. *Lord Chatham: His Early Life and Connections*. New York: Harper & Brothers Publishers, 1910.

Sanders, Lloyd. *Patron and Place-hunter: A Study of George Bubb Dodington, Lord Melcombe*. London: John Lane, 1919.

Seton, Sir Bruce Gordon, Bt. of Abercorn, and Arnot, Jean Gordon (eds.). *The Prisoners of the '45*. Edited for the Scottish History Society. Third Series. Vol. XIII–XV. Edinburgh: The University Press, 1928–1929.

Sherrard, O. A. *Lord Chatham*. London: The Bodley Head, 1952–1958.

Smollett, Tobias S. *A Complete History of England from the Descent of Julius Caesar, to the Treaty of Aix la Chapelle, 1748*. London: Richard Baldwin, 1760.

————. *The History of England, Written Originally in French by Rapin de Thoyras: Translated into English, with Additional Notes; and Continued from the Revolution to the Accession of King George II by N. Tindal: . . . With the Reign of George II: by T. Smollett, M. D*. London: John Harrison, 1789.

Stevens, David Harrison. *Party Politics and English Journalism, 1702–1742*. Chicago: University of Chicago Press, 1916.

Sutherland, Lucy S. *The City of London and the Opposition to Government, 1768–1774*. London: Athlone Press, 1959.

Sykes, Norman. *Church and State in England in the Eighteenth Century*. Cambridge: University Press, 1934.

Taylor, G. R. Stirling. *Robert Walpole; and His Age*. London: Jonathan Cape, 1931.

Thomson, Mark A. *Secretaries of State 1681–1782*. Oxford: The Clarendon Press, 1932.

Torrens, W. M. *History of Cabinets from the Union with Scotland to the Acquisition of Canada and Bengal*. London: W. H. Allen & Co., Limited, 1894.

Turberville, A. S. *The House of Lords in the Eighteenth Century*. Oxford: The Clarendon Press, 1927.

Turner, Edward Raymond. *The Cabinet Council of England in the Seventeenth and Eighteenth Centuries, 1622–1784*. Edited by Gaudence Megaro. Baltimore: Johns Hopkins Press, 1930–1932.

Vaucher, Paul. *Robert Walpole et la politique Fleury, 1731–1742*. Paris: Plon-Nourrit et Cie, 1924.

Ward, W. R. *Georgian Oxford: University Politics in the Eighteenth Century*. Oxford: The Clarendon Press, 1958.

———. *The English Land Tax in the Eighteenth Century.* Oxford: University Press, 1953.

Watson, J. Steven. *The Reign of George III, 1760–1815.* Oxford: The Clarendon Press, 1960.

Wiggin, Lewis M. *The Faction of Cousins: A Political Account of the Grenvilles, 1733–1763.* New Haven: Yale University Press, 1958.

Williams, Basil. *Carteret and Newcastle: A Contrast in Contemporaries.* Cambridge: University Press, 1943.

———. *The Life of William Pitt, Earl of Chatham.* London: Longmans, Green, and Co., 1915.

———. *The Whig Supremacy.* Oxford: The Clarendon Press, 1936.

Wilson, Arthur McCandless. *French Foreign Policy during the Administration of Cardinal Fleury, 1726–1743.* Cambridge: Harvard University Press, 1936.

SECONDARY WORKS: ARTICLES

Andrews, Charles M. "Anglo-French Commercial Rivalry, 1700–1750: The Western Phase, I," *American Historical Review,* XX (1915), 539.

———. "Anglo-French Commercial Rivalry, 1700–1750: The Western Phase, II," *American Historical Review,* XX (1915), 761.

Anson, W. R. "The Cabinet in the Seventeenth and Eighteenth Centuries," *English Historical Review,* XXIX, 56.

———. "The Cabinet, Its Development, 1688–1760," *English Historical Review,* XXIX, 325.

Barnes, D. G. "The Duke of Newcastle, Ecclesiastical Minister, 1724–1754," *Pacific Historical Review,* III (1934), 164–191.

———. "Henry Pelham and the Duke of Newcastle," *The Journal of British Studies,* No. 2 (May 1962), 62–77.

Bateman, B. "Clerical Preferment Under the Duke of Newcastle," *English Historical Review,* VII, 685.

Bellot, H. Hale. "Journal of the Commissioners for Trade and Plantations, 1722/23–1749," *English Historical Review,* XLVII, 469.

———. "Journal of the Commissioners for Trade and Plantations, 1749/50–1758," *English Historical Review,* XLIX, 136.

Brown, Vera L. "South Sea Company and Contraband Trade," *American Historical Review,* XXXI (1926), 662–678.

Buffington, Arthur H. "The Canada Expedition of 1746," *American Historical Review,* XLV (1940), 552.

Carter, Alice. "Analysis of Public Indebtedness in Eighteenth Century England," *Bulletin of the Institute of Historical Research,* XXIV, 173.

Chance, James Frederick. "The Antecedents of the Treaty of Hanover," *English Historical Review,* XXVIII, 691.

Clark, Dora Mae. "The Office of Secretary to the Treasury in the Eighteenth Century," *American Historical Review,* XLII (1937), 22.

Gipson, Lawrence H. "British Diplomacy in the Light of the Anglo-Spanish New World Issues, 1750–1757," *American Historical Review,* XLV (1940), 552.

Graham, G. S. "The Naval Defence of British North America, 1739–1763," *Transactions of the Royal Historical Society,* Fourth Series, XXX (1948).

Hertz, G. B. "The Old Colonial System," *English Historical Review,* XXII, 618.

Horn, D. B. "Cabinet Controversy on Subsidy Treaties in Time of Peace, 1749–50," *English Historical Review*, XLV, 463.

———. "The Origins of the Proposed Election of a King of the Romans, 1748–50," *English Historical Review*, XLII, 361.

———. "Saxony in the War of the Austrian Succession," *English Historical Review*, XLIV, 33.

Laughton, J. K. "Jenkins' Ear," *English Historical Review*, IV, 741.

Lodge, Sir Richard. "The English Factory at Lisbon," *Transactions of the Royal Historical Society*, Fourth Series, XVI (1933).

———. "English Neutrality in the War of the Polish Succession," *Transactions of the Royal Historical Society*, Fourth Series, XIV (1931).

———. "The Hanau Controversy in 1744 and the Fall of Carteret," *English Historical Review*, XXXVIII, 509.

———. "Lord Hyndford's Embassy to Russia, 1744–1749," *English Historical Review*, XLVIII, 389.

———. "The Mission of Henry Legge to Berlin, 1748," *Transactions of the Royal Historical Society*, Fourth Series, XIV, 1931.

———. "The Private Correspondence of Benjamin Keene," *English Historical Review*, XLIX, 344.

———. "Russia, Prussia and Great Britain, 1742–44," *English Historical Review*, XLV, 579.

———. "The So-called 'Treaty' of Hanau," *English Historical Review*, XXXVIII, 384.

Nulle, Stebelton H. "Duke of Newcastle and the Election of 1727," *Journal of Modern History*, IX (1937), 1–22.

Pares, Richard. "American Versus Continental Warfare, 1739–63," *English Historical Review*, LI, 429.

Roberts, R. A. "The Birth of an American State: Georgia, An Effort of Philanthropy and Protestant Propaganda," *Transactions of the Royal Historical Society*, Fourth Series, VI (1923).

Ropes, Arthur R. "The Causes of the Seven Years' War," *Transactions of the Royal Historical Society*, New Series, IV (1889).

Sedgwick, R. R. "The Inner Cabinet, 1739–41," *English Historical Review*, XXXIV, 290.

Sykes, Norman. "The Duke of Newcastle as an Ecclesiastical Minister," *English Historical Review*, LVII, 59.

Temperley, H. W. V. "Causes of the War of Jenkins' Ear, 1739," *Transactions of the Royal Historical Society*, Third Series, III (1909).

Turner, Edward R. "The Lords Justices of England," *English Historical Review*, XXIX, 453.

Williams, Basil. "Carteret and the So-called Treaty of Hanau," *English Historical Review*, XLIX, 684.

———. "Duke of Newcastle and the Election of 1734," *English Historical Review*, XII (1897), 448–488.

———. "The Foreign Office of the First Two Georges," *Blackwood's Magazine*, CLXXI, No. 1,095 (Jan. 1907), 92–106.

———. "Foreign Policy of England under Walpole, 1721–1731," *English Historical Review*, Part I, Vol. XV (1900), Part II, Vol. XVI (1901).

Index

Index

For the convenience of the reader, peers and courtesy lords are listed under the title or name which is best known to modern readers, not necessarily under their family names.